VIZ GRAPHIC NOVEL

Descendants of Darkness

Yami no Matsuei

ita

2

Descendants of Darkness
Yami no Matsuei
Vol. 2
Shôjo Edition

Story & Art by
Yoko Matsushita

English Adaptation/Kelly Sue DeConnick
Translation/David Ury
Touch-Up & Lettering/Gia Cam Luc
Graphics & Cover Design/Hidemi Sahara
Editors/Eric Searleman & Richard Kadrey

Editor in Chief, Books/Alvin Lu
Editor in Chief, Magazines/Marc Weidenbaum
VP of Publishing Licensing/Rika Inouye
VP of Sales/Gonzalo Ferreyra
Sr. VP of Marketing/Liza Coppola
Publisher/Hyoe Narita

Printed in the U.S.A.

Published by VIZ Media, LLC
P.O. Box 77064
San Francisco, CA 94107

Shôjo Edition
10 9 8 7 6 5 4
First printing, October 2004
Fourth printing, May 2008

For advertising rates or media kit, e-mail advertising@viz.com

www.viz.com   store.viz.com

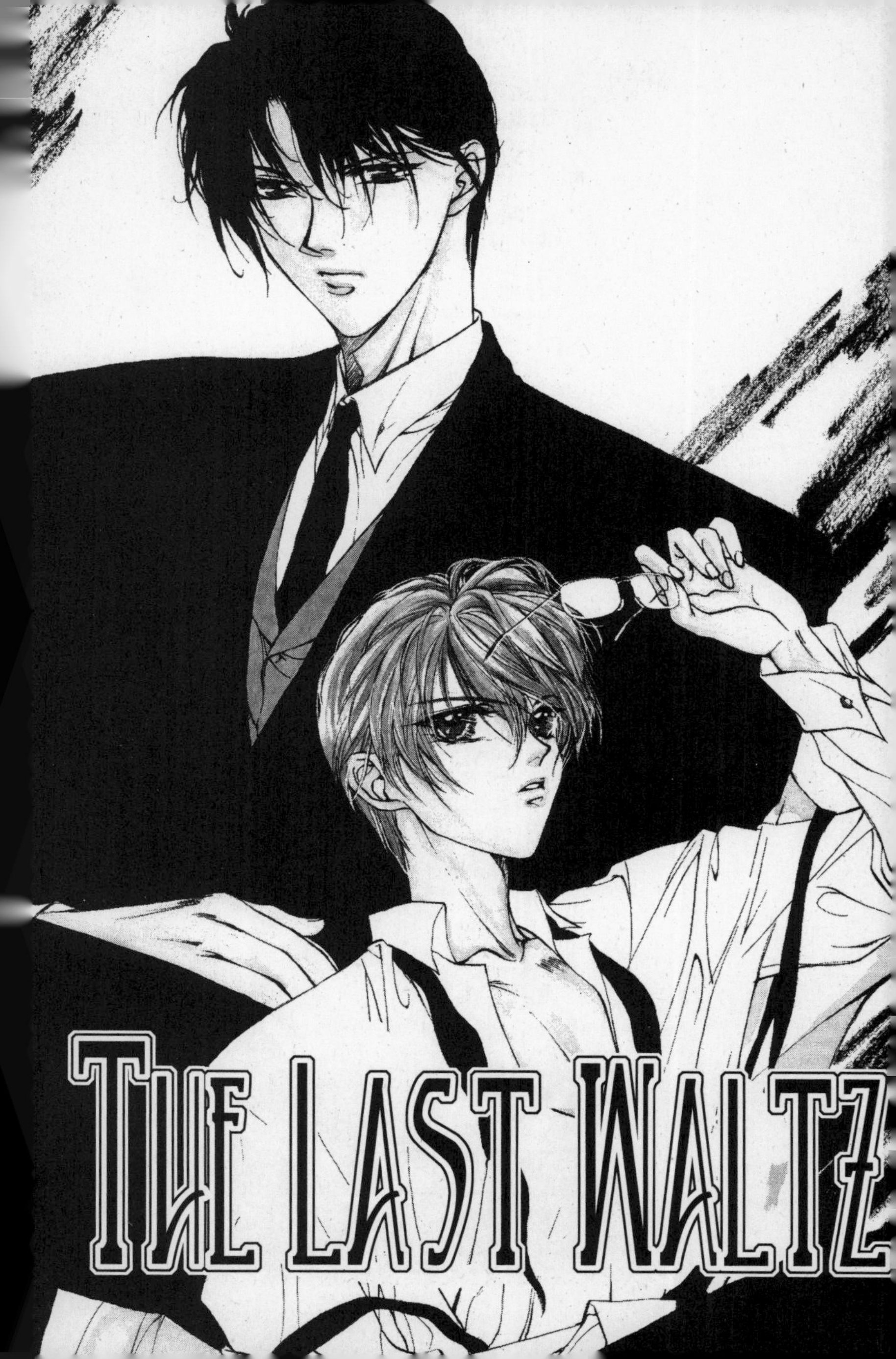
THE LAST WALTZ

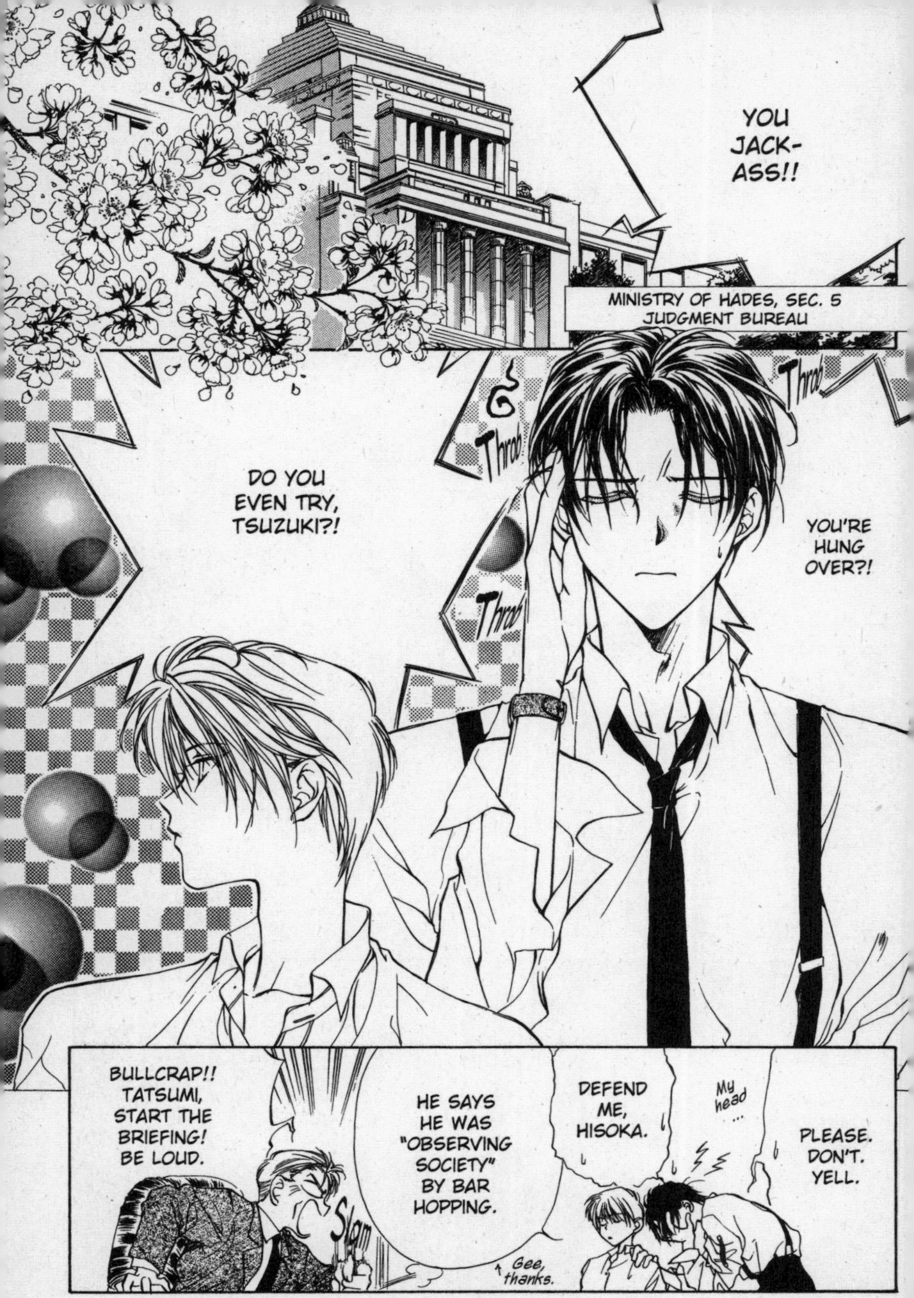
YOU JACK-ASS!!
MINISTRY OF HADES, SEC. 5 JUDGMENT BUREAU
Throb
Throb
Throb
YOU'RE HUNG OVER?!
DO YOU EVEN TRY, TSUZUKI?!
PLEASE. DON'T. YELL.
My head ...
DEFEND ME, HISOKA.
HE SAYS HE WAS "OBSERVING SOCIETY" BY BAR HOPPING.
Gee, thanks.
Slam
BULLCRAP!! TATSUMI, START THE BRIEFING! BE LOUD.

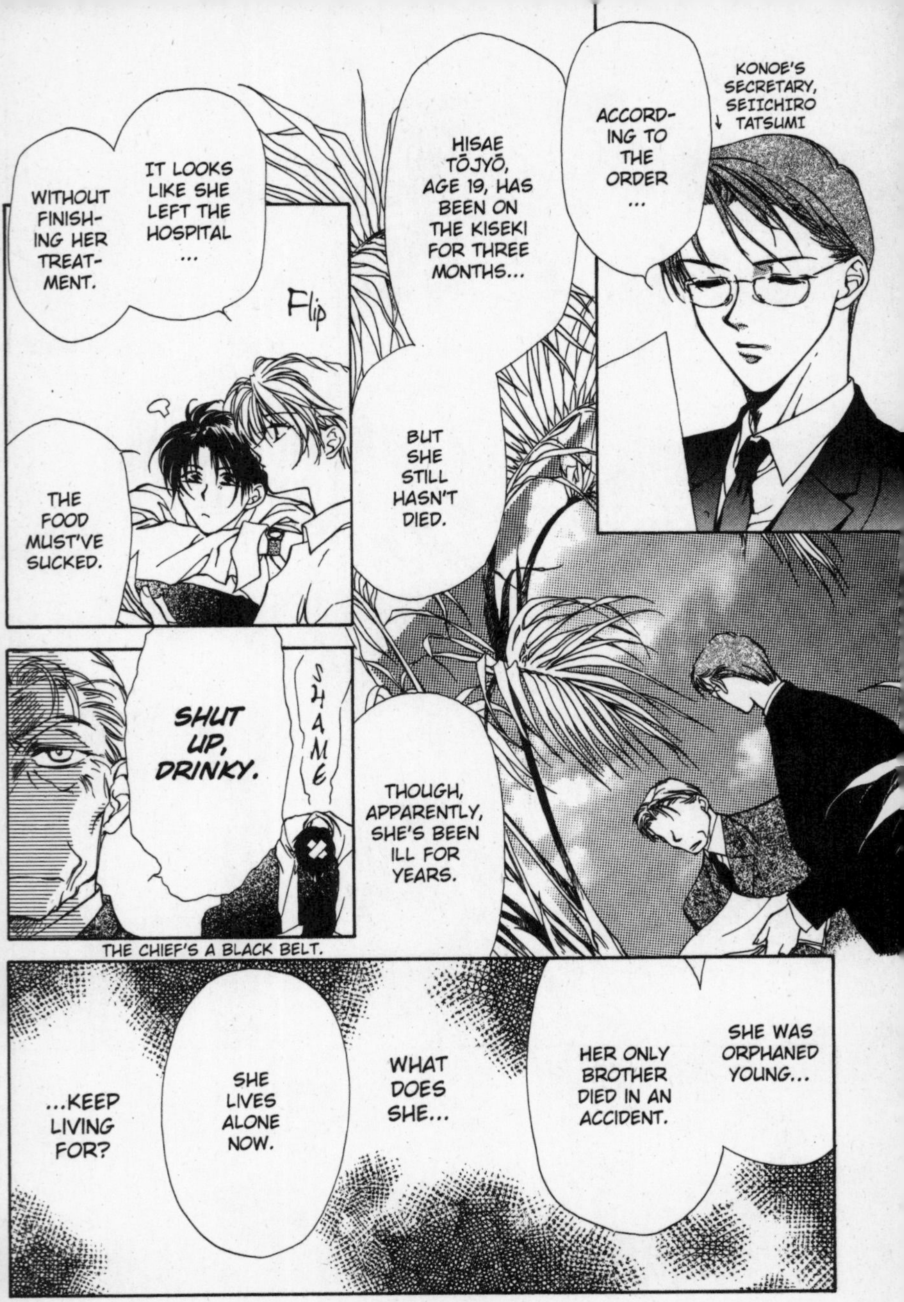

KONOE'S SECRETARY, SEIICHIRO TATSUMI
ACCORDING TO THE ORDER ...
HISAE TŌJYŌ, AGE 19, HAS BEEN ON THE KISEKI FOR THREE MONTHS...
BUT SHE STILL HASN'T DIED.
IT LOOKS LIKE SHE LEFT THE HOSPITAL ...
WITHOUT FINISHING HER TREATMENT.
Flip
THE FOOD MUST'VE SUCKED.
THOUGH, APPARENTLY, SHE'S BEEN ILL FOR YEARS.
SHAME
SHUT UP, DRINKY.
THE CHIEF'S A BLACK BELT.
SHE WAS ORPHANED YOUNG...
HER ONLY BROTHER DIED IN AN ACCIDENT.
WHAT DOES SHE...
SHE LIVES ALONE NOW.
...KEEP LIVING FOR?

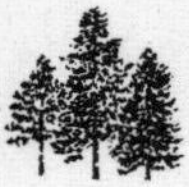

Matsushita, here. Let me begin by saying thank you, as always, and welcome to Vol. 2 of Descendants of Darkness.

If you're looking carefully, you'll notice a few changes to the art in this volume. Chief Konoe has lost weight, for instance. (Good work, Chief! Way to keep that cholesterol down! Ha ha.)

No bonus story this time, which some of you will appreciate and some of you will find disappointing, I'm sure. To the latter group, I offer my apologies. I hope everyone else enjoys the gallery art that I included instead.

And for those of you who'd like to know a little about me:

PROFILE

Yoko Matsushita
Birth Place: Kumamoto Prefecture
Birthday: June 23rd
Astrological Sign & Blood Type: Cancer & AB
Hobbies: Video Games yup, Video Games!!!
...I like coffee more than black tea. It's bad for my stomach, I know.

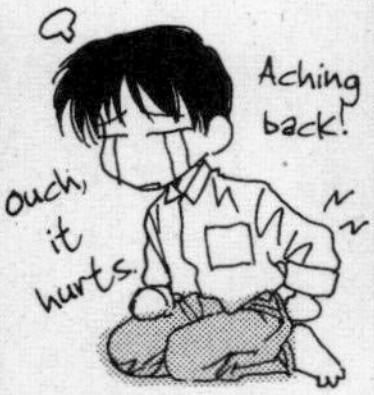
Aching back!
ouch, it hurts.

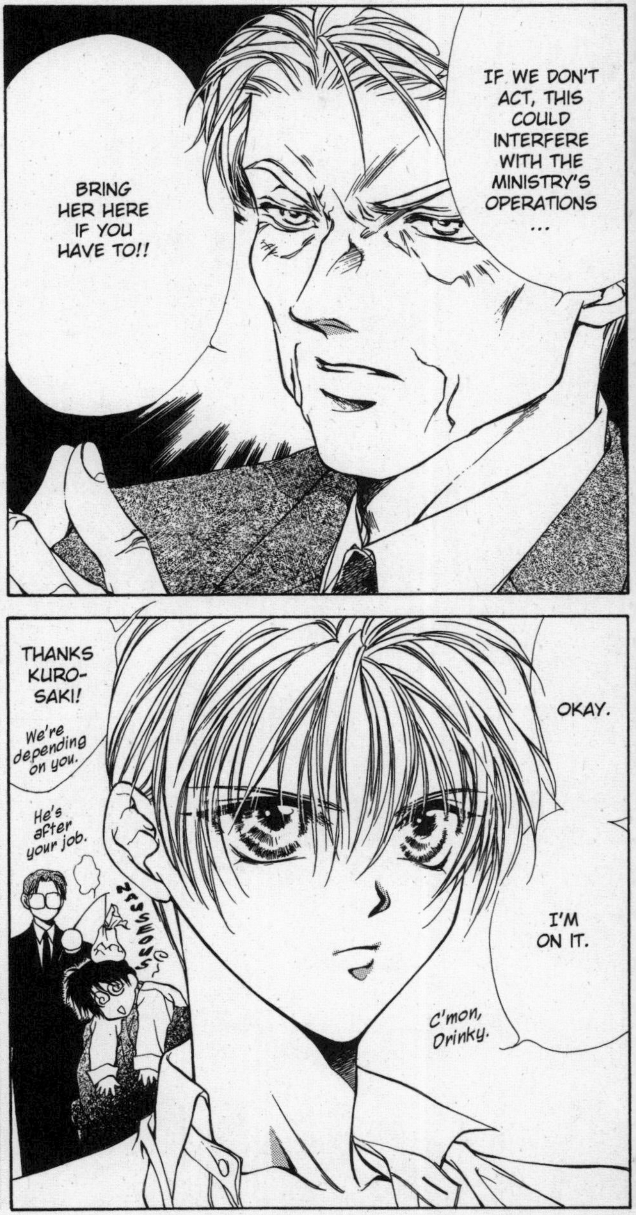
IF WE DON'T ACT, THIS COULD INTERFERE WITH THE MINISTRY'S OPERATIONS ...
BRING HER HERE IF YOU HAVE TO!!
OKAY.
THANKS KURO-SAKI!
We're depending on you.
He's after your job.
I'M ON IT.
NAUSEOUS
C'mon, Drinky.

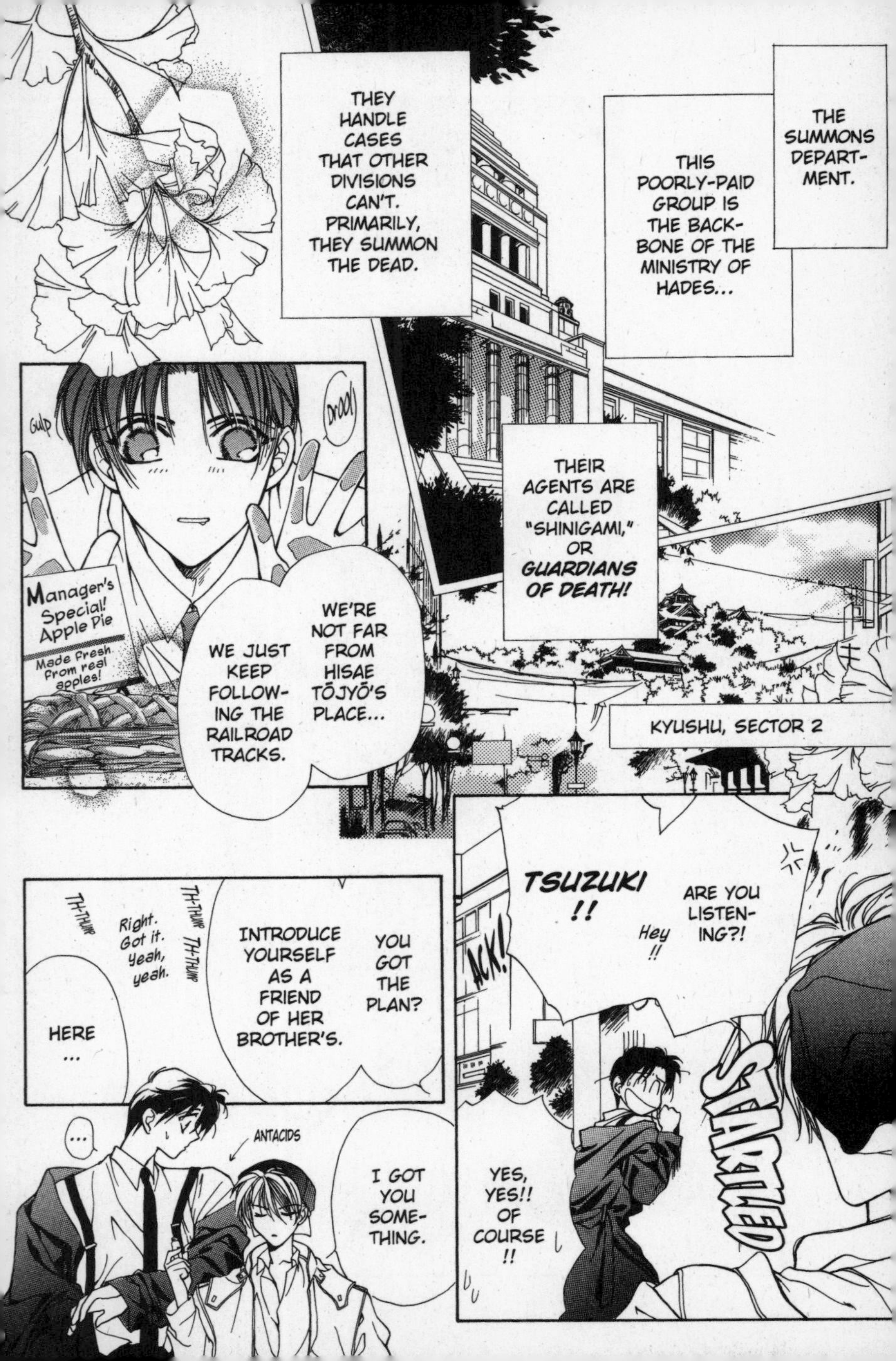
THE SUMMONS DEPARTMENT.
THIS POORLY-PAID GROUP IS THE BACKBONE OF THE MINISTRY OF HADES...
THEY HANDLE CASES THAT OTHER DIVISIONS CAN'T. PRIMARILY, THEY SUMMON THE DEAD.
THEIR AGENTS ARE CALLED "SHINIGAMI," OR *GUARDIANS OF DEATH!*
KYUSHU, SECTOR 2
DROOL
GULP
Manager's Special! Apple Pie
Made Fresh from real apples!
WE'RE NOT FAR FROM HISAE TŌJYŌ'S PLACE...
WE JUST KEEP FOLLOWING THE RAILROAD TRACKS.
ARE YOU LISTENING?!
TSUZUKI!!
Hey!!
ACK!
STARTLED
YES, YES!! OF COURSE!!
YOU GOT THE PLAN?
INTRODUCE YOURSELF AS A FRIEND OF HER BROTHER'S.
TH-THUMP TH-THUMP
TH-THUMP
Right. Got it. Yeah, yeah.
HERE...
I GOT YOU SOMETHING.
ANTACIDS
...

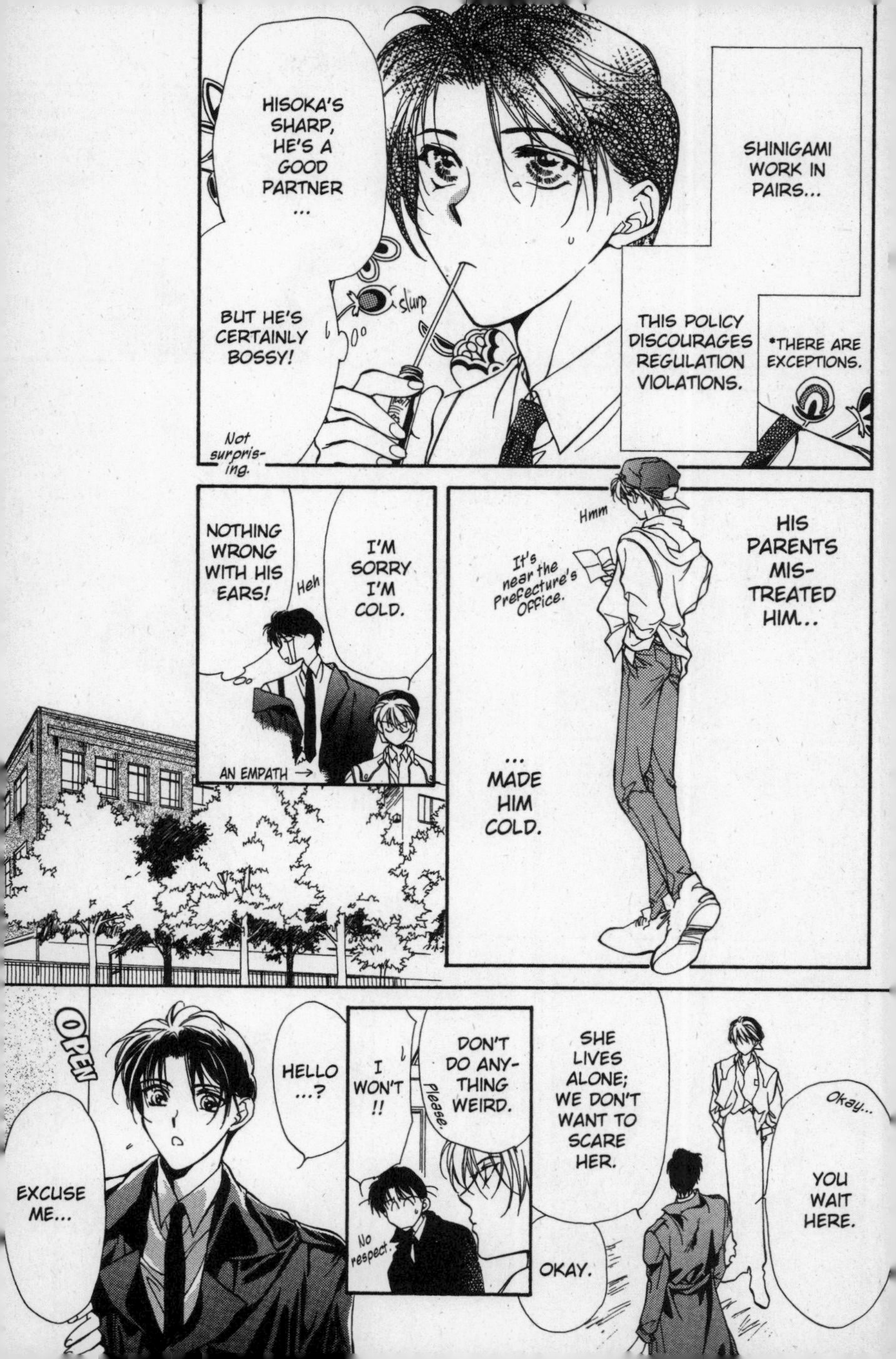

SHINIGAMI WORK IN PAIRS...
THIS POLICY DISCOURAGES REGULATION VIOLATIONS.
*THERE ARE EXCEPTIONS.
HISOKA'S SHARP, HE'S A GOOD PARTNER ...
slurp
BUT HE'S CERTAINLY BOSSY!
Not surprising.
HIS PARENTS MISTREATED HIM...
Hmm
It's near the Prefecture's Office.
... MADE HIM COLD.
I'M SORRY I'M COLD.
Heh
NOTHING WRONG WITH HIS EARS!
AN EMPATH →
Okay...
YOU WAIT HERE.
SHE LIVES ALONE; WE DON'T WANT TO SCARE HER.
OKAY.
DON'T DO ANYTHING WEIRD.
Please.
I WON'T !!
No respect.
HELLO ...?
OPEN
EXCUSE ME...

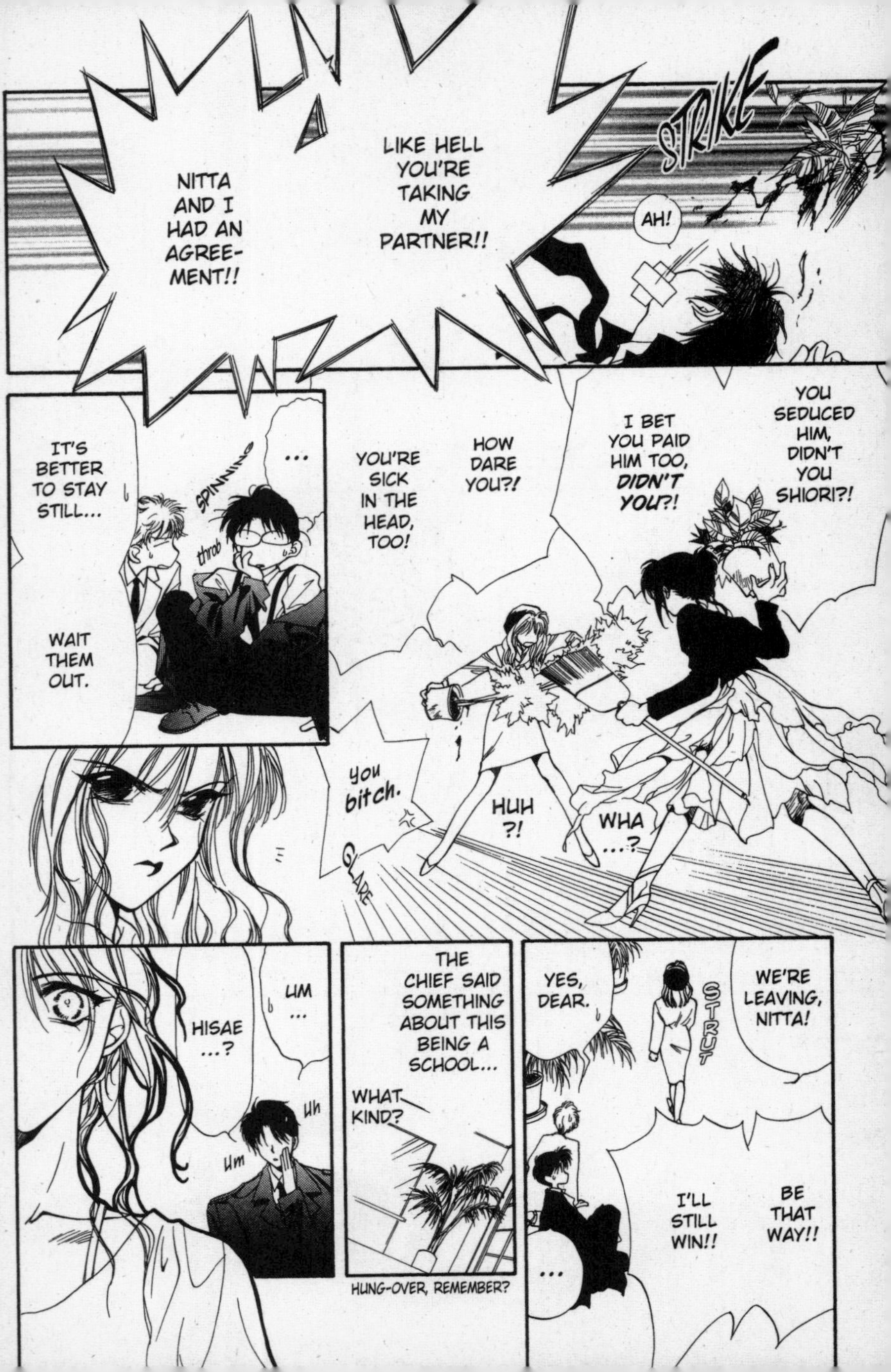
STRIKE
AH!
LIKE HELL YOU'RE TAKING MY PARTNER!!
NITTA AND I HAD AN AGREE-MENT!!
YOU SEDUCED HIM, DIDN'T YOU SHIORI?!
I BET YOU PAID HIM TOO, DIDN'T YOU?!
HOW DARE YOU?!
YOU'RE SICK IN THE HEAD, TOO!
WHA ...?
HUH ?!
...
SPINNING
throb
IT'S BETTER TO STAY STILL...
WAIT THEM OUT.
you bitch.
GLARE
WE'RE LEAVING, NITTA!
STRUT
YES, DEAR.
BE THAT WAY!!
I'LL STILL WIN!!
...
THE CHIEF SAID SOMETHING ABOUT THIS BEING A SCHOOL...
WHAT KIND?
HUNG-OVER, REMEMBER?
UM ...
HISAE ...?
uh
um

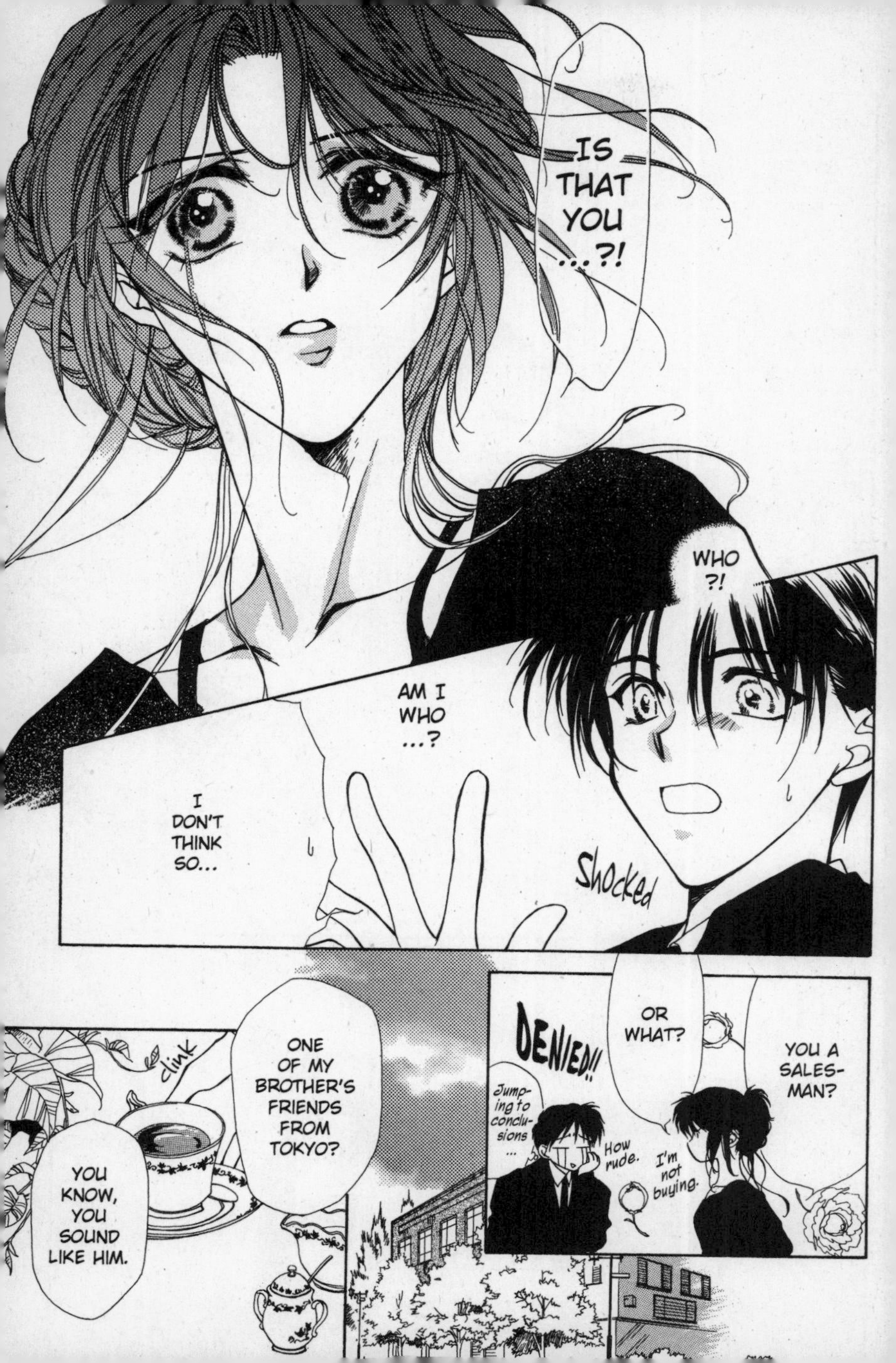
IS THAT YOU ...?!
WHO ?!
AM I WHO ...?
I DON'T THINK SO...
Shocked
YOU A SALES-MAN?
OR WHAT?
DENIED!!
I'm not buying.
How rude.
Jumping to conclusions ...
ONE OF MY BROTHER'S FRIENDS FROM TOKYO?
clink
YOU KNOW, YOU SOUND LIKE HIM.

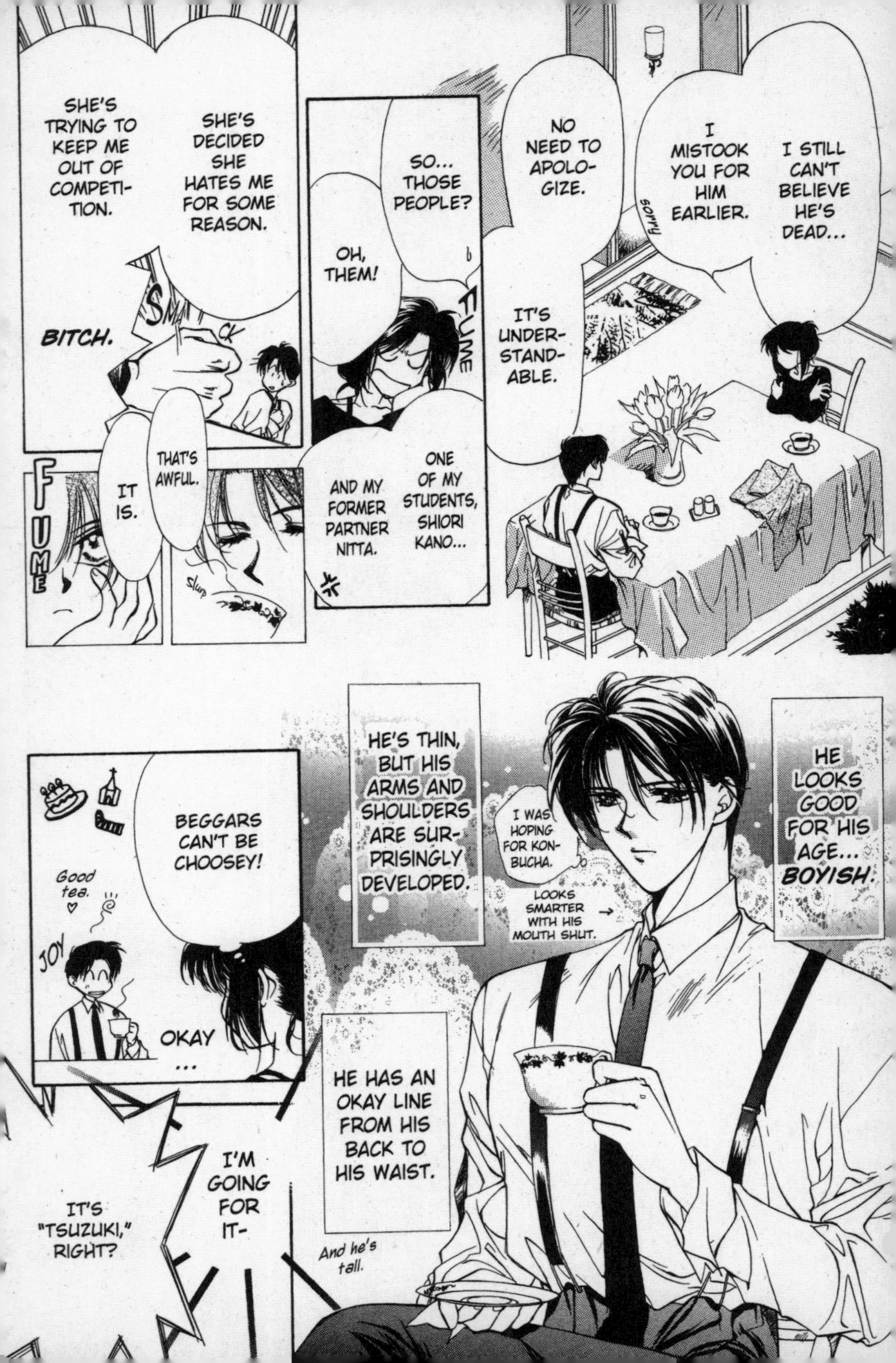

I STILL CAN'T BELIEVE HE'S DEAD...
I MISTOOK YOU FOR HIM EARLIER.
SORRY
NO NEED TO APOLOGIZE.
IT'S UNDERSTANDABLE.
SO... THOSE PEOPLE?
OH, THEM!
FUME
ONE OF MY STUDENTS, SHIORI KANO...
AND MY FORMER PARTNER NITTA.
SHE'S DECIDED SHE HATES ME FOR SOME REASON.
SHE'S TRYING TO KEEP ME OUT OF COMPETITION.
SMACK
BITCH.
THAT'S AWFUL.
slurp
IT IS.
FUME
HE LOOKS GOOD FOR HIS AGE... BOYISH.
HE'S THIN, BUT HIS ARMS AND SHOULDERS ARE SURPRISINGLY DEVELOPED.
I WAS HOPING FOR KONBUCHA.
LOOKS SMARTER WITH HIS MOUTH SHUT.
HE HAS AN OKAY LINE FROM HIS BACK TO HIS WAIST.
And he's tall.
BEGGARS CAN'T BE CHOOSEY!
Good tea.
JOY
OKAY ...
I'M GOING FOR IT-
IT'S "TSUZUKI," RIGHT?

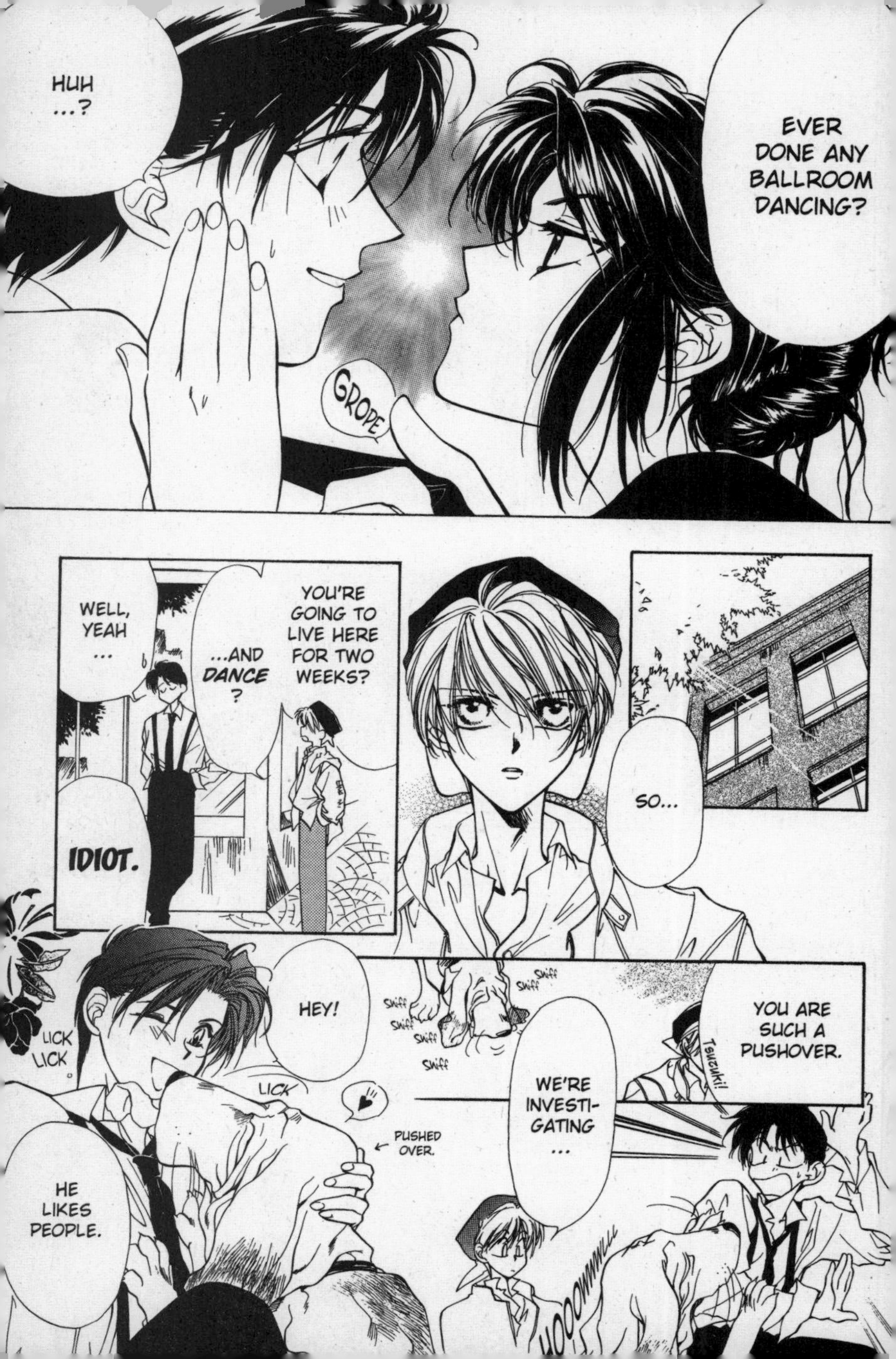

EVER DONE ANY BALLROOM DANCING?
GROPE
HUH ...?
SO...
YOU'RE GOING TO LIVE HERE FOR TWO WEEKS?
...AND *DANCE*?
WELL, YEAH ...
IDIOT.
YOU ARE SUCH A PUSHOVER.
TSUZUKI!!
WE'RE INVESTI-GATING ...
HOOOWWWLLL
Sniff Sniff
Sniff Sniff Sniff
Sniff
HEY!
LICK LICK
LICK
PUSHED OVER.
HE LIKES PEOPLE.

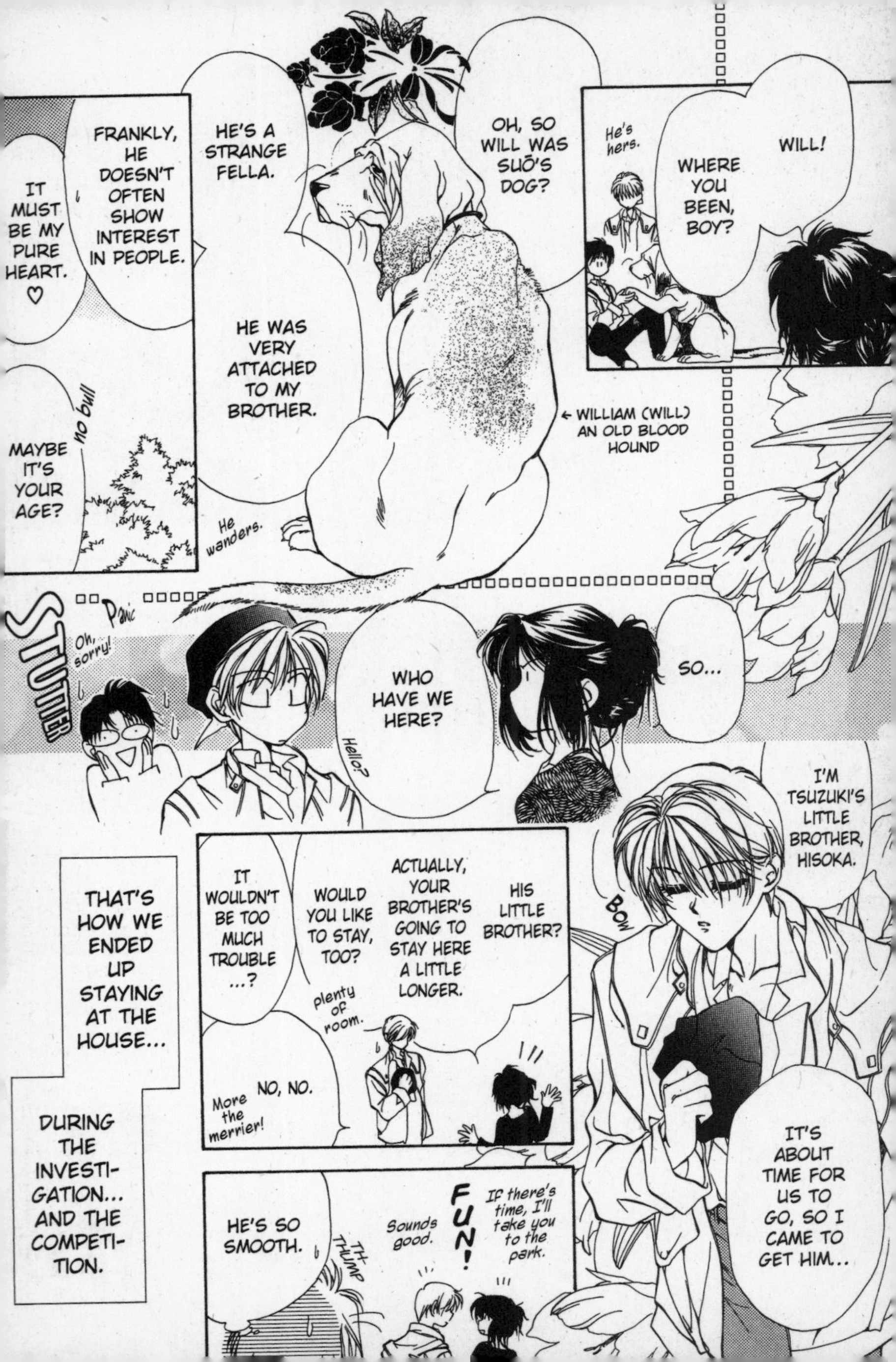
WILL!
WHERE YOU BEEN, BOY?
He's hers.
OH, SO WILL WAS SUŌ'S DOG?
HE'S A STRANGE FELLA.
← WILLIAM (WILL) AN OLD BLOOD HOUND
HE WAS VERY ATTACHED TO MY BROTHER.
He wanders.
FRANKLY, HE DOESN'T OFTEN SHOW INTEREST IN PEOPLE.
IT MUST BE MY PURE HEART. ♡
no bull
MAYBE IT'S YOUR AGE?
SO...
WHO HAVE WE HERE?
Hello?
Panic
Oh, sorry!
STUTTER
I'M TSUZUKI'S LITTLE BROTHER, HISOKA.
BOW
IT'S ABOUT TIME FOR US TO GO, SO I CAME TO GET HIM...
HIS LITTLE BROTHER?
ACTUALLY, YOUR BROTHER'S GOING TO STAY HERE A LITTLE LONGER.
WOULD YOU LIKE TO STAY, TOO?
IT WOULDN'T BE TOO MUCH TROUBLE ...?
plenty of room.
NO, NO.
More the merrier!
THAT'S HOW WE ENDED UP STAYING AT THE HOUSE...
If there's time, I'll take you to the park.
FUN!
Sounds good.
HE'S SO SMOOTH.
TH THUMP
DURING THE INVESTIGATION... AND THE COMPETITION.

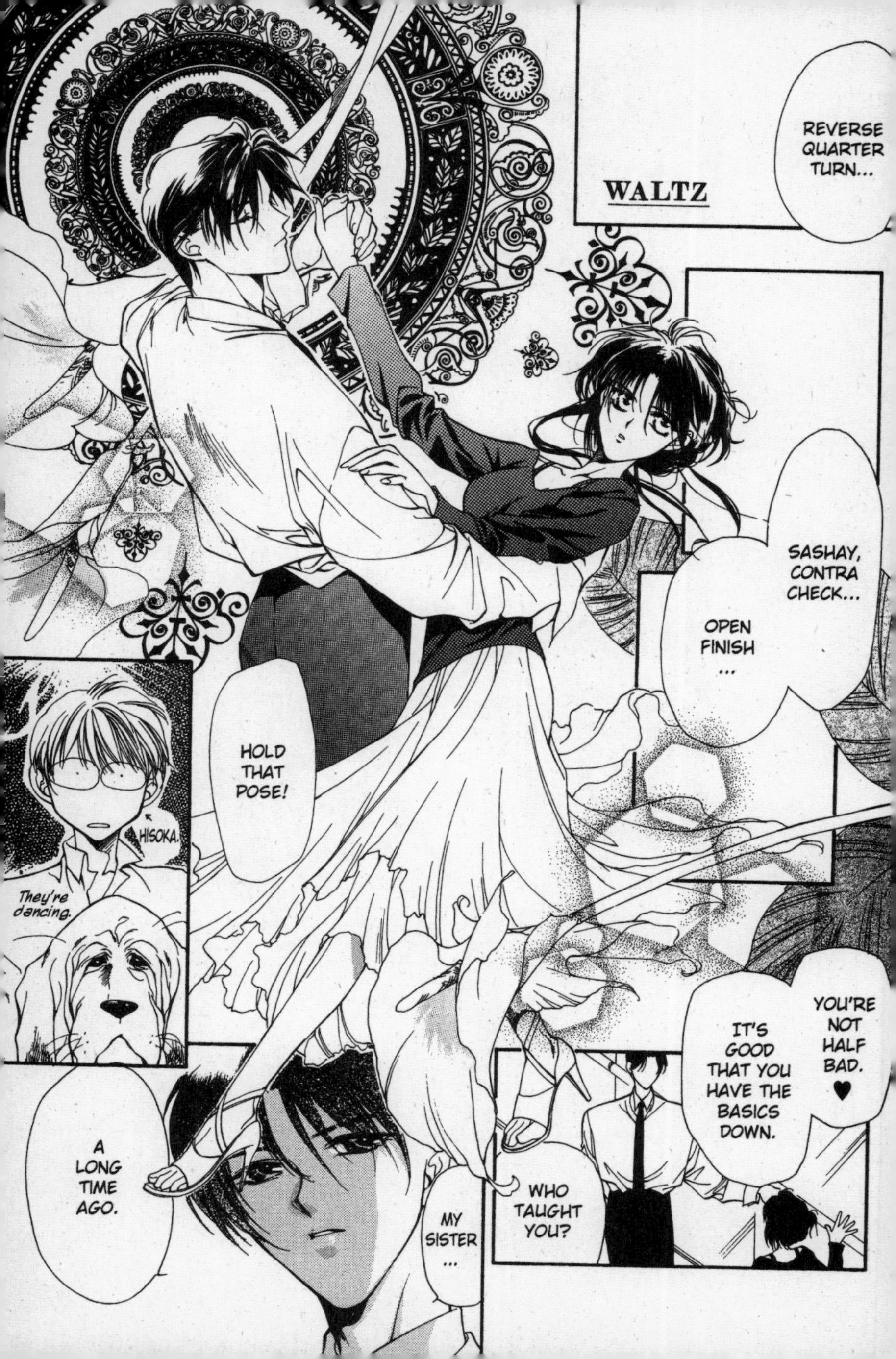
REVERSE QUARTER TURN...
WALTZ
SASHAY, CONTRA CHECK...
OPEN FINISH ...
HOLD THAT POSE!
HISOKA.
They're dancing.
YOU'RE NOT HALF BAD. ♥
IT'S GOOD THAT YOU HAVE THE BASICS DOWN.
WHO TAUGHT YOU?
MY SISTER ...
A LONG TIME AGO.

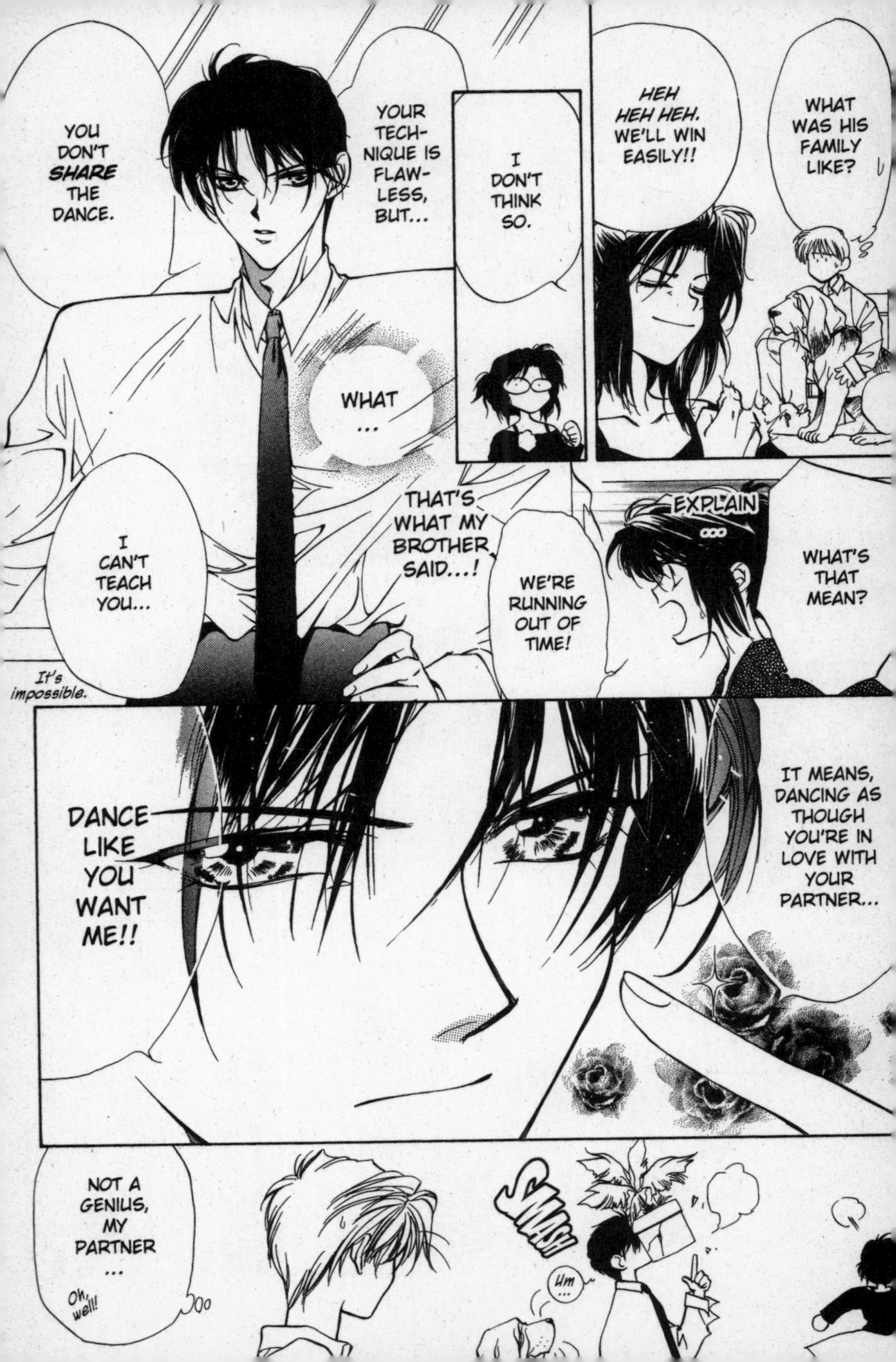
WHAT WAS HIS FAMILY LIKE?
HEH HEH HEH. WE'LL WIN EASILY!!
I DON'T THINK SO.
WHAT'S THAT MEAN?
EXPLAIN ...
WE'RE RUNNING OUT OF TIME!
THAT'S WHAT MY BROTHER SAID...!
YOUR TECHNIQUE IS FLAWLESS, BUT...
YOU DON'T SHARE THE DANCE.
WHAT ...
I CAN'T TEACH YOU...
It's impossible.
IT MEANS, DANCING AS THOUGH YOU'RE IN LOVE WITH YOUR PARTNER...
DANCE LIKE YOU WANT ME!!
SMASH
Um ...
NOT A GENIUS, MY PARTNER ...
Oh, well!

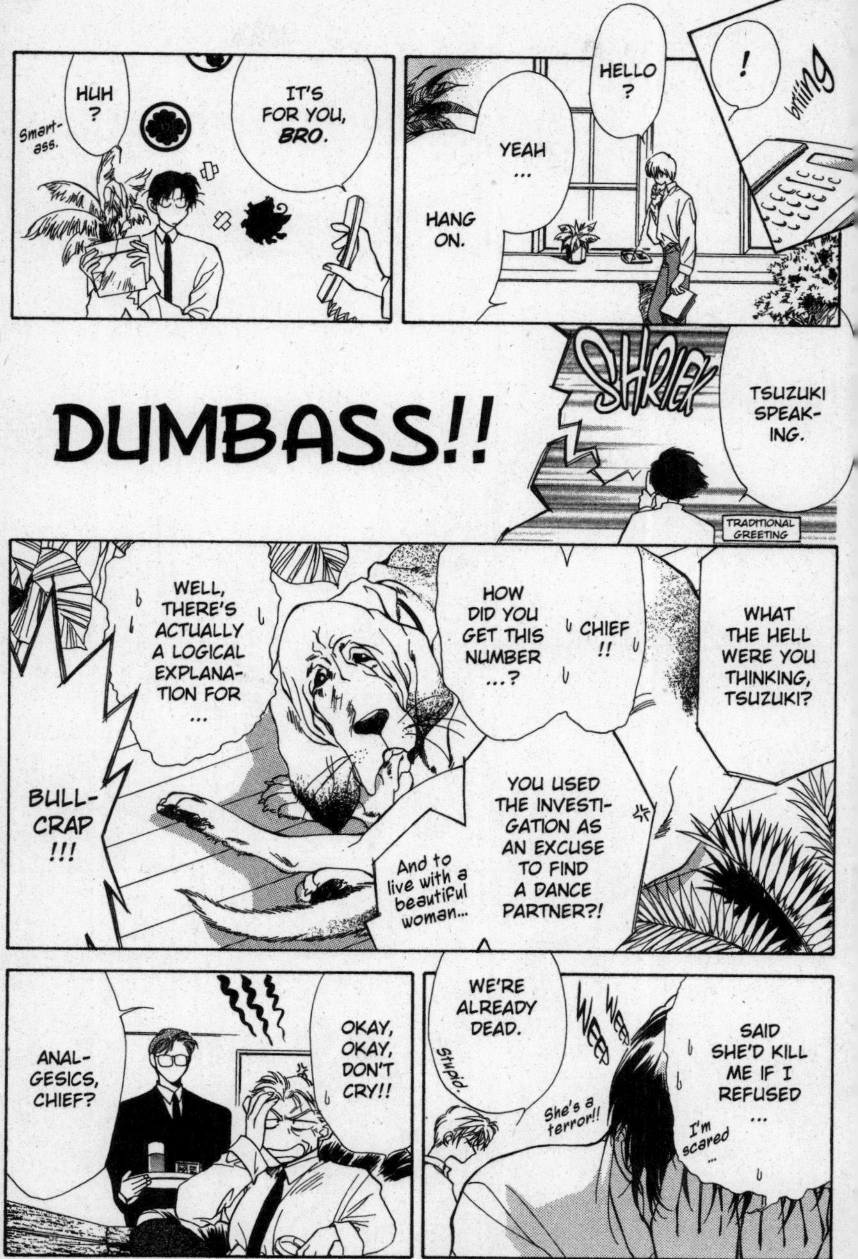
!
brriing
HELLO ?
YEAH ...
HANG ON.
IT'S FOR YOU, BRO.
HUH ?
Smart-ass.
SHRIEK
TSUZUKI SPEAK-ING.
TRADITIONAL GREETING
DUMBASS!!
WHAT THE HELL WERE YOU THINKING, TSUZUKI?
CHIEF !!
HOW DID YOU GET THIS NUMBER ...?
YOU USED THE INVESTI-GATION AS AN EXCUSE TO FIND A DANCE PARTNER?!
And to live with a beautiful woman...
WELL, THERE'S ACTUALLY A LOGICAL EXPLANA-TION FOR ...
BULL-CRAP !!!
SAID SHE'D KILL ME IF I REFUSED ...
I'm scared ...
WEEP WEEP
She's a terror!!
WE'RE ALREADY DEAD.
Stupid.
OKAY, OKAY, DON'T CRY!!
ANAL-GESICS, CHIEF?

LIVE FROM THE JUDGMENT BUREAU

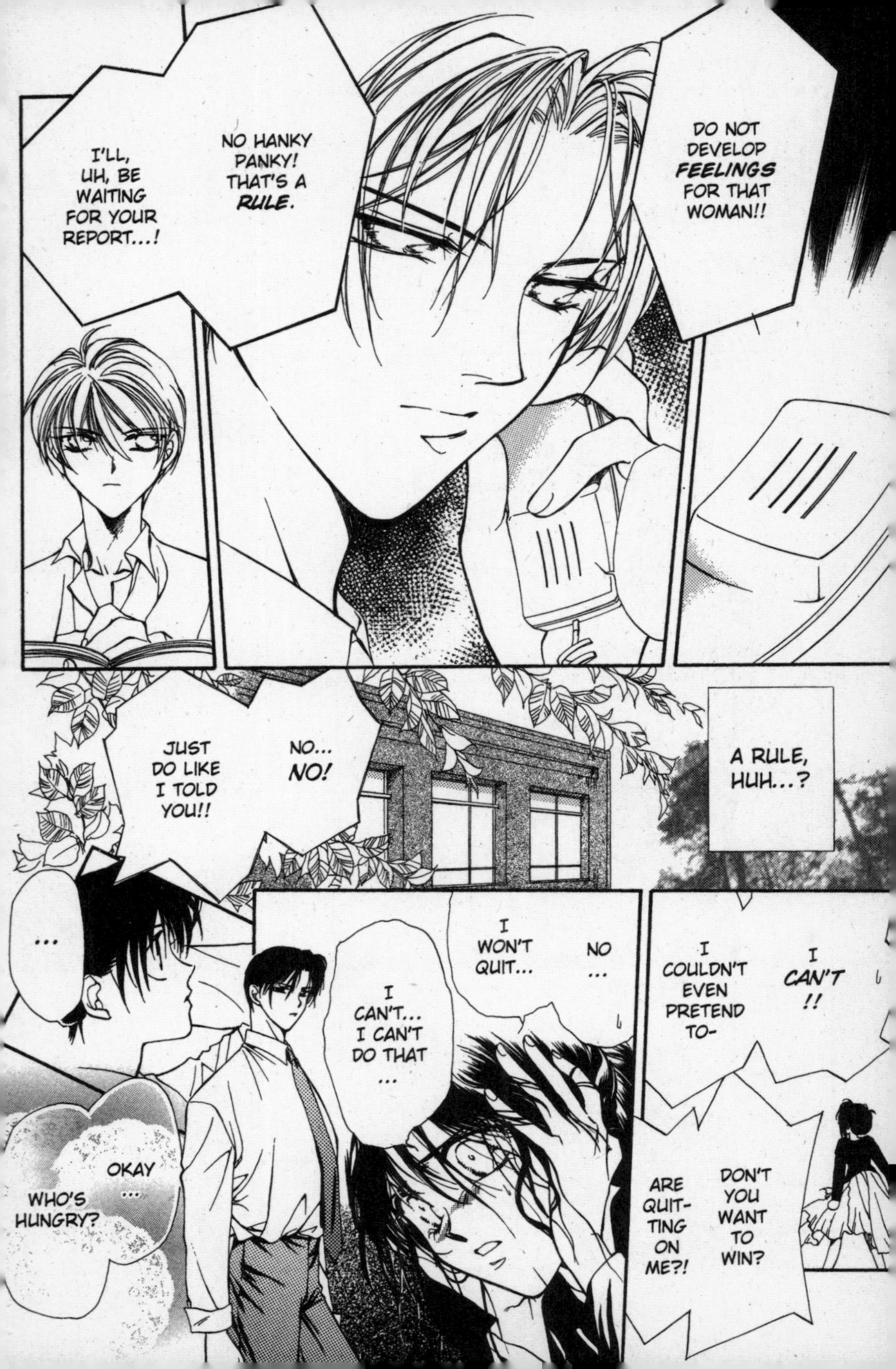
DO NOT DEVELOP FEELINGS FOR THAT WOMAN!!
NO HANKY PANKY! THAT'S A RULE.
I'LL, UH, BE WAITING FOR YOUR REPORT...!
A RULE, HUH...?
NO... NO!
JUST DO LIKE I TOLD YOU!!
I CAN'T!!
I COULDN'T EVEN PRETEND TO-
DON'T YOU WANT TO WIN?
ARE QUITTING ON ME?!
NO...
I WON'T QUIT...
I CAN'T... I CAN'T DO THAT...
...
OKAY...
WHO'S HUNGRY?

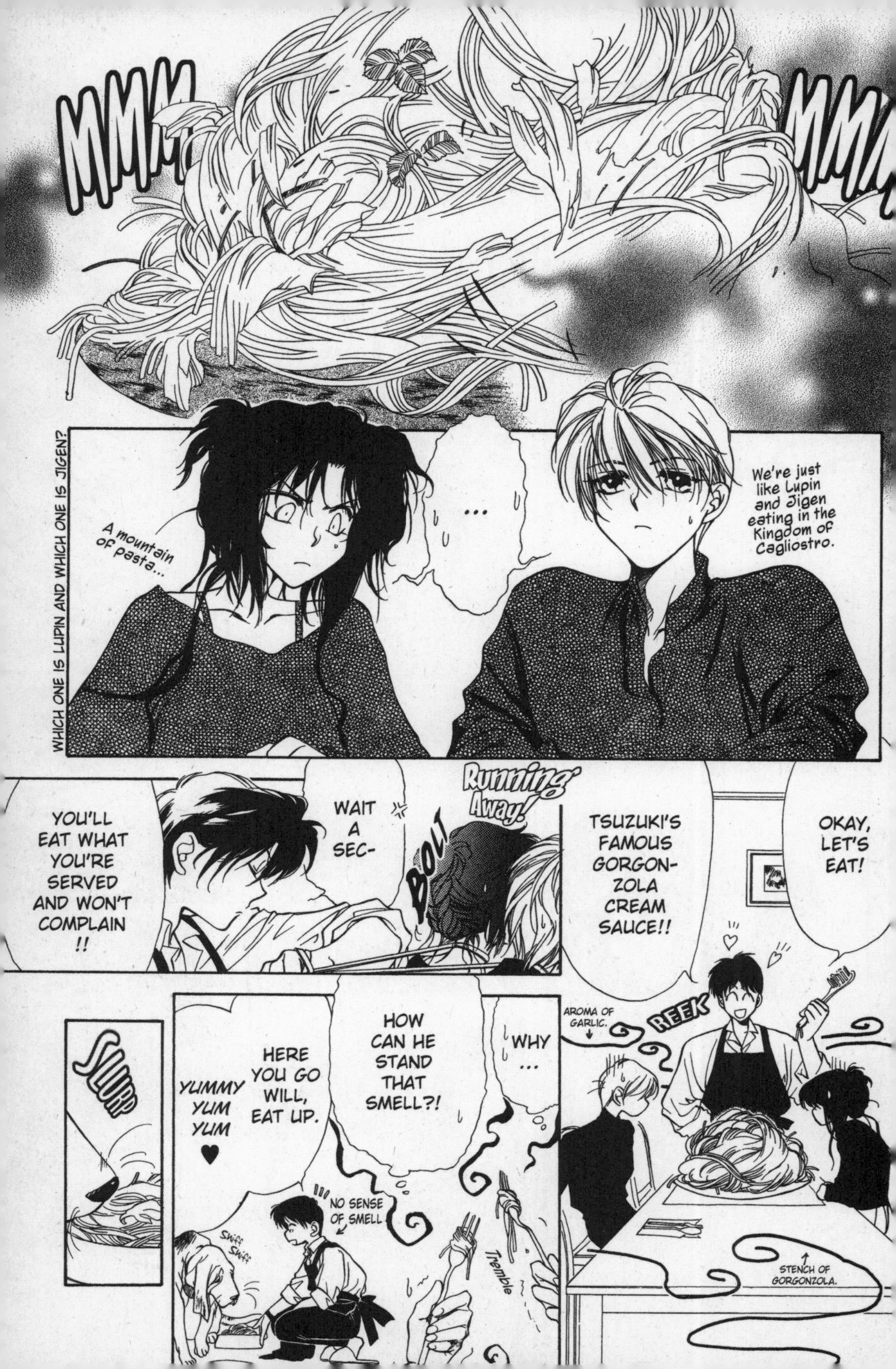
MMM
MMM
We're just like Lupin and Jigen eating in the Kingdom of Cagliostro.
...
A mountain of pasta...
WHICH ONE IS LUPIN AND WHICH ONE IS JIGEN?
OKAY, LET'S EAT!
TSUZUKI'S FAMOUS GORGONZOLA CREAM SAUCE!!
REEK
AROMA OF GARLIC.
STENCH OF GORGONZOLA.
Running Away!
BOLT
WAIT A SEC-
YOU'LL EAT WHAT YOU'RE SERVED AND WON'T COMPLAIN !!
WHY ...
HOW CAN HE STAND THAT SMELL?!
Tremble
HERE YOU GO WILL, EAT UP.
YUMMY YUM YUM ♥
NO SENSE OF SMELL
Sniff Sniff
SLURP

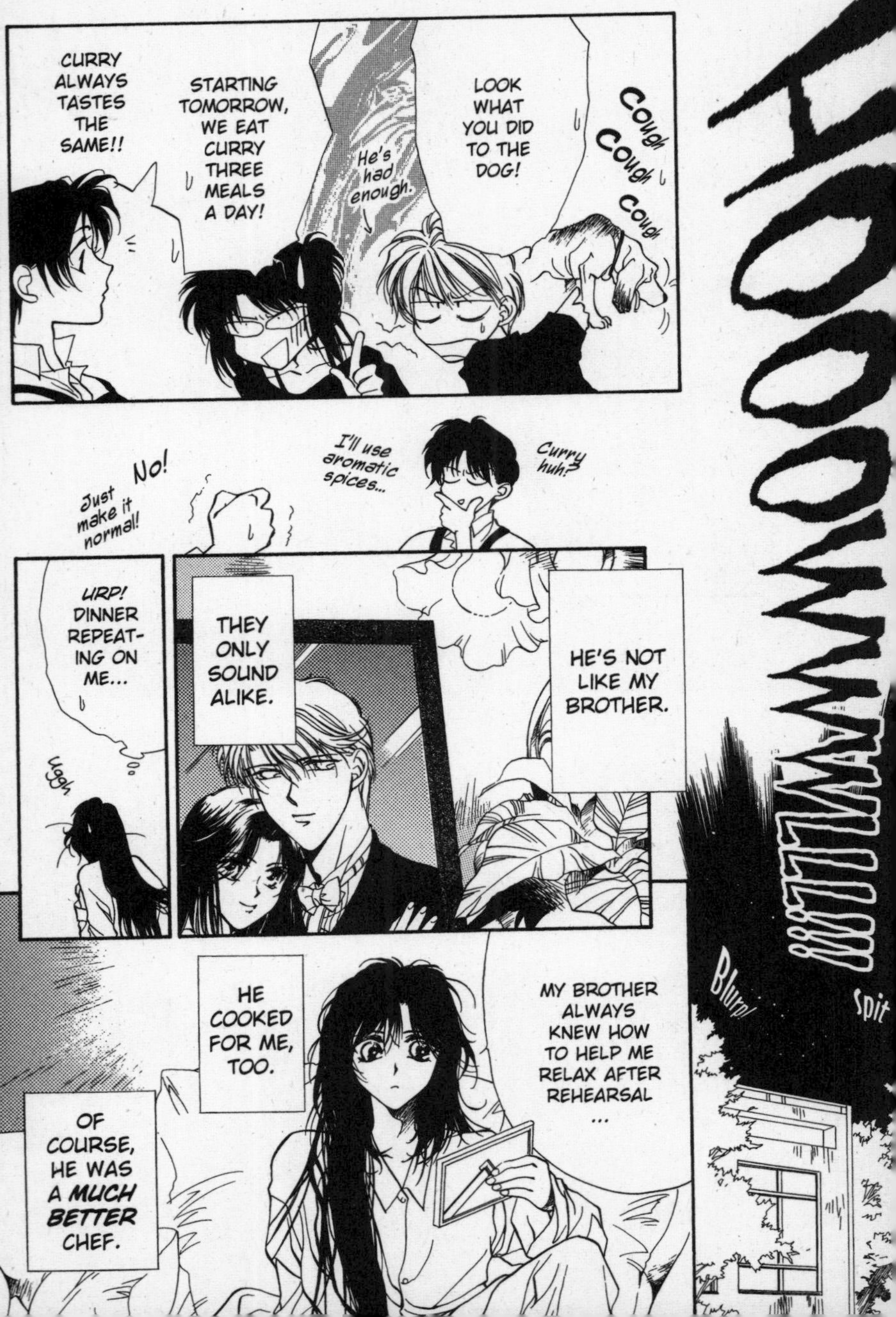
HOOWWWLLL!!
Blurp!
spit
Cough Cough Cough
LOOK WHAT YOU DID TO THE DOG!
He's had enough.
STARTING TOMORROW, WE EAT CURRY THREE MEALS A DAY!
CURRY ALWAYS TASTES THE SAME!!
Curry huh?
I'll use aromatic spices...
No!
Just make it normal!
HE'S NOT LIKE MY BROTHER.
THEY ONLY SOUND ALIKE.
URP! DINNER REPEAT-ING ON ME...
Uggh
MY BROTHER ALWAYS KNEW HOW TO HELP ME RELAX AFTER REHEARSAL ...
HE COOKED FOR ME, TOO.
OF COURSE, HE WAS A *MUCH BETTER* CHEF.

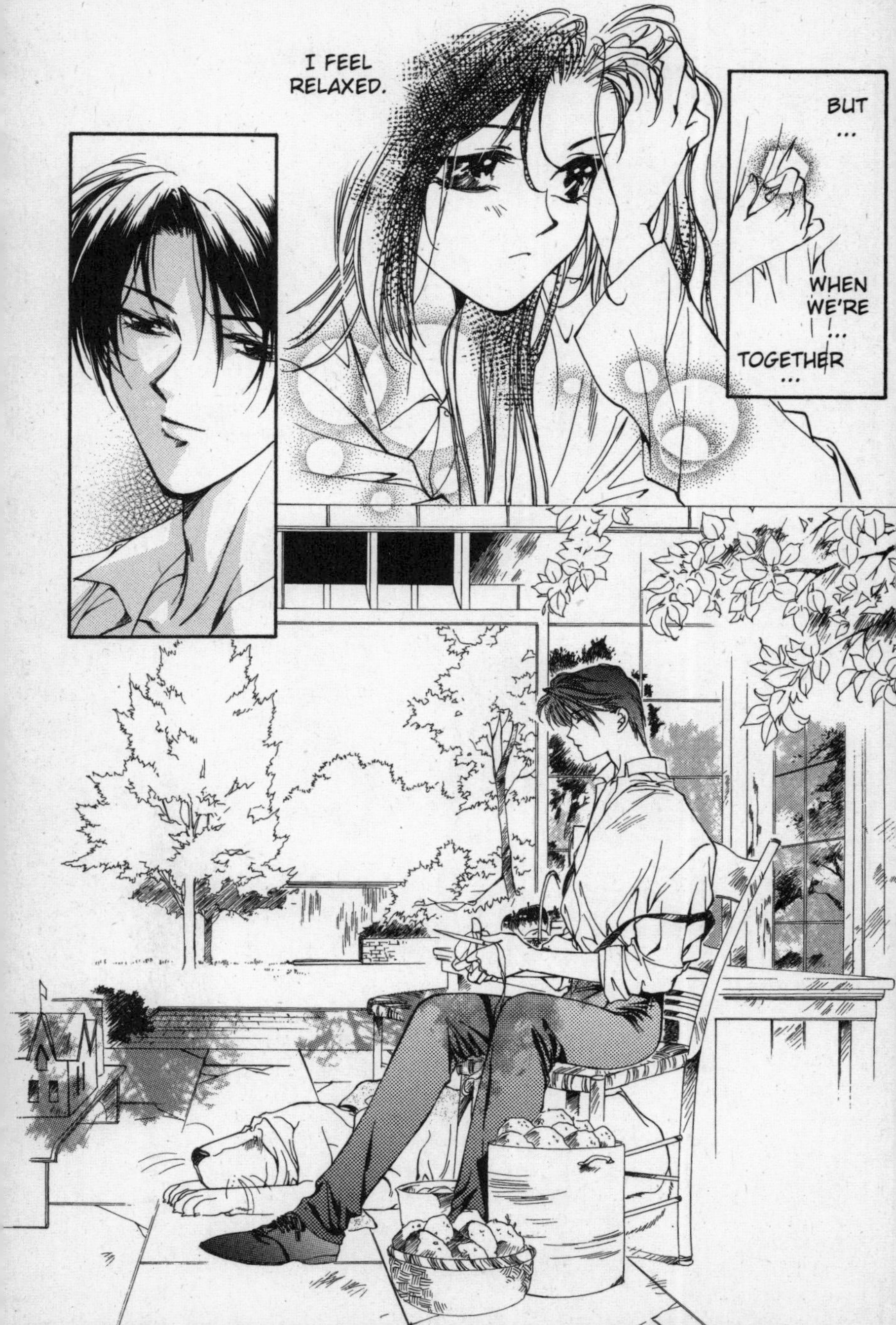
I FEEL RELAXED.
BUT ...
WHEN WE'RE ...
TOGETHER ...

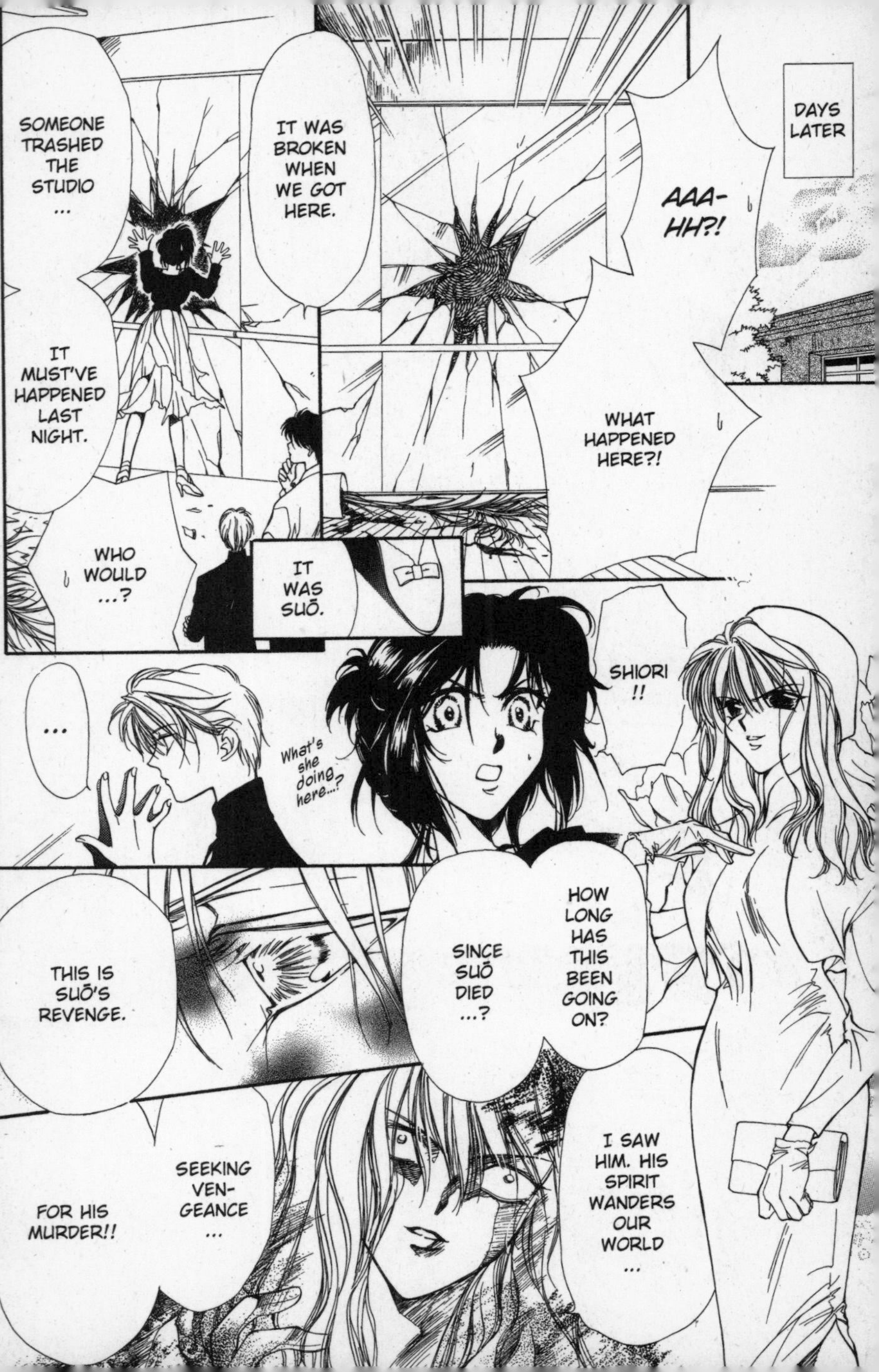
DAYS LATER
AAA-HH?!
WHAT HAPPENED HERE?!
IT WAS BROKEN WHEN WE GOT HERE.
SOMEONE TRASHED THE STUDIO ...
IT MUST'VE HAPPENED LAST NIGHT.
WHO WOULD ...?
IT WAS SUŌ.
SHIORI !!
What's she doing here...?
...
HOW LONG HAS THIS BEEN GOING ON?
SINCE SUŌ DIED ...?
THIS IS SUŌ'S REVENGE.
I SAW HIM. HIS SPIRIT WANDERS OUR WORLD ...
SEEKING VEN- GEANCE ...
FOR HIS MURDER!!

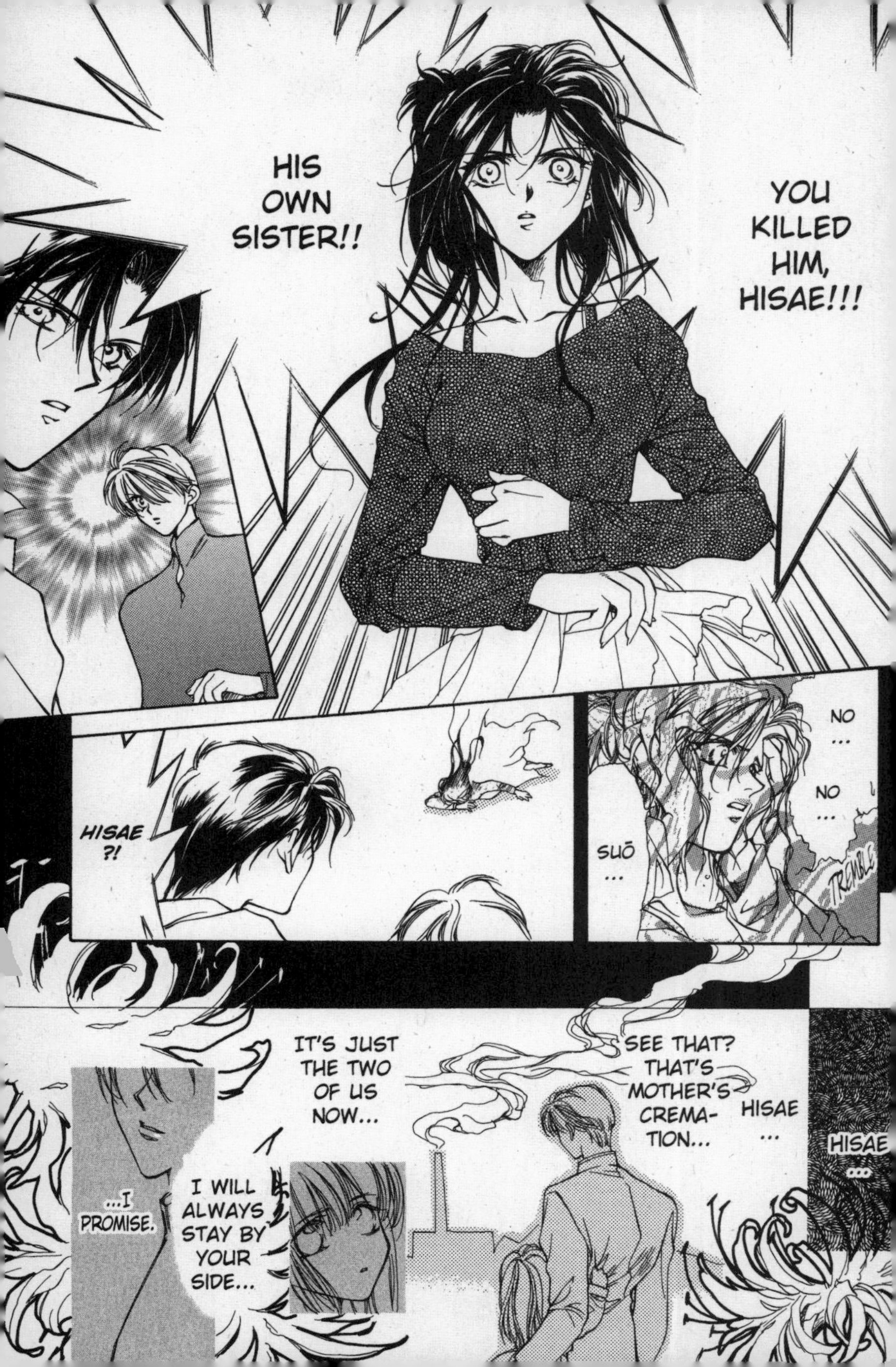
YOU KILLED HIM, HISAE!!!
HIS OWN SISTER!!
NO ... NO ...
SUŌ ...
TREMBLE
HISAE ?!
HISAE ...
HISAE ...
SEE THAT? THAT'S MOTHER'S CREMATION...
IT'S JUST THE TWO OF US NOW...
I WILL ALWAYS STAY BY YOUR SIDE...
...I PROMISE.

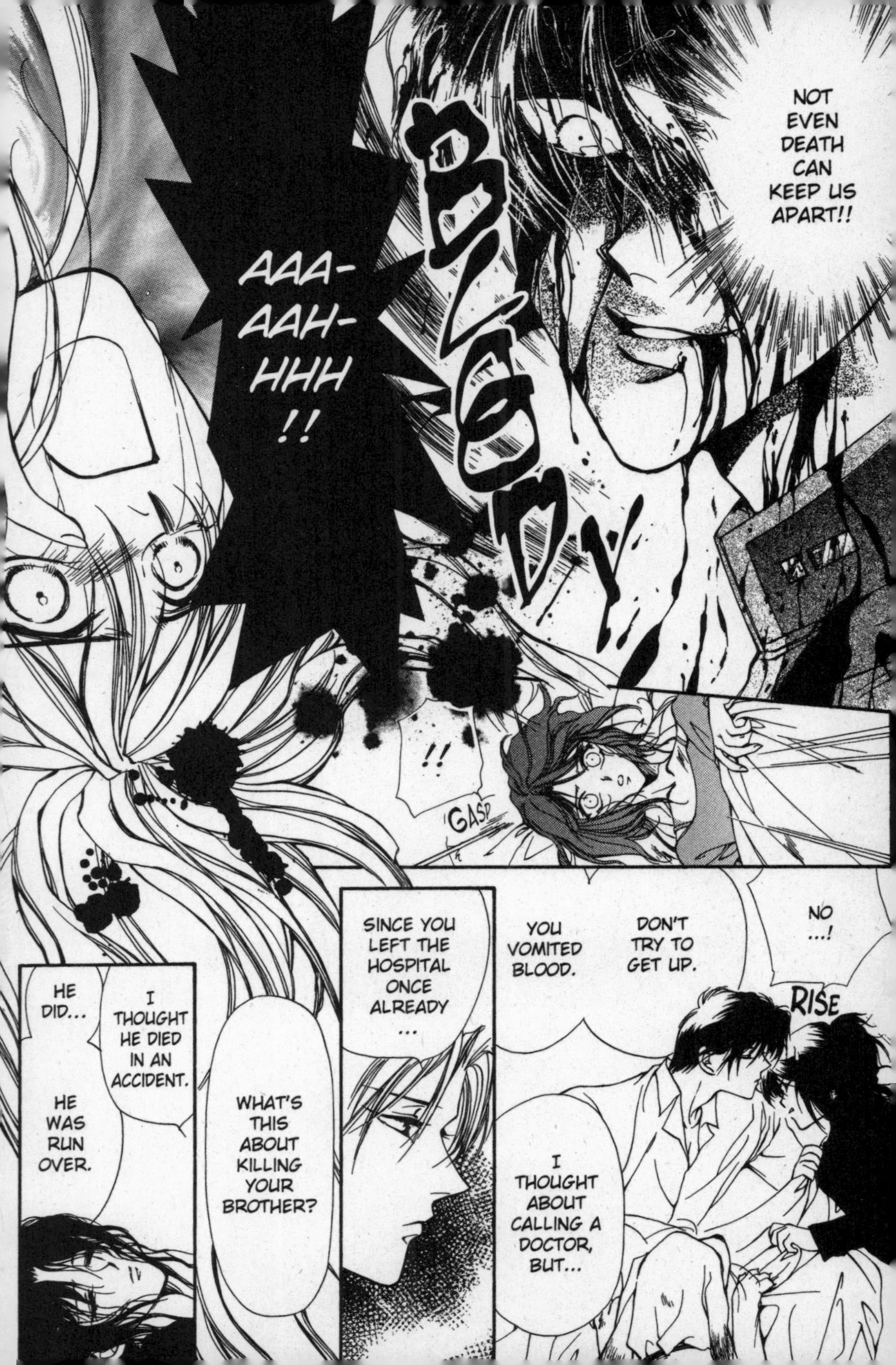

NOT EVEN DEATH CAN KEEP US APART!!
AAA-AAH-HHH!!
!!
GASP
NO ...!
RISE
DON'T TRY TO GET UP.
YOU VOMITED BLOOD.
I THOUGHT ABOUT CALLING A DOCTOR, BUT...
SINCE YOU LEFT THE HOSPITAL ONCE ALREADY ...
WHAT'S THIS ABOUT KILLING YOUR BROTHER?
I THOUGHT HE DIED IN AN ACCIDENT.
HE DID...
HE WAS RUN OVER.

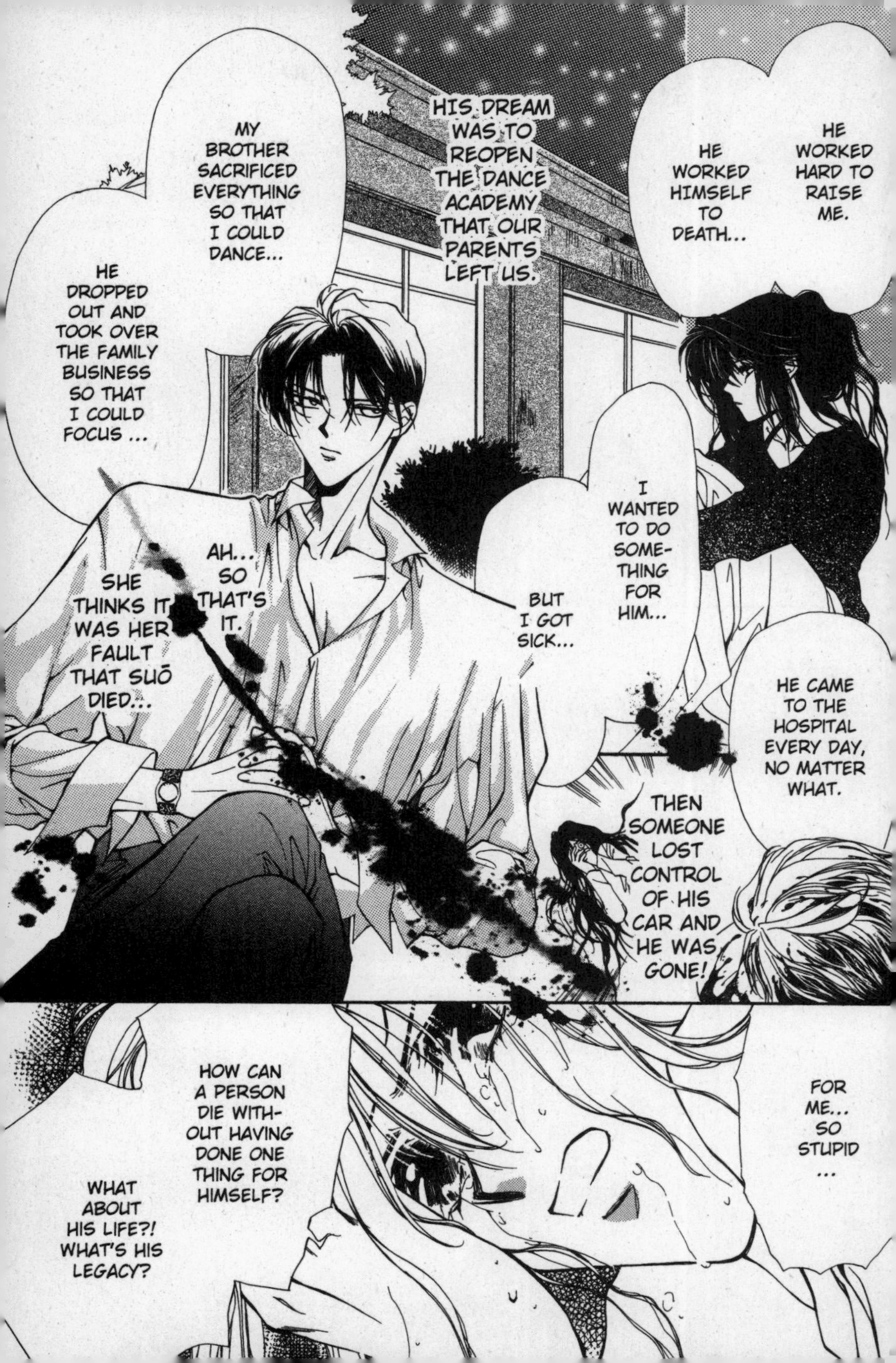
HE WORKED HARD TO RAISE ME.
HE WORKED HIMSELF TO DEATH...
HIS DREAM WAS TO REOPEN THE DANCE ACADEMY THAT OUR PARENTS LEFT US.
MY BROTHER SACRIFICED EVERYTHING SO THAT I COULD DANCE...
HE DROPPED OUT AND TOOK OVER THE FAMILY BUSINESS SO THAT I COULD FOCUS ...
I WANTED TO DO SOME-THING FOR HIM...
BUT I GOT SICK...
AH... SO THAT'S IT.
SHE THINKS IT WAS HER FAULT THAT SUŌ DIED...
HE CAME TO THE HOSPITAL EVERY DAY, NO MATTER WHAT.
THEN SOMEONE LOST CONTROL OF HIS CAR AND HE WAS GONE!
FOR ME... SO STUPID ...
HOW CAN A PERSON DIE WITH-OUT HAVING DONE ONE THING FOR HIMSELF?
WHAT ABOUT HIS LIFE?! WHAT'S HIS LEGACY?

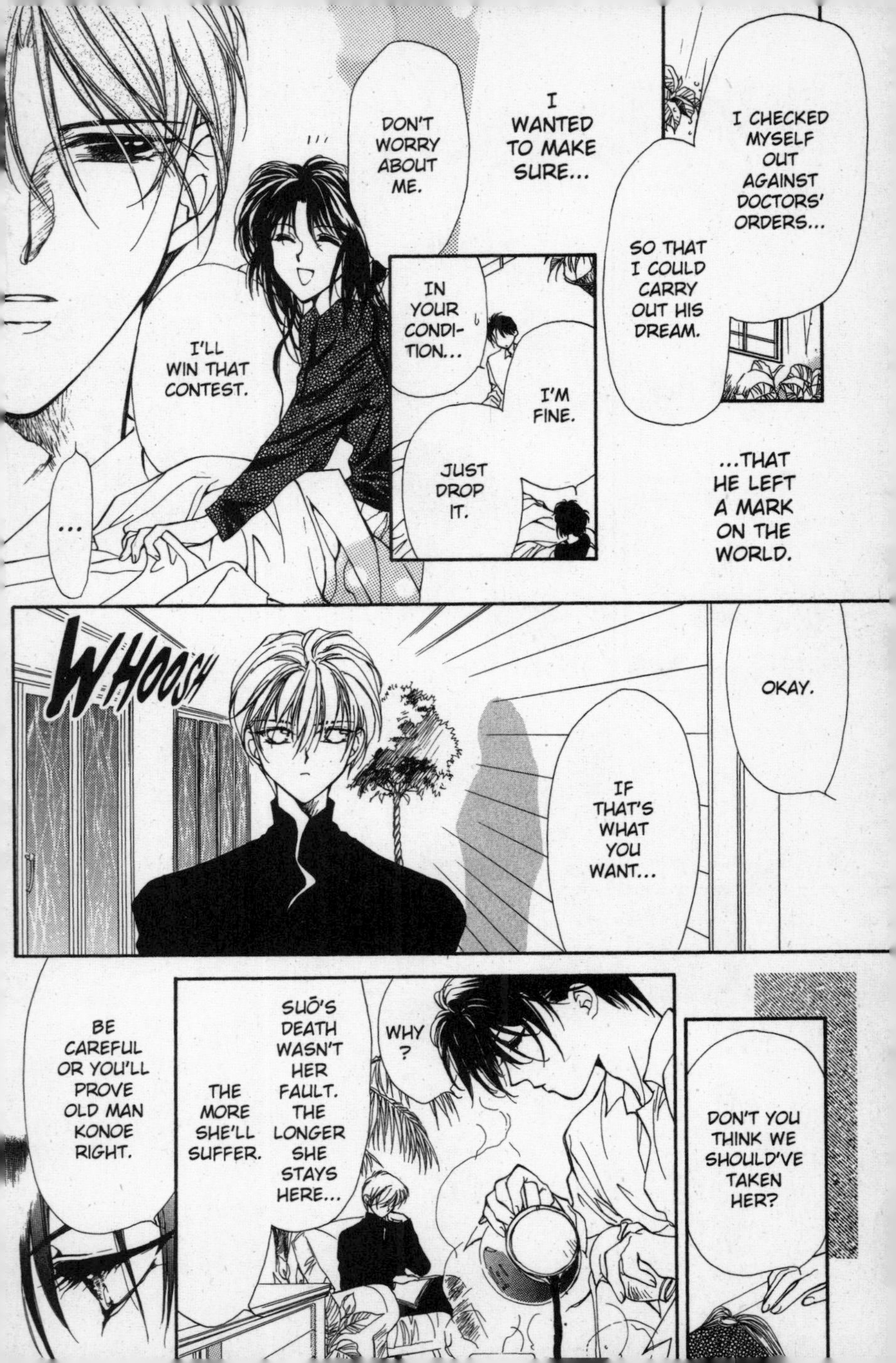
I CHECKED MYSELF OUT AGAINST DOCTORS' ORDERS...
SO THAT I COULD CARRY OUT HIS DREAM.
I WANTED TO MAKE SURE...
...THAT HE LEFT A MARK ON THE WORLD.
IN YOUR CONDITION...
I'M FINE.
JUST DROP IT.
DON'T WORRY ABOUT ME.
I'LL WIN THAT CONTEST.
...
OKAY.
IF THAT'S WHAT YOU WANT...
WHOOSH
DON'T YOU THINK WE SHOULD'VE TAKEN HER?
WHY?
SUŌ'S DEATH WASN'T HER FAULT. THE LONGER SHE STAYS HERE...
THE MORE SHE'LL SUFFER.
BE CAREFUL OR YOU'LL PROVE OLD MAN KONOE RIGHT.

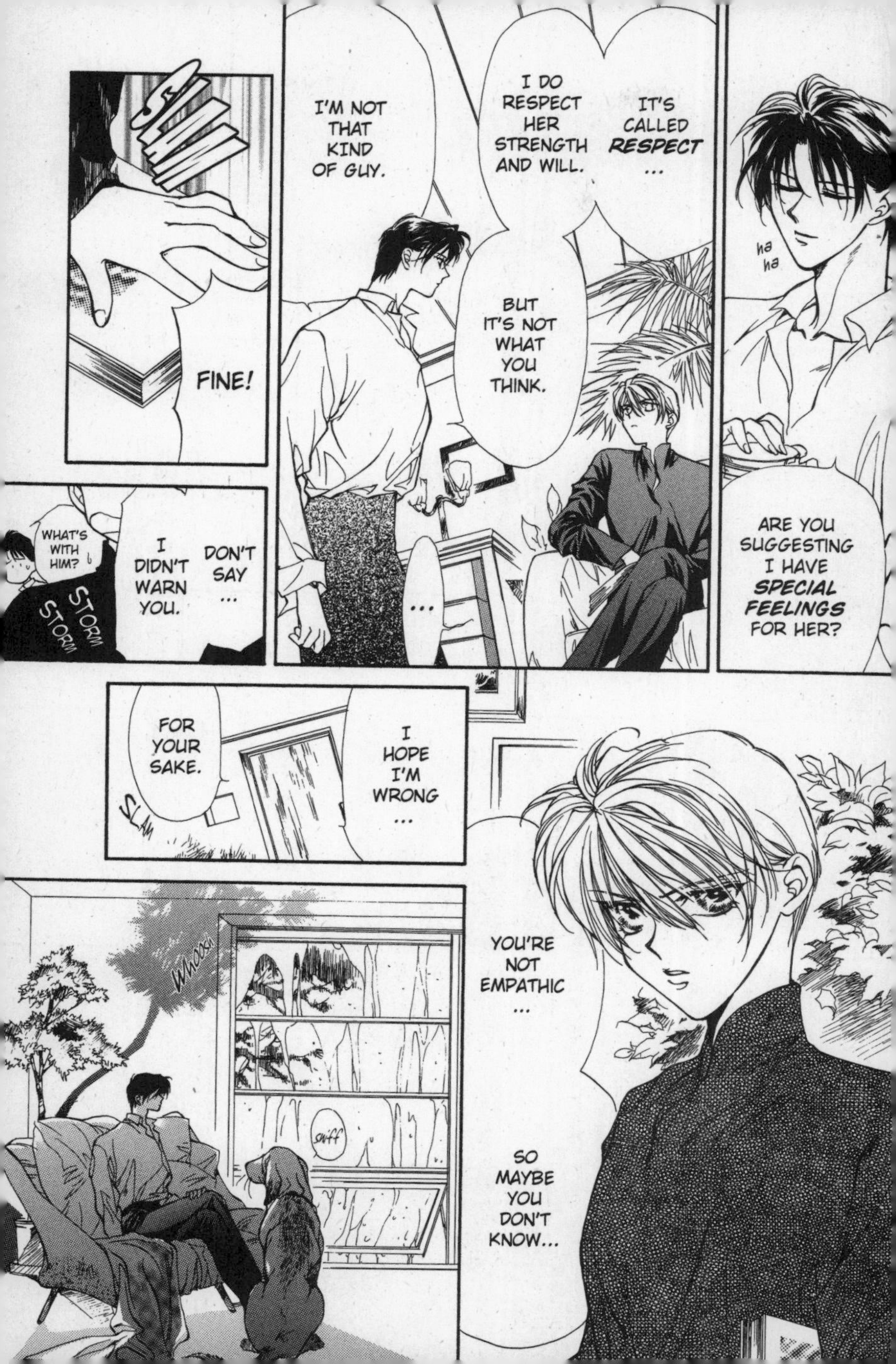
ha ha
ARE YOU SUGGESTING I HAVE SPECIAL FEELINGS FOR HER?
IT'S CALLED RESPECT ...
I DO RESPECT HER STRENGTH AND WILL.
I'M NOT THAT KIND OF GUY.
BUT IT'S NOT WHAT YOU THINK.
...
FINE!
DON'T SAY ...
I DIDN'T WARN YOU.
WHAT'S WITH HIM?
STORM STORM
YOU'RE NOT EMPATHIC ...
SO MAYBE YOU DON'T KNOW...
I HOPE I'M WRONG ...
FOR YOUR SAKE.
SLAM
WHOOSH
sniff

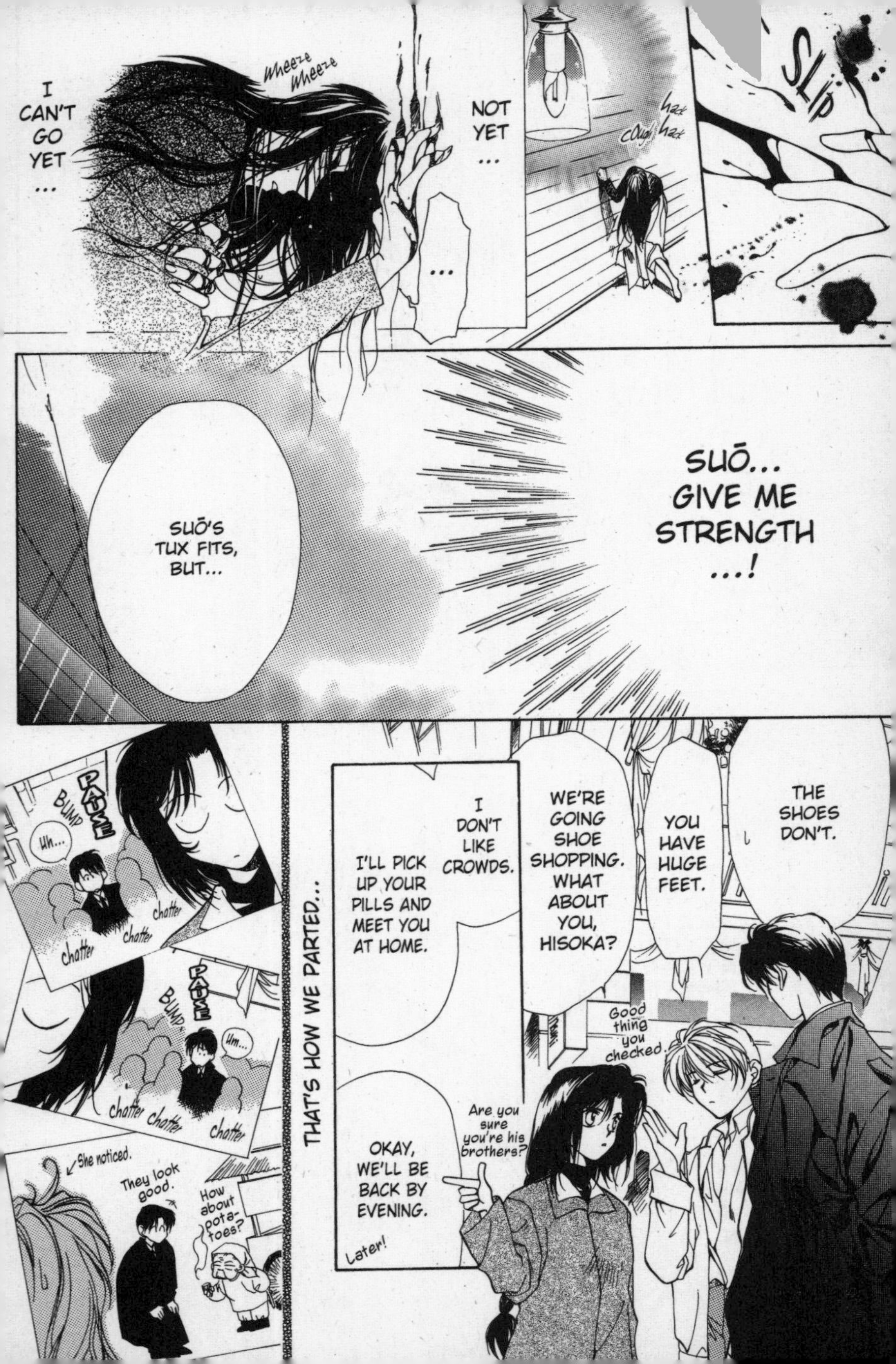
SLIP
hack hack
cough
NOT YET ...
I CAN'T GO YET ...
Wheeze Wheeze
...
SUŌ... GIVE ME STRENGTH ...!
SUŌ'S TUX FITS, BUT...
THE SHOES DON'T.
YOU HAVE HUGE FEET.
Good thing you checked.
WE'RE GOING SHOE SHOPPING. WHAT ABOUT YOU, HISOKA?
I DON'T LIKE CROWDS.
I'LL PICK UP YOUR PILLS AND MEET YOU AT HOME.
Are you sure you're his brothers?
OKAY, WE'LL BE BACK BY EVENING.
Later!
THAT'S HOW WE PARTED...
PAUSE
BUMP
Uh...
chatter chatter chatter
PAUSE
BUMP
Um...
chatter chatter chatter
She noticed.
They look good.
How about pota-toes?

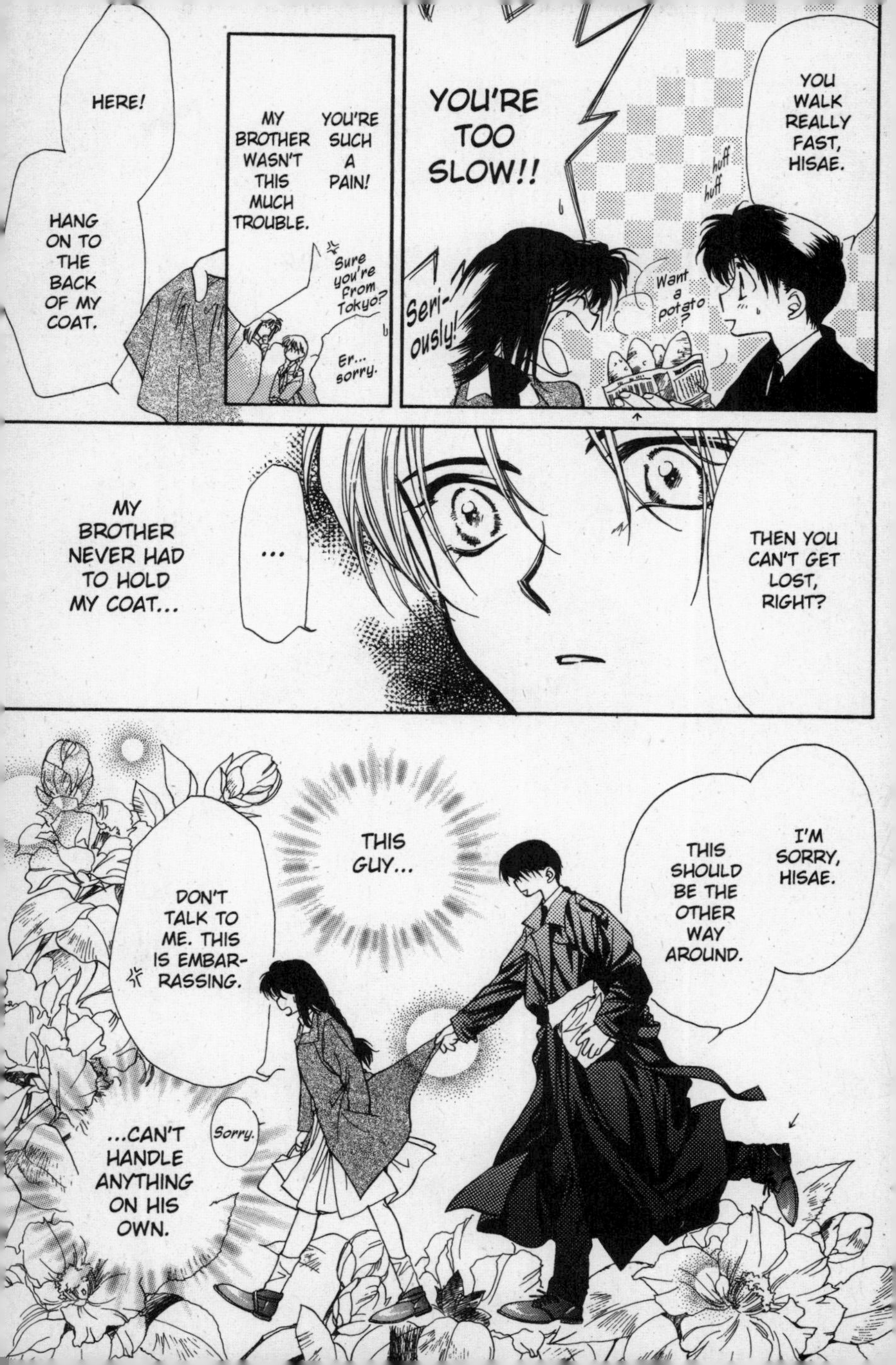
YOU WALK REALLY FAST, HISAE.
huff huff
YOU'RE TOO SLOW!!
Want a potato?
Seri-ously!
YOU'RE SUCH A PAIN!
MY BROTHER WASN'T THIS MUCH TROUBLE.
Sure you're from Tokyo?
Er... sorry.
HERE!
HANG ON TO THE BACK OF MY COAT.
THEN YOU CAN'T GET LOST, RIGHT?
...
MY BROTHER NEVER HAD TO HOLD MY COAT...
I'M SORRY, HISAE.
THIS SHOULD BE THE OTHER WAY AROUND.
THIS GUY...
DON'T TALK TO ME. THIS IS EMBARRASSING.
Sorry.
...CAN'T HANDLE ANYTHING ON HIS OWN.

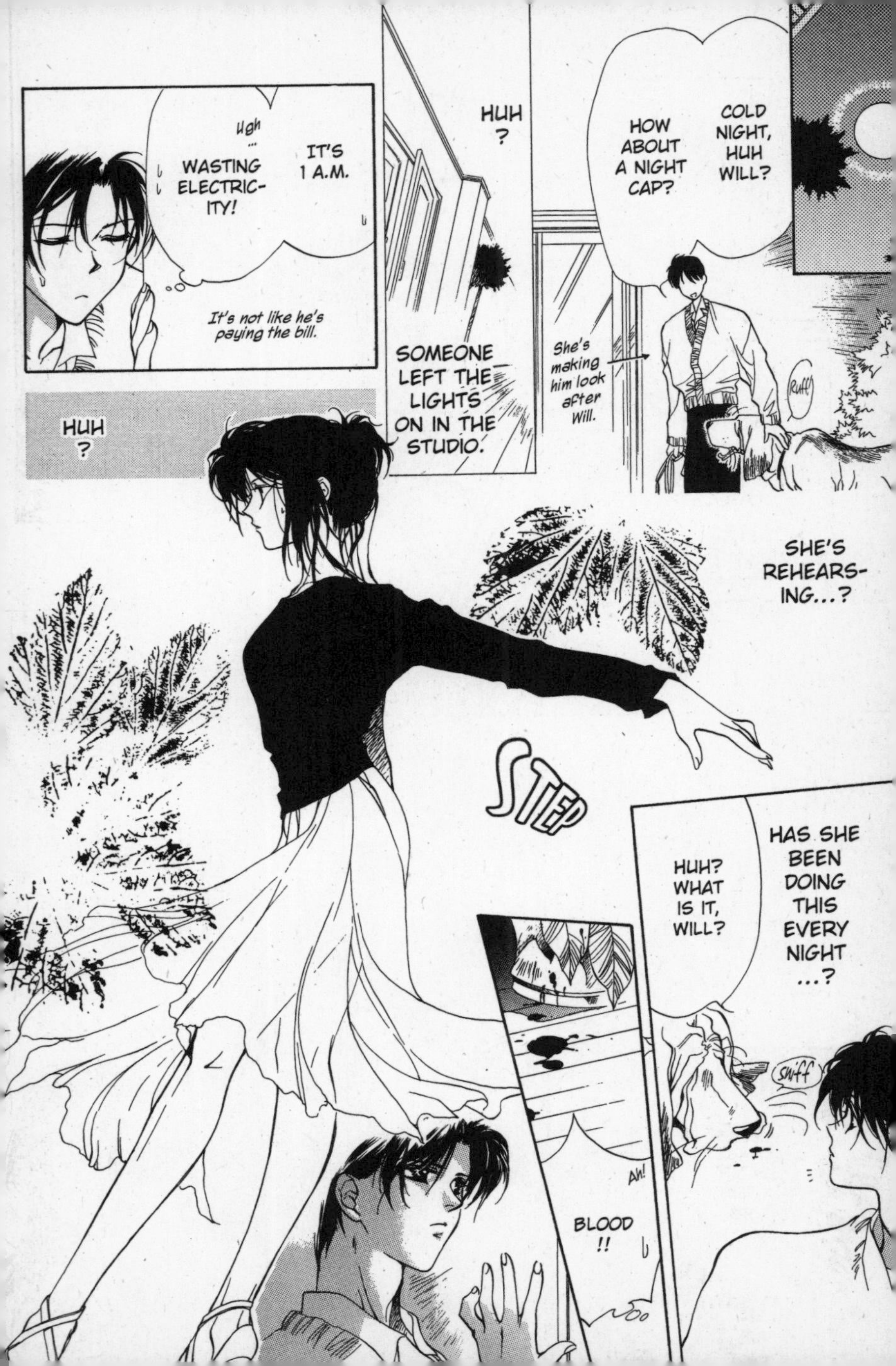

COLD NIGHT, HUH WILL?
HOW ABOUT A NIGHT CAP?
She's making him look after Will.
Ruff!
HUH ?
SOMEONE LEFT THE LIGHTS ON IN THE STUDIO.
IT'S 1 A.M.
Ugh ... WASTING ELECTRIC-ITY!
It's not like he's paying the bill.
HUH ?
SHE'S REHEARS-ING...?
STEP
HAS SHE BEEN DOING THIS EVERY NIGHT ...?
HUH? WHAT IS IT, WILL?
sniff
Ah!
BLOOD !!

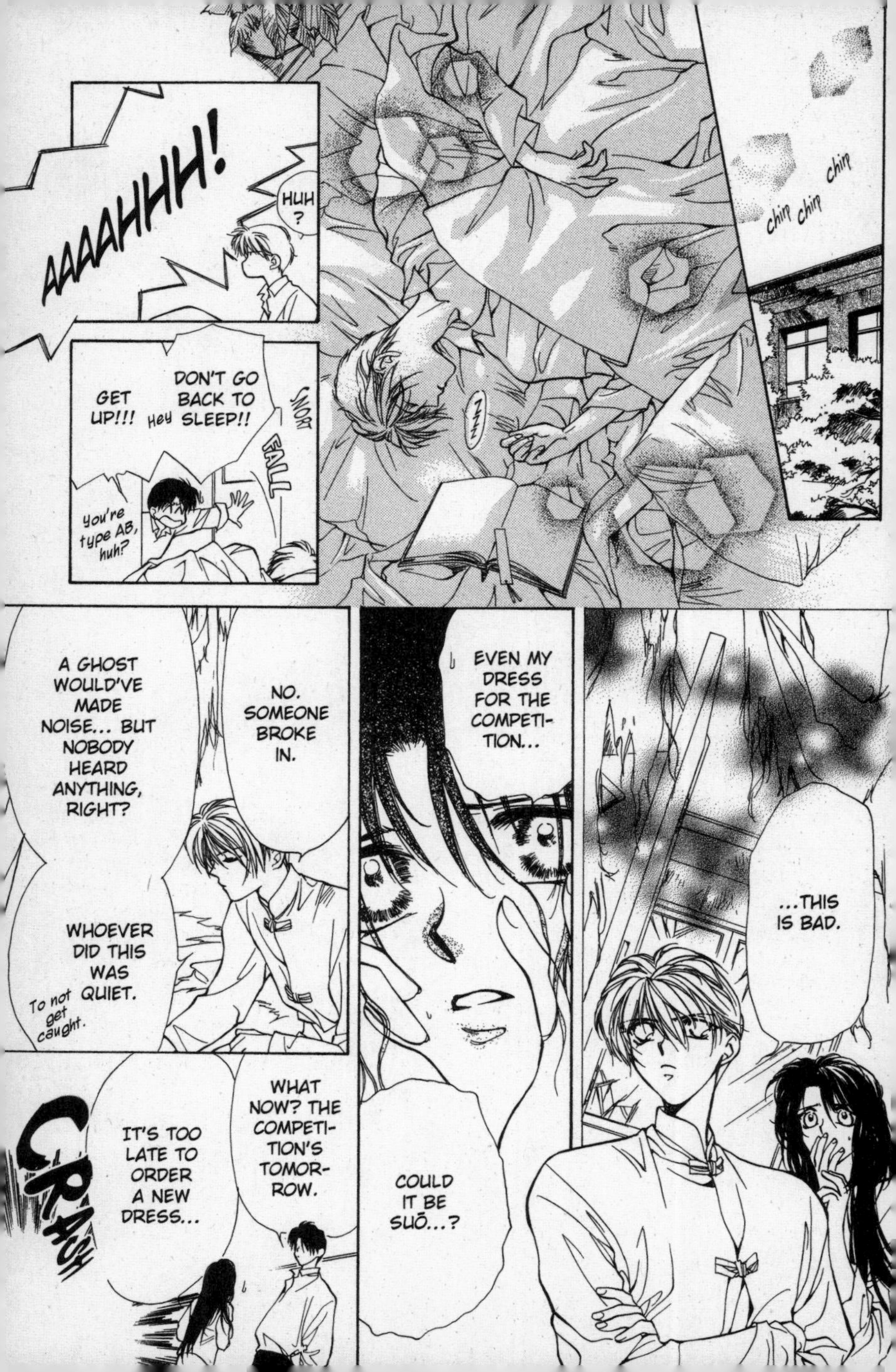
Chirp chirp chirp
ZZZ
AAAAHHH!
HUH ?
DON'T GO BACK TO SLEEP!!
Hey
GET UP!!!
SNORT
FALL
you're type AB, huh?
...THIS IS BAD.
EVEN MY DRESS FOR THE COMPETITION...
COULD IT BE SUŌ...?
NO. SOMEONE BROKE IN.
A GHOST WOULD'VE MADE NOISE... BUT NOBODY HEARD ANYTHING, RIGHT?
WHOEVER DID THIS WAS QUIET.
To not get caught.
WHAT NOW? THE COMPETITION'S TOMORROW.
IT'S TOO LATE TO ORDER A NEW DRESS...
CRASH

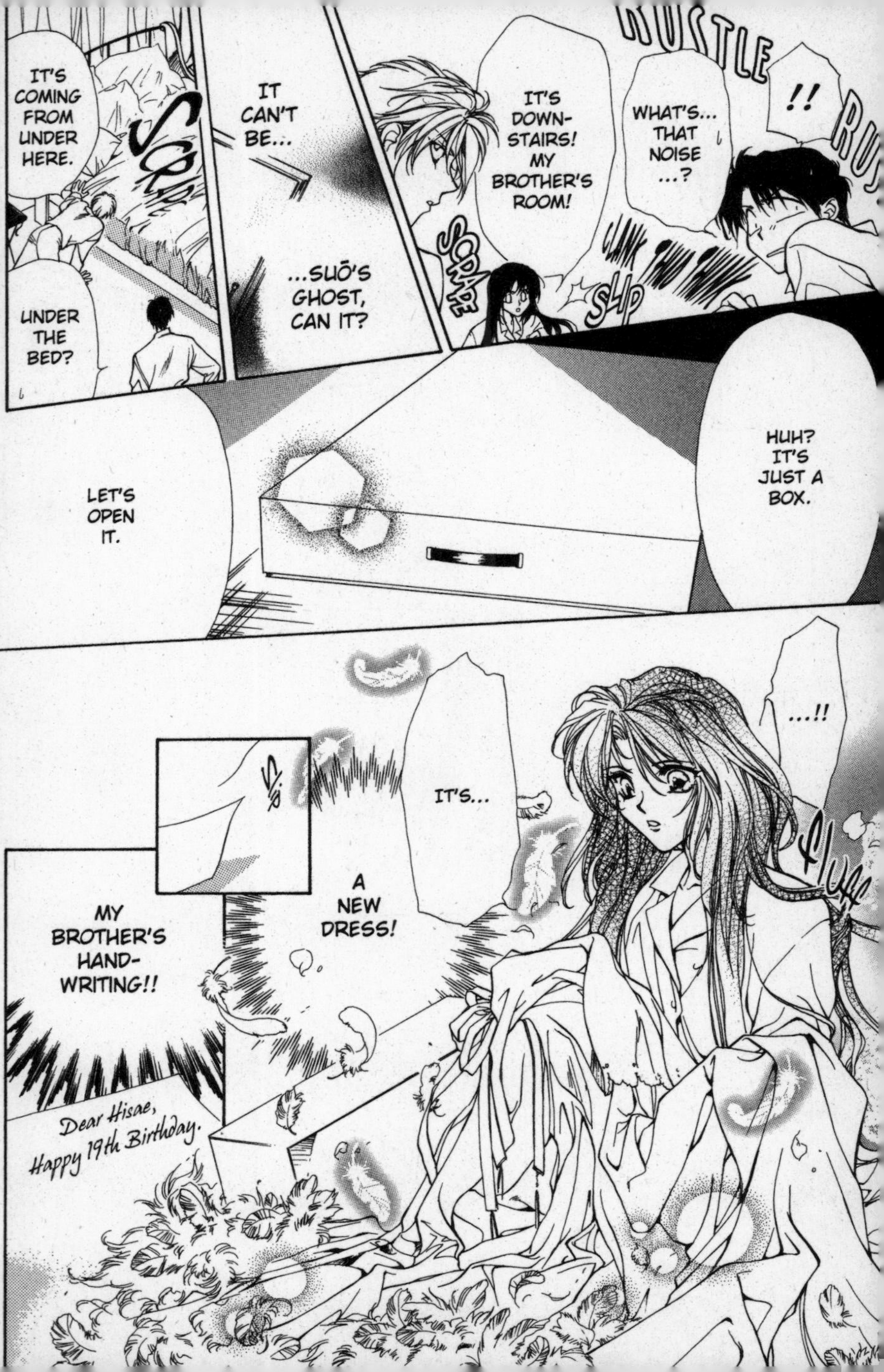
RUSTLE
RUS
!!
WHAT'S... THAT NOISE ...?
IT'S DOWN-STAIRS! MY BROTHER'S ROOM!
CLANK
SLIP
SCRAPE
IT CAN'T BE...
...SUŌ'S GHOST, CAN IT?
IT'S COMING FROM UNDER HERE.
SCRP
UNDER THE BED?
HUH? IT'S JUST A BOX.
LET'S OPEN IT.
...!!
FLUFF
IT'S...
A NEW DRESS!
SLIP
MY BROTHER'S HAND-WRITING!!
Dear Hisae, Happy 19th Birthday.

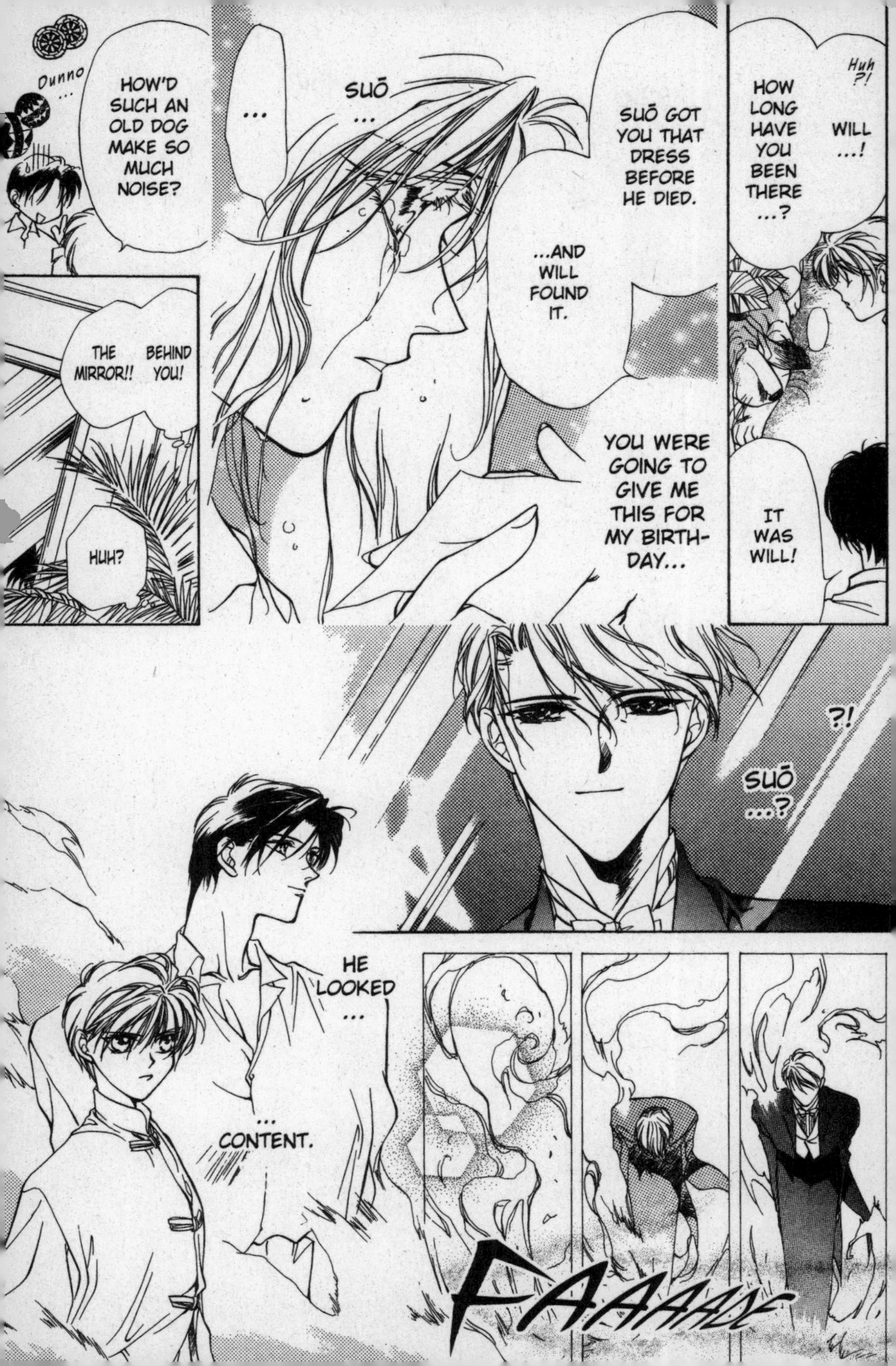
Huh ?!
WILL ...!
HOW LONG HAVE YOU BEEN THERE ...?
IT WAS WILL!
SUŌ GOT YOU THAT DRESS BEFORE HE DIED.
...AND WILL FOUND IT.
YOU WERE GOING TO GIVE ME THIS FOR MY BIRTH-DAY...
SUŌ ...
...
HOW'D SUCH AN OLD DOG MAKE SO MUCH NOISE?
Dunno ...
BEHIND YOU!
THE MIRROR!!
HUH?
?!
SUŌ ...?
HE LOOKED ...
... CONTENT.

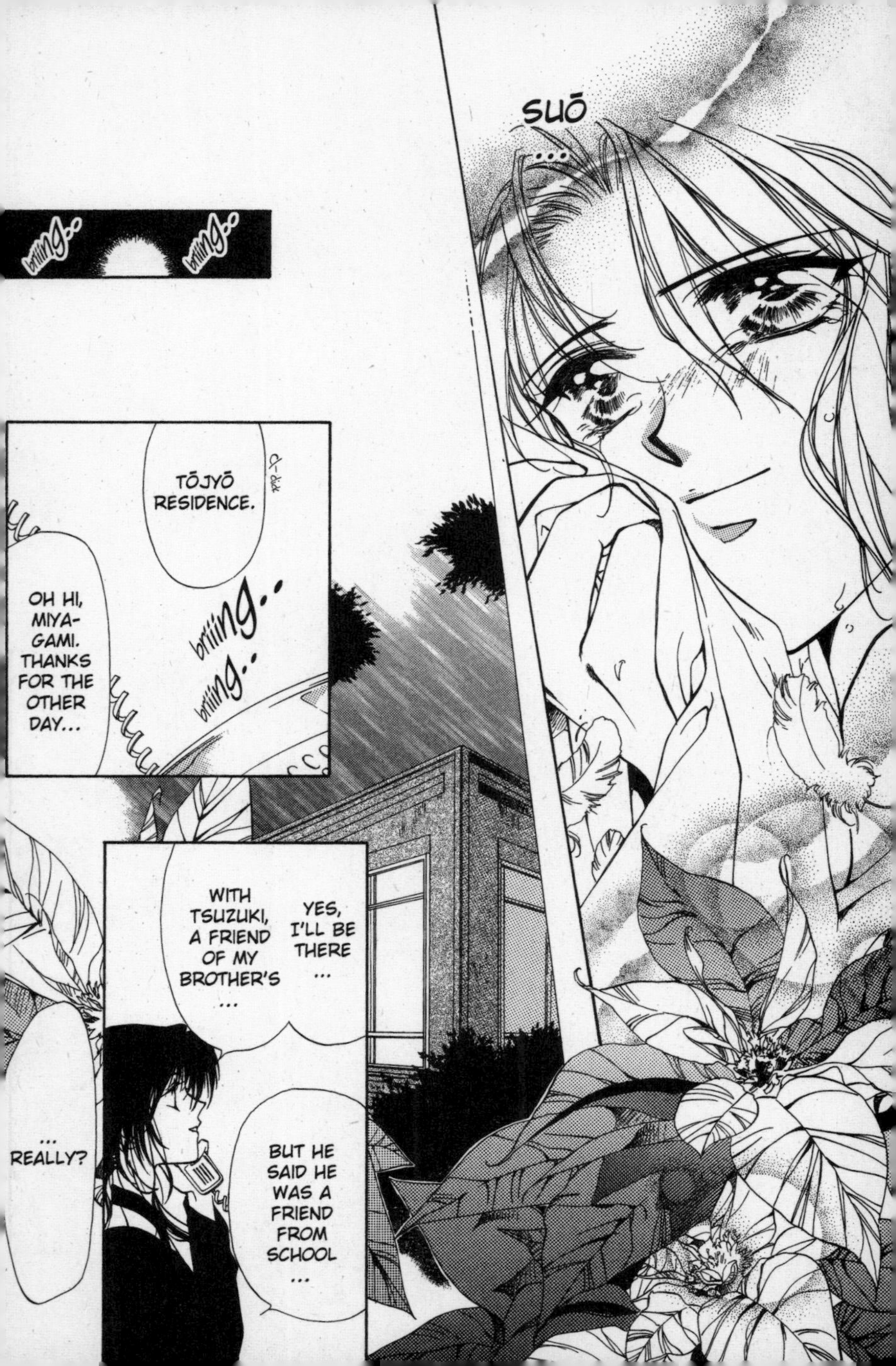
SUŌ ...
briiing.. briiing..
cl-click
TŌJYŌ RESIDENCE.
briiing.. briiing..
OH HI, MIYA-GAMI. THANKS FOR THE OTHER DAY...
YES, I'LL BE THERE ...
WITH TSUZUKI, A FRIEND OF MY BROTHER'S ...
BUT HE SAID HE WAS A FRIEND FROM SCHOOL ...
... REALLY?

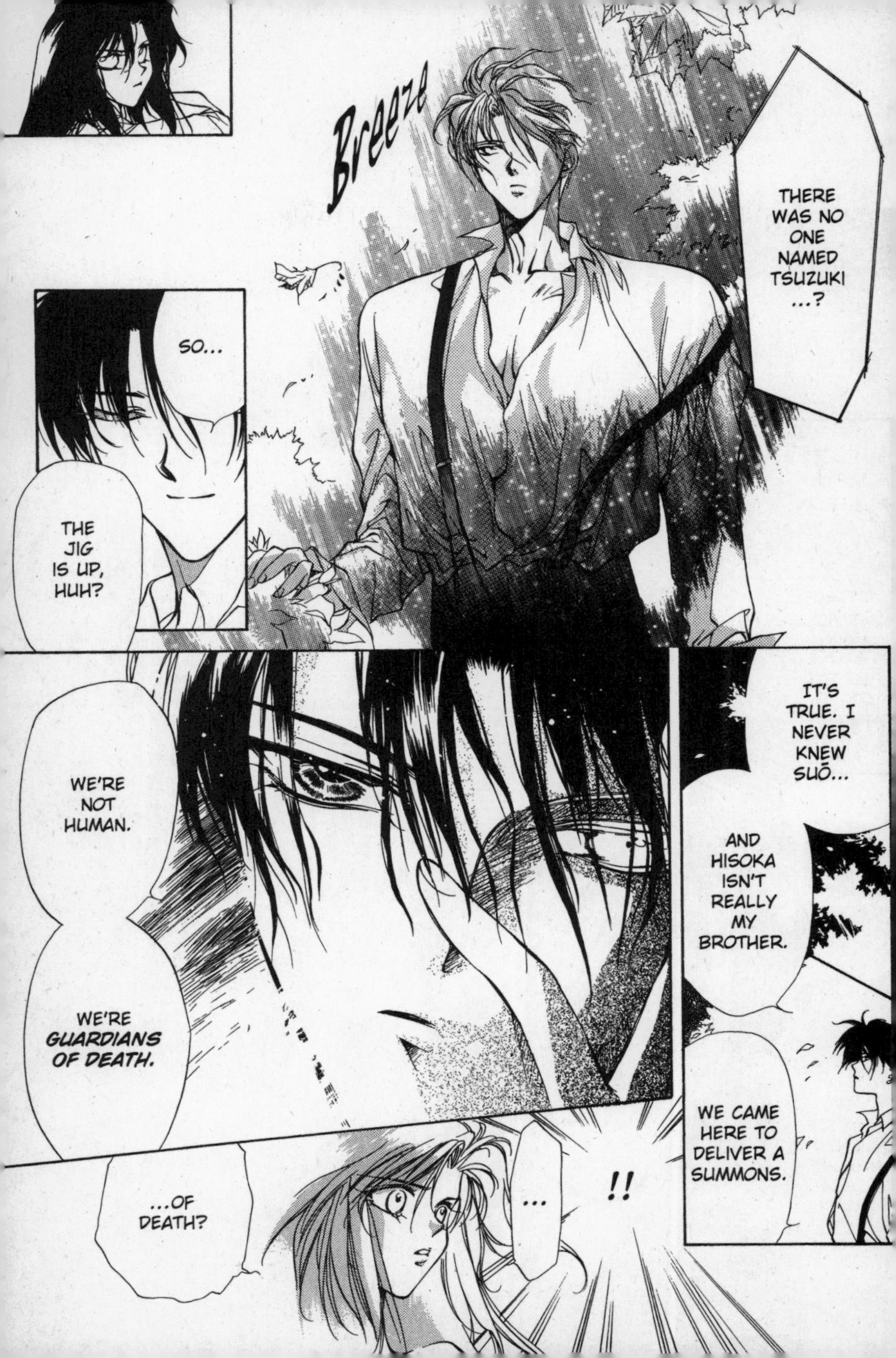
Breeze
THERE WAS NO ONE NAMED TSUZUKI ...?
SO...
THE JIG IS UP, HUH?
IT'S TRUE. I NEVER KNEW SUŌ...
AND HISOKA ISN'T REALLY MY BROTHER.
WE CAME HERE TO DELIVER A SUMMONS.
WE'RE NOT HUMAN.
WE'RE *GUARDIANS OF DEATH*.
!!
...
...OF DEATH?

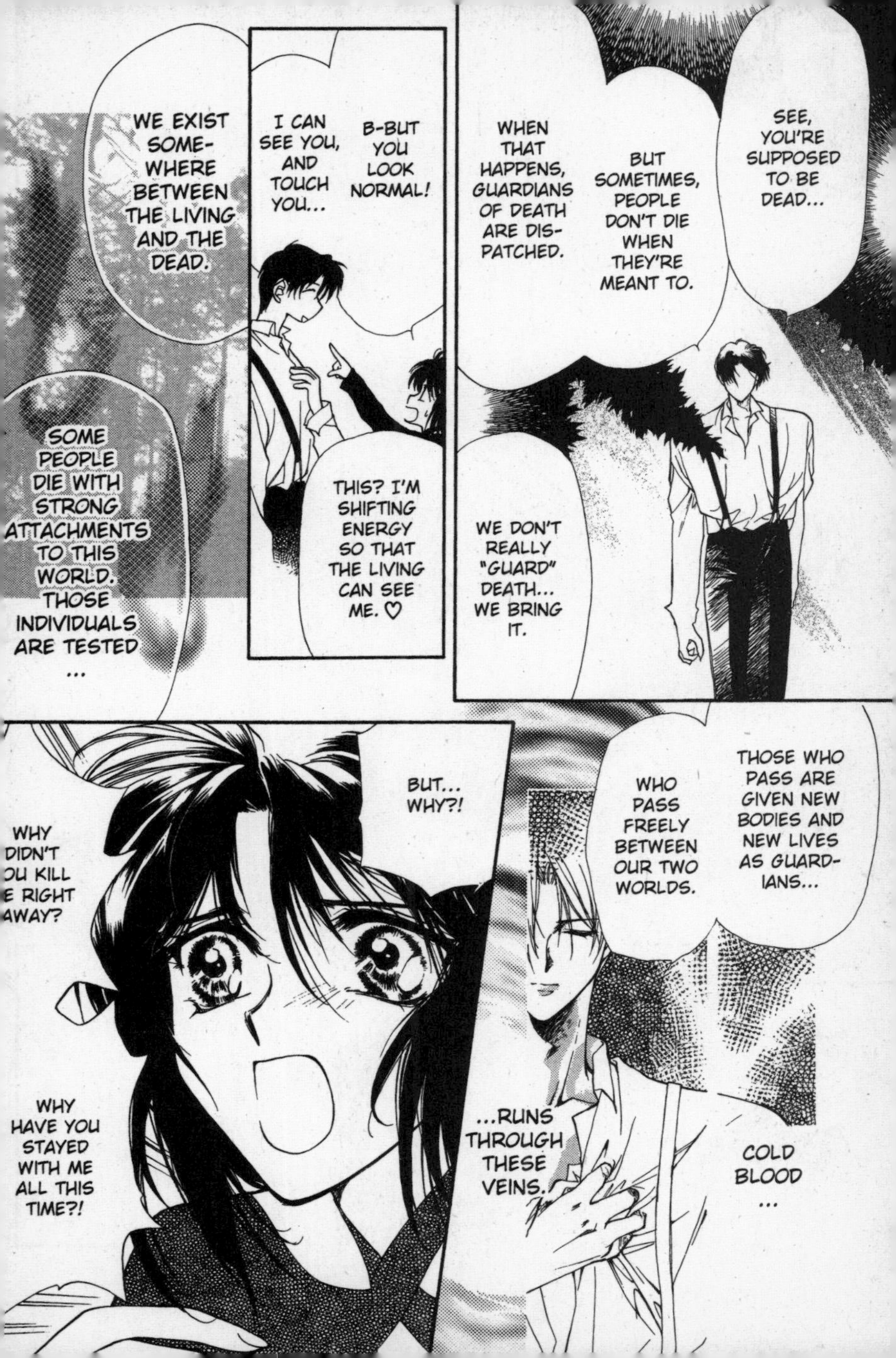
SEE, YOU'RE SUPPOSED TO BE DEAD...
BUT SOMETIMES, PEOPLE DON'T DIE WHEN THEY'RE MEANT TO.
WHEN THAT HAPPENS, GUARDIANS OF DEATH ARE DISPATCHED.
WE DON'T REALLY "GUARD" DEATH... WE BRING IT.
B-BUT YOU LOOK NORMAL!
I CAN SEE YOU, AND TOUCH YOU...
THIS? I'M SHIFTING ENERGY SO THAT THE LIVING CAN SEE ME. ♡
WE EXIST SOME-WHERE BETWEEN THE LIVING AND THE DEAD.
SOME PEOPLE DIE WITH STRONG ATTACHMENTS TO THIS WORLD. THOSE INDIVIDUALS ARE TESTED ...
THOSE WHO PASS ARE GIVEN NEW BODIES AND NEW LIVES AS GUARD-IANS...
WHO PASS FREELY BETWEEN OUR TWO WORLDS.
COLD BLOOD ...
...RUNS THROUGH THESE VEINS.
BUT... WHY?!
WHY DIDN'T OU KILL E RIGHT AWAY?
WHY HAVE YOU STAYED WITH ME ALL THIS TIME?!

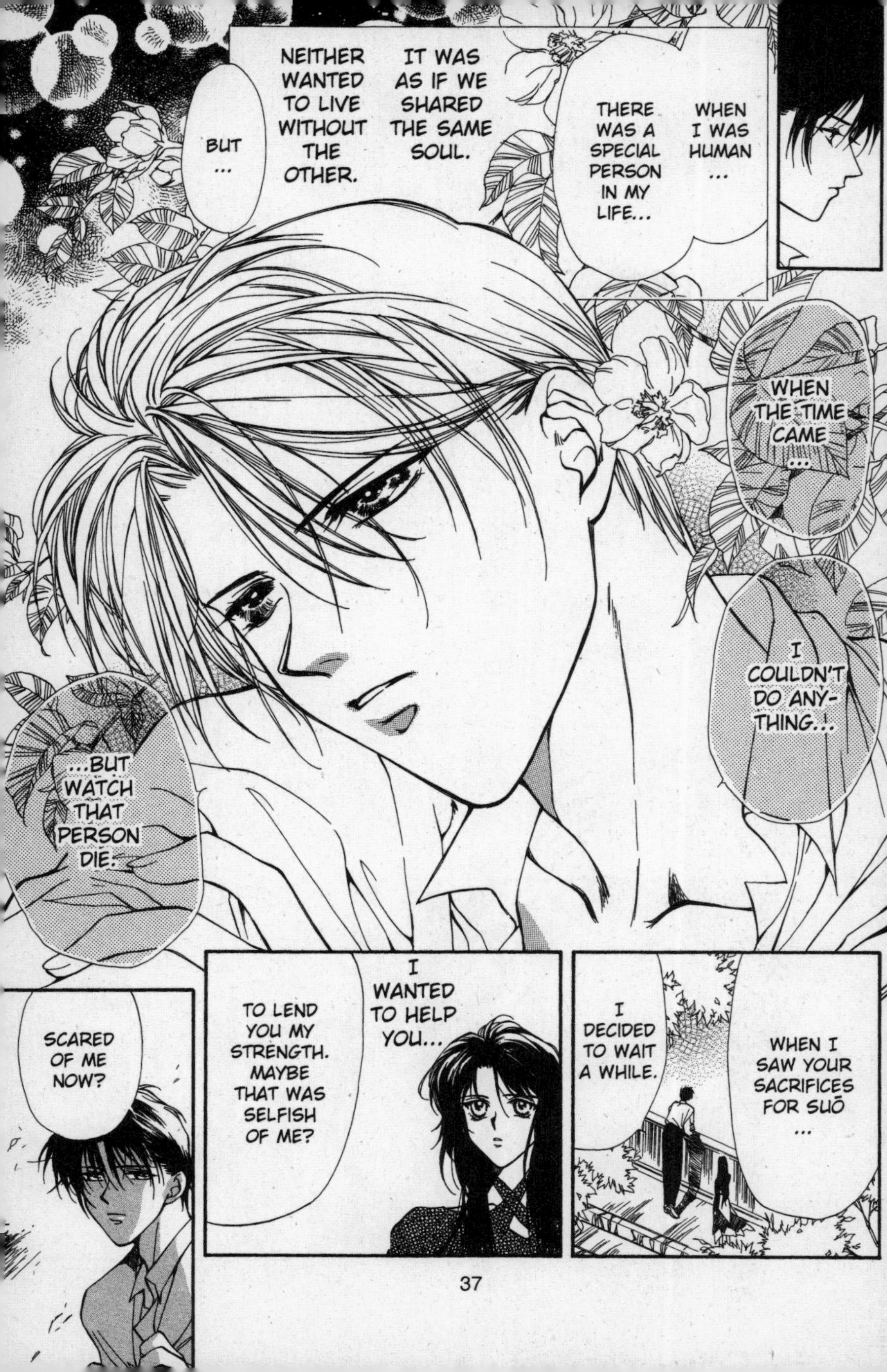
WHEN I WAS HUMAN ...
THERE WAS A SPECIAL PERSON IN MY LIFE...
IT WAS AS IF WE SHARED THE SAME SOUL.
NEITHER WANTED TO LIVE WITHOUT THE OTHER.
BUT ...
WHEN THE TIME CAME ...
I COULDN'T DO ANY-THING...
...BUT WATCH THAT PERSON DIE.
WHEN I SAW YOUR SACRIFICES FOR SUŌ ...
I DECIDED TO WAIT A WHILE.
I WANTED TO HELP YOU...
TO LEND YOU MY STRENGTH. MAYBE THAT WAS SELFISH OF ME?
SCARED OF ME NOW?

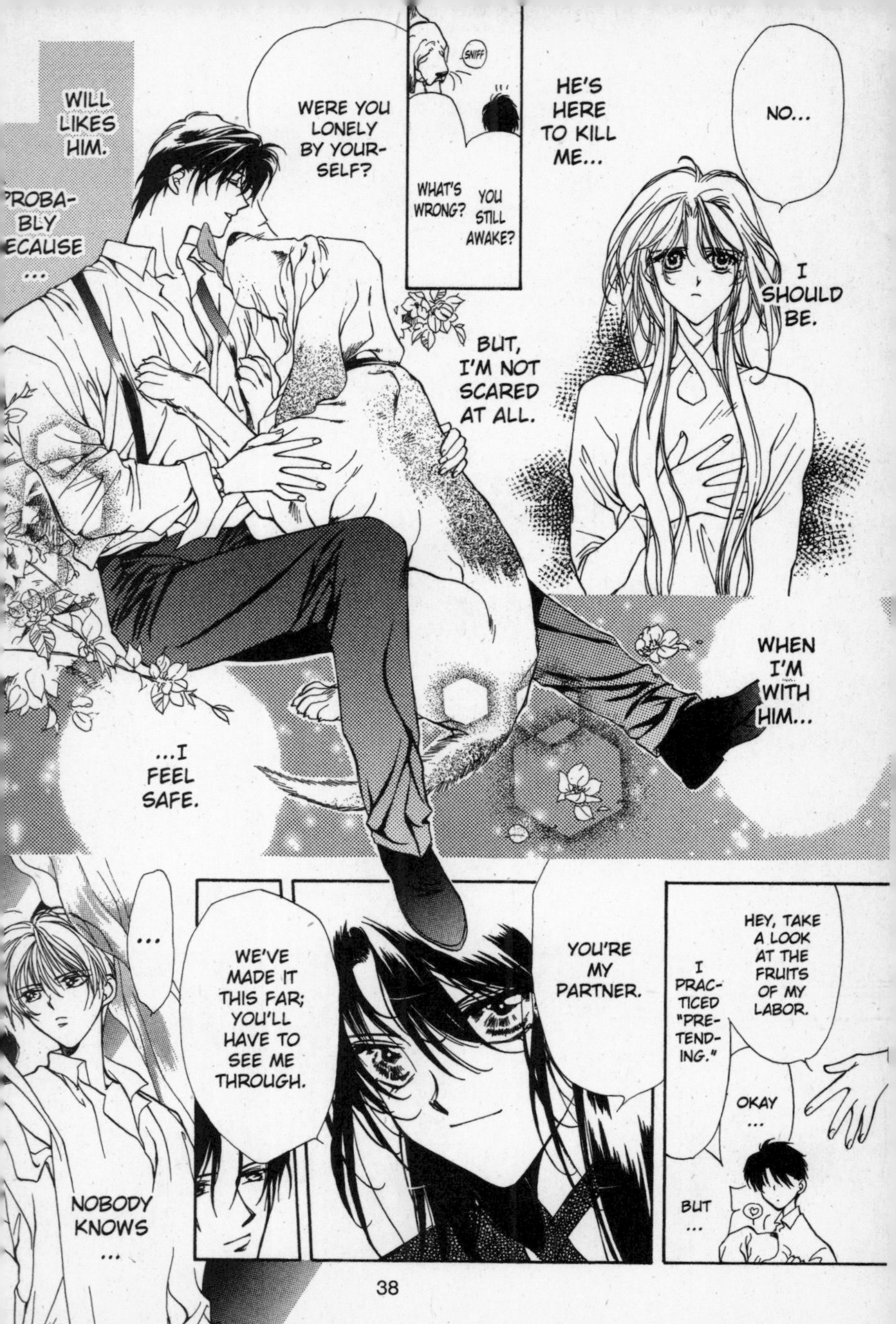

NO...
I SHOULD BE.
HE'S HERE TO KILL ME...
BUT, I'M NOT SCARED AT ALL.
SNIFF
YOU STILL AWAKE?
WHAT'S WRONG?
WERE YOU LONELY BY YOURSELF?
WILL LIKES HIM.
ROBA-BLY ECAUSE ...
WHEN I'M WITH HIM...
...I FEEL SAFE.
HEY, TAKE A LOOK AT THE FRUITS OF MY LABOR.
I PRACTICED "PRETENDING."
OKAY ...
BUT ...
YOU'RE MY PARTNER.
WE'VE MADE IT THIS FAR; YOU'LL HAVE TO SEE ME THROUGH.
...
NOBODY KNOWS ...

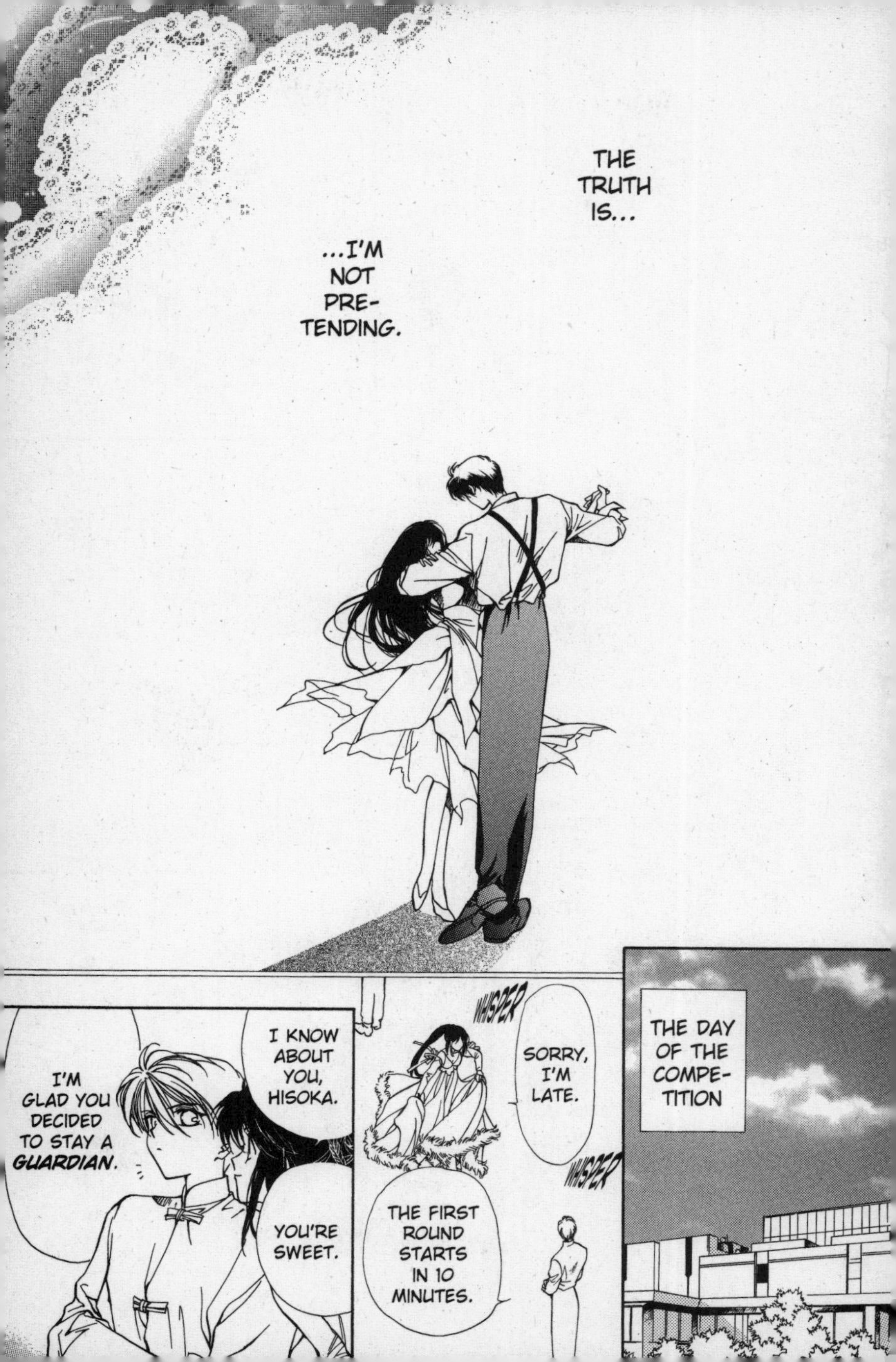

THE TRUTH IS...
...I'M NOT PRE-TENDING.
THE DAY OF THE COMPE-TITION
WHISPER
SORRY, I'M LATE.
WHISPER
THE FIRST ROUND STARTS IN 10 MINUTES.
I KNOW ABOUT YOU, HISOKA.
I'M GLAD YOU DECIDED TO STAY A **GUARDIAN**.
YOU'RE SWEET.

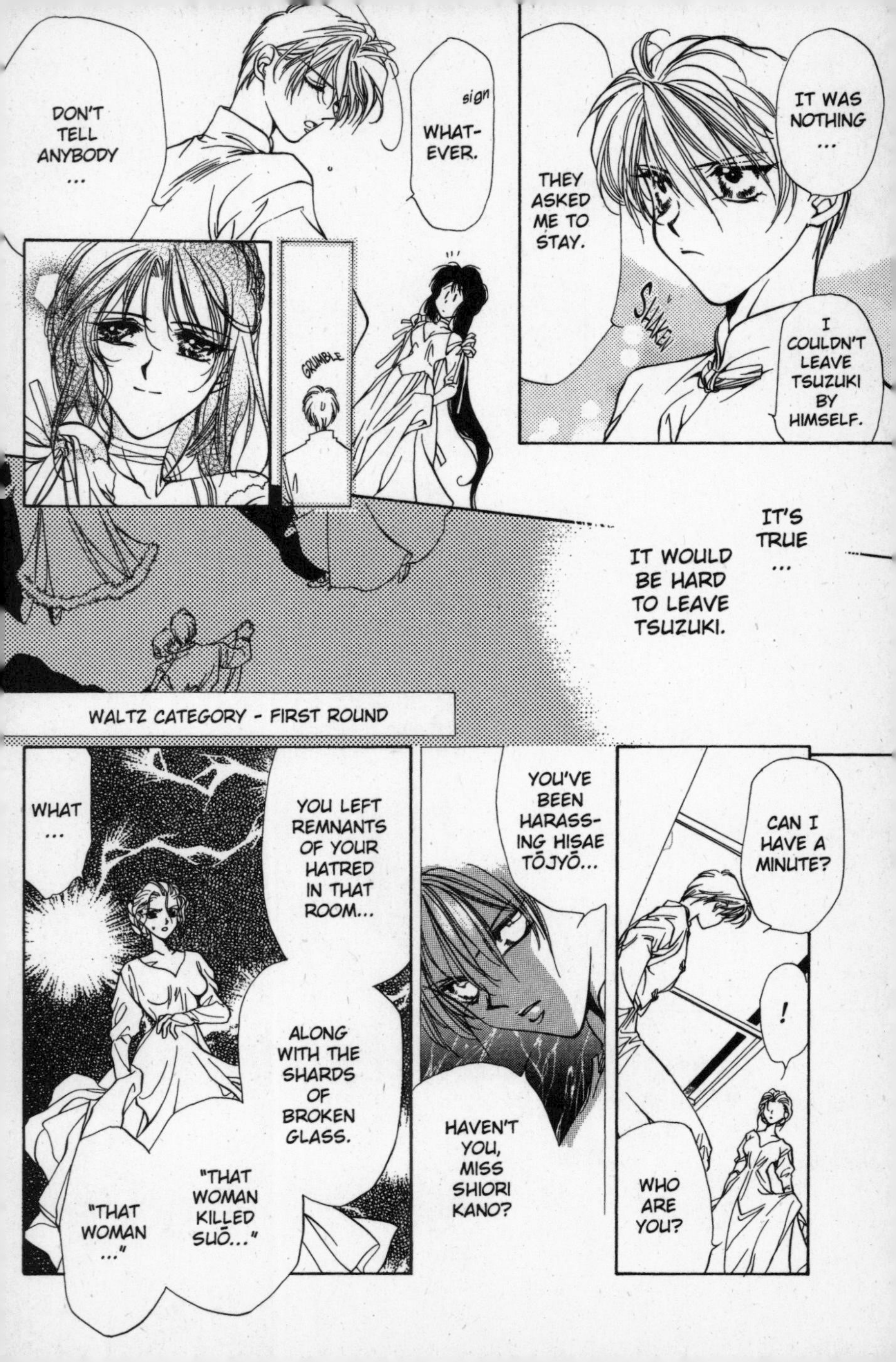

IT WAS NOTHING ...
THEY ASKED ME TO STAY.
SHAKEN
I COULDN'T LEAVE TSUZUKI BY HIMSELF.
sign
WHAT-EVER.
DON'T TELL ANYBODY ...
IT'S TRUE ...
IT WOULD BE HARD TO LEAVE TSUZUKI.
GRUMBLE
WALTZ CATEGORY - FIRST ROUND
CAN I HAVE A MINUTE?
!
WHO ARE YOU?
YOU'VE BEEN HARASS-ING HISAE TŌJYŌ...
HAVEN'T YOU, MISS SHIORI KANO?
YOU LEFT REMNANTS OF YOUR HATRED IN THAT ROOM...
WHAT ...
ALONG WITH THE SHARDS OF BROKEN GLASS.
"THAT WOMAN KILLED SUŌ..."
"THAT WOMAN ..."

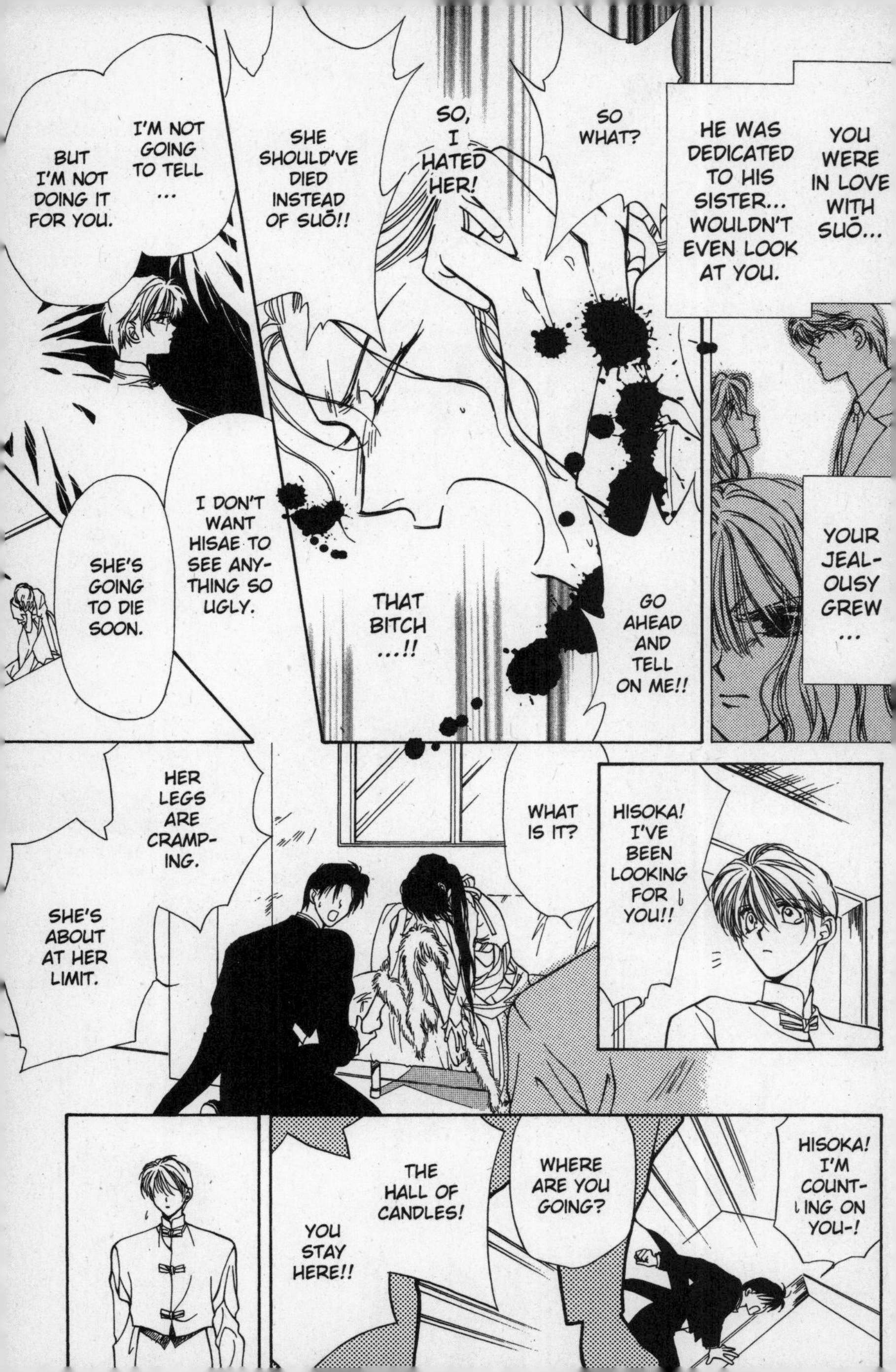
YOU WERE IN LOVE WITH SUŌ...
HE WAS DEDICATED TO HIS SISTER... WOULDN'T EVEN LOOK AT YOU.
YOUR JEAL-OUSY GREW...
SO WHAT?
SO, I HATED HER!
SHE SHOULD'VE DIED INSTEAD OF SUŌ!!
GO AHEAD AND TELL ON ME!!
THAT BITCH...!!
I'M NOT GOING TO TELL...
BUT I'M NOT DOING IT FOR YOU.
I DON'T WANT HISAE TO SEE ANY-THING SO UGLY.
SHE'S GOING TO DIE SOON.
HISOKA! I'VE BEEN LOOKING FOR YOU!!
WHAT IS IT?
HER LEGS ARE CRAMP-ING.
SHE'S ABOUT AT HER LIMIT.
HISOKA! I'M COUNT-ING ON YOU-!
WHERE ARE YOU GOING?
THE HALL OF CANDLES!
YOU STAY HERE!!

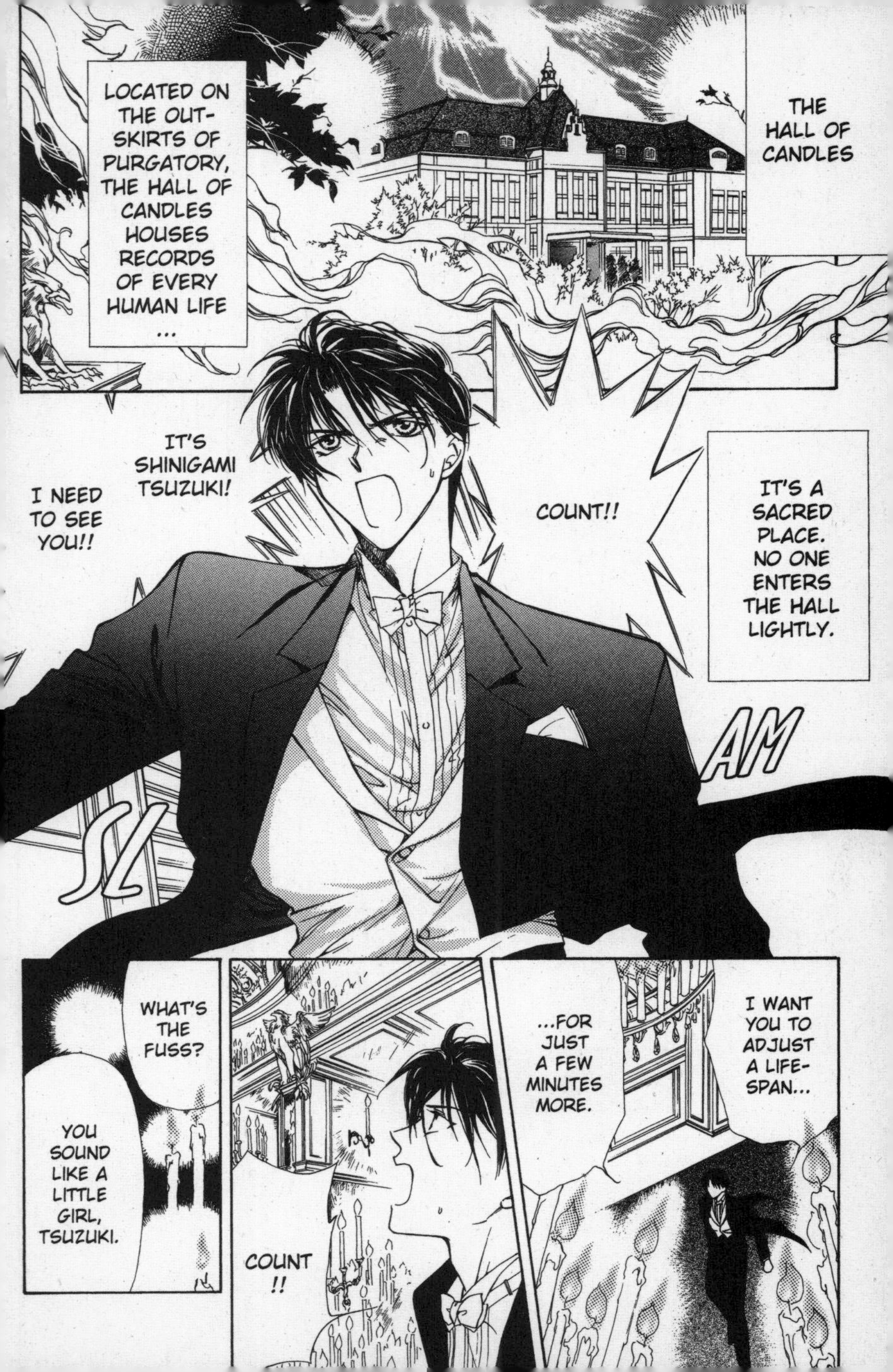
THE HALL OF CANDLES
LOCATED ON THE OUT-SKIRTS OF PURGATORY, THE HALL OF CANDLES HOUSES RECORDS OF EVERY HUMAN LIFE ...
IT'S A SACRED PLACE. NO ONE ENTERS THE HALL LIGHTLY.
COUNT!!
IT'S SHINIGAMI TSUZUKI!
I NEED TO SEE YOU!!
SL
AM
I WANT YOU TO ADJUST A LIFE-SPAN...
...FOR JUST A FEW MINUTES MORE.
COUNT !!
WHAT'S THE FUSS?
YOU SOUND LIKE A LITTLE GIRL, TSUZUKI.

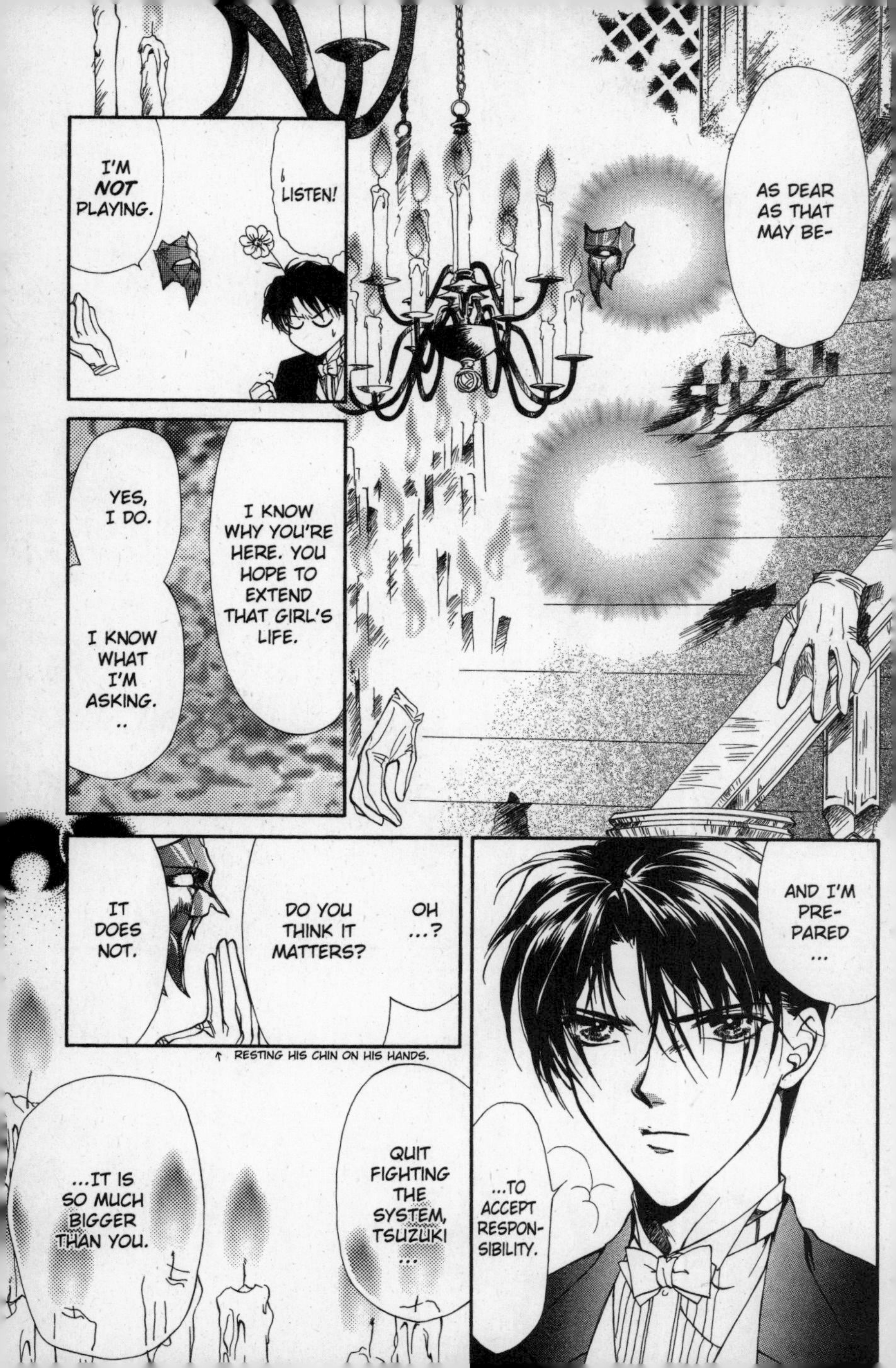
LISTEN!
I'M *NOT* PLAYING.
I KNOW WHY YOU'RE HERE. YOU HOPE TO EXTEND THAT GIRL'S LIFE.
YES, I DO.
I KNOW WHAT I'M ASKING. ..
AS DEAR AS THAT MAY BE-
AND I'M PRE-PARED ...
...TO ACCEPT RESPON-SIBILITY.
OH ...?
DO YOU THINK IT MATTERS?
IT DOES NOT.
↑ RESTING HIS CHIN ON HIS HANDS.
QUIT FIGHTING THE SYSTEM, TSUZUKI ...
...IT IS SO MUCH BIGGER THAN YOU.

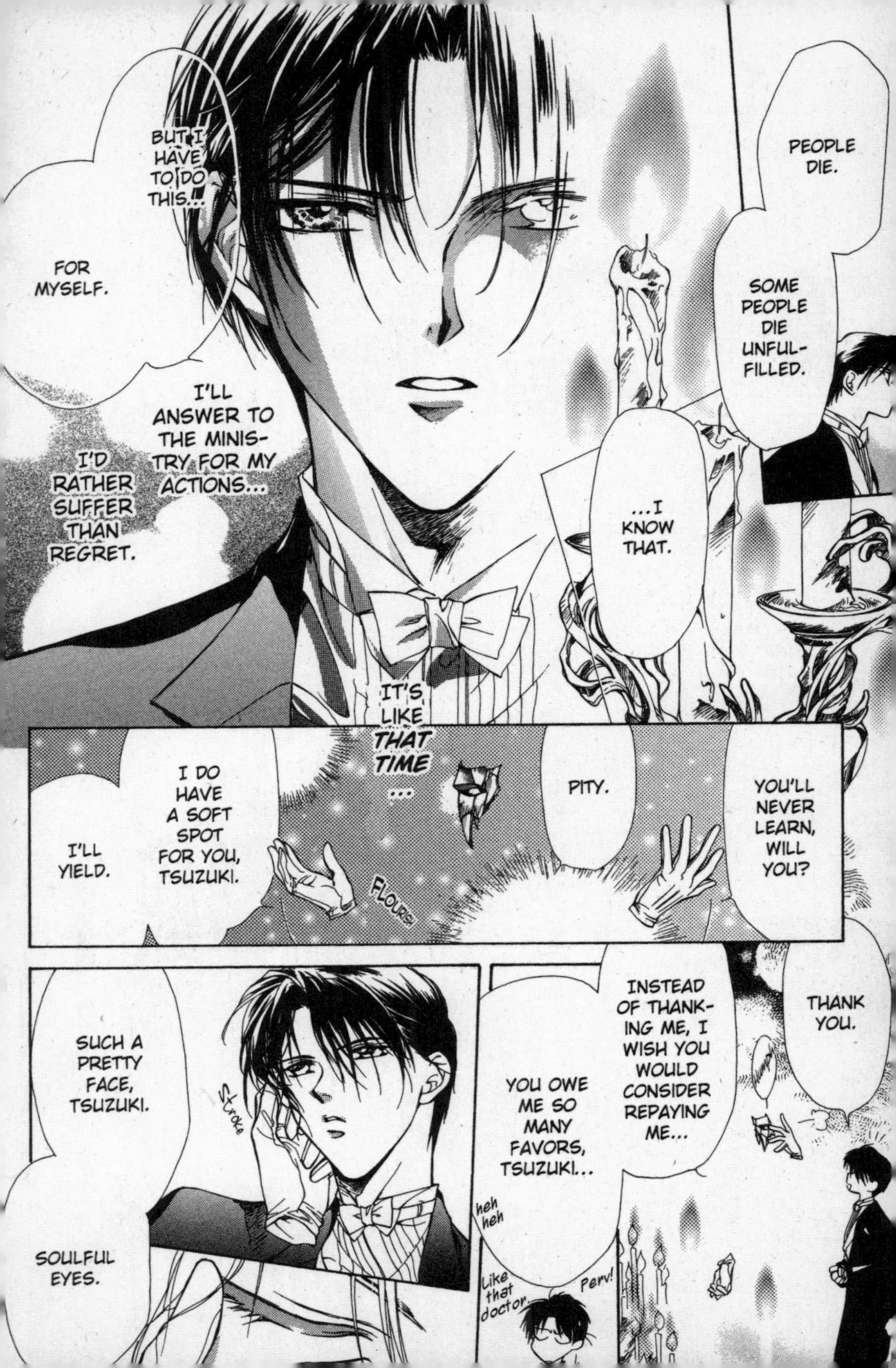
PEOPLE DIE.
SOME PEOPLE DIE UNFULFILLED.
...I KNOW THAT.
BUT I HAVE TO DO THIS...
FOR MYSELF.
I'LL ANSWER TO THE MINISTRY FOR MY ACTIONS...
I'D RATHER SUFFER THAN REGRET.
IT'S LIKE *THAT TIME*...
YOU'LL NEVER LEARN, WILL YOU?
PITY.
FLOURISH
I DO HAVE A SOFT SPOT FOR YOU, TSUZUKI.
I'LL YIELD.
THANK YOU.
INSTEAD OF THANKING ME, I WISH YOU WOULD CONSIDER REPAYING ME...
YOU OWE ME SO MANY FAVORS, TSUZUKI...
heh heh
Perv!
Like that doctor.
SUCH A PRETTY FACE, TSUZUKI.
Stroke
SOULFUL EYES.

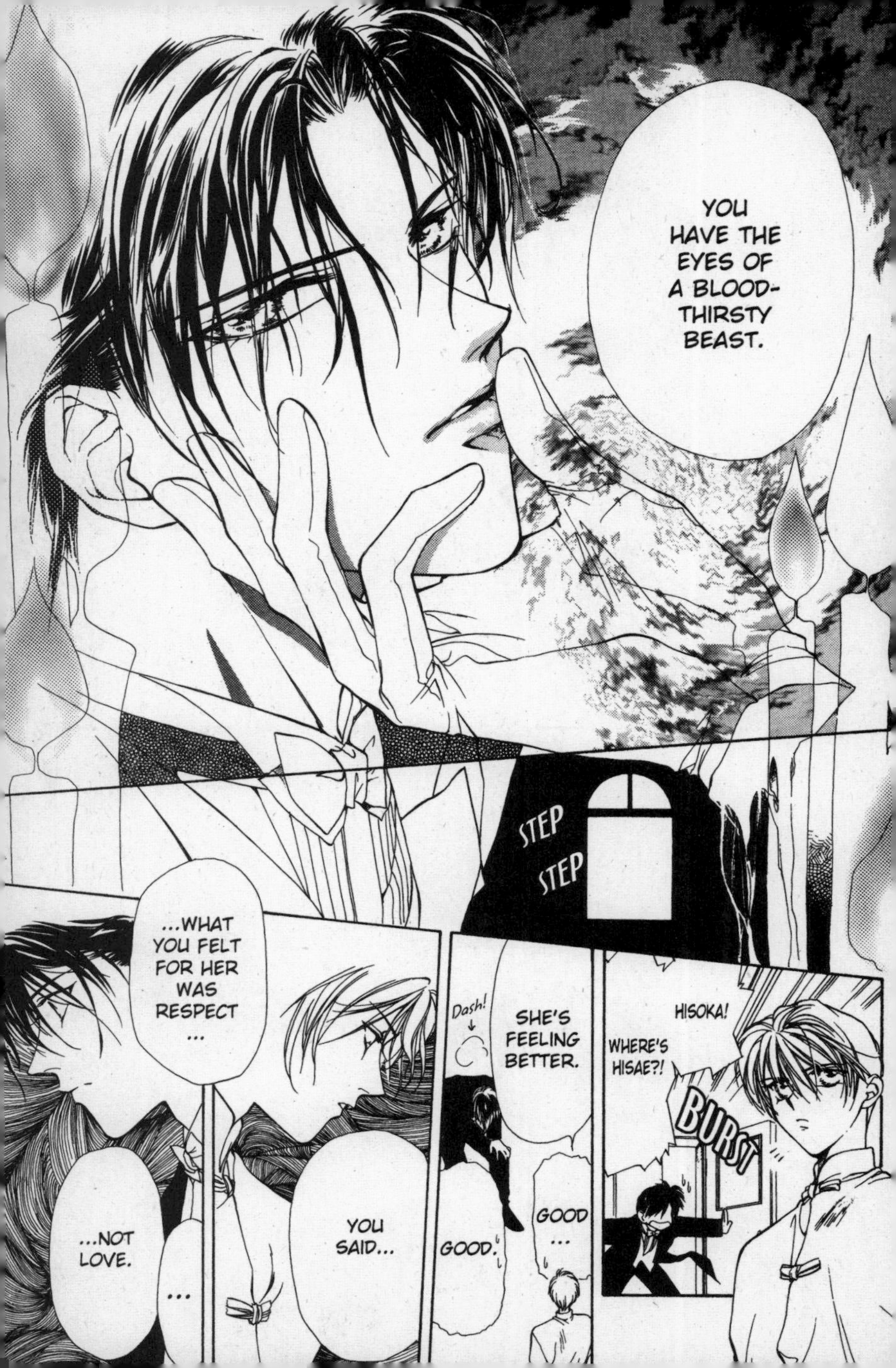
YOU HAVE THE EYES OF A BLOOD-THIRSTY BEAST.
STEP
STEP
HISOKA!
WHERE'S HISAE?!
BURST
SHE'S FEELING BETTER.
Dash!
GOOD...
GOOD.
...WHAT YOU FELT FOR HER WAS RESPECT ...
YOU SAID...
...
...NOT LOVE.

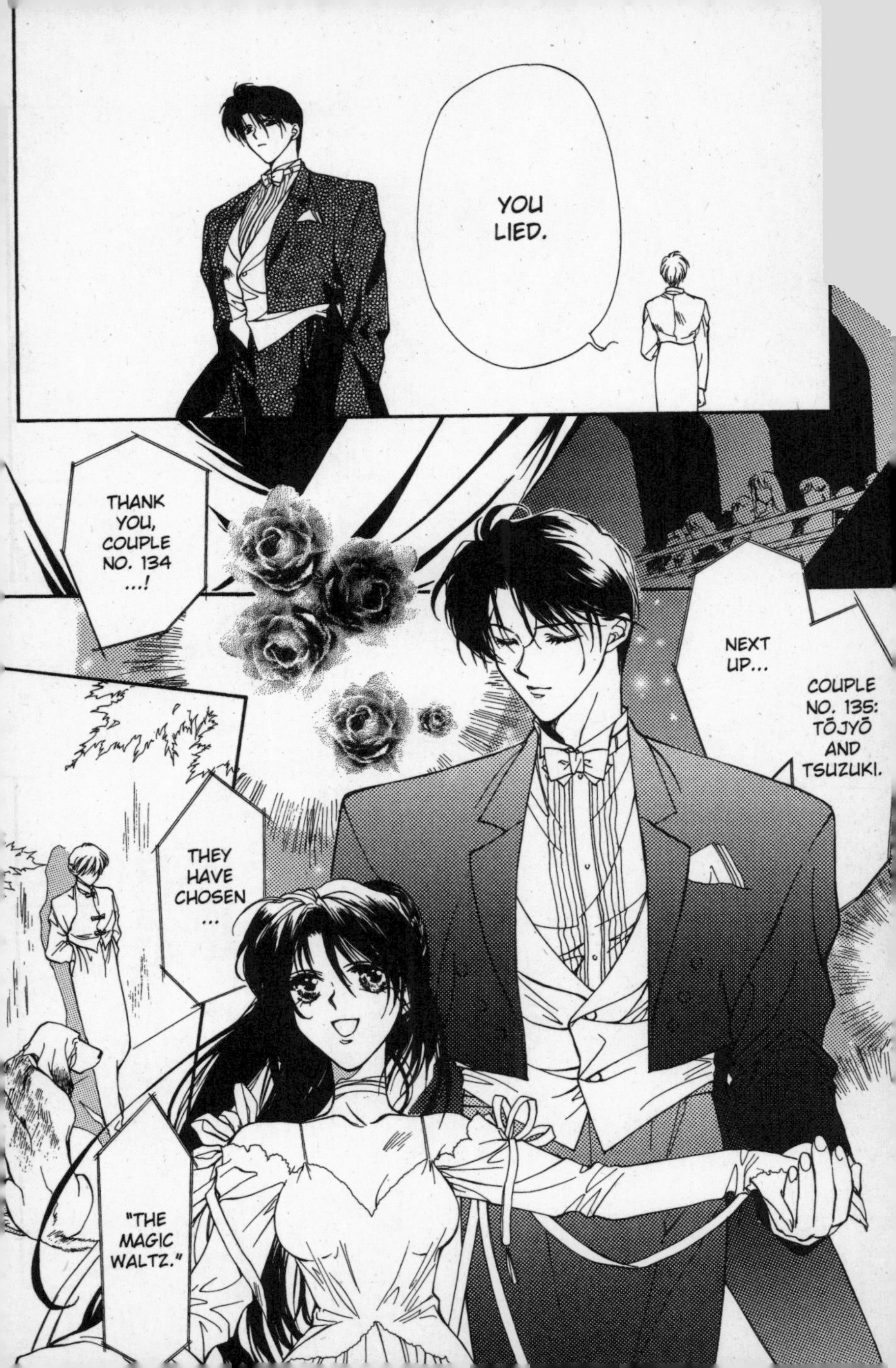
YOU LIED.
THANK YOU, COUPLE NO. 134 ...!
NEXT UP...
COUPLE NO. 135: TŌJYŌ AND TSUZUKI.
THEY HAVE CHOSEN ...
"THE MAGIC WALTZ."

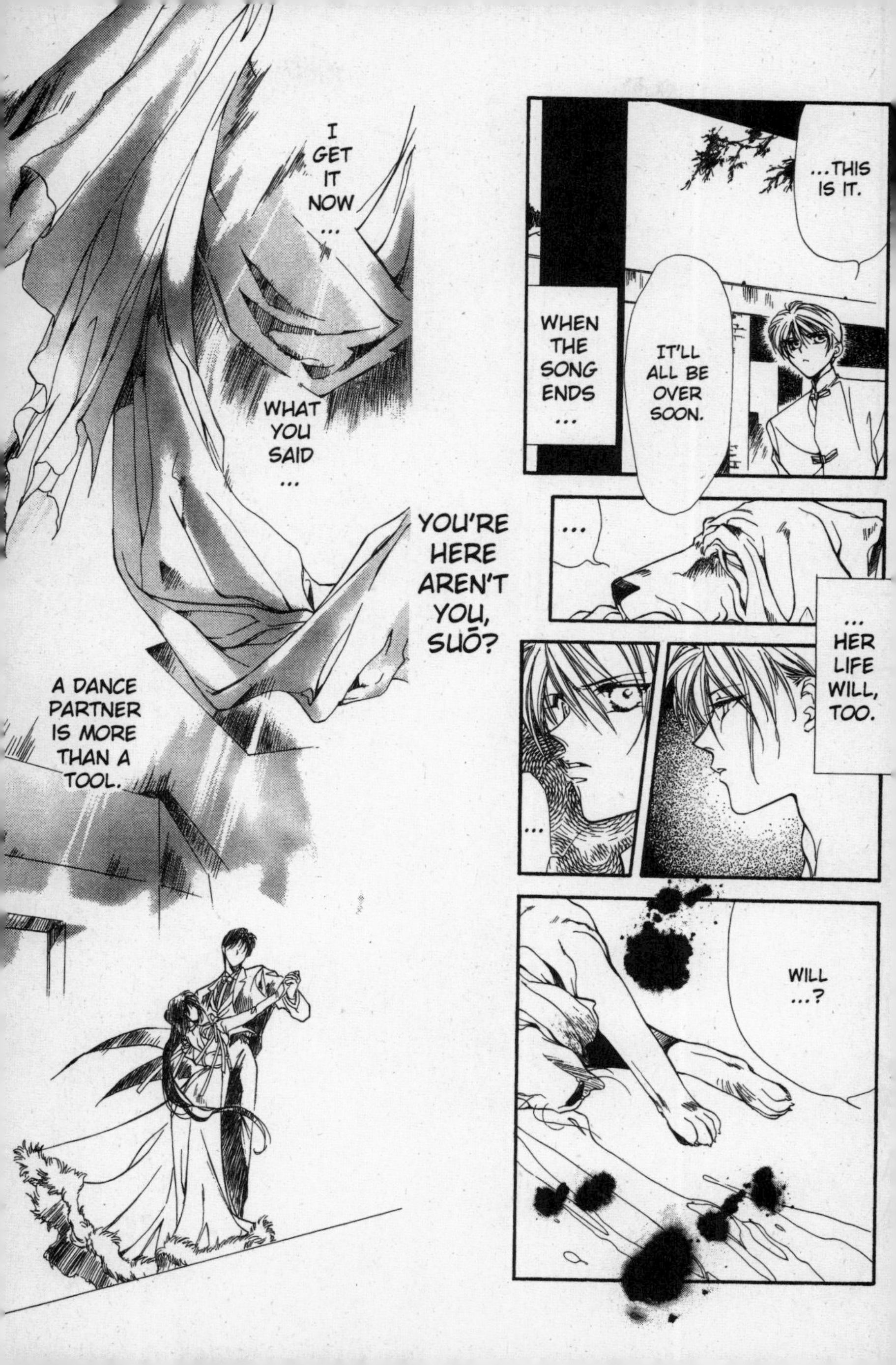
...THIS IS IT.
IT'LL ALL BE OVER SOON.
WHEN THE SONG ENDS ...
...
... HER LIFE WILL, TOO.
...
WILL ...?
I GET IT NOW ...
WHAT YOU SAID ...
YOU'RE HERE AREN'T YOU, SUŌ?
A DANCE PARTNER IS MORE THAN A TOOL.

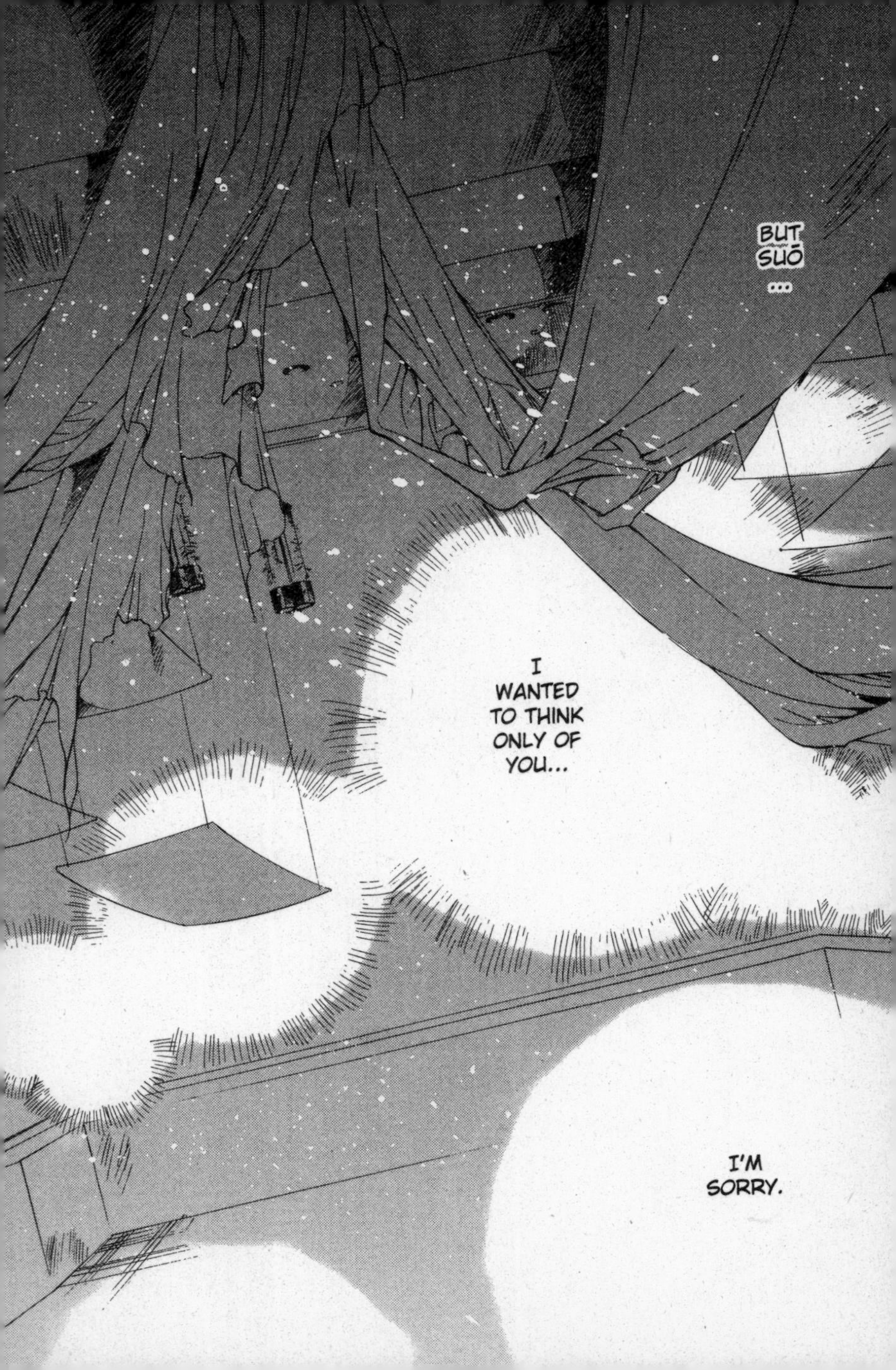
BUT SUŌ ...
I WANTED TO THINK ONLY OF YOU...
I'M SORRY.

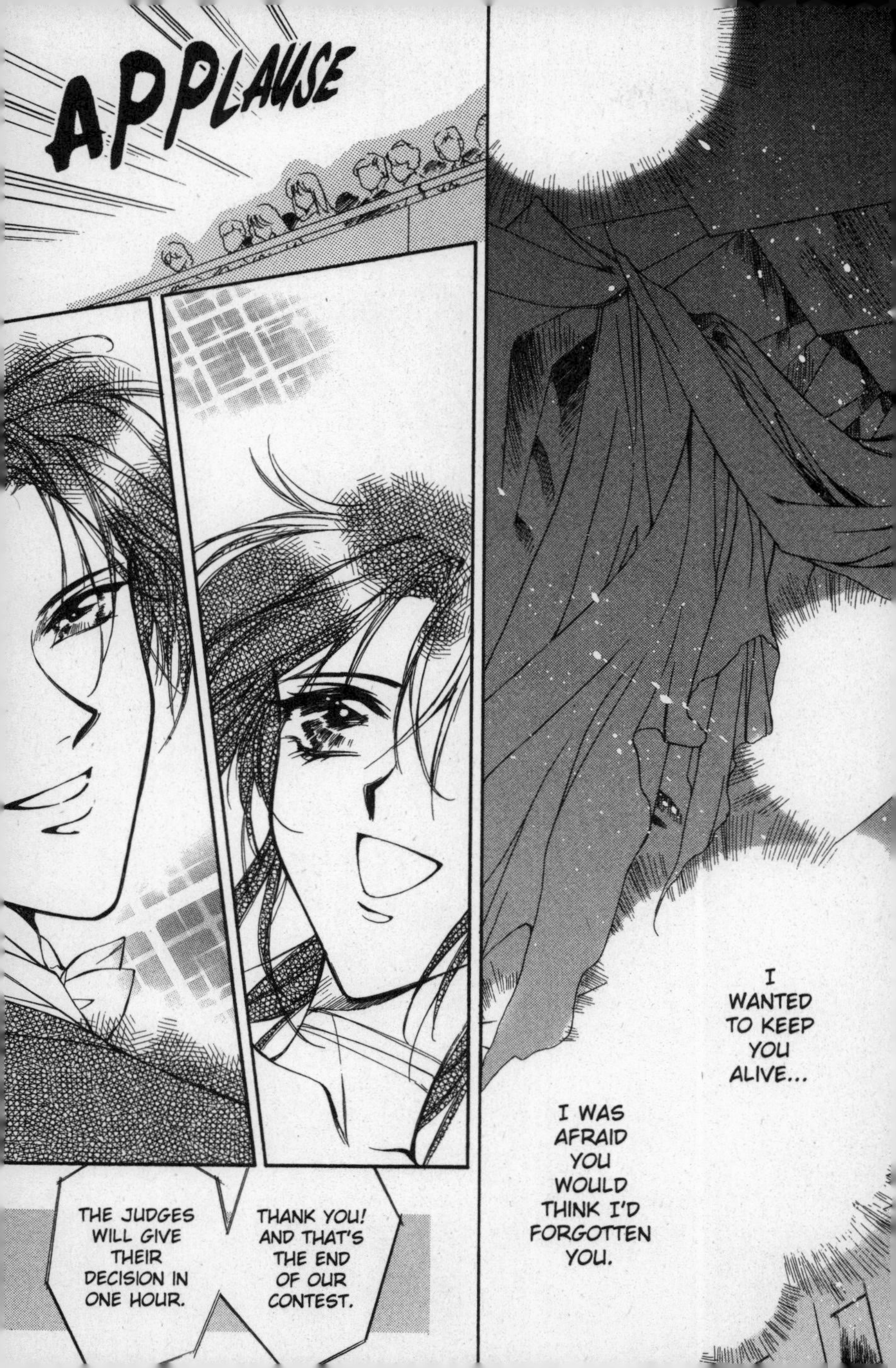
I WANTED TO KEEP YOU ALIVE...
I WAS AFRAID YOU WOULD THINK I'D FORGOTTEN YOU.
APPLAUSE
THANK YOU! AND THAT'S THE END OF OUR CONTEST.
THE JUDGES WILL GIVE THEIR DECISION IN ONE HOUR.

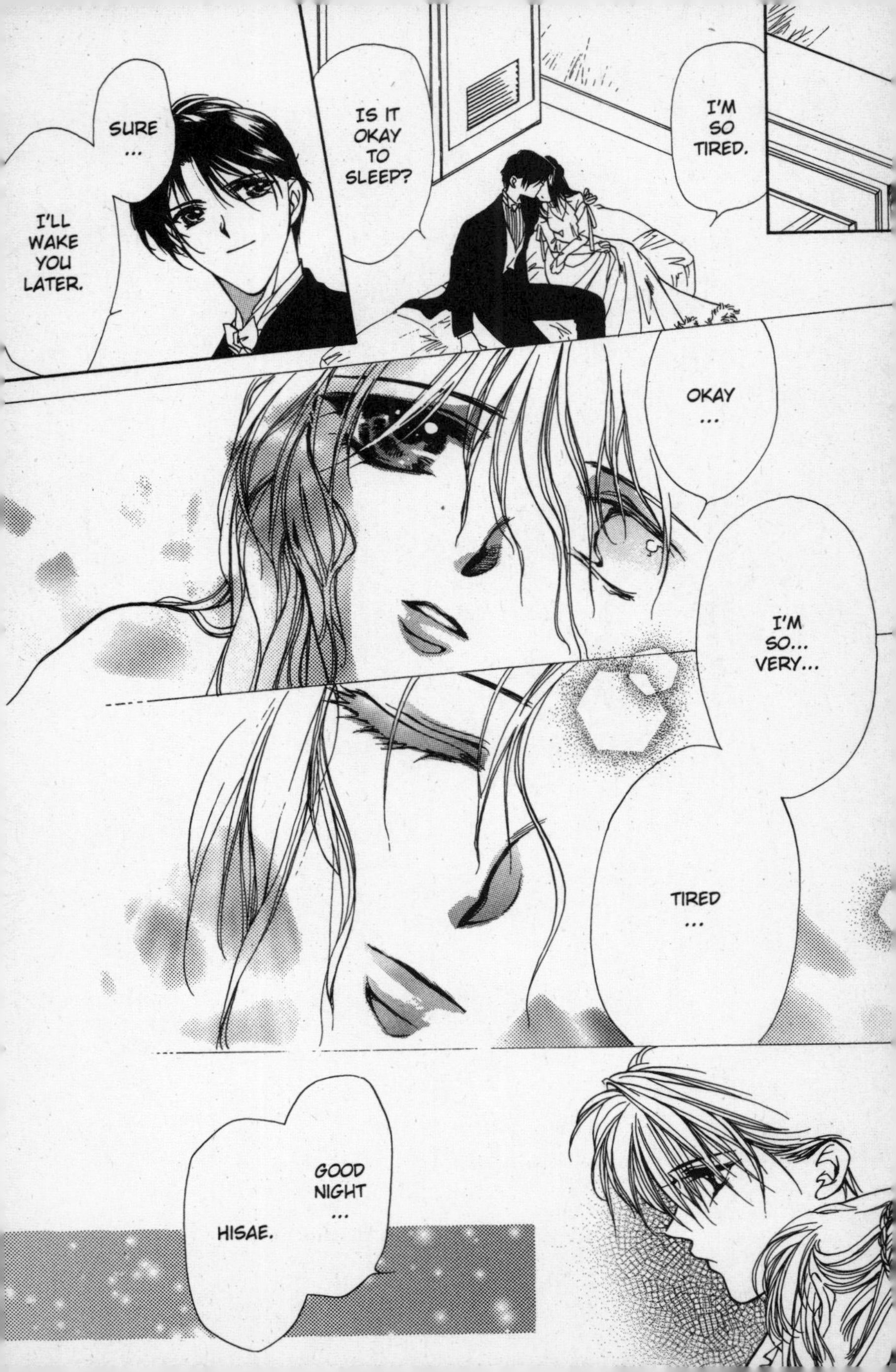
I'M SO TIRED.
IS IT OKAY TO SLEEP?
SURE ...
I'LL WAKE YOU LATER.
OKAY ...
I'M SO... VERY...
TIRED ...
GOOD NIGHT ...
HISAE.

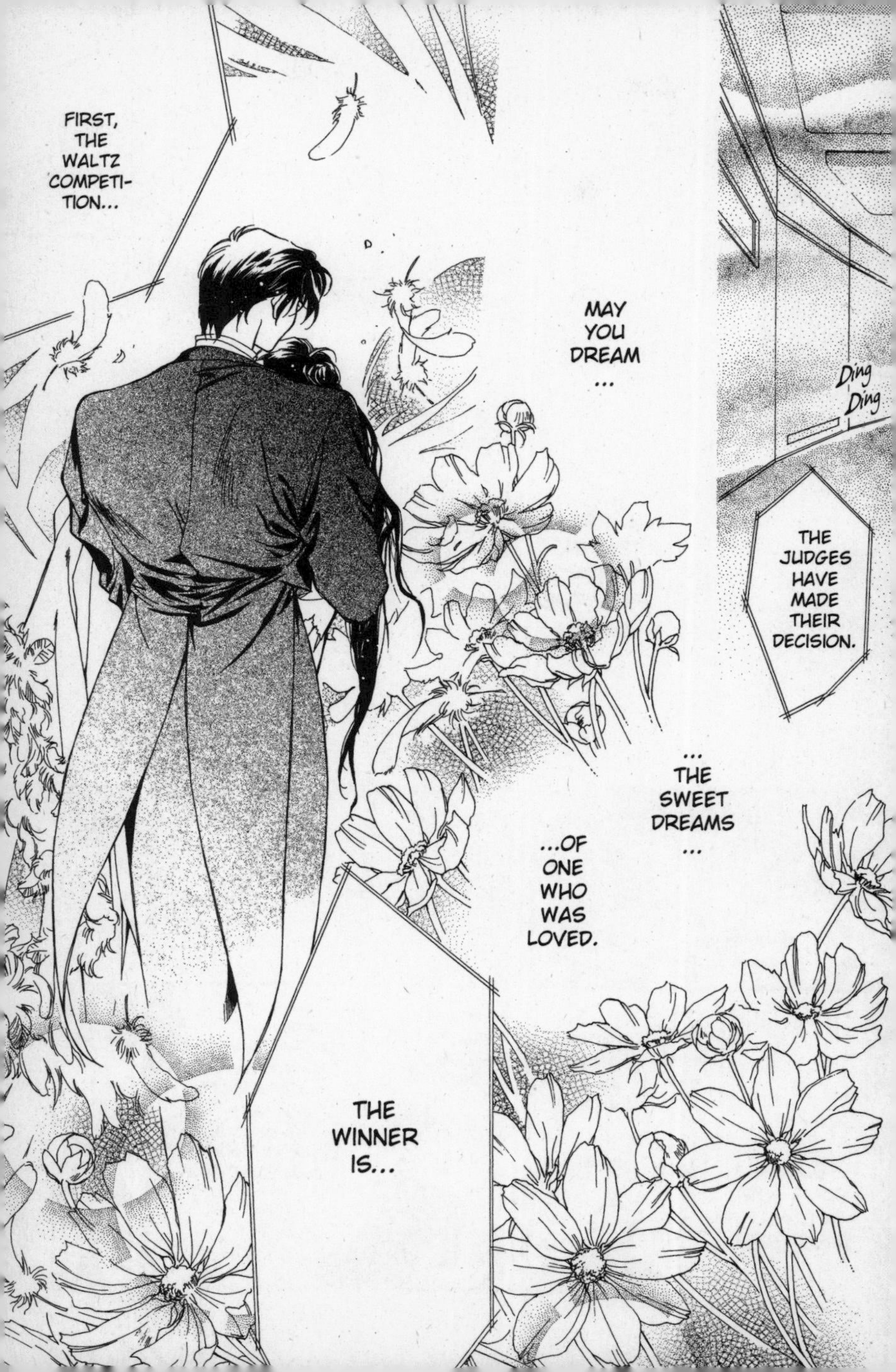
Ding Ding
THE JUDGES HAVE MADE THEIR DECISION.
MAY YOU DREAM ...
... THE SWEET DREAMS ...
...OF ONE WHO WAS LOVED.
FIRST, THE WALTZ COMPETI-TION...
THE WINNER IS...

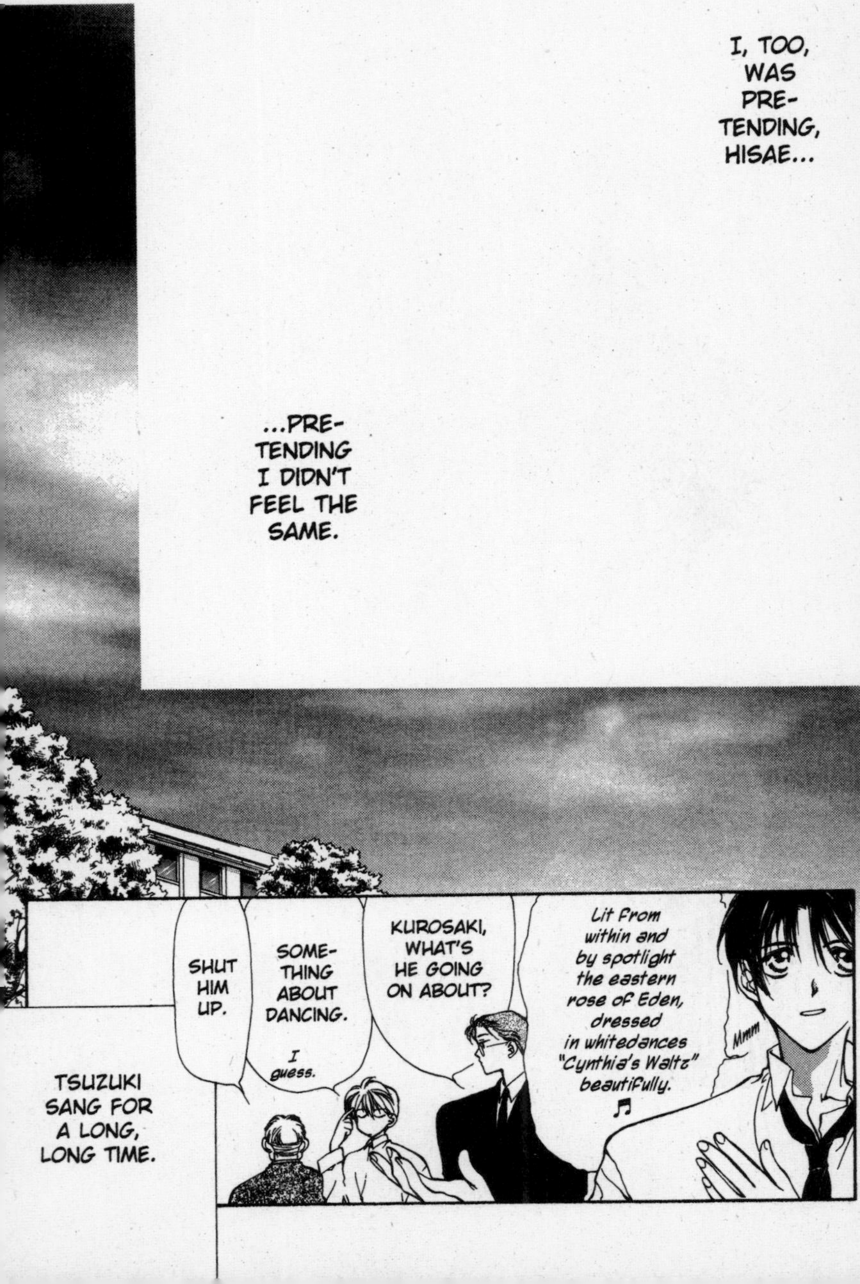
I, TOO, WAS PRE-TENDING, HISAE...
...PRE-TENDING I DIDN'T FEEL THE SAME.
Lit from within and by spotlight the eastern rose of Eden, dressed in whitedances "Cynthia's Waltz" beautifully. ♫
Mmm
KUROSAKI, WHAT'S HE GOING ON ABOUT?
SOME-THING ABOUT DANCING.
I guess.
SHUT HIM UP.
TSUZUKI SANG FOR A LONG, LONG TIME.

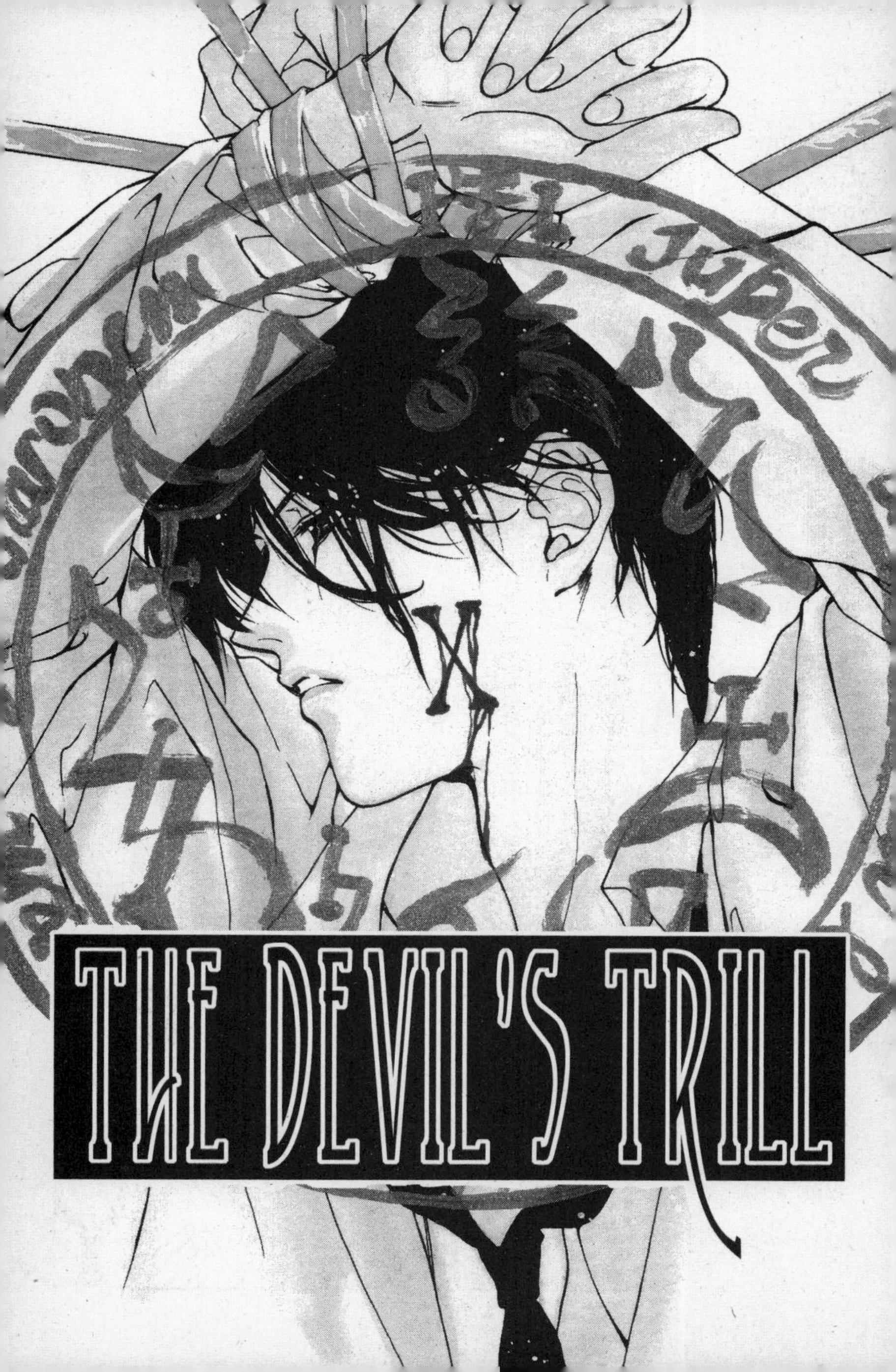
THE DEVIL'S TRILL

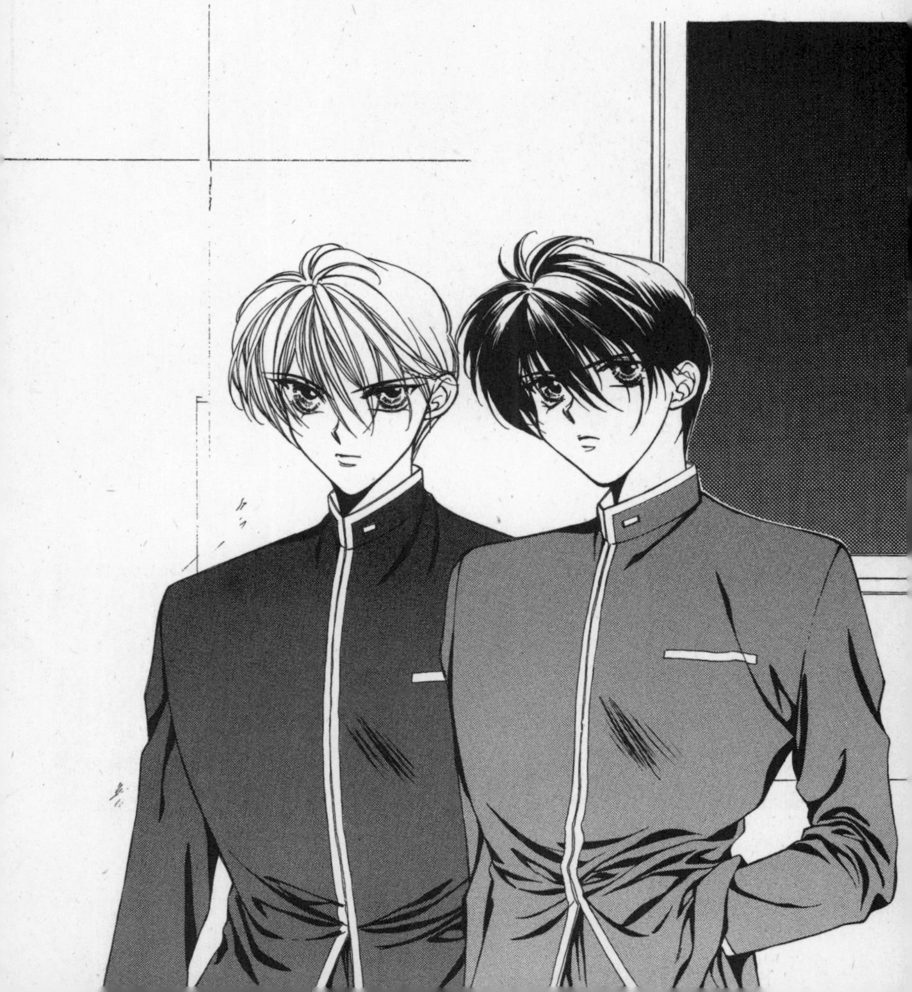

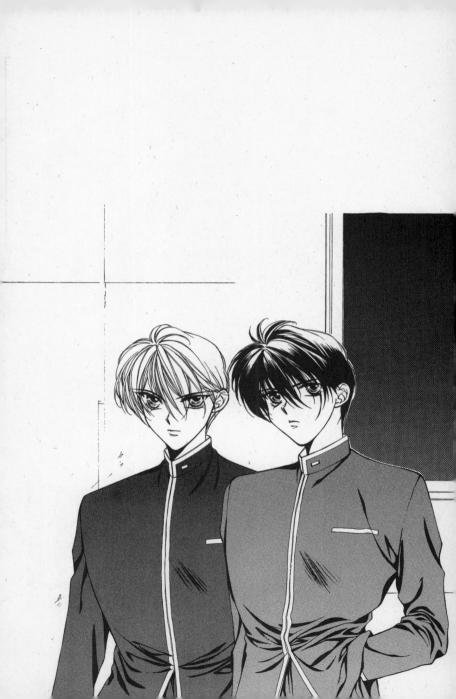

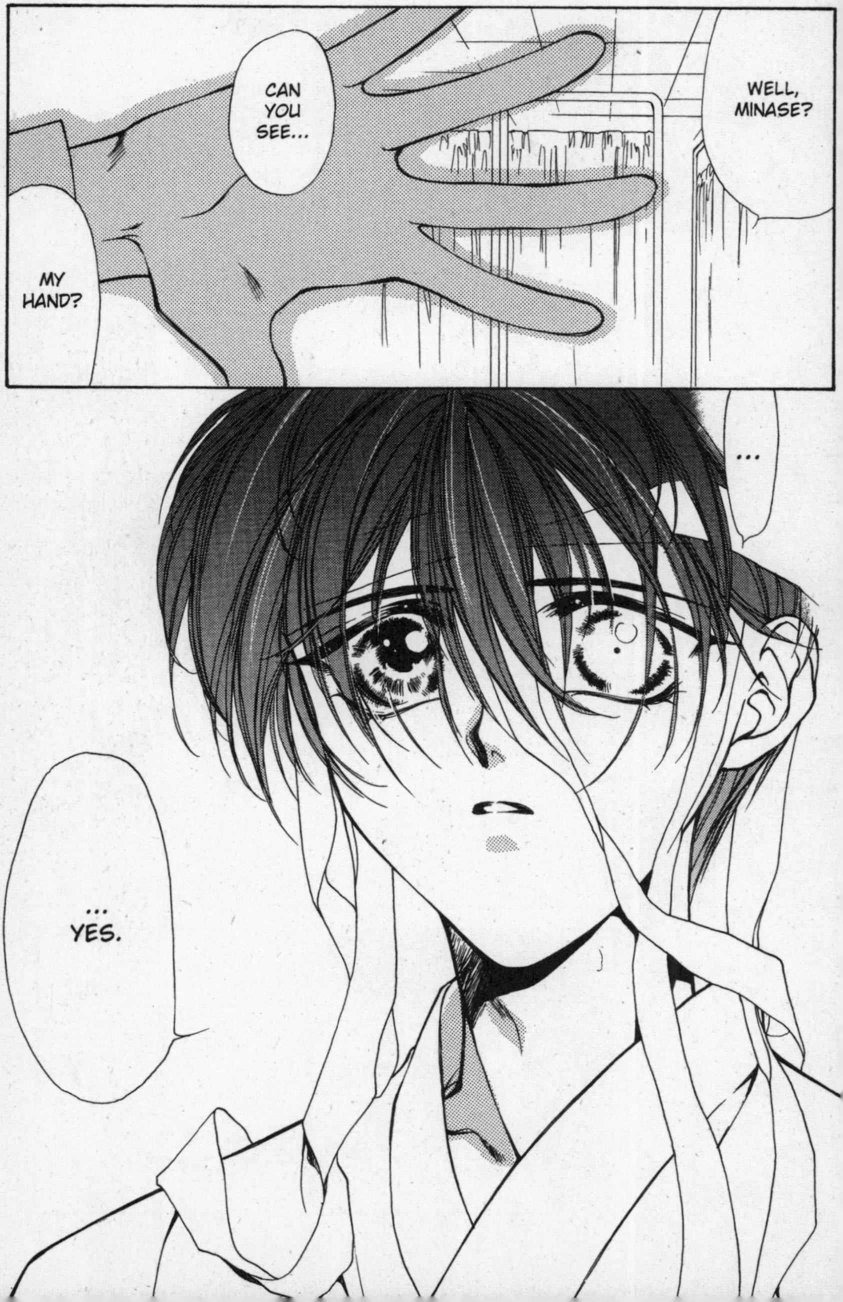
WELL, MINASE?
CAN YOU SEE...
MY HAND?
...
... YES.

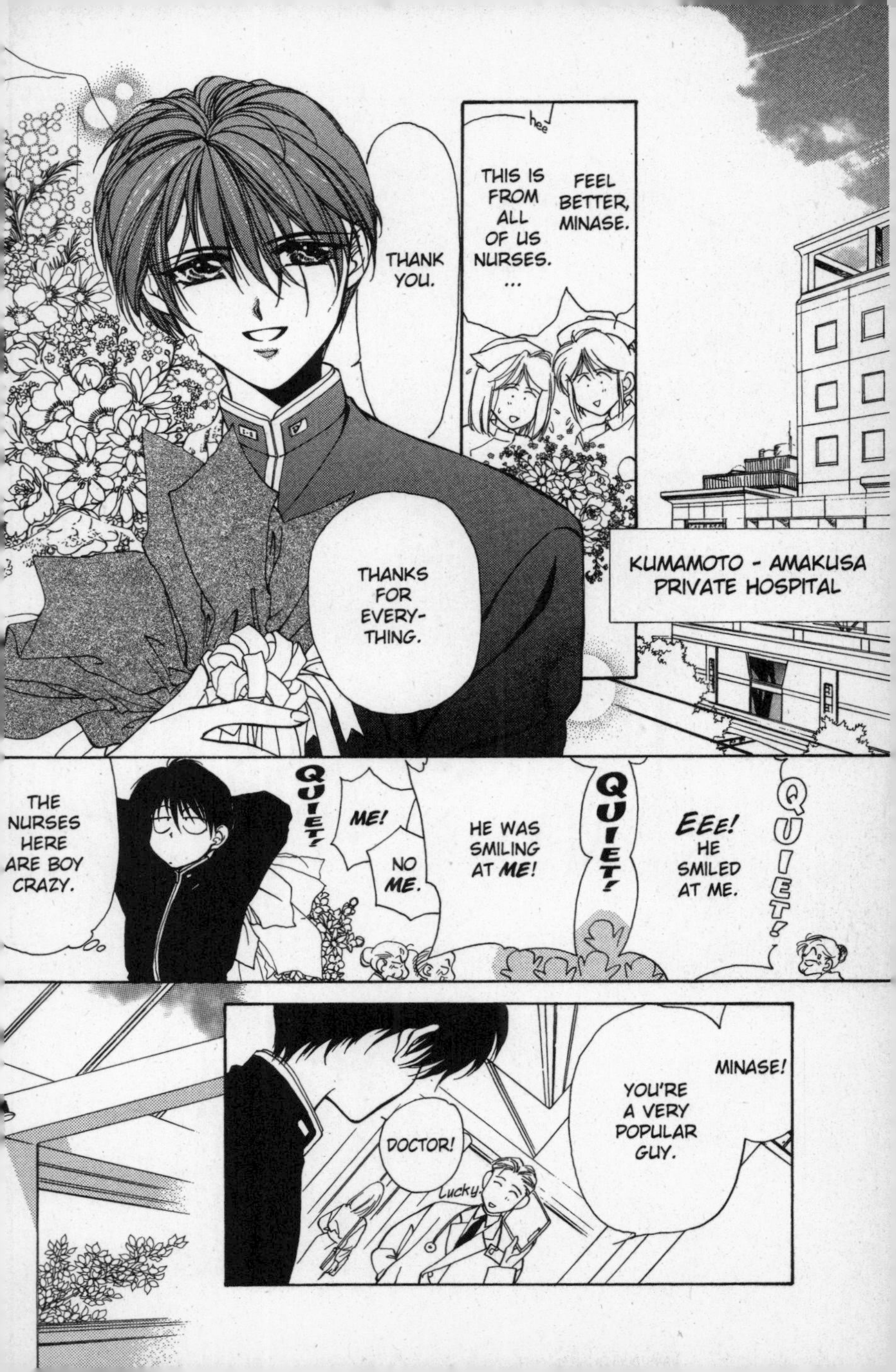
KUMAMOTO - AMAKUSA PRIVATE HOSPITAL
hee
FEEL BETTER, MINASE.
THIS IS FROM ALL OF US NURSES. ...
THANK YOU.
THANKS FOR EVERYTHING.
QUIET!
EEE! HE SMILED AT ME.
QUIET!
HE WAS SMILING AT ME!
NO ME.
ME!
QUIET!
THE NURSES HERE ARE BOY CRAZY.
MINASE!
YOU'RE A VERY POPULAR GUY.
Lucky
DOCTOR!

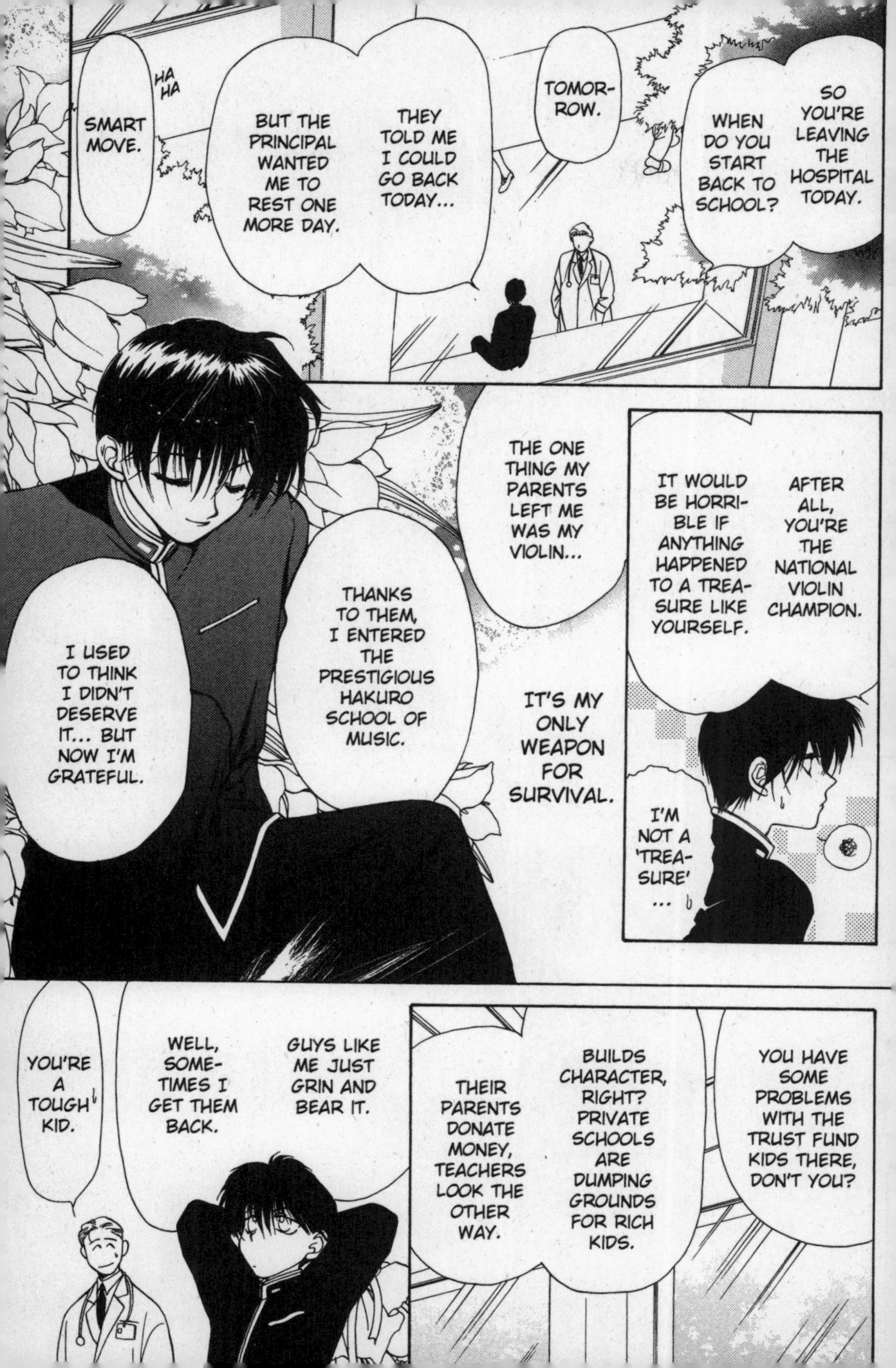
SO YOU'RE LEAVING THE HOSPITAL TODAY.
WHEN DO YOU START BACK TO SCHOOL?
TOMORROW.
THEY TOLD ME I COULD GO BACK TODAY...
BUT THE PRINCIPAL WANTED ME TO REST ONE MORE DAY.
HA HA
SMART MOVE.
AFTER ALL, YOU'RE THE NATIONAL VIOLIN CHAMPION.
IT WOULD BE HORRIBLE IF ANYTHING HAPPENED TO A TREASURE LIKE YOURSELF.
I'M NOT A 'TREASURE'...
THE ONE THING MY PARENTS LEFT ME WAS MY VIOLIN...
IT'S MY ONLY WEAPON FOR SURVIVAL.
THANKS TO THEM, I ENTERED THE PRESTIGIOUS HAKURO SCHOOL OF MUSIC.
I USED TO THINK I DIDN'T DESERVE IT... BUT NOW I'M GRATEFUL.
YOU HAVE SOME PROBLEMS WITH THE TRUST FUND KIDS THERE, DON'T YOU?
BUILDS CHARACTER, RIGHT? PRIVATE SCHOOLS ARE DUMPING GROUNDS FOR RICH KIDS.
THEIR PARENTS DONATE MONEY, TEACHERS LOOK THE OTHER WAY.
GUYS LIKE ME JUST GRIN AND BEAR IT.
WELL, SOMETIMES I GET THEM BACK.
YOU'RE A TOUGH KID.

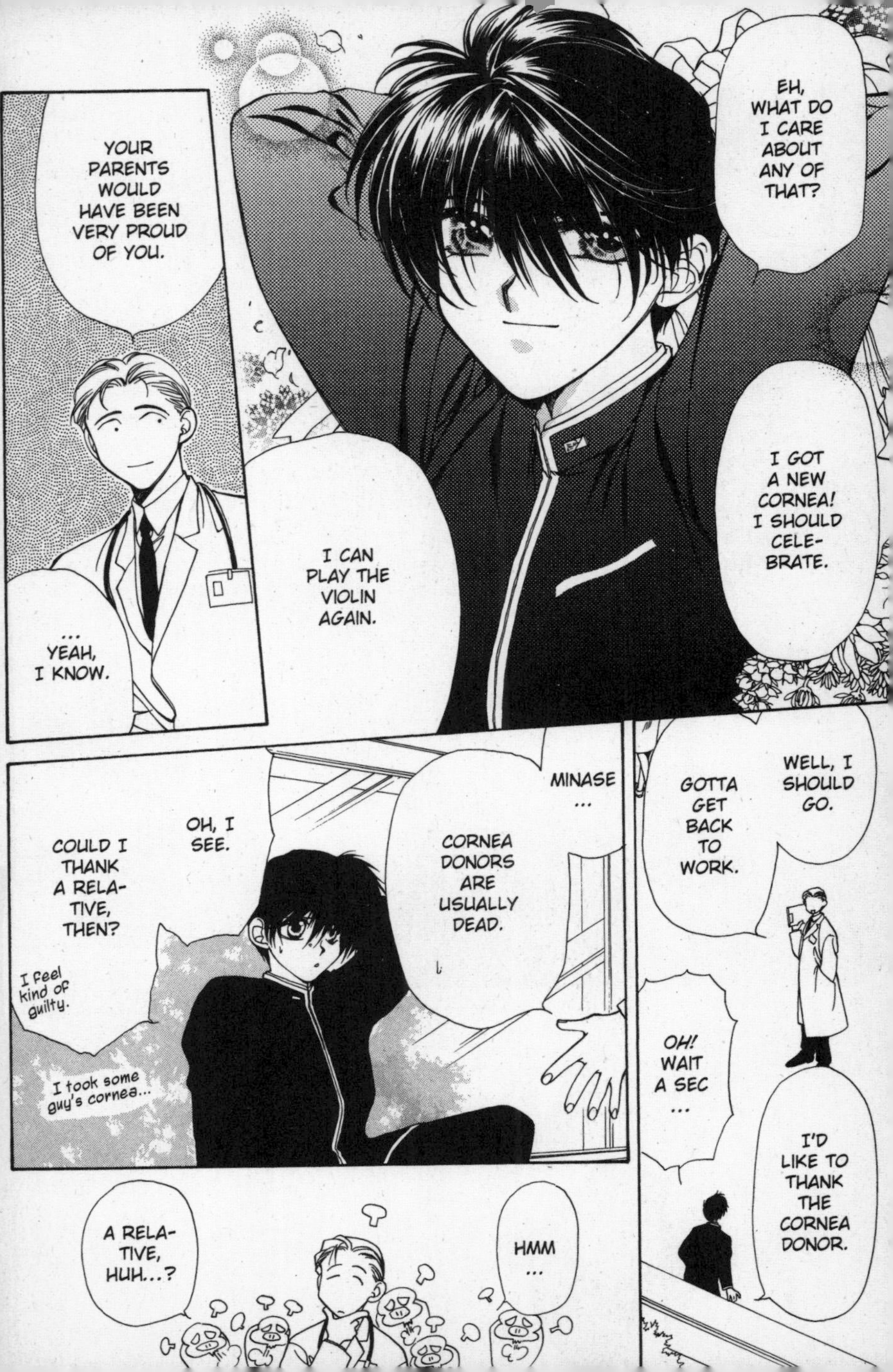
EH, WHAT DO I CARE ABOUT ANY OF THAT?
I GOT A NEW CORNEA! I SHOULD CELE-BRATE.
I CAN PLAY THE VIOLIN AGAIN.
YOUR PARENTS WOULD HAVE BEEN VERY PROUD OF YOU.
... YEAH, I KNOW.
WELL, I SHOULD GO.
GOTTA GET BACK TO WORK.
OH! WAIT A SEC ...
I'D LIKE TO THANK THE CORNEA DONOR.
MINASE ...
CORNEA DONORS ARE USUALLY DEAD.
OH, I SEE.
COULD I THANK A RELA-TIVE, THEN?
I feel kind of guilty.
I took some guy's cornea...
HMM ...
A RELA-TIVE, HUH...?

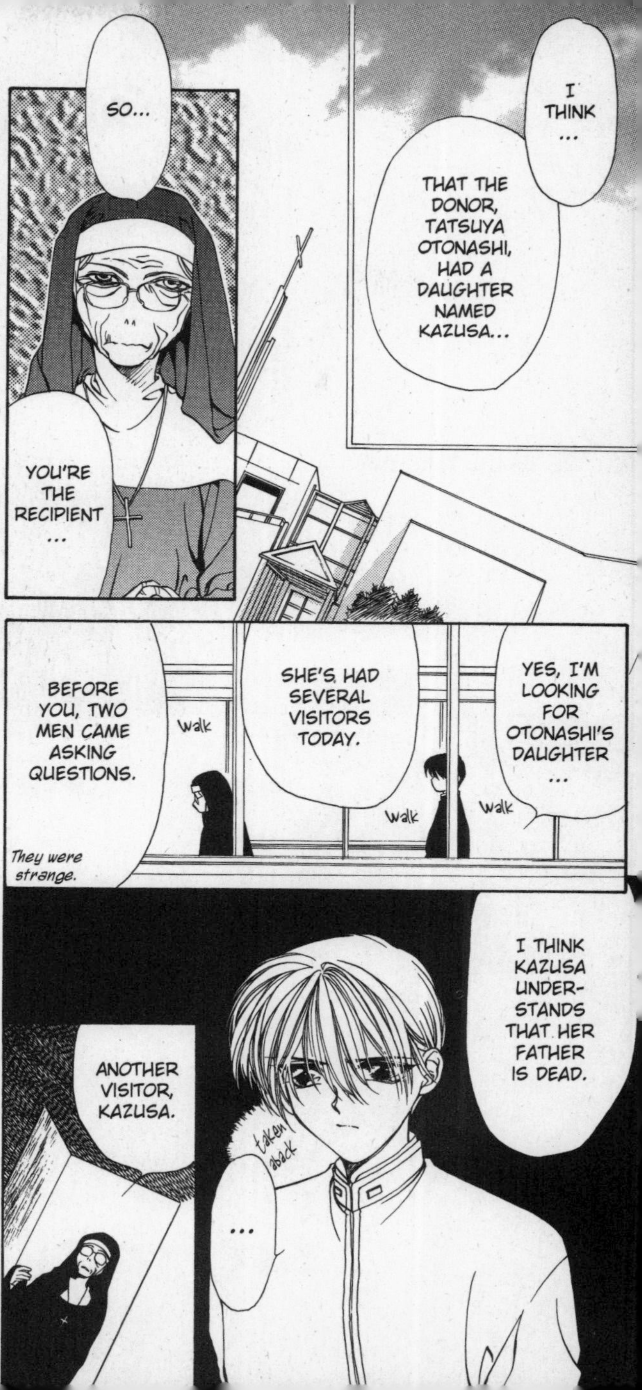
I THINK ...
THAT THE DONOR, TATSUYA OTONASHI, HAD A DAUGHTER NAMED KAZUSA...
SO...
YOU'RE THE RECIPIENT ...
YES, I'M LOOKING FOR OTONASHI'S DAUGHTER ...
Walk
SHE'S HAD SEVERAL VISITORS TODAY.
Walk
BEFORE YOU, TWO MEN CAME ASKING QUESTIONS.
Walk
They were strange.
I THINK KAZUSA UNDERSTANDS THAT HER FATHER IS DEAD.
taken aback
...
ANOTHER VISITOR, KAZUSA.

Flipping through an encyclopedia one day, I found an entry on the Tartini sonata The Devil's Trill and I fell in love with the name. I had planned to use it in a short story, but it soon grew into a four part series. I tried to write a story based on the composers claim that the devil had appeared to him in a dream and inspired the piece. There might be some, um, vagaries as a result. Please try not to think too hard about the dialogue. Seriously.

Oh, our heroes dont appear for quite a while. I thought it might be nice to start the story somewhere other than The Ministry... Apparently that freaked some readers out.

I'm sorry.

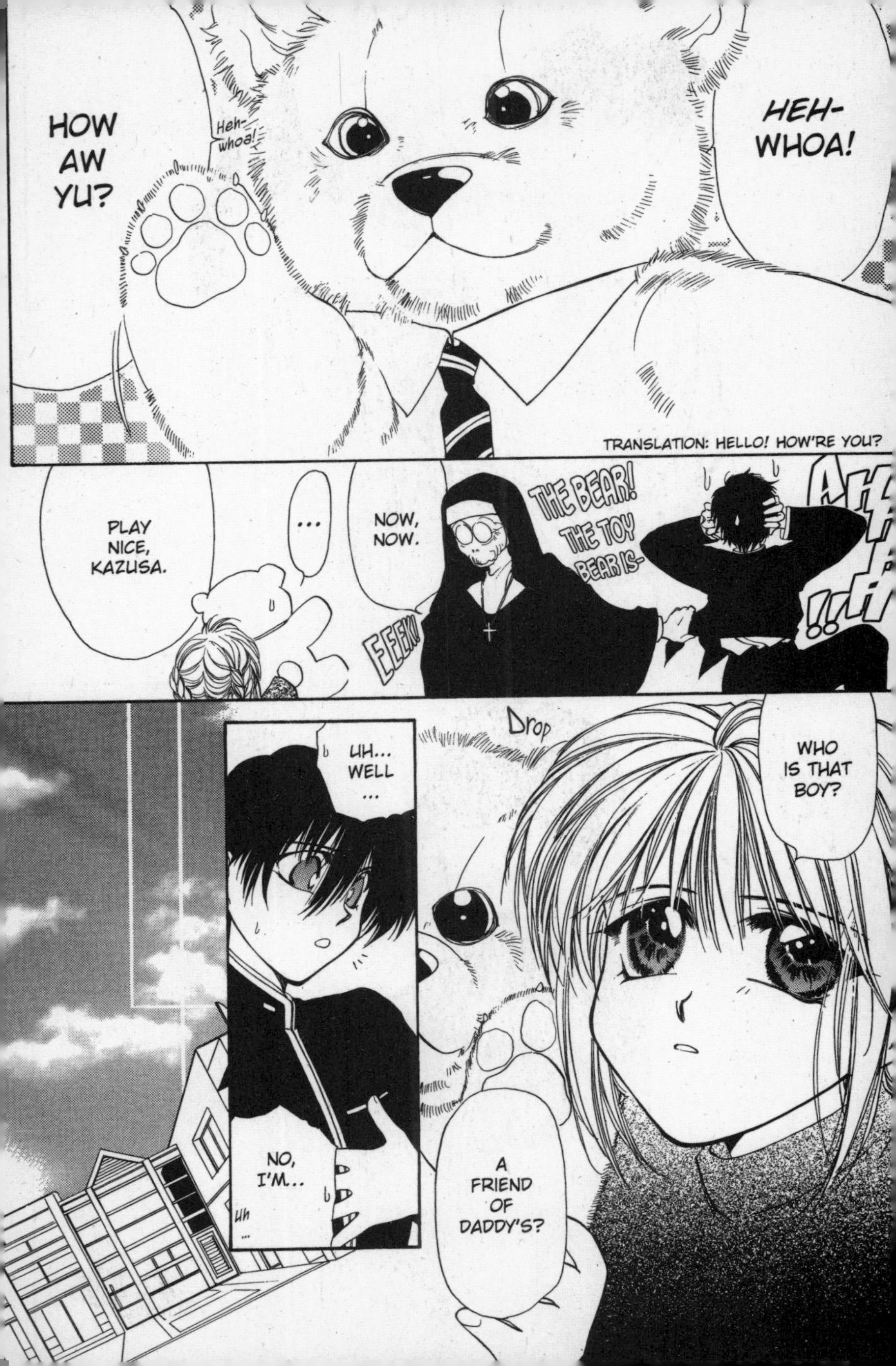
HEH-WHOA!
Heh-whoa!
HOW AW YU?
TRANSLATION: HELLO! HOW'RE YOU?
THE BEAR! THE TOY BEAR IS-
EEEK!
NOW, NOW.
...
PLAY NICE, KAZUSA.
WHO IS THAT BOY?
Drop
UH... WELL ...
A FRIEND OF DADDY'S?
NO, I'M...
Uh ...

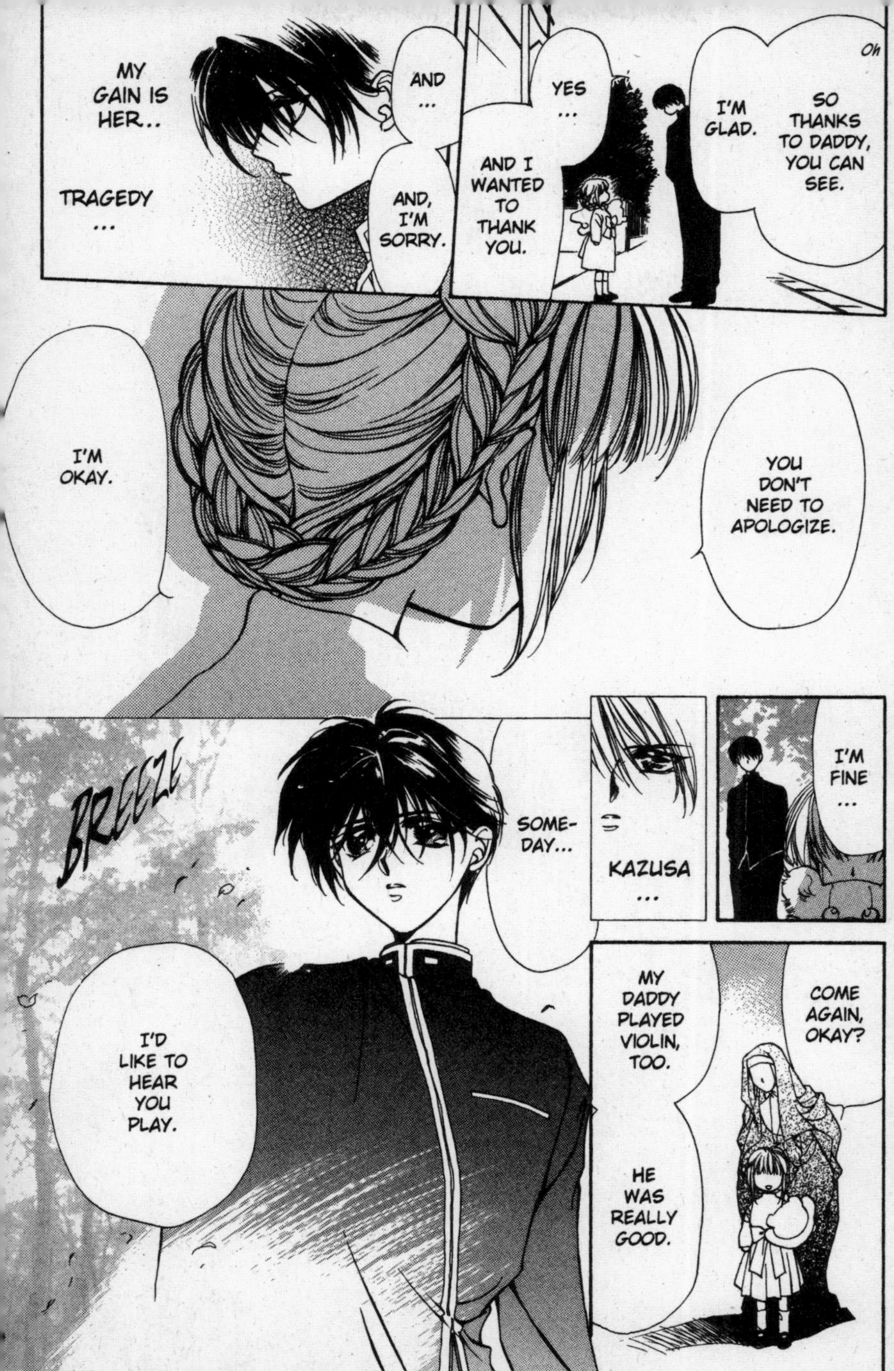
Oh
SO THANKS TO DADDY, YOU CAN SEE.
I'M GLAD.
YES ...
AND I WANTED TO THANK YOU.
AND ...
AND, I'M SORRY.
MY GAIN IS HER...
TRAGEDY ...
YOU DON'T NEED TO APOLOGIZE.
I'M OKAY.
I'M FINE ...
KAZUSA ...
COME AGAIN, OKAY?
MY DADDY PLAYED VIOLIN, TOO.
HE WAS REALLY GOOD.
SOME-DAY...
BREEZE
I'D LIKE TO HEAR YOU PLAY.

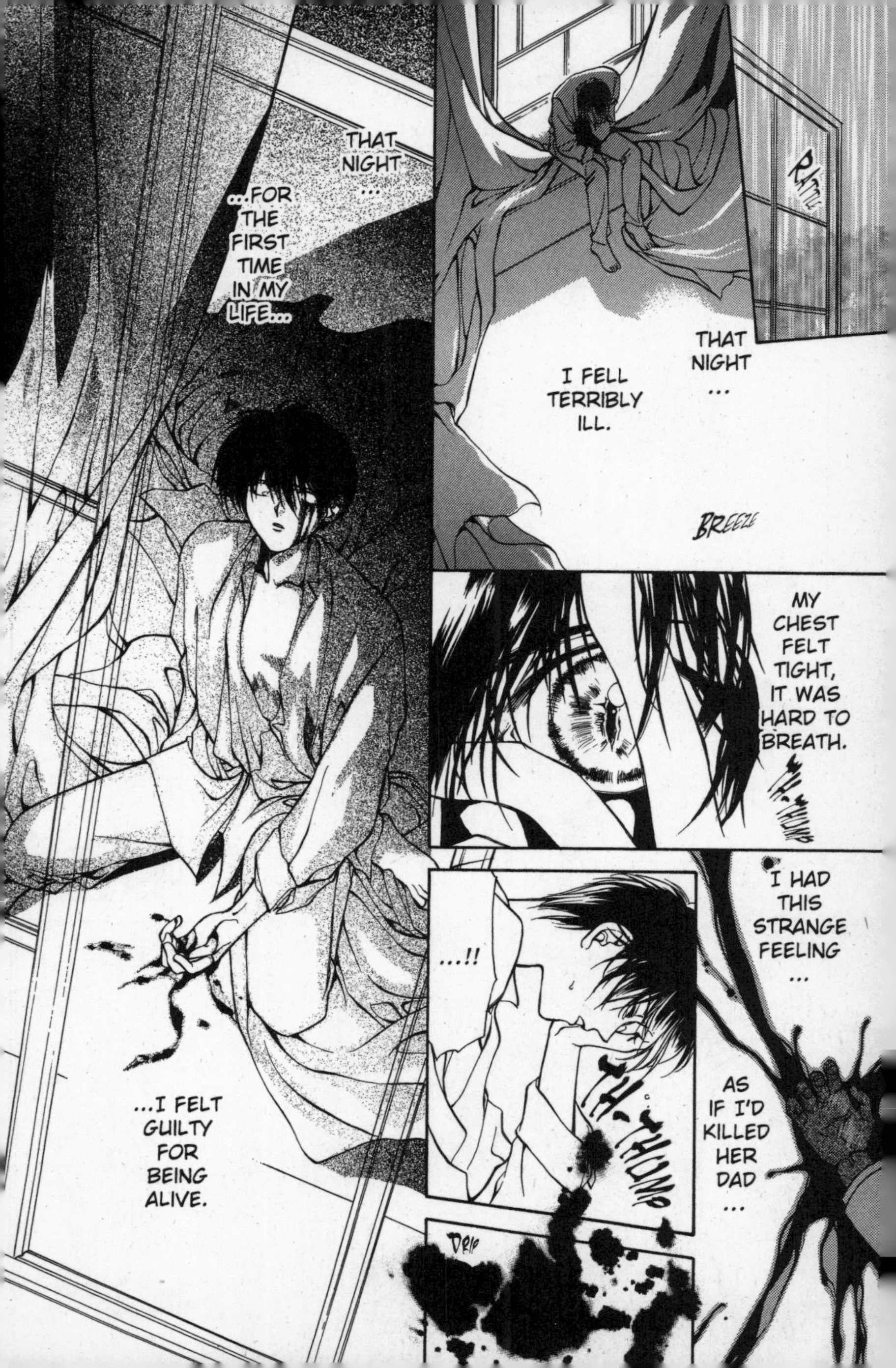
RATTLE
THAT NIGHT ...
I FELL TERRIBLY ILL.
BREEZE
MY CHEST FELT TIGHT, IT WAS HARD TO BREATH.
TH-THUMP
I HAD THIS STRANGE FEELING ...
AS IF I'D KILLED HER DAD ...
...!!
TH-THUMP
DRIP
THAT NIGHT ...
...FOR THE FIRST TIME IN MY LIFE...
...I FELT GUILTY FOR BEING ALIVE.

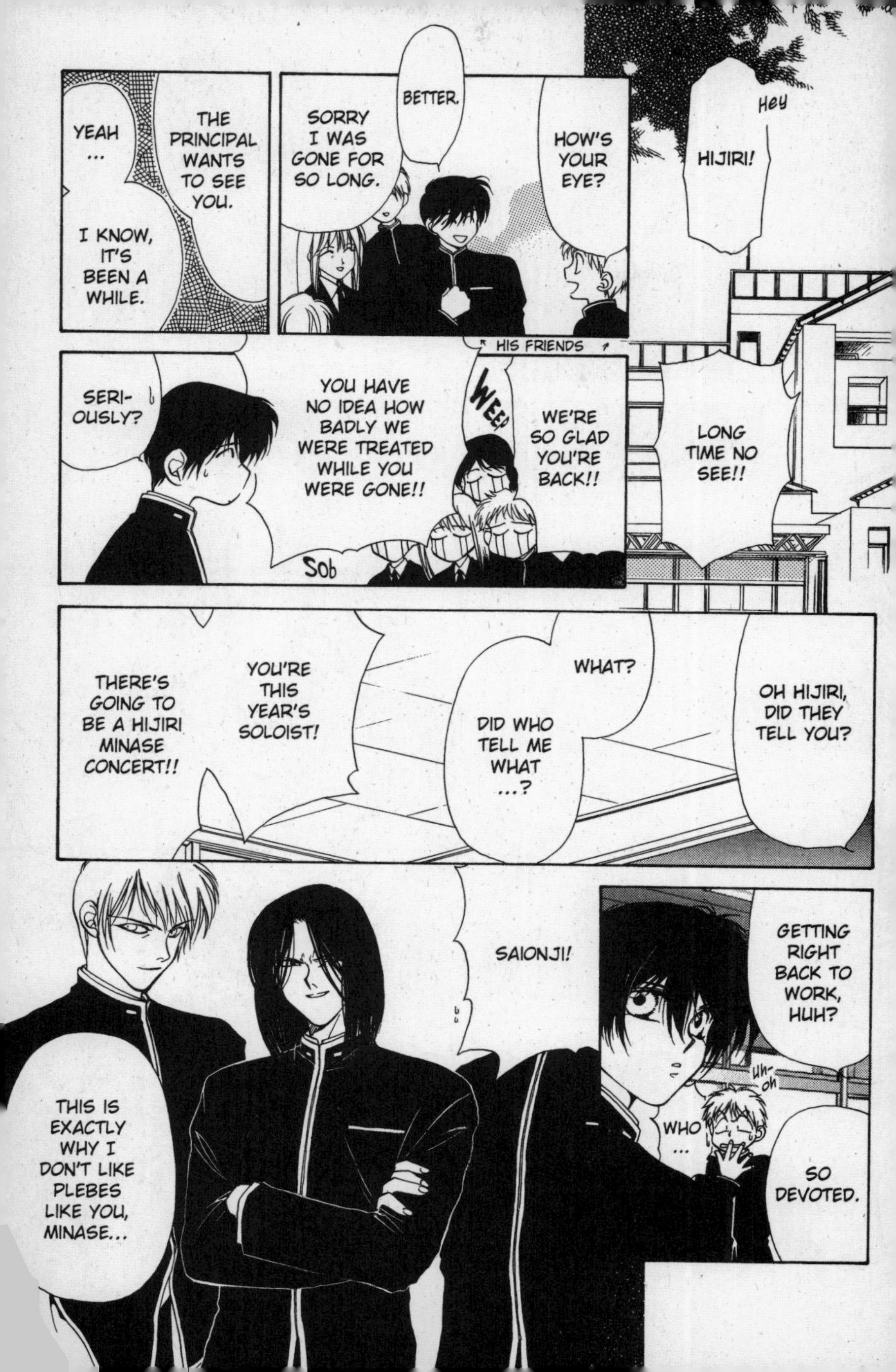

Hey
HIJIRI!
LONG TIME NO SEE!!
HOW'S YOUR EYE?
BETTER.
SORRY I WAS GONE FOR SO LONG.
THE PRINCIPAL WANTS TO SEE YOU.
YEAH ...
I KNOW, IT'S BEEN A WHILE.
HIS FRIENDS
WE'RE SO GLAD YOU'RE BACK!!
WEEP
YOU HAVE NO IDEA HOW BADLY WE WERE TREATED WHILE YOU WERE GONE!!
Sob
SERI-OUSLY?
OH HIJIRI, DID THEY TELL YOU?
WHAT?
DID WHO TELL ME WHAT ...?
YOU'RE THIS YEAR'S SOLOIST!
THERE'S GOING TO BE A HIJIRI MINASE CONCERT!!
GETTING RIGHT BACK TO WORK, HUH?
SO DEVOTED.
Uh-oh
WHO ...
SAIONJI!
THIS IS EXACTLY WHY I DON'T LIKE PLEBES LIKE YOU, MINASE...

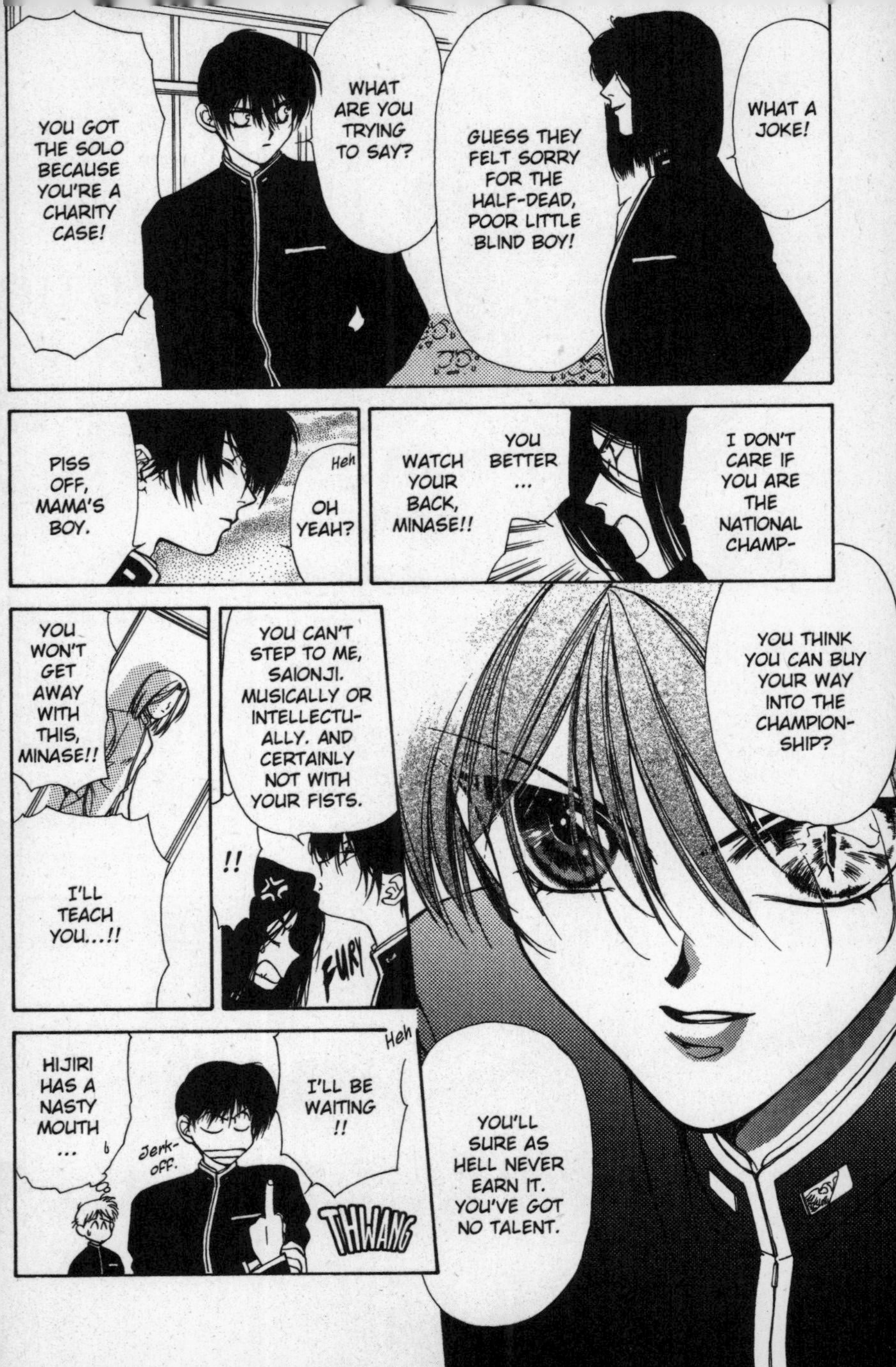
WHAT A JOKE!
GUESS THEY FELT SORRY FOR THE HALF-DEAD, POOR LITTLE BLIND BOY!
WHAT ARE YOU TRYING TO SAY?
YOU GOT THE SOLO BECAUSE YOU'RE A CHARITY CASE!
I DON'T CARE IF YOU ARE THE NATIONAL CHAMP-
YOU BETTER ...
WATCH YOUR BACK, MINASE!!
Heh
OH YEAH?
PISS OFF, MAMA'S BOY.
YOU THINK YOU CAN BUY YOUR WAY INTO THE CHAMPION-SHIP?
YOU'LL SURE AS HELL NEVER EARN IT. YOU'VE GOT NO TALENT.
YOU CAN'T STEP TO ME, SAIONJI. MUSICALLY OR INTELLECTU-ALLY. AND CERTAINLY NOT WITH YOUR FISTS.
!!
FURY
YOU WON'T GET AWAY WITH THIS, MINASE!!
I'LL TEACH YOU...!!
Heh
I'LL BE WAITING !!
THWANG
Jerk-off.
HIJIRI HAS A NASTY MOUTH ...

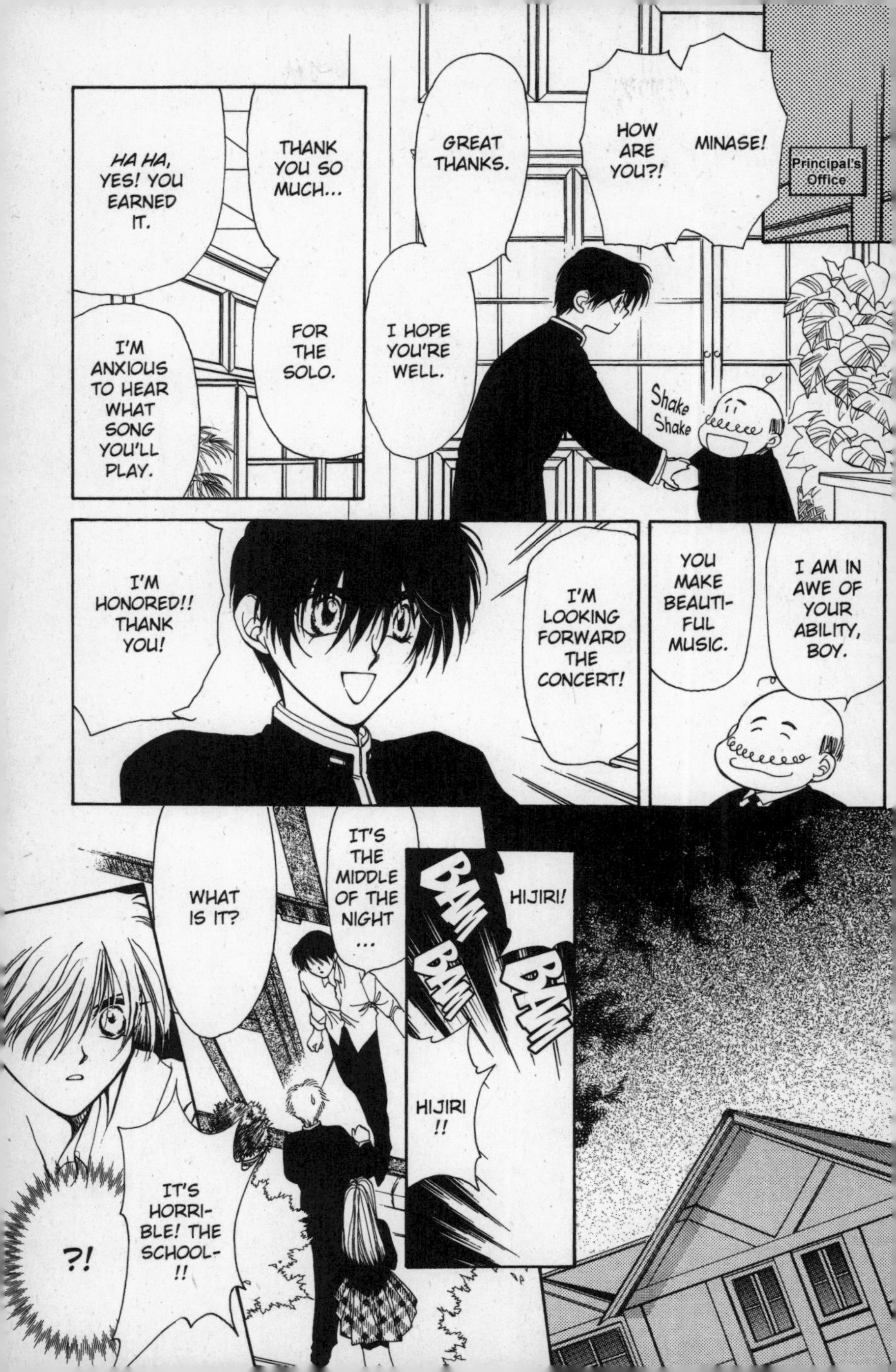
Principal's Office
MINASE!
HOW ARE YOU?!
Shake Shake
GREAT THANKS.
I HOPE YOU'RE WELL.
THANK YOU SO MUCH...
FOR THE SOLO.
HA HA, YES! YOU EARNED IT.
I'M ANXIOUS TO HEAR WHAT SONG YOU'LL PLAY.
I AM IN AWE OF YOUR ABILITY, BOY.
YOU MAKE BEAUTI-FUL MUSIC.
I'M LOOKING FORWARD THE CONCERT!
I'M HONORED!! THANK YOU!
HIJIRI!
BAM BAM
BAM BAM
HIJIRI !!
IT'S THE MIDDLE OF THE NIGHT ...
WHAT IS IT?
IT'S HORRI-BLE! THE SCHOOL-!!
?!

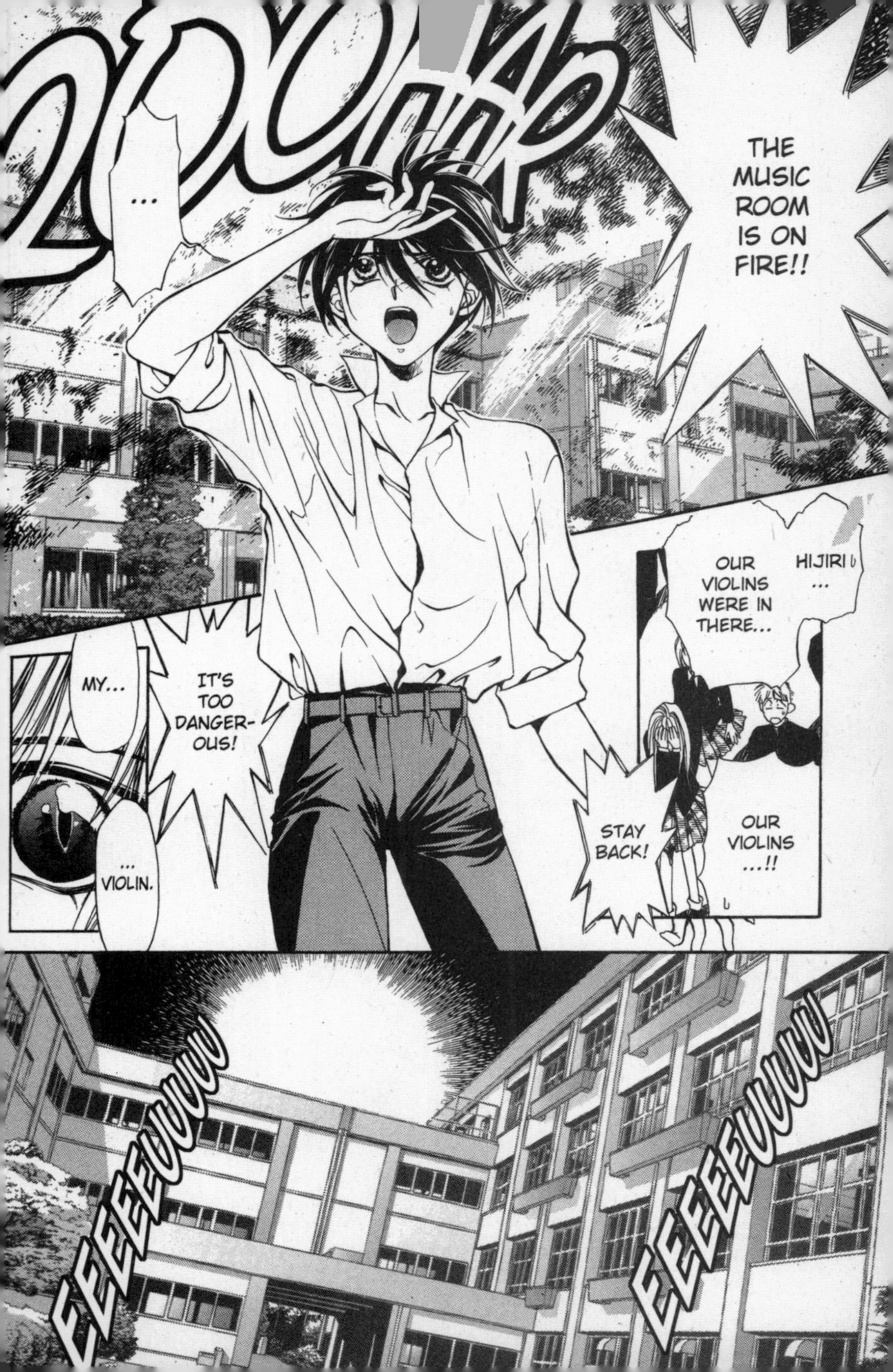
THE MUSIC ROOM IS ON FIRE!!
...
HIJIRI ...
OUR VIOLINS WERE IN THERE...
OUR VIOLINS ...!!
STAY BACK!
IT'S TOO DANGER-OUS!
MY...
... VIOLIN.

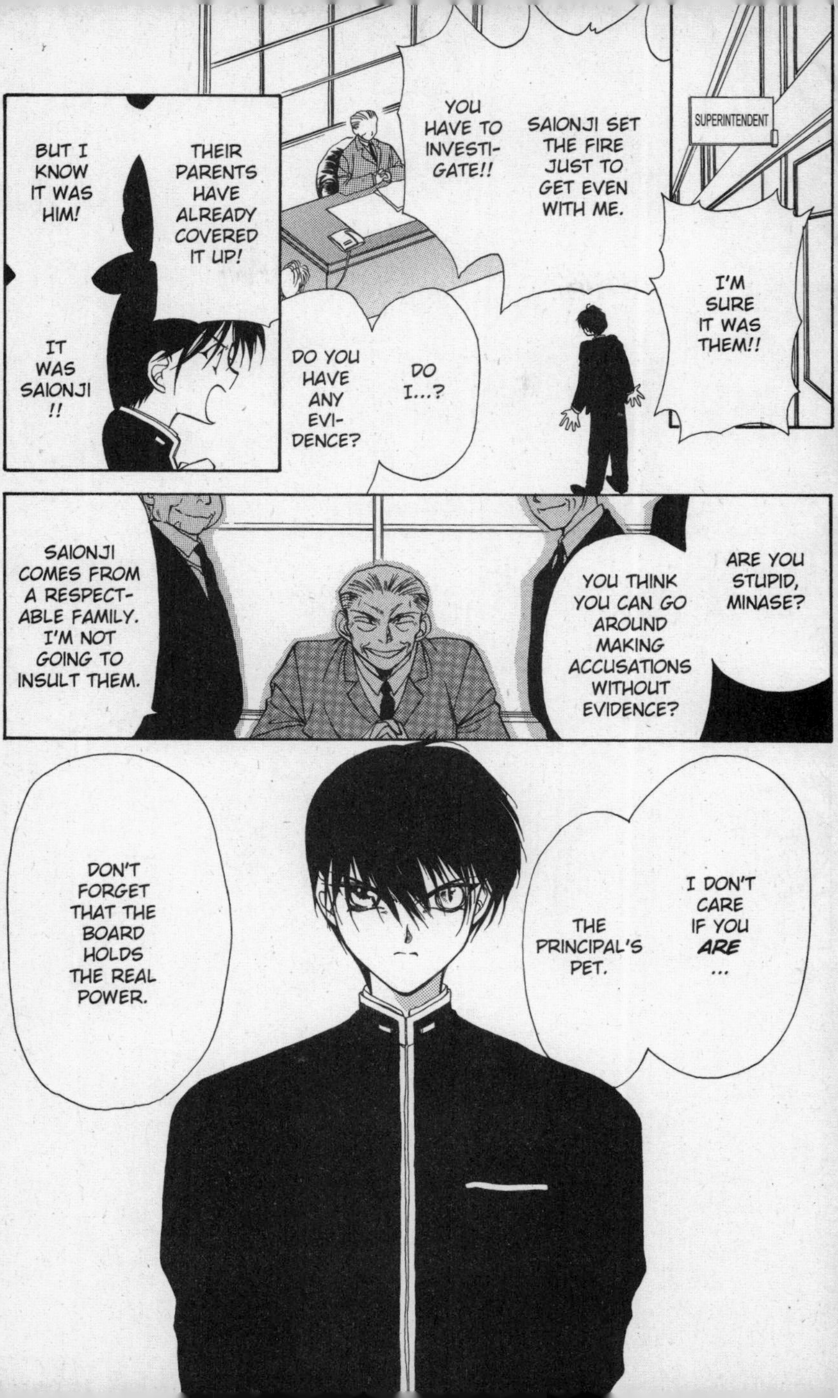
SUPERINTENDENT
SAIONJI SET THE FIRE JUST TO GET EVEN WITH ME.
YOU HAVE TO INVESTIGATE!!
I'M SURE IT WAS THEM!!
DO I...?
DO YOU HAVE ANY EVIDENCE?
THEIR PARENTS HAVE ALREADY COVERED IT UP!
BUT I KNOW IT WAS HIM!
IT WAS SAIONJI!!
ARE YOU STUPID, MINASE?
YOU THINK YOU CAN GO AROUND MAKING ACCUSATIONS WITHOUT EVIDENCE?
SAIONJI COMES FROM A RESPECTABLE FAMILY. I'M NOT GOING TO INSULT THEM.
I DON'T CARE IF YOU *ARE*...
THE PRINCIPAL'S PET.
DON'T FORGET THAT THE BOARD HOLDS THE REAL POWER.

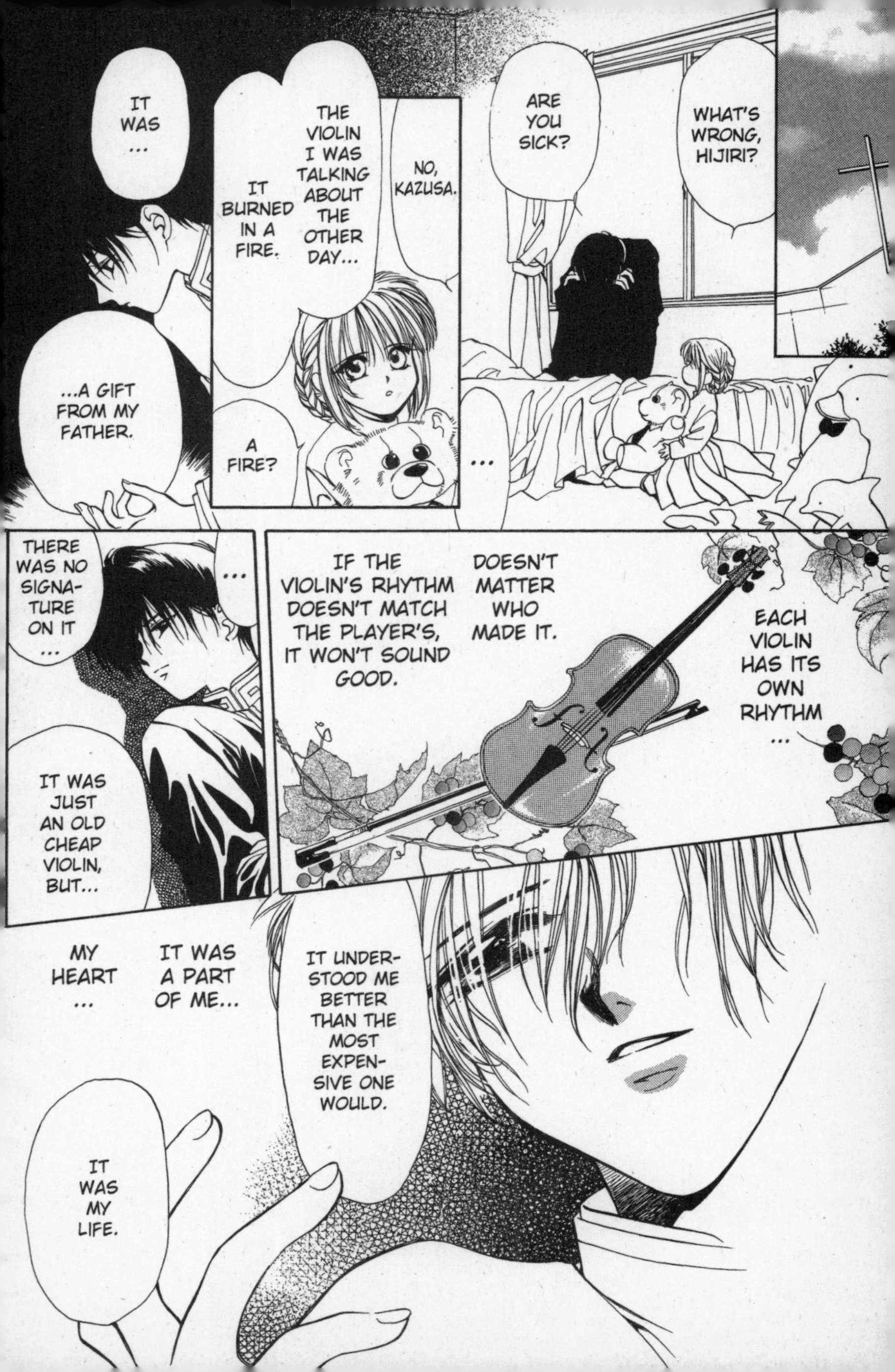

WHAT'S WRONG, HIJIRI?
ARE YOU SICK?
...
NO, KAZUSA.
THE VIOLIN I WAS TALKING ABOUT THE OTHER DAY...
IT BURNED IN A FIRE.
A FIRE?
IT WAS...
...A GIFT FROM MY FATHER.
EACH VIOLIN HAS ITS OWN RHYTHM...
DOESN'T MATTER WHO MADE IT.
IF THE VIOLIN'S RHYTHM DOESN'T MATCH THE PLAYER'S, IT WON'T SOUND GOOD.
...
THERE WAS NO SIGNATURE ON IT...
IT WAS JUST AN OLD CHEAP VIOLIN, BUT...
IT UNDERSTOOD ME BETTER THAN THE MOST EXPENSIVE ONE WOULD.
IT WAS A PART OF ME...
MY HEART...
IT WAS MY LIFE.

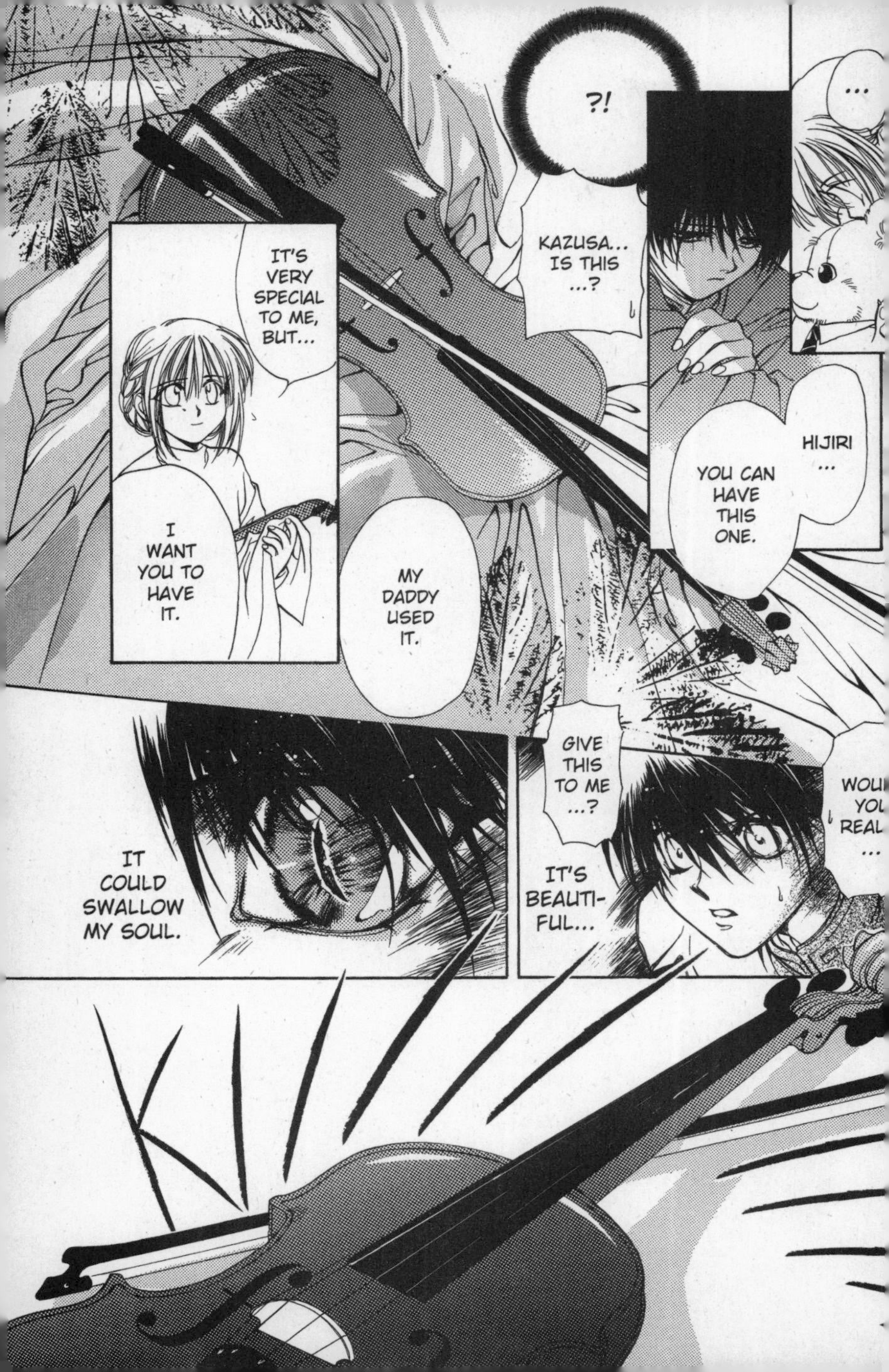
...
?!
KAZUSA... IS THIS ...?
HIJIRI ...
YOU CAN HAVE THIS ONE.
IT'S VERY SPECIAL TO ME, BUT...
I WANT YOU TO HAVE IT.
MY DADDY USED IT.
WOU YOU REAL ...
GIVE THIS TO ME ...?
IT'S BEAUTIFUL...
IT COULD SWALLOW MY SOUL.

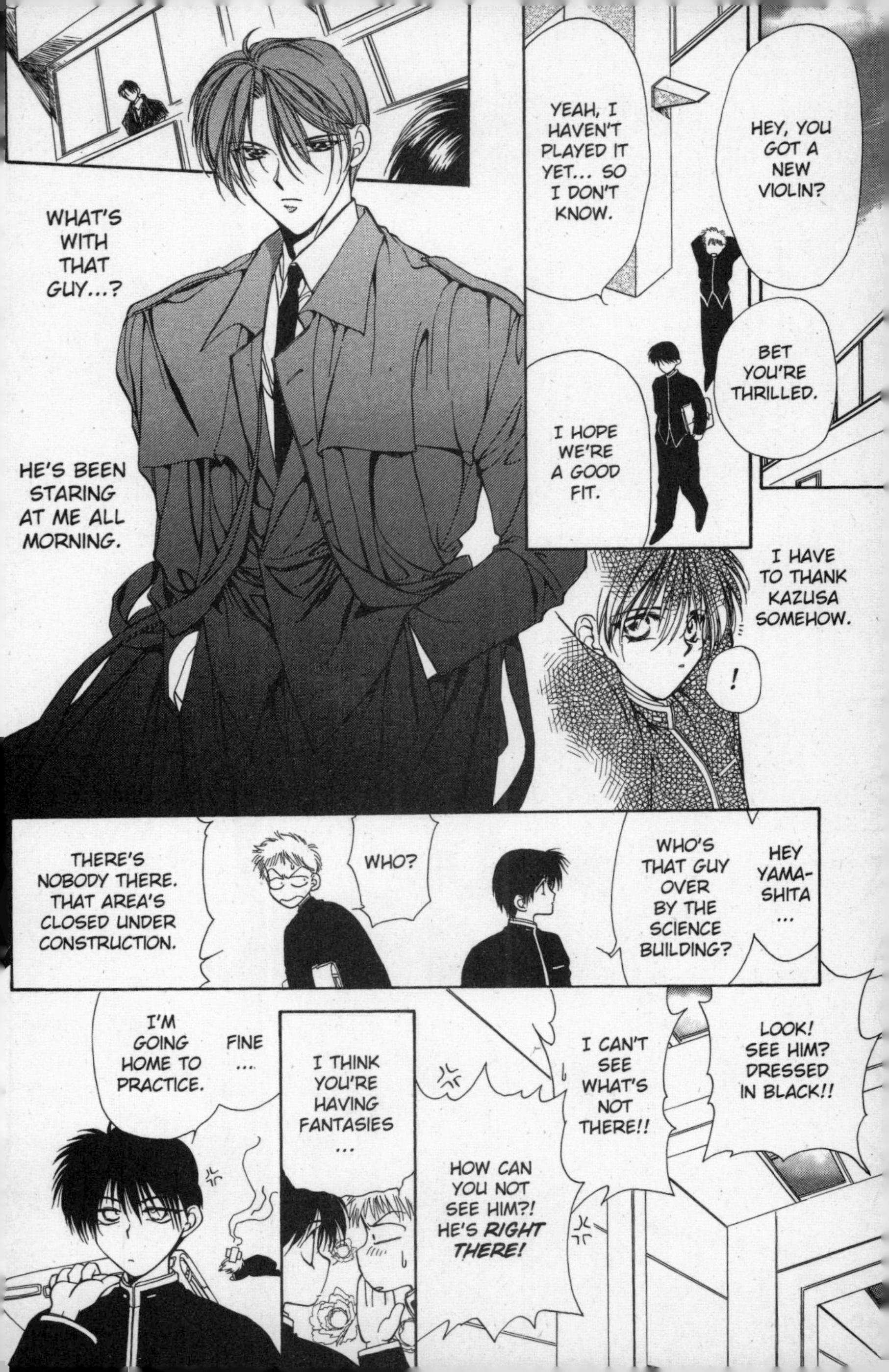
HEY, YOU GOT A NEW VIOLIN?
YEAH, I HAVEN'T PLAYED IT YET... SO I DON'T KNOW.
BET YOU'RE THRILLED.
I HOPE WE'RE A GOOD FIT.
I HAVE TO THANK KAZUSA SOMEHOW.
!
WHAT'S WITH THAT GUY...?
HE'S BEEN STARING AT ME ALL MORNING.
HEY YAMA-SHITA...
WHO'S THAT GUY OVER BY THE SCIENCE BUILDING?
WHO?
THERE'S NOBODY THERE. THAT AREA'S CLOSED UNDER CONSTRUCTION.
LOOK! SEE HIM? DRESSED IN BLACK!!
I CAN'T SEE WHAT'S NOT THERE!!
HOW CAN YOU NOT SEE HIM?! HE'S *RIGHT THERE!*
I THINK YOU'RE HAVING FANTASIES...
FINE...
I'M GOING HOME TO PRACTICE.

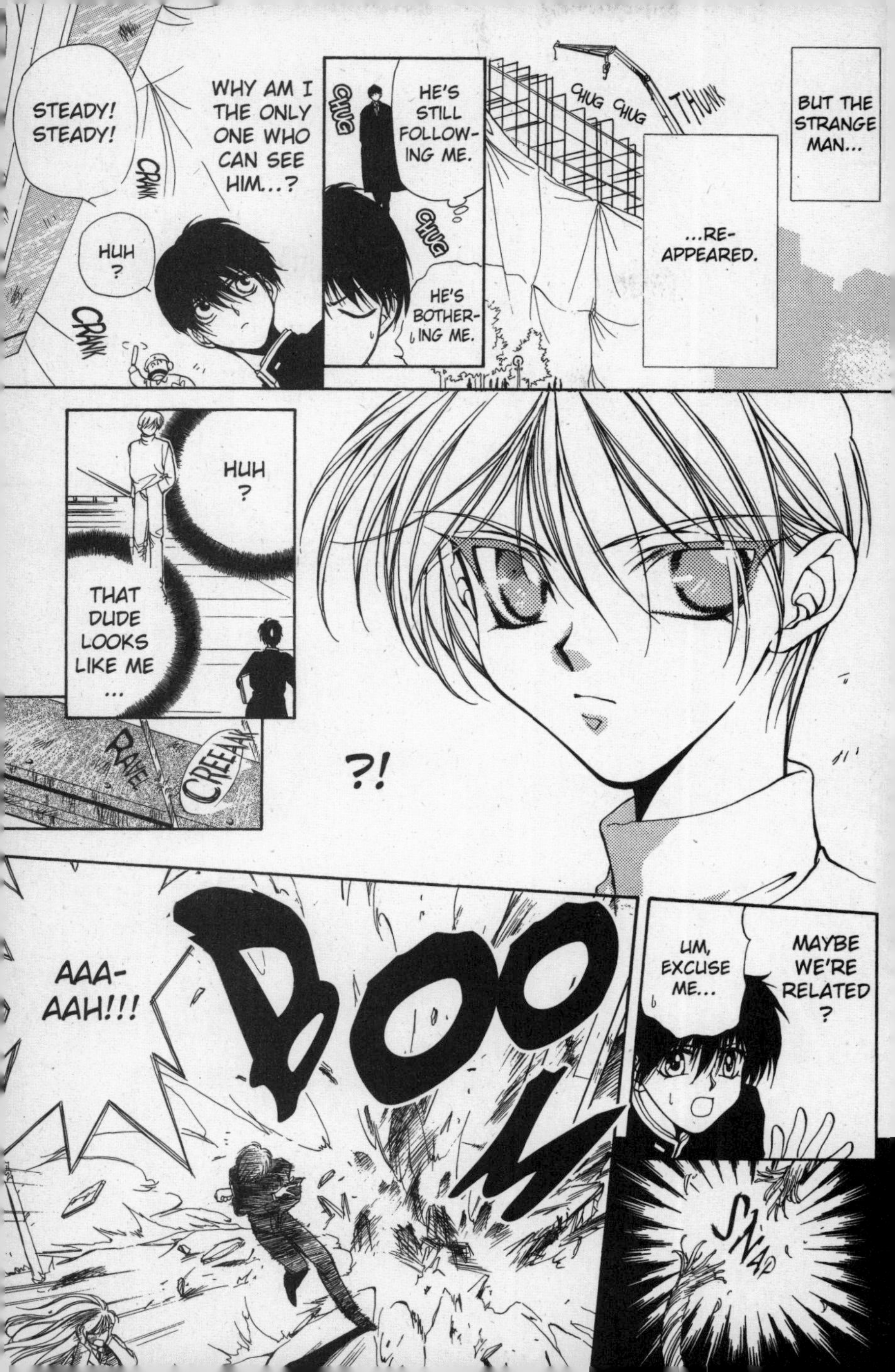
BUT THE STRANGE MAN...
THUNK
CHUG CHUG
...RE-APPEARED.
HE'S STILL FOLLOW-ING ME.
CHUG
CHUG
HE'S BOTHER-ING ME.
WHY AM I THE ONLY ONE WHO CAN SEE HIM...?
STEADY! STEADY!
CRANK
HUH?
CRANK
?!
HUH?
THAT DUDE LOOKS LIKE ME...
CREEAAK
MAYBE WE'RE RELATED?
UM, EXCUSE ME...
SNAP
BOOM
AAA-AAH!!!

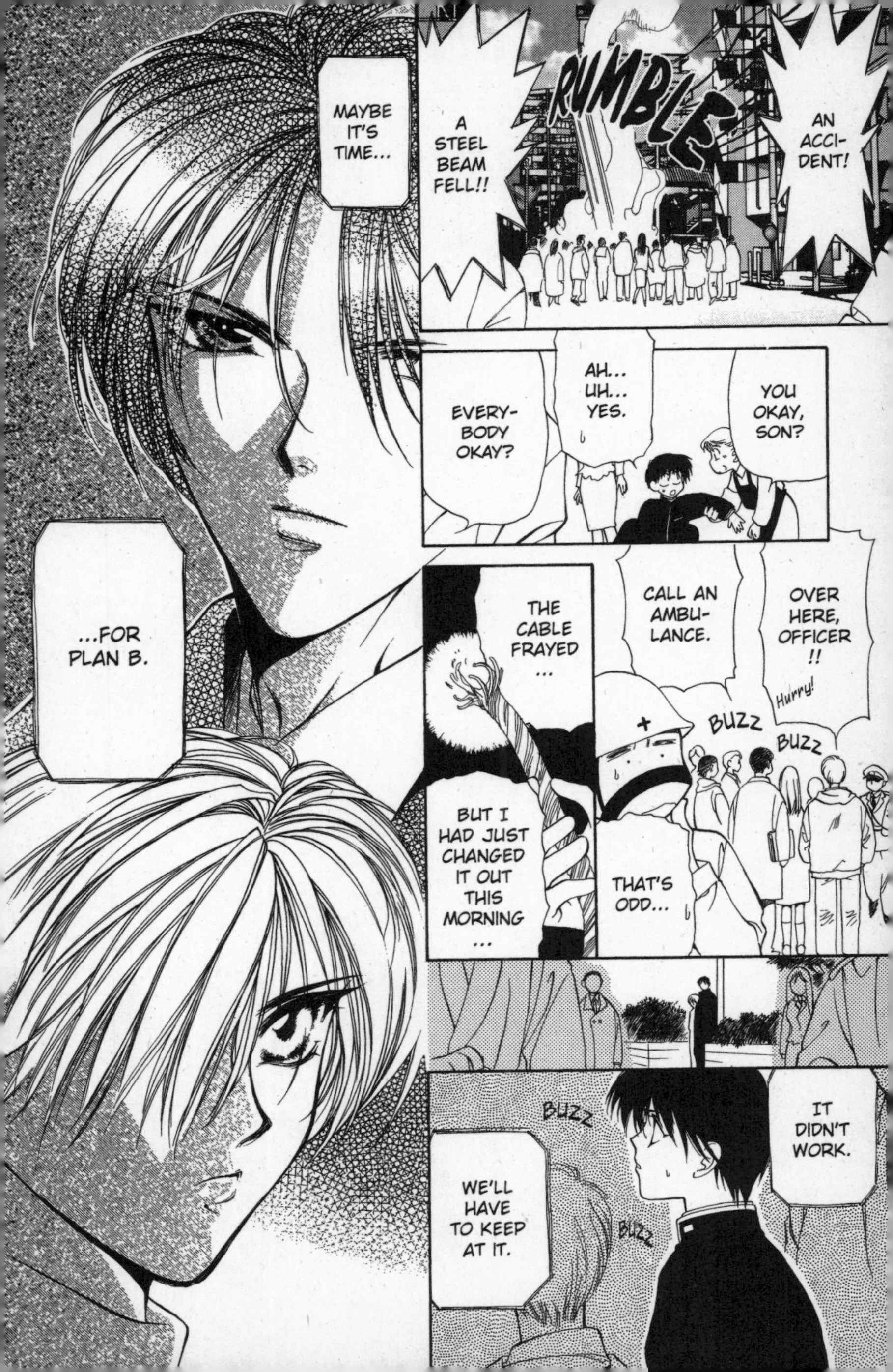
AN ACCI-DENT!
RUMBLE
A STEEL BEAM FELL!!
YOU OKAY, SON?
AH... UH... YES.
EVERY-BODY OKAY?
OVER HERE, OFFICER !!
Hurry!
CALL AN AMBU-LANCE.
BUZZ
BUZZ
THAT'S ODD...
THE CABLE FRAYED ...
BUT I HAD JUST CHANGED IT OUT THIS MORNING ...
IT DIDN'T WORK.
BUZZ
WE'LL HAVE TO KEEP AT IT.
BUZZ
MAYBE IT'S TIME...
...FOR PLAN B.

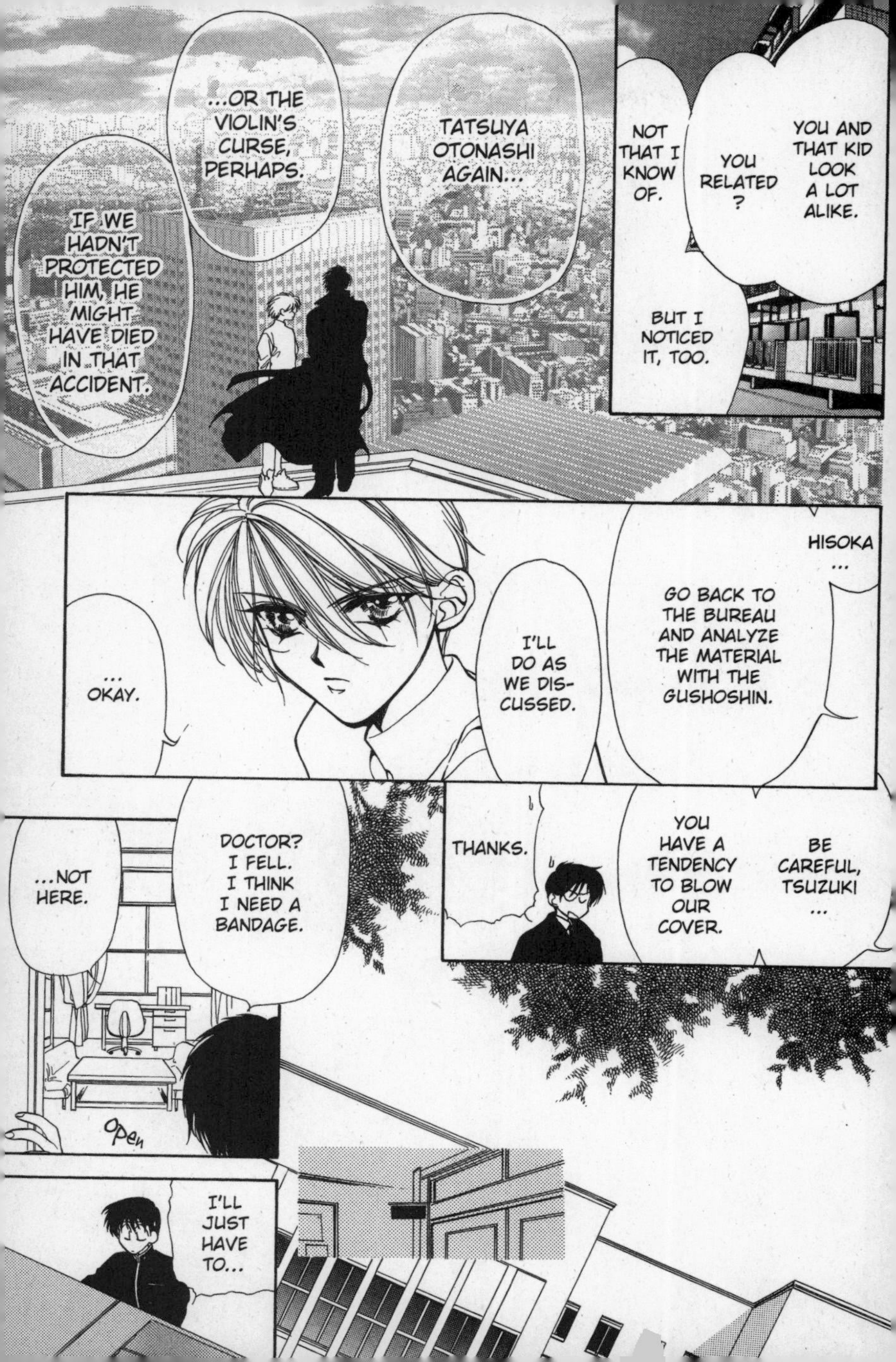
YOU AND THAT KID LOOK A LOT ALIKE.
YOU RELATED ?
NOT THAT I KNOW OF.
BUT I NOTICED IT, TOO.
TATSUYA OTONASHI AGAIN...
...OR THE VIOLIN'S CURSE, PERHAPS.
IF WE HADN'T PROTECTED HIM, HE MIGHT HAVE DIED IN THAT ACCIDENT.
HISOKA ...
GO BACK TO THE BUREAU AND ANALYZE THE MATERIAL WITH THE GUSHOSHIN.
I'LL DO AS WE DIS-CUSSED.
... OKAY.
BE CAREFUL, TSUZUKI ...
YOU HAVE A TENDENCY TO BLOW OUR COVER.
THANKS.
DOCTOR? I FELL. I THINK I NEED A BANDAGE.
...NOT HERE.
Open
I'LL JUST HAVE TO...

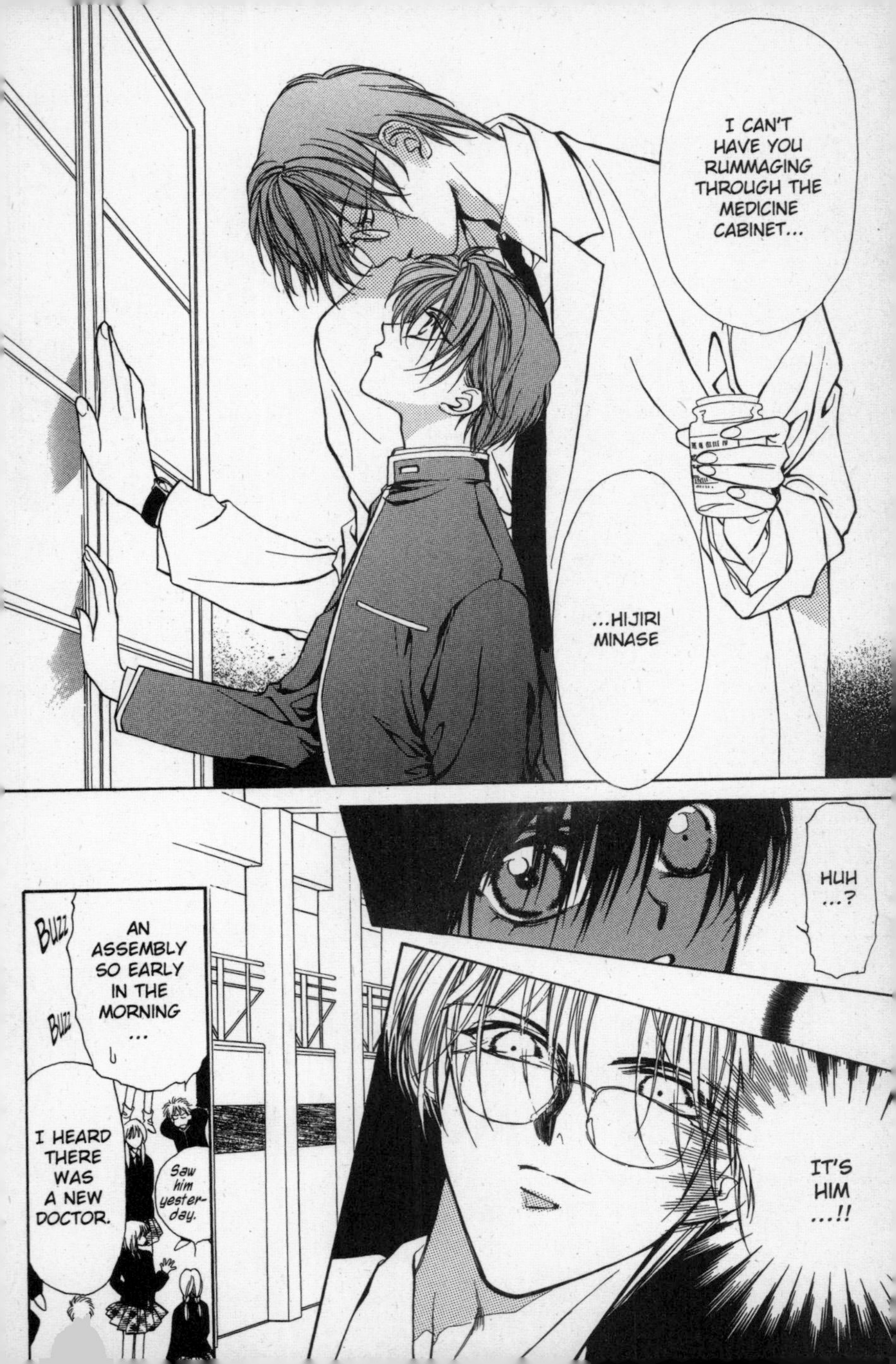
I CAN'T HAVE YOU RUMMAGING THROUGH THE MEDICINE CABINET...
...HIJIRI MINASE
HUH ...?
IT'S HIM ...!!
AN ASSEMBLY SO EARLY IN THE MORNING ...
Buzz
Buzz
Saw him yester-day.
I HEARD THERE WAS A NEW DOCTOR.

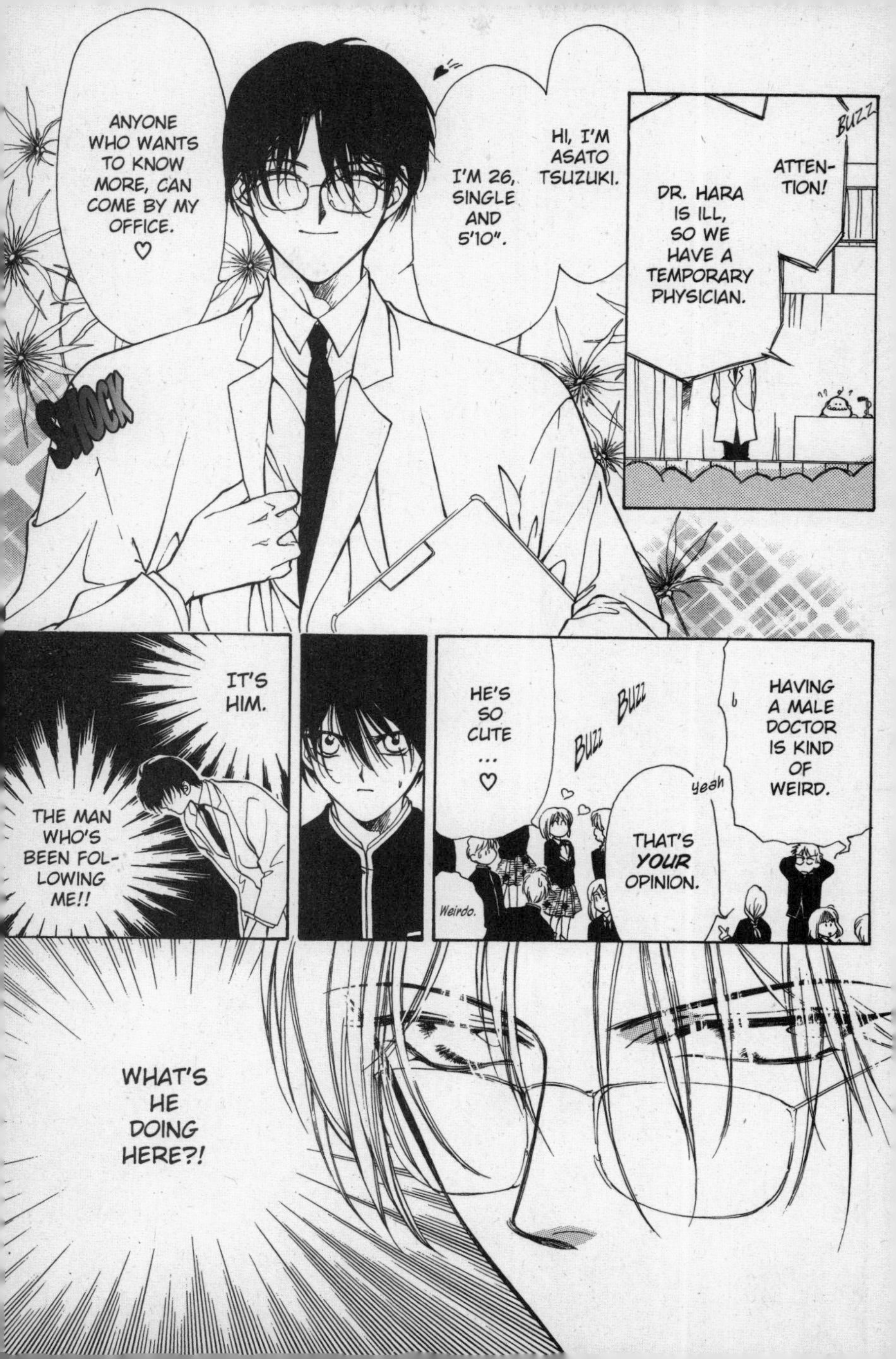
BUZZ
ATTENTION!
DR. HARA IS ILL, SO WE HAVE A TEMPORARY PHYSICIAN.
HI, I'M ASATO TSUZUKI.
I'M 26, SINGLE AND 5'10".
ANYONE WHO WANTS TO KNOW MORE, CAN COME BY MY OFFICE. ♡
SHOCK
HAVING A MALE DOCTOR IS KIND OF WEIRD.
yeah
THAT'S YOUR OPINION.
Buzz Buzz
HE'S SO CUTE ... ♡
Weirdo.
IT'S HIM.
THE MAN WHO'S BEEN FOLLOWING ME!!
WHAT'S HE DOING HERE?!

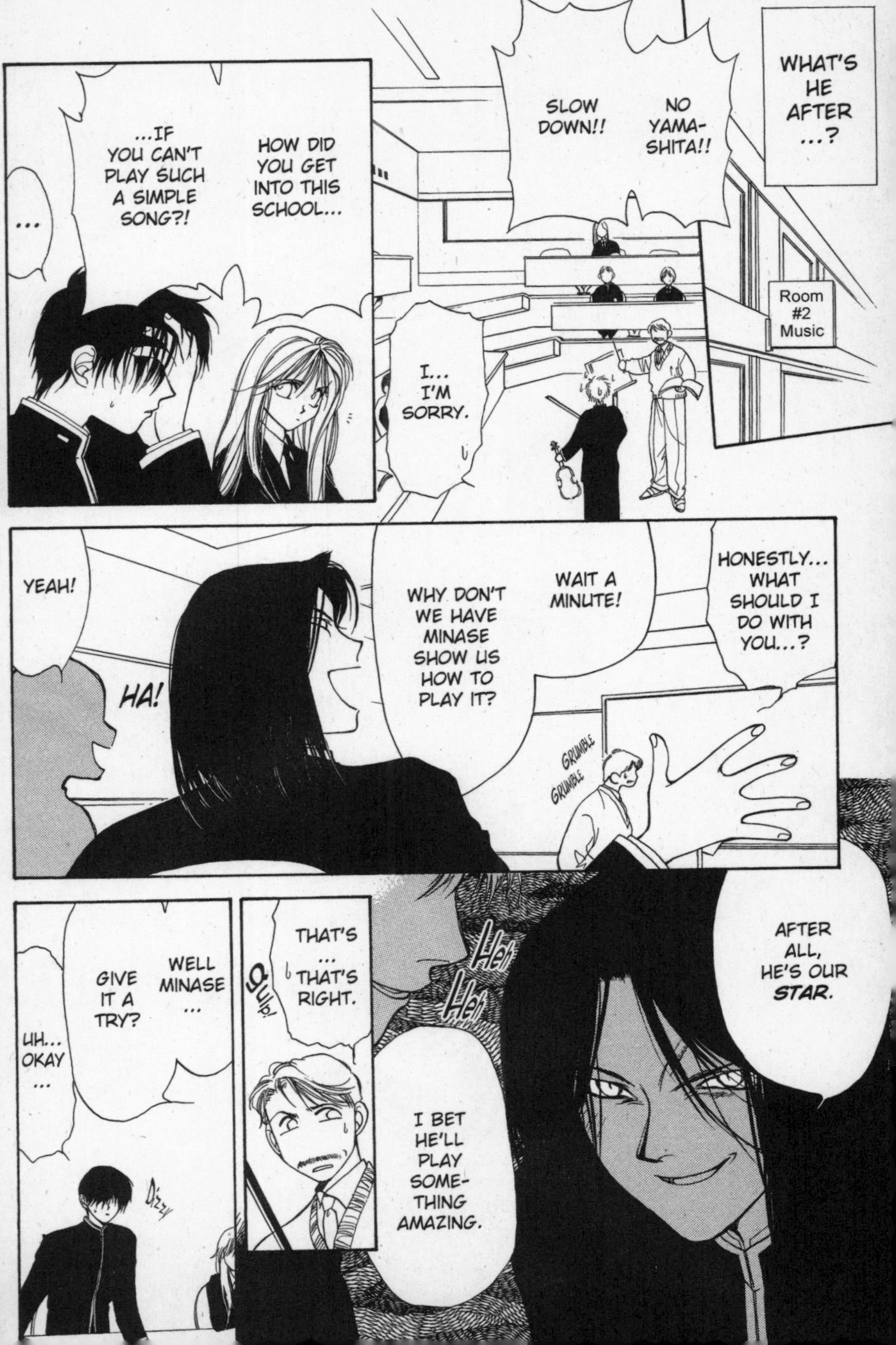

WHAT'S HE AFTER ...?
NO YAMA-SHITA!!
SLOW DOWN!!
Room #2 Music
I... I'M SORRY.
HOW DID YOU GET INTO THIS SCHOOL...
...IF YOU CAN'T PLAY SUCH A SIMPLE SONG?!
...
HONESTLY... WHAT SHOULD I DO WITH YOU...?
GRUMBLE GRUMBLE
WAIT A MINUTE!
WHY DON'T WE HAVE MINASE SHOW US HOW TO PLAY IT?
HA!
YEAH!
AFTER ALL, HE'S OUR STAR.
HEH HEH
I BET HE'LL PLAY SOME-THING AMAZING.
THAT'S ... THAT'S RIGHT.
GULP!
WELL MINASE ...
GIVE IT A TRY?
UH... OKAY ...
DIZZY

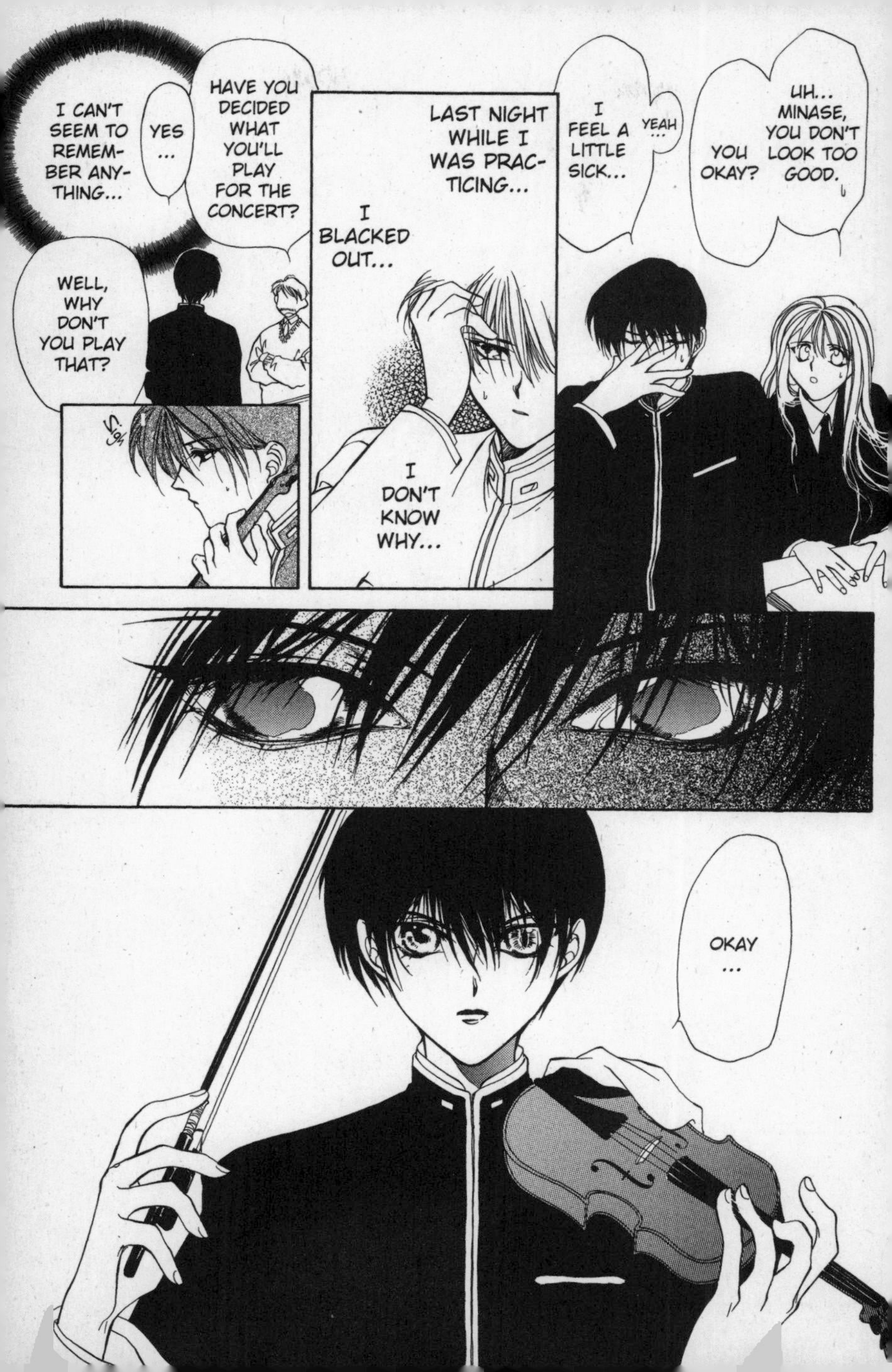
UH... MINASE, YOU DON'T LOOK TOO GOOD.
YOU OKAY?
YEAH...
I FEEL A LITTLE SICK...
LAST NIGHT WHILE I WAS PRACTICING...
I BLACKED OUT...
I DON'T KNOW WHY...
HAVE YOU DECIDED WHAT YOU'LL PLAY FOR THE CONCERT?
YES...
I CAN'T SEEM TO REMEMBER ANYTHING...
WELL, WHY DON'T YOU PLAY THAT?
Sigh
OKAY...

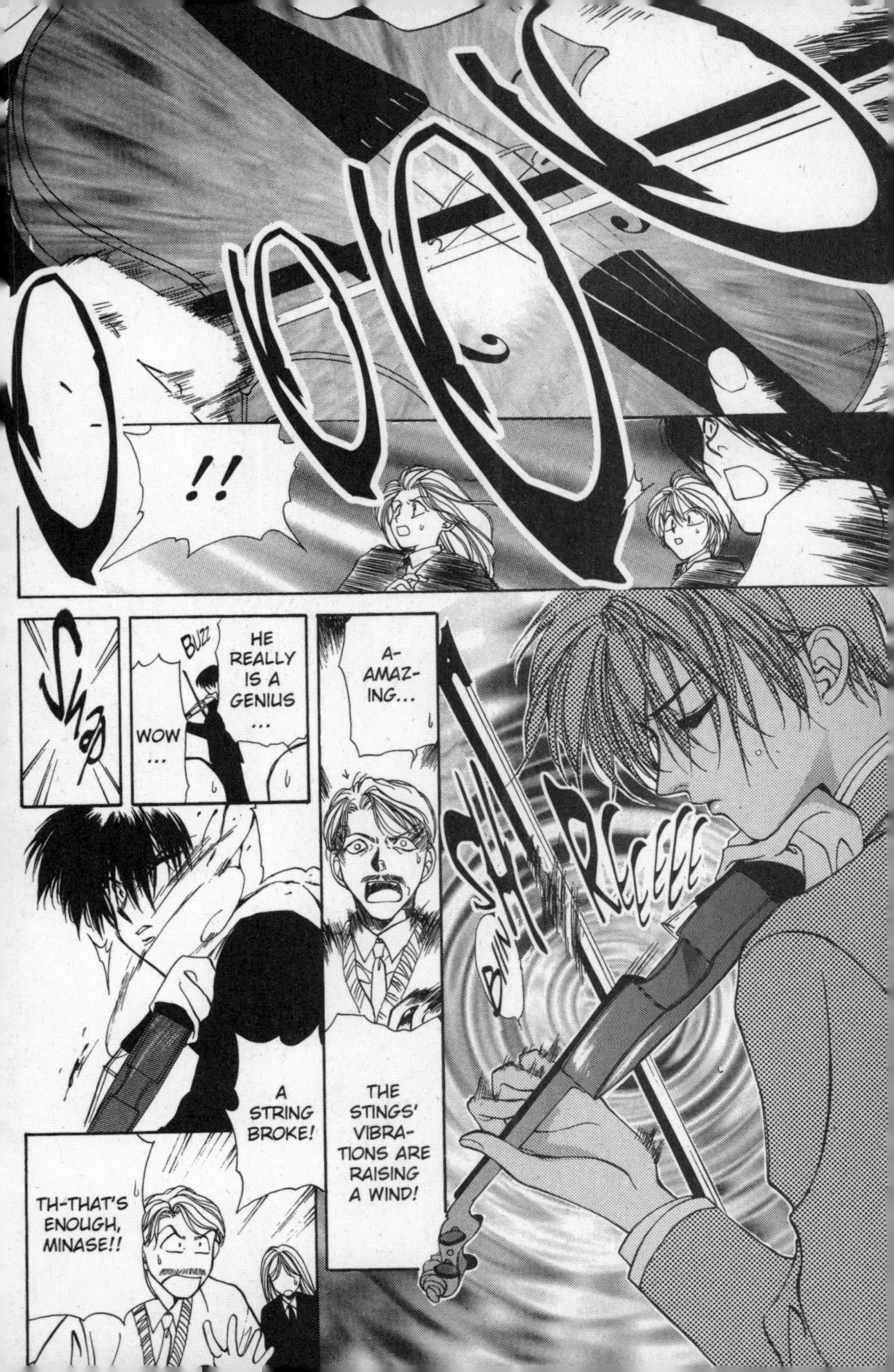
!!
A-
AMAZ-
ING...
HE
REALLY
IS A
GENIUS
...
WOW
...
BUZZ
Snap
THE
STINGS'
VIBRA-
TIONS ARE
RAISING
A WIND!
A
STRING
BROKE!
TH-THAT'S
ENOUGH,
MINASE!!

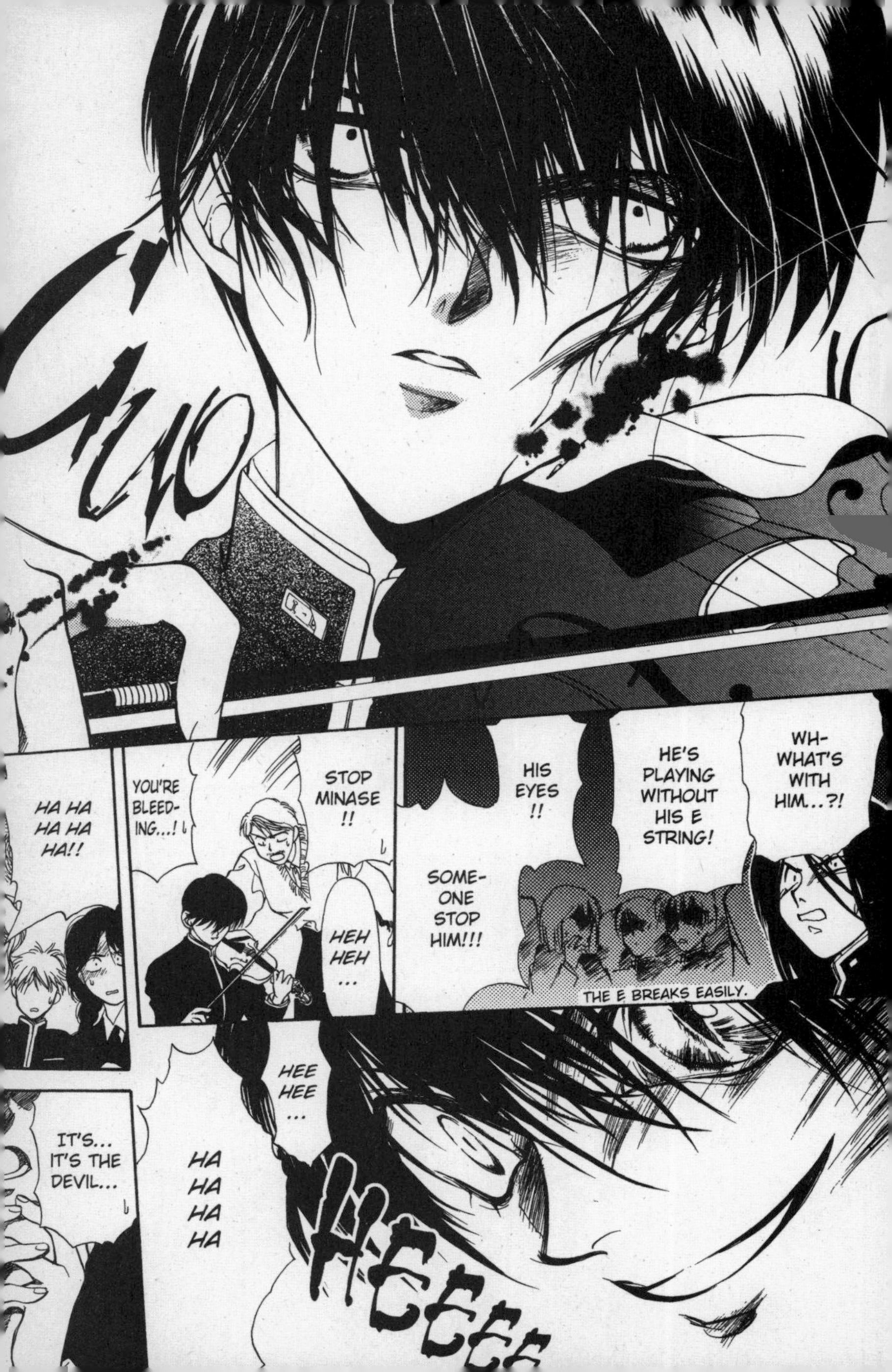
WH- WHAT'S WITH HIM...?!
HE'S PLAYING WITHOUT HIS E STRING!
HIS EYES !!
SOME-ONE STOP HIM!!!
THE E BREAKS EASILY.
STOP MINASE !!
YOU'RE BLEED-ING...!
HEH HEH ...
HA HA HA HA HA!!
HEE HEE ...
HA HA HA HA
IT'S... IT'S THE DEVIL...
HEEEE

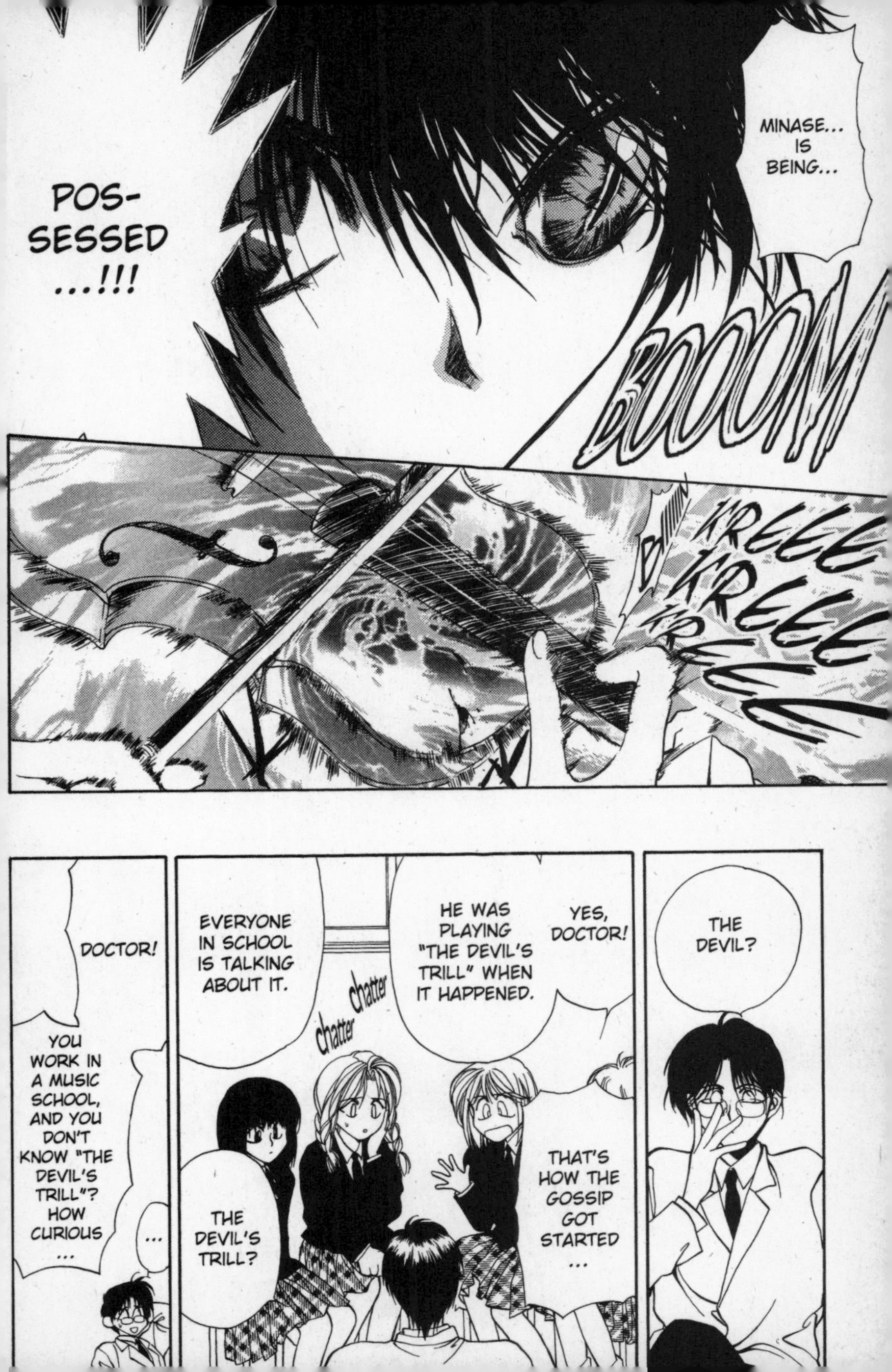
MINASE... IS BEING...
POS-SESSED ...!!!
BOOOM
KREEE
KREEE
THE DEVIL?
YES, DOCTOR!
HE WAS PLAYING "THE DEVIL'S TRILL" WHEN IT HAPPENED.
EVERYONE IN SCHOOL IS TALKING ABOUT IT.
chatter
chatter
THAT'S HOW THE GOSSIP GOT STARTED ...
THE DEVIL'S TRILL?
DOCTOR!
YOU WORK IN A MUSIC SCHOOL, AND YOU DON'T KNOW "THE DEVIL'S TRILL"? HOW CURIOUS ...
...

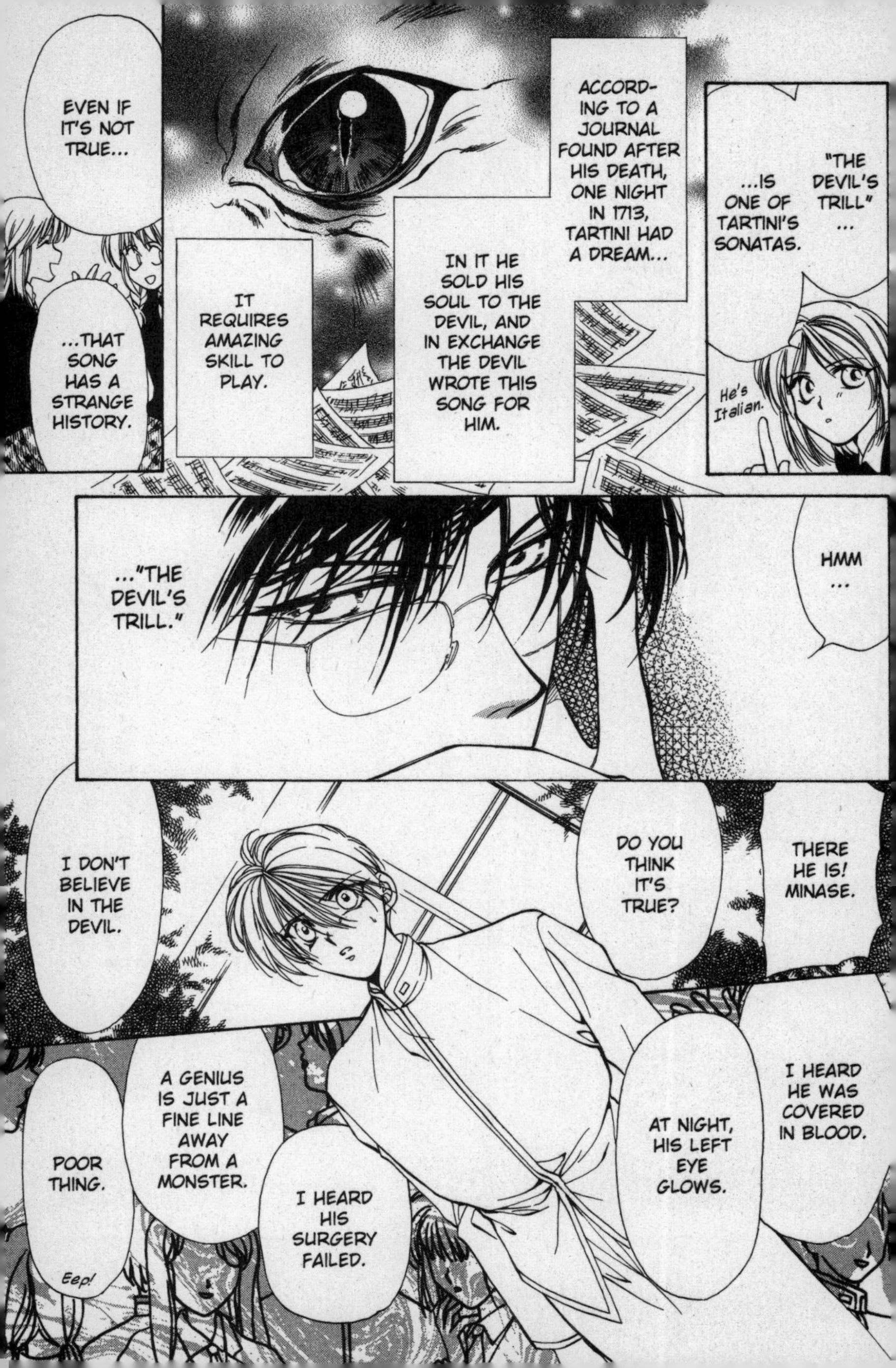
"THE DEVIL'S TRILL" ...
...IS ONE OF TARTINI'S SONATAS.
He's Italian.
ACCORD-ING TO A JOURNAL FOUND AFTER HIS DEATH, ONE NIGHT IN 1713, TARTINI HAD A DREAM...
IN IT HE SOLD HIS SOUL TO THE DEVIL, AND IN EXCHANGE THE DEVIL WROTE THIS SONG FOR HIM.
IT REQUIRES AMAZING SKILL TO PLAY.
EVEN IF IT'S NOT TRUE...
...THAT SONG HAS A STRANGE HISTORY.
HMM ...
..."THE DEVIL'S TRILL."
THERE HE IS! MINASE.
DO YOU THINK IT'S TRUE?
I DON'T BELIEVE IN THE DEVIL.
I HEARD HE WAS COVERED IN BLOOD.
AT NIGHT, HIS LEFT EYE GLOWS.
I HEARD HIS SURGERY FAILED.
A GENIUS IS JUST A FINE LINE AWAY FROM A MONSTER.
POOR THING.
Eep!

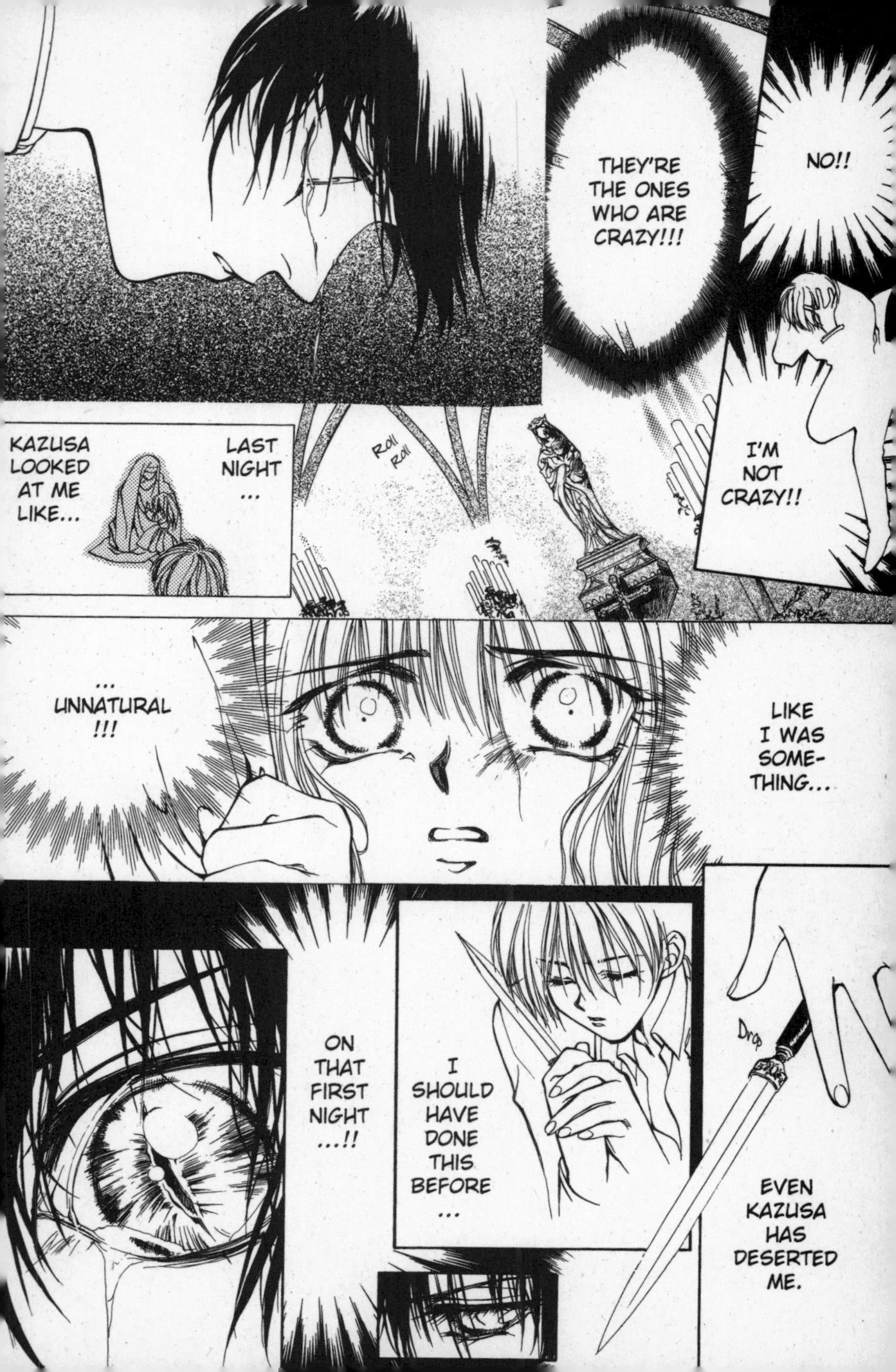
NO!!
I'M NOT CRAZY!!
THEY'RE THE ONES WHO ARE CRAZY!!!
Roll Roll
LAST NIGHT ...
KAZUSA LOOKED AT ME LIKE...
LIKE I WAS SOME-THING...
... UNNATURAL !!!
EVEN KAZUSA HAS DESERTED ME.
Drop
I SHOULD HAVE DONE THIS BEFORE ...
ON THAT FIRST NIGHT ...!!

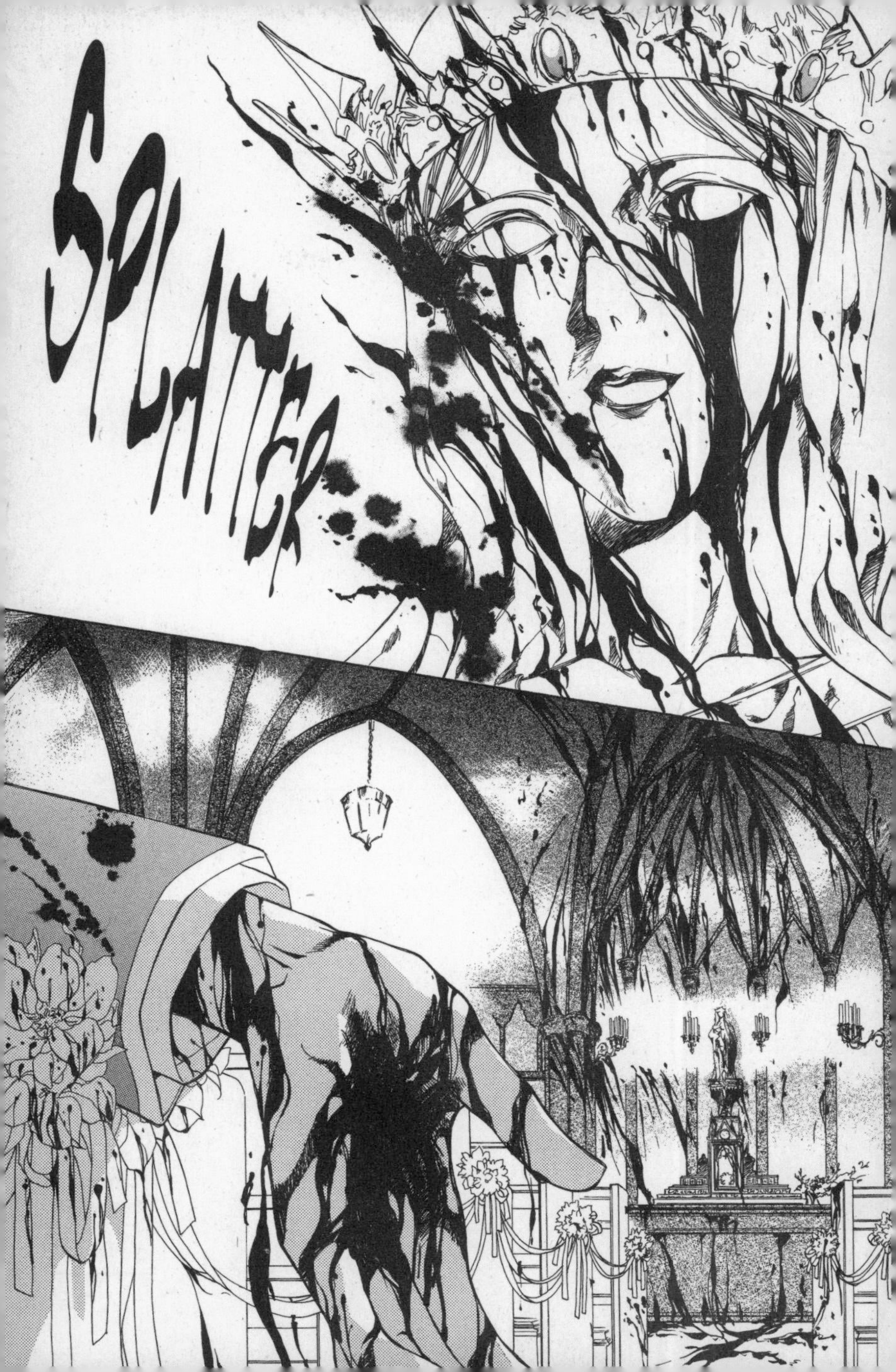
SPLATTER

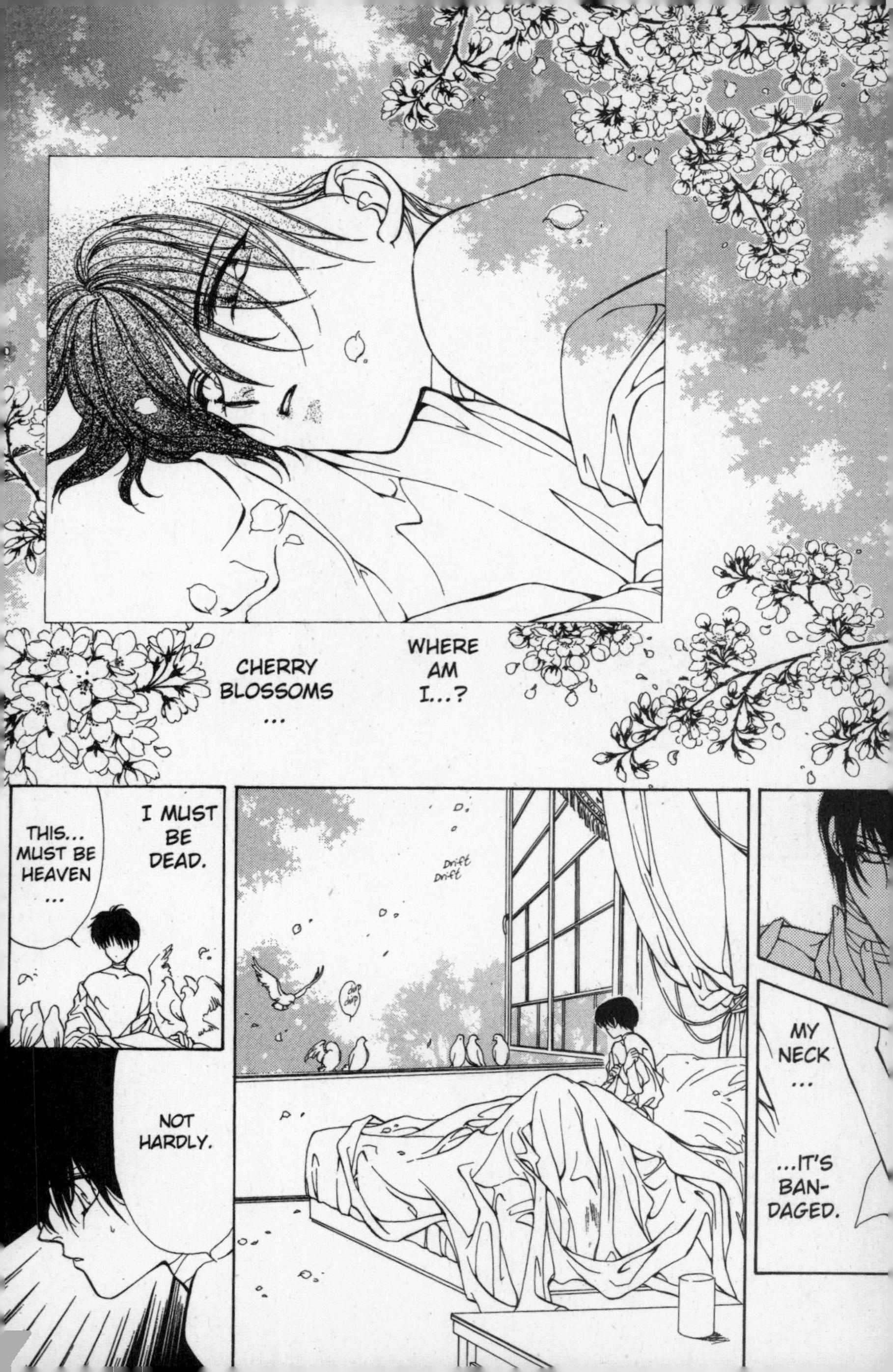
WHERE AM I...?
CHERRY BLOSSOMS ...
MY NECK ...
...IT'S BAN-DAGED.
Drift Drift
I MUST BE DEAD.
THIS... MUST BE HEAVEN ...
NOT HARDLY.

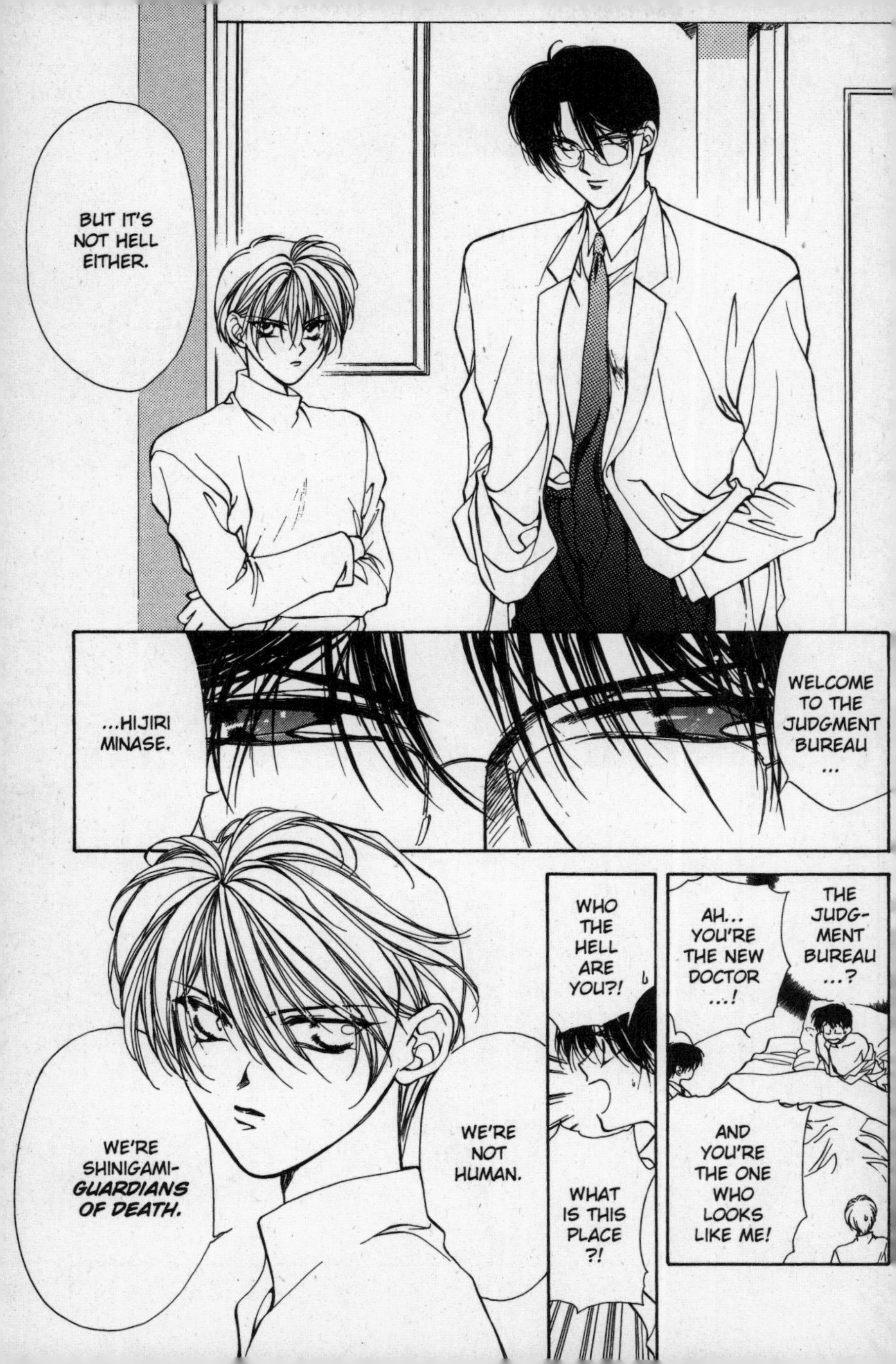
BUT IT'S NOT HELL EITHER.
WELCOME TO THE JUDGMENT BUREAU ...
...HIJIRI MINASE.
THE JUDGMENT BUREAU ...?
AH... YOU'RE THE NEW DOCTOR ...!
AND YOU'RE THE ONE WHO LOOKS LIKE ME!
WHO THE HELL ARE YOU?!
WHAT IS THIS PLACE ?!
WE'RE NOT HUMAN.
WE'RE SHINIGAMI-*GUARDIANS OF DEATH.*

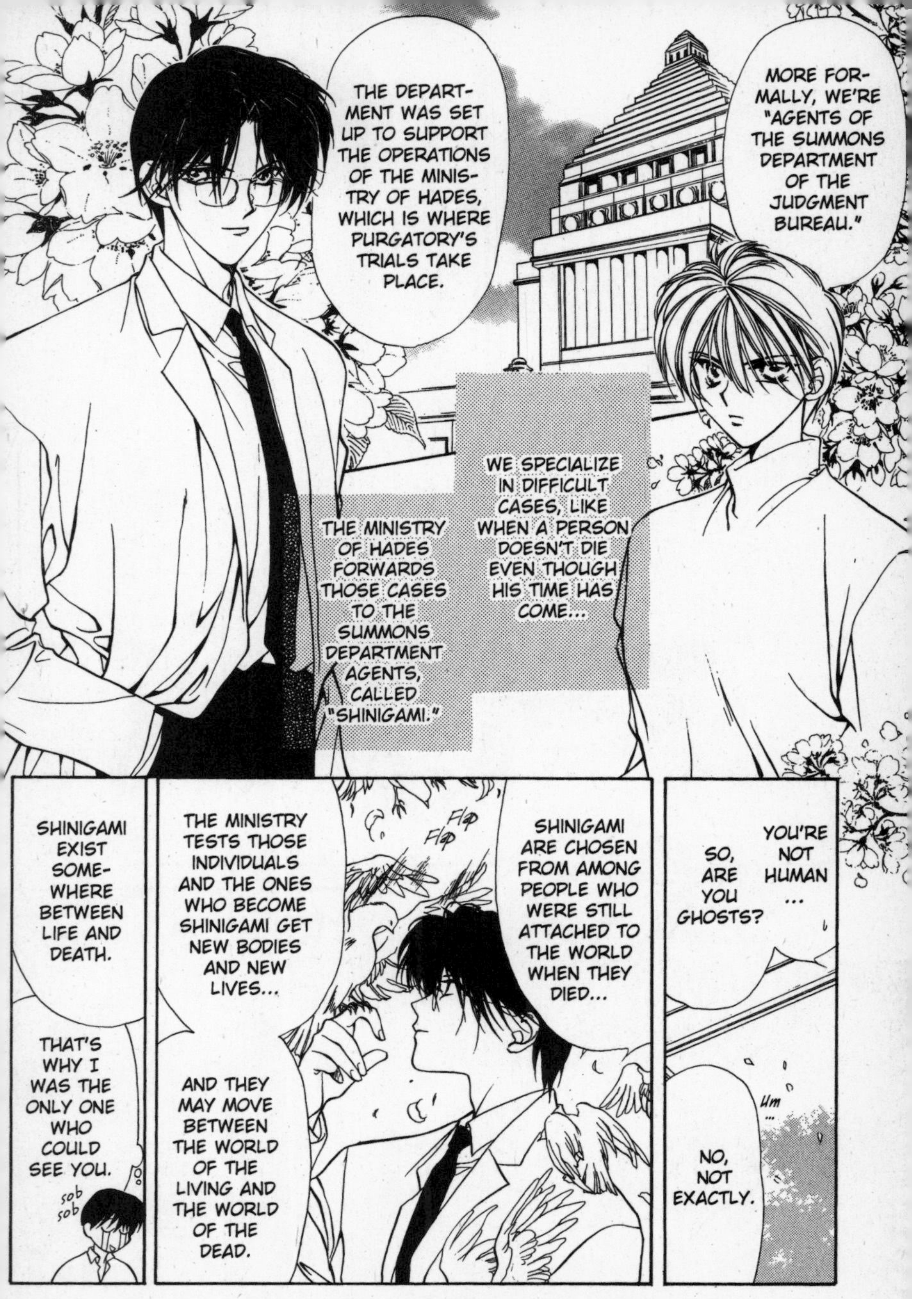
MORE FOR-MALLY, WE'RE "AGENTS OF THE SUMMONS DEPARTMENT OF THE JUDGMENT BUREAU."
THE DEPART-MENT WAS SET UP TO SUPPORT THE OPERATIONS OF THE MINIS-TRY OF HADES, WHICH IS WHERE PURGATORY'S TRIALS TAKE PLACE.
WE SPECIALIZE IN DIFFICULT CASES, LIKE WHEN A PERSON DOESN'T DIE EVEN THOUGH HIS TIME HAS COME...
THE MINISTRY OF HADES FORWARDS THOSE CASES TO THE SUMMONS DEPARTMENT AGENTS, CALLED "SHINIGAMI."
YOU'RE NOT HUMAN ...
SO, ARE YOU GHOSTS?
Um ...
NO, NOT EXACTLY.
SHINIGAMI ARE CHOSEN FROM AMONG PEOPLE WHO WERE STILL ATTACHED TO THE WORLD WHEN THEY DIED...
Flap Flap
THE MINISTRY TESTS THOSE INDIVIDUALS AND THE ONES WHO BECOME SHINIGAMI GET NEW BODIES AND NEW LIVES...
AND THEY MAY MOVE BETWEEN THE WORLD OF THE LIVING AND THE WORLD OF THE DEAD.
SHINIGAMI EXIST SOME-WHERE BETWEEN LIFE AND DEATH.
THAT'S WHY I WAS THE ONLY ONE WHO COULD SEE YOU.
sob sob

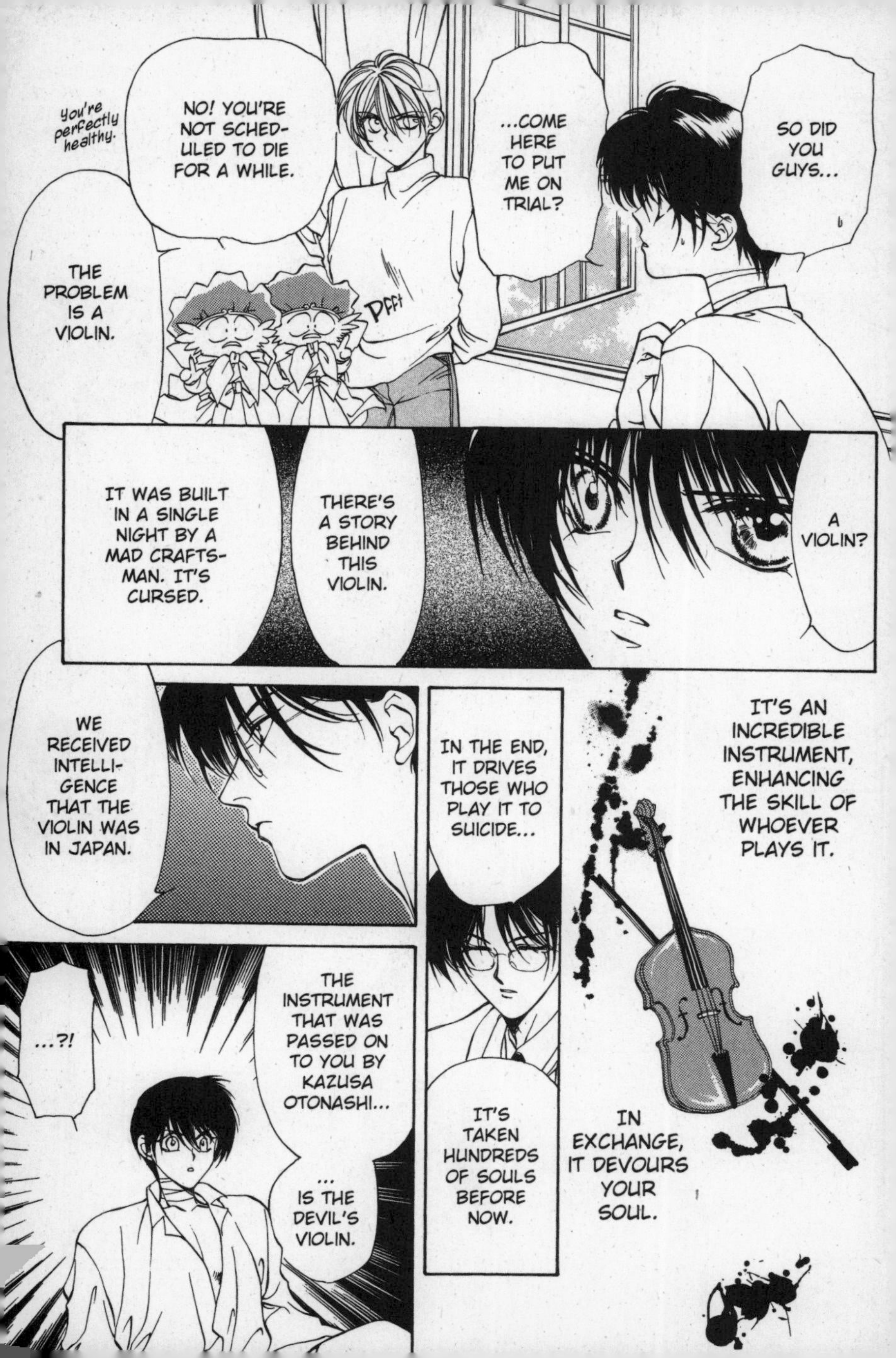
SO DID YOU GUYS...
...COME HERE TO PUT ME ON TRIAL?
NO! YOU'RE NOT SCHED-ULED TO DIE FOR A WHILE.
You're perfectly healthy.
PFFt
THE PROBLEM IS A VIOLIN.
A VIOLIN?
THERE'S A STORY BEHIND THIS VIOLIN.
IT WAS BUILT IN A SINGLE NIGHT BY A MAD CRAFTS-MAN. IT'S CURSED.
IT'S AN INCREDIBLE INSTRUMENT, ENHANCING THE SKILL OF WHOEVER PLAYS IT.
IN EXCHANGE, IT DEVOURS YOUR SOUL.
IN THE END, IT DRIVES THOSE WHO PLAY IT TO SUICIDE...
IT'S TAKEN HUNDREDS OF SOULS BEFORE NOW.
WE RECEIVED INTELLI-GENCE THAT THE VIOLIN WAS IN JAPAN.
THE INSTRUMENT THAT WAS PASSED ON TO YOU BY KAZUSA OTONASHI...
... IS THE DEVIL'S VIOLIN.
...?!

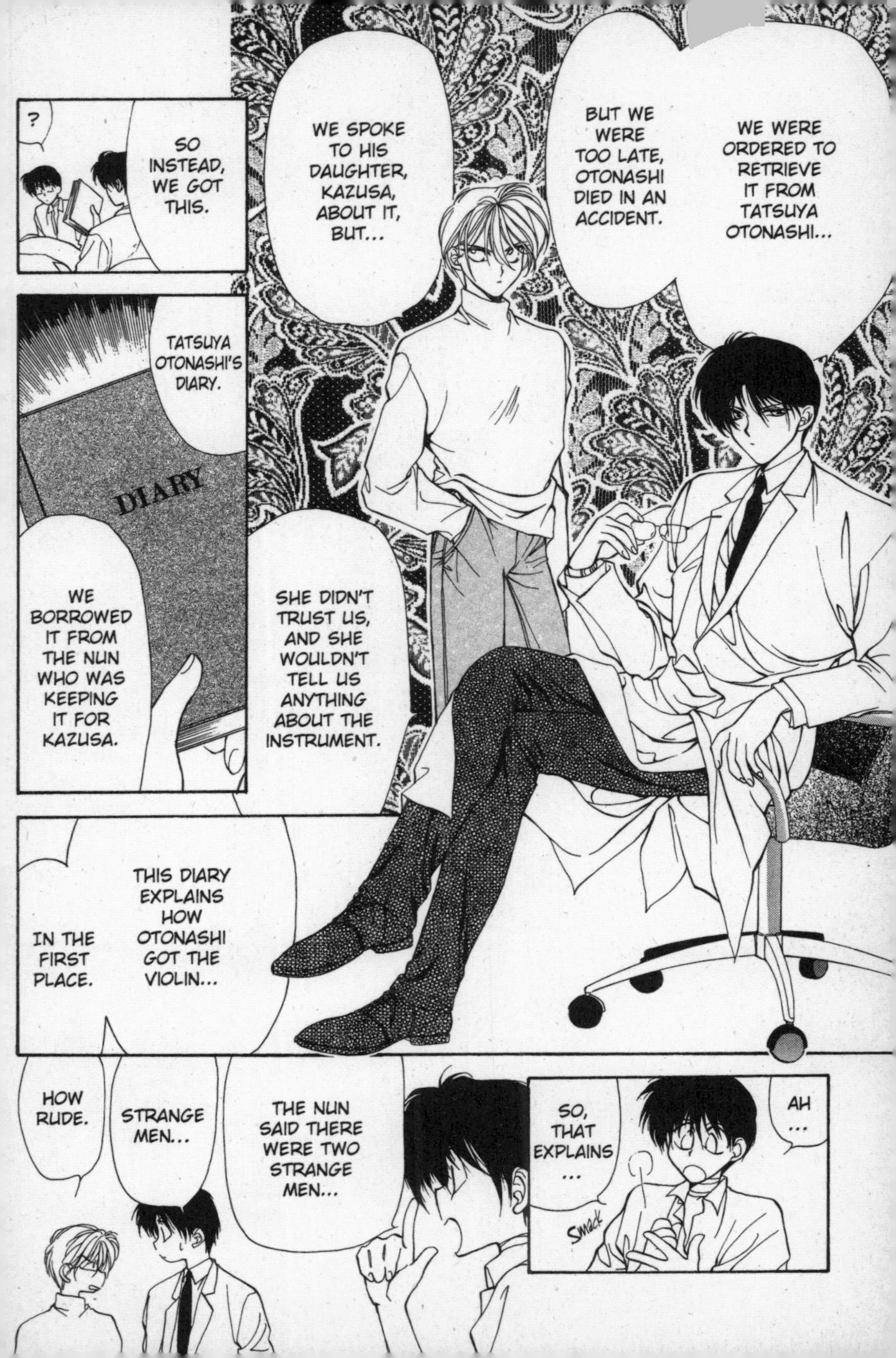
WE WERE ORDERED TO RETRIEVE IT FROM TATSUYA OTONASHI...
BUT WE WERE TOO LATE, OTONASHI DIED IN AN ACCIDENT.
WE SPOKE TO HIS DAUGHTER, KAZUSA, ABOUT IT, BUT...
SHE DIDN'T TRUST US, AND SHE WOULDN'T TELL US ANYTHING ABOUT THE INSTRUMENT.
?
SO INSTEAD, WE GOT THIS.
TATSUYA OTONASHI'S DIARY.
DIARY
WE BORROWED IT FROM THE NUN WHO WAS KEEPING IT FOR KAZUSA.
THIS DIARY EXPLAINS HOW OTONASHI GOT THE VIOLIN...
IN THE FIRST PLACE.
AH ...
SO, THAT EXPLAINS ...
SMACK
THE NUN SAID THERE WERE TWO STRANGE MEN...
STRANGE MEN...
HOW RUDE.

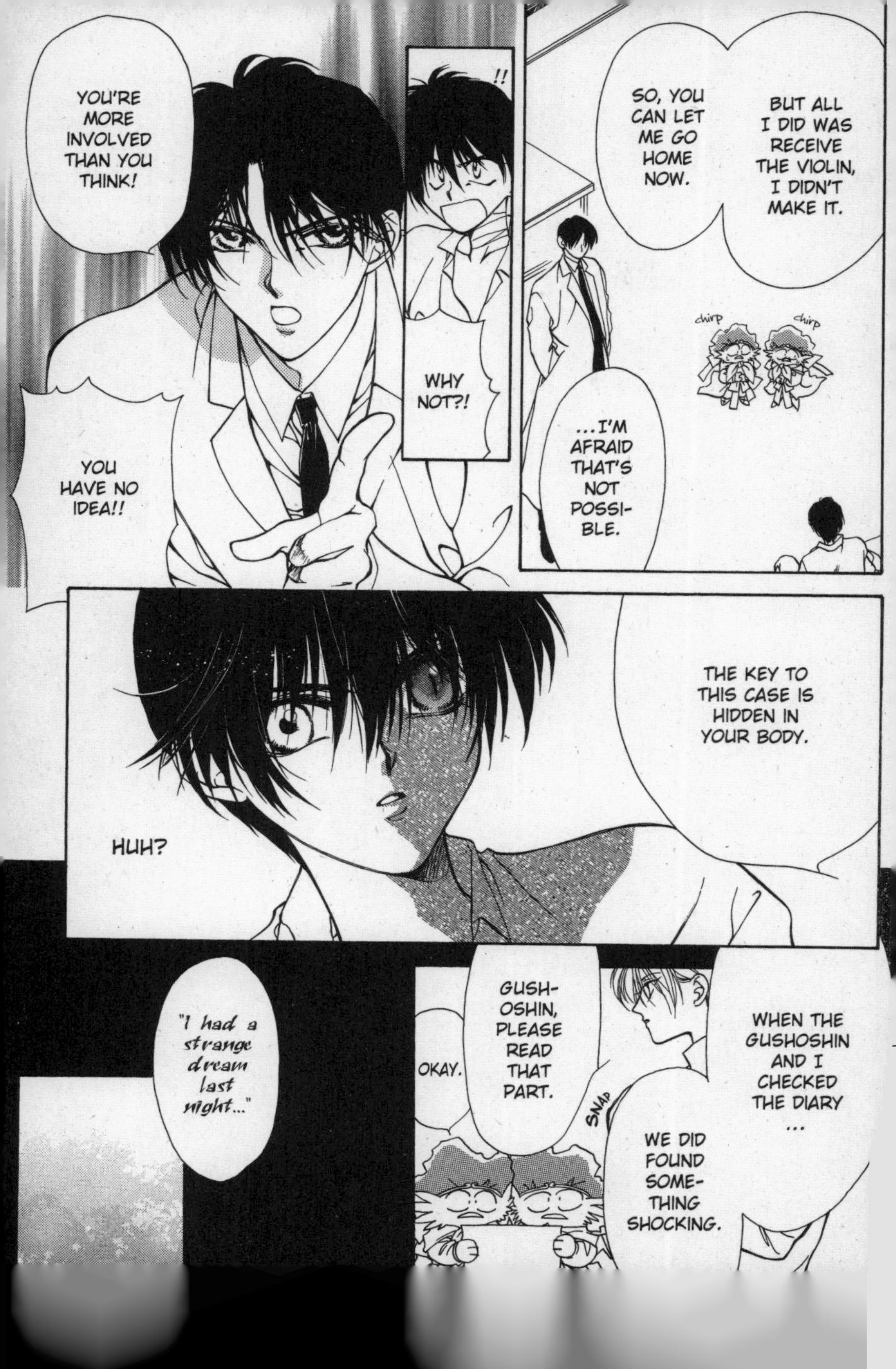
BUT ALL I DID WAS RECEIVE THE VIOLIN, I DIDN'T MAKE IT.
SO, YOU CAN LET ME GO HOME NOW.
chirp
chirp
...I'M AFRAID THAT'S NOT POSSI-BLE.
!!
WHY NOT?!
YOU'RE MORE INVOLVED THAN YOU THINK!
YOU HAVE NO IDEA!!
THE KEY TO THIS CASE IS HIDDEN IN YOUR BODY.
HUH?
WHEN THE GUSHOSHIN AND I CHECKED THE DIARY ...
WE DID FOUND SOME-THING SHOCKING.
SNAP
GUSH-OSHIN, PLEASE READ THAT PART.
OKAY.
"I had a strange dream last night..."

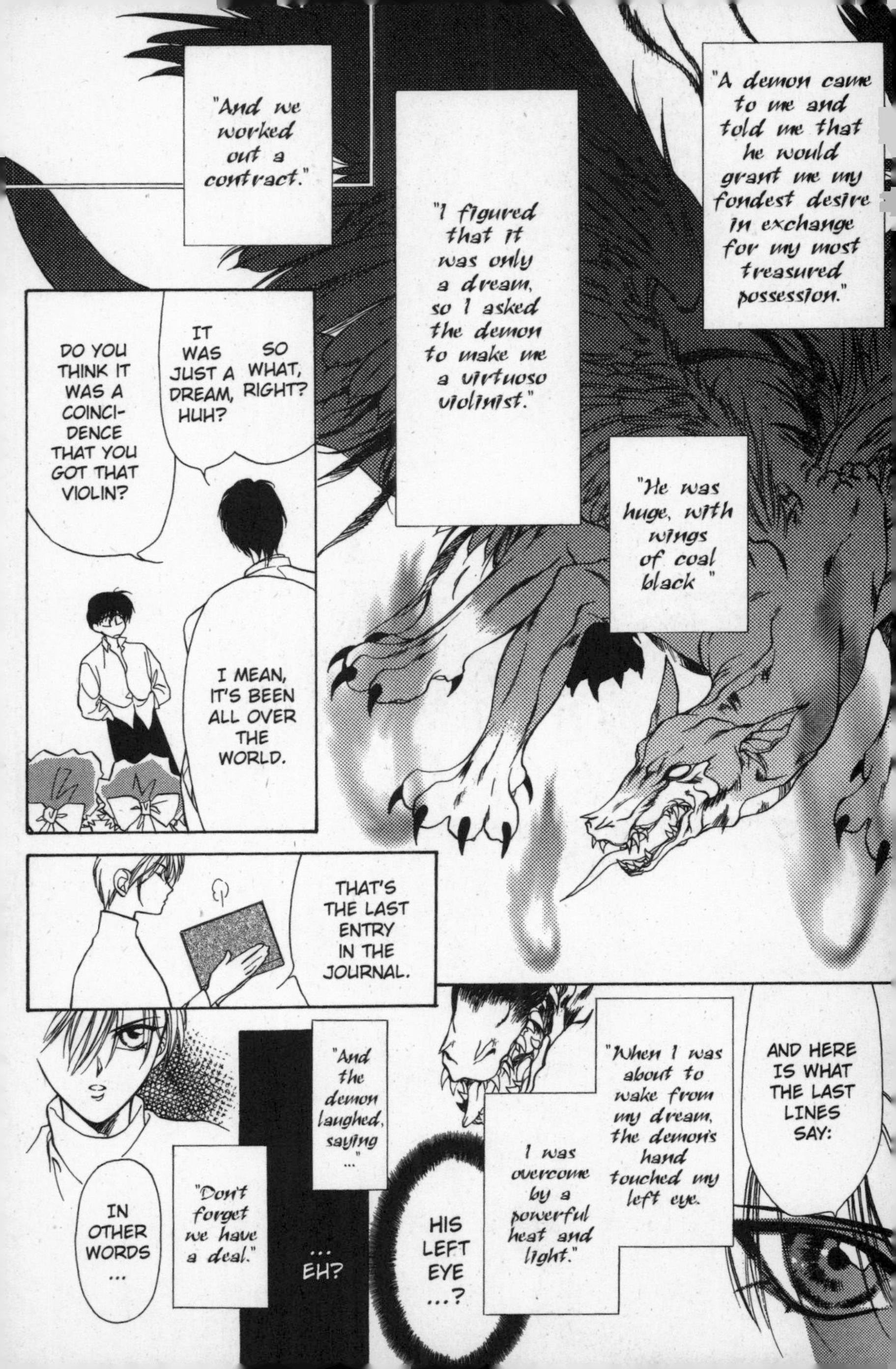
"A demon came to me and told me that he would grant me my fondest desire in exchange for my most treasured possession."
"I figured that it was only a dream, so I asked the demon to make me a virtuoso violinist."
"And we worked out a contract."
"He was huge, with wings of coal black"
SO WHAT, RIGHT?
IT WAS JUST A DREAM, HUH?
DO YOU THINK IT WAS A COINCIDENCE THAT YOU GOT THAT VIOLIN?
I MEAN, IT'S BEEN ALL OVER THE WORLD.
THAT'S THE LAST ENTRY IN THE JOURNAL.
AND HERE IS WHAT THE LAST LINES SAY:
"When I was about to wake from my dream, the demon's hand touched my left eye.
I was overcome by a powerful heat and light."
HIS LEFT EYE ...?
"And the demon laughed, saying" ...
"Don't forget we have a deal."
... EH?
IN OTHER WORDS ...

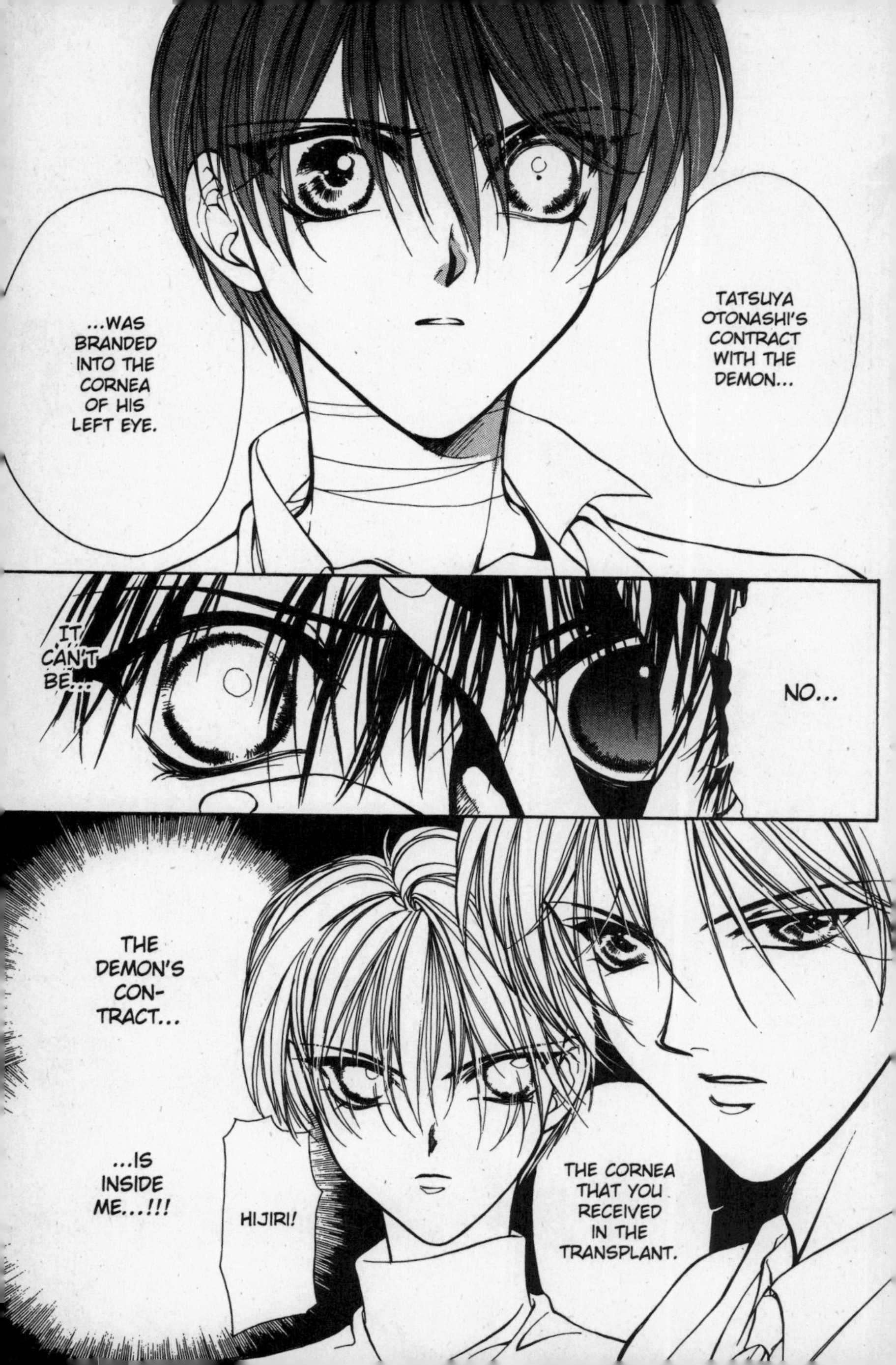
TATSUYA OTONASHI'S CONTRACT WITH THE DEMON...
...WAS BRANDED INTO THE CORNEA OF HIS LEFT EYE.
NO...
IT CAN'T BE...
THE CORNEA THAT YOU RECEIVED IN THE TRANSPLANT.
HIJIRI!
THE DEMON'S CON-TRACT...
...IS INSIDE ME...!!!

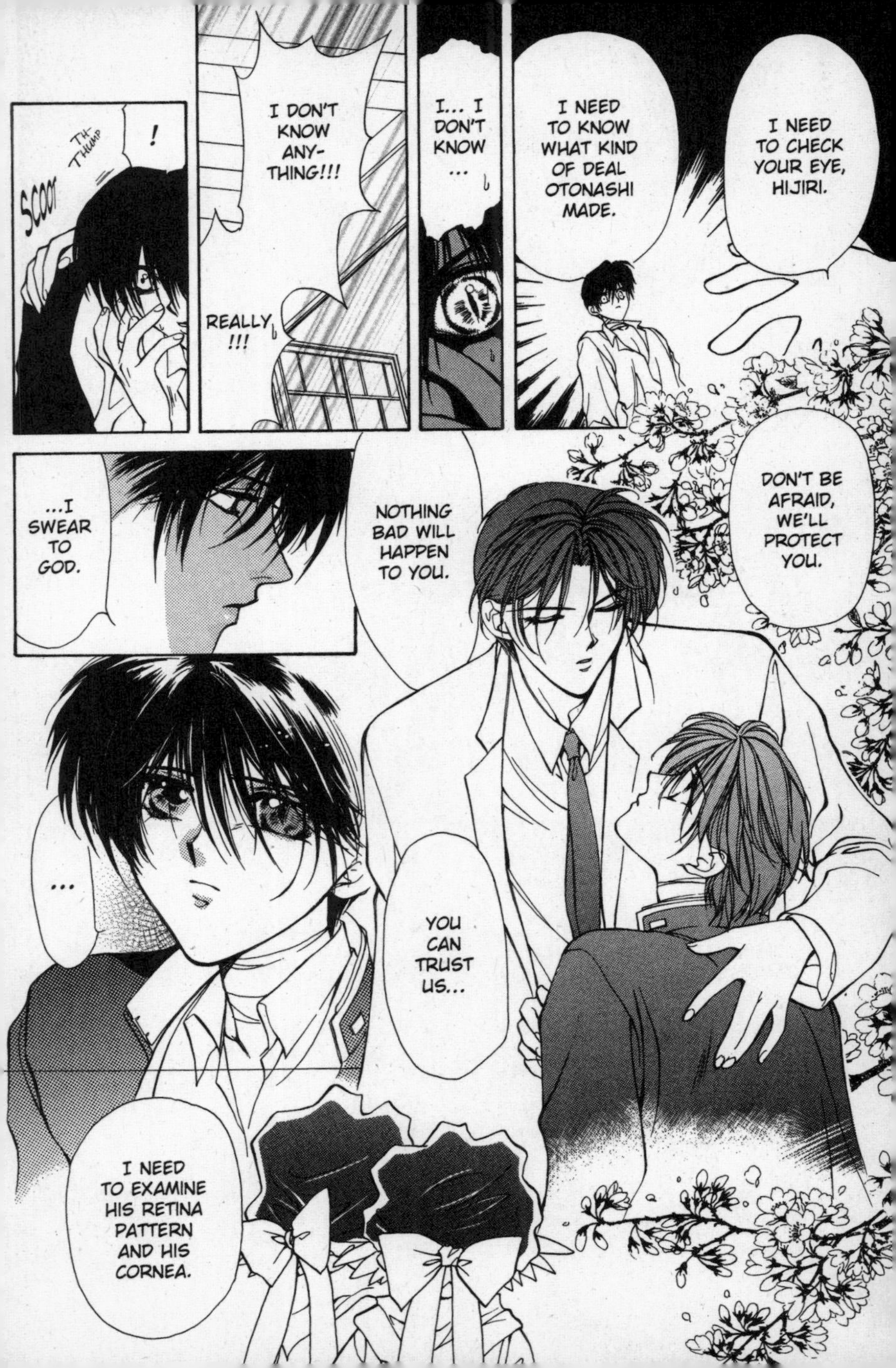
I NEED TO CHECK YOUR EYE, HIJIRI.
I NEED TO KNOW WHAT KIND OF DEAL OTONASHI MADE.
I... I DON'T KNOW ...
I DON'T KNOW ANY-THING!!!
REALLY!!!
TH-THUMP
!
SCOOT
DON'T BE AFRAID, WE'LL PROTECT YOU.
NOTHING BAD WILL HAPPEN TO YOU.
...I SWEAR TO GOD.
YOU CAN TRUST US...
...
I NEED TO EXAMINE HIS RETINA PATTERN AND HIS CORNEA.

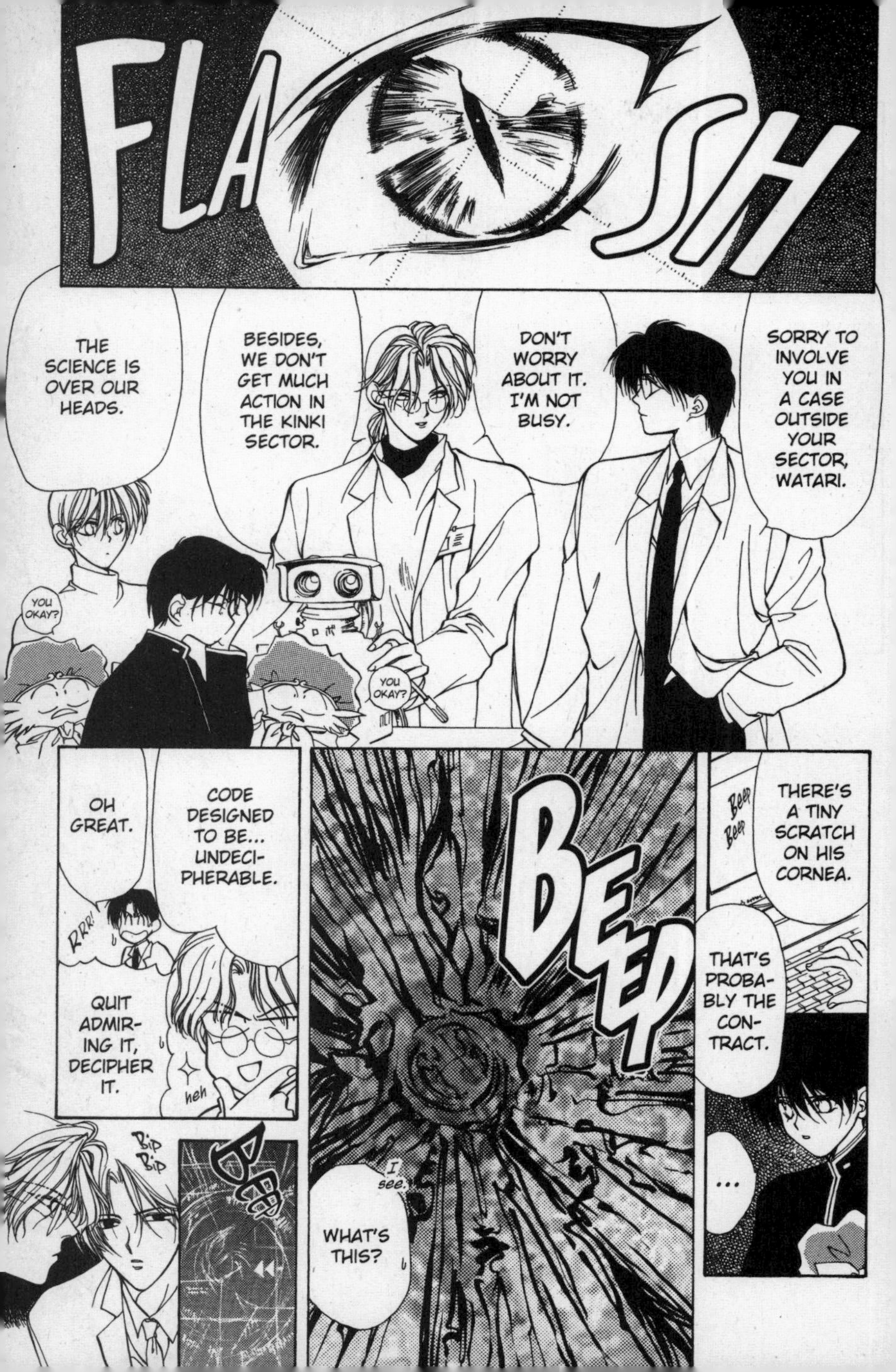
FLASH
SORRY TO INVOLVE YOU IN A CASE OUTSIDE YOUR SECTOR, WATARI.
DON'T WORRY ABOUT IT. I'M NOT BUSY.
BESIDES, WE DON'T GET MUCH ACTION IN THE KINKI SECTOR.
THE SCIENCE IS OVER OUR HEADS.
YOU OKAY?
ロボ
YOU OKAY?
Beep Beep
THERE'S A TINY SCRATCH ON HIS CORNEA.
THAT'S PROBABLY THE CONTRACT.
...
BEEP
I see.
WHAT'S THIS?
CODE DESIGNED TO BE... UNDECIPHERABLE.
OH GREAT.
RRR!
QUIT ADMIR-ING IT, DECIPHER IT.
heh
Bip Bip
BEEP

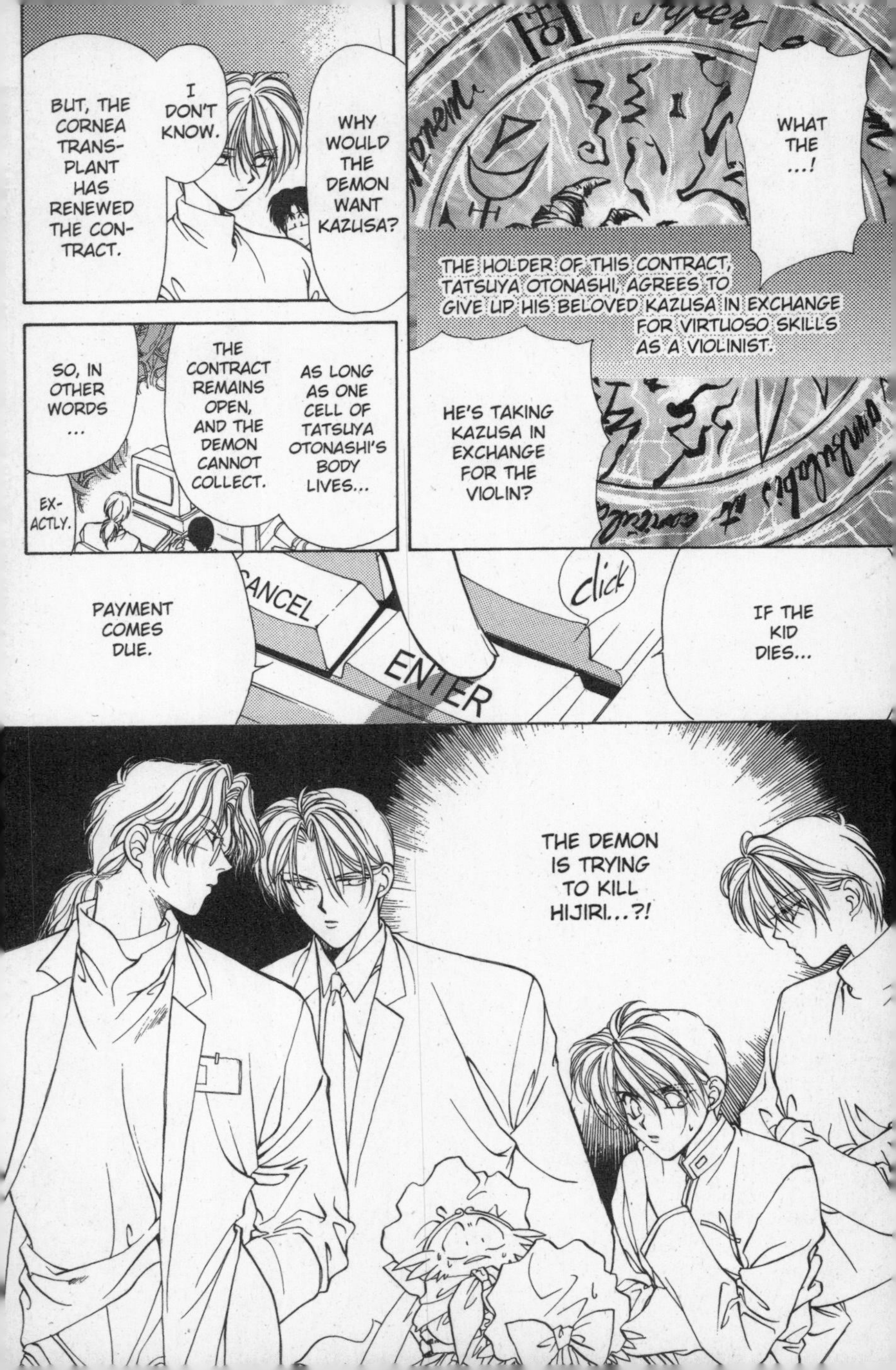
WHAT THE ...!
THE HOLDER OF THIS CONTRACT, TATSUYA OTONASHI, AGREES TO GIVE UP HIS BELOVED KAZUSA IN EXCHANGE FOR VIRTUOSO SKILLS AS A VIOLINIST.
HE'S TAKING KAZUSA IN EXCHANGE FOR THE VIOLIN?
WHY WOULD THE DEMON WANT KAZUSA?
I DON'T KNOW.
BUT, THE CORNEA TRANSPLANT HAS RENEWED THE CONTRACT.
AS LONG AS ONE CELL OF TATSUYA OTONASHI'S BODY LIVES...
THE CONTRACT REMAINS OPEN, AND THE DEMON CANNOT COLLECT.
SO, IN OTHER WORDS ...
EX-ACTLY.
IF THE KID DIES...
click
CANCEL
ENTER
PAYMENT COMES DUE.
THE DEMON IS TRYING TO KILL HIJIRI...?!

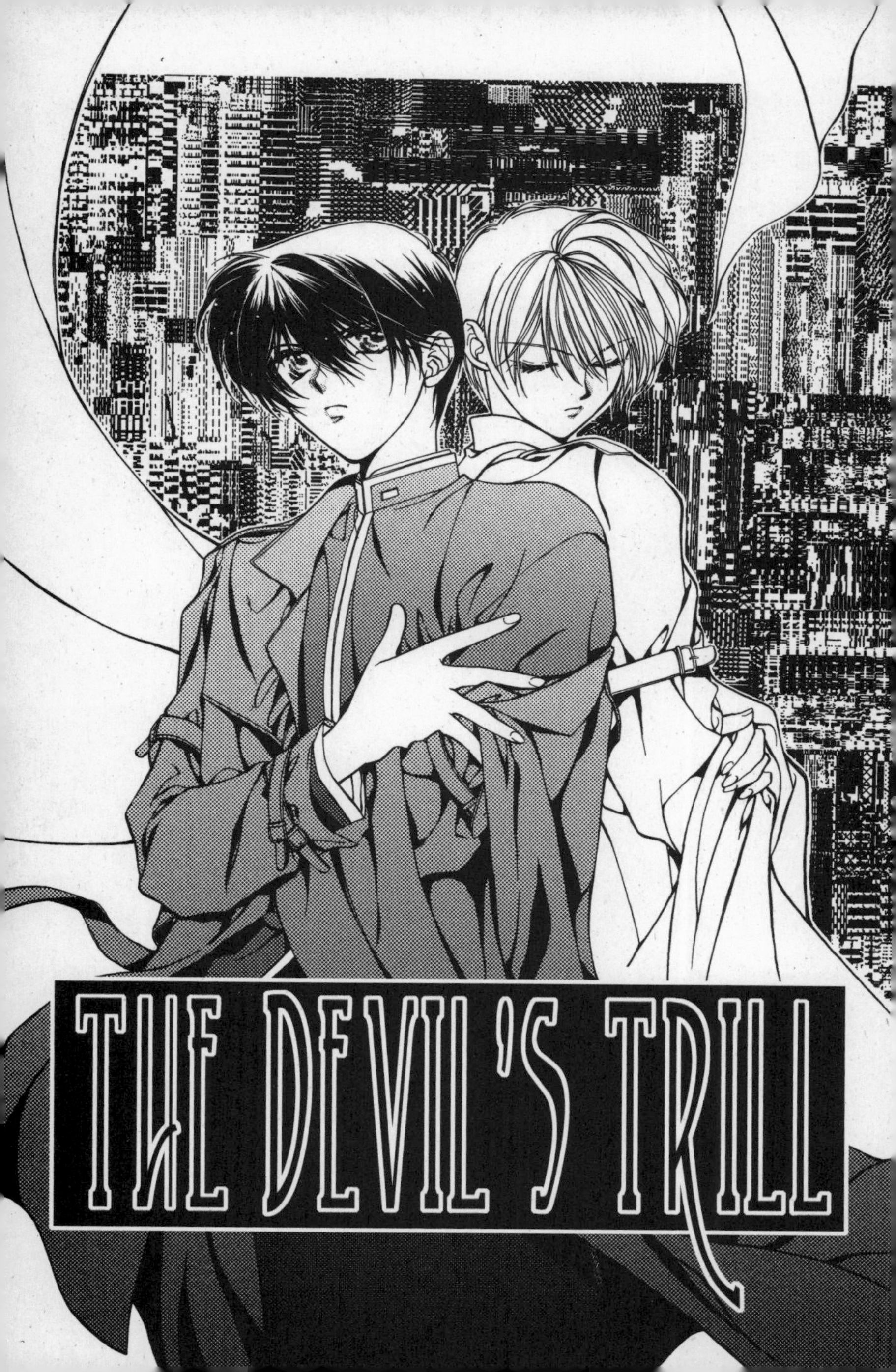
THE DEVIL'S TRILL

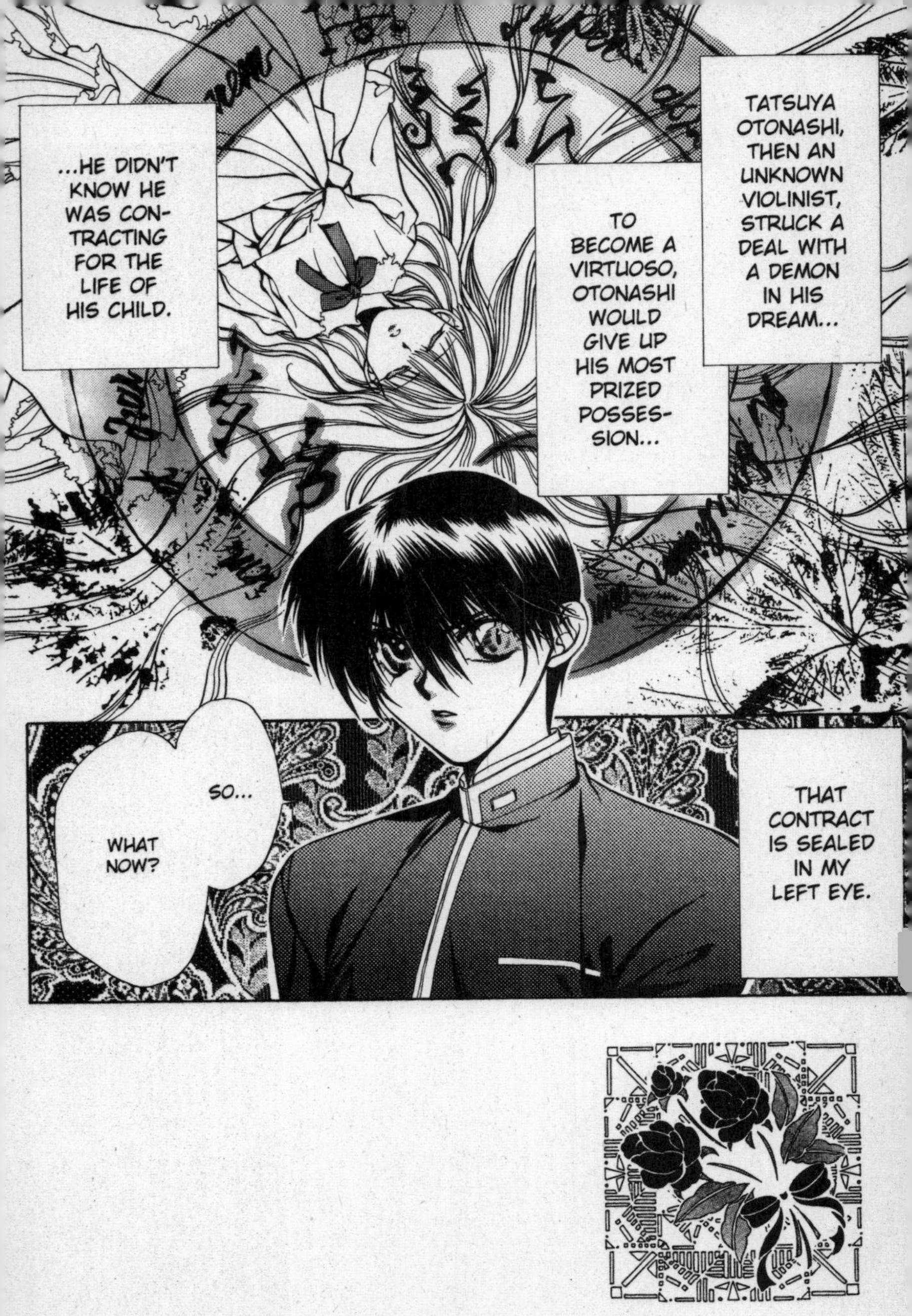
TATSUYA OTONASHI, THEN AN UNKNOWN VIOLINIST, STRUCK A DEAL WITH A DEMON IN HIS DREAM...
TO BECOME A VIRTUOSO, OTONASHI WOULD GIVE UP HIS MOST PRIZED POSSES-SION...
...HE DIDN'T KNOW HE WAS CON-TRACTING FOR THE LIFE OF HIS CHILD.
THAT CONTRACT IS SEALED IN MY LEFT EYE.
SO...
WHAT NOW?

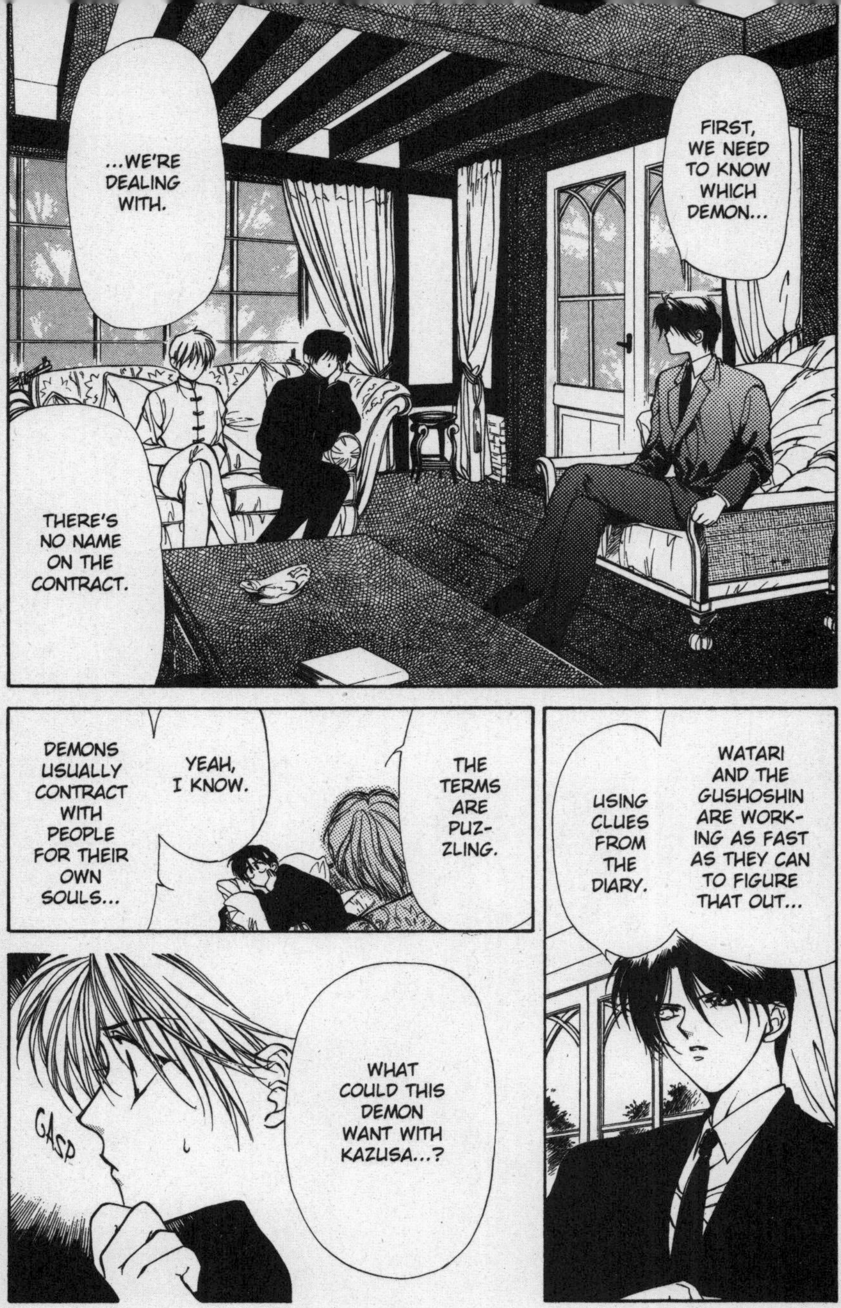
FIRST, WE NEED TO KNOW WHICH DEMON...
...WE'RE DEALING WITH.
THERE'S NO NAME ON THE CONTRACT.
WATARI AND THE GUSHOSHIN ARE WORKING AS FAST AS THEY CAN TO FIGURE THAT OUT...
USING CLUES FROM THE DIARY.
THE TERMS ARE PUZZLING.
YEAH, I KNOW.
DEMONS USUALLY CONTRACT WITH PEOPLE FOR THEIR OWN SOULS...
WHAT COULD THIS DEMON WANT WITH KAZUSA...?
GASP

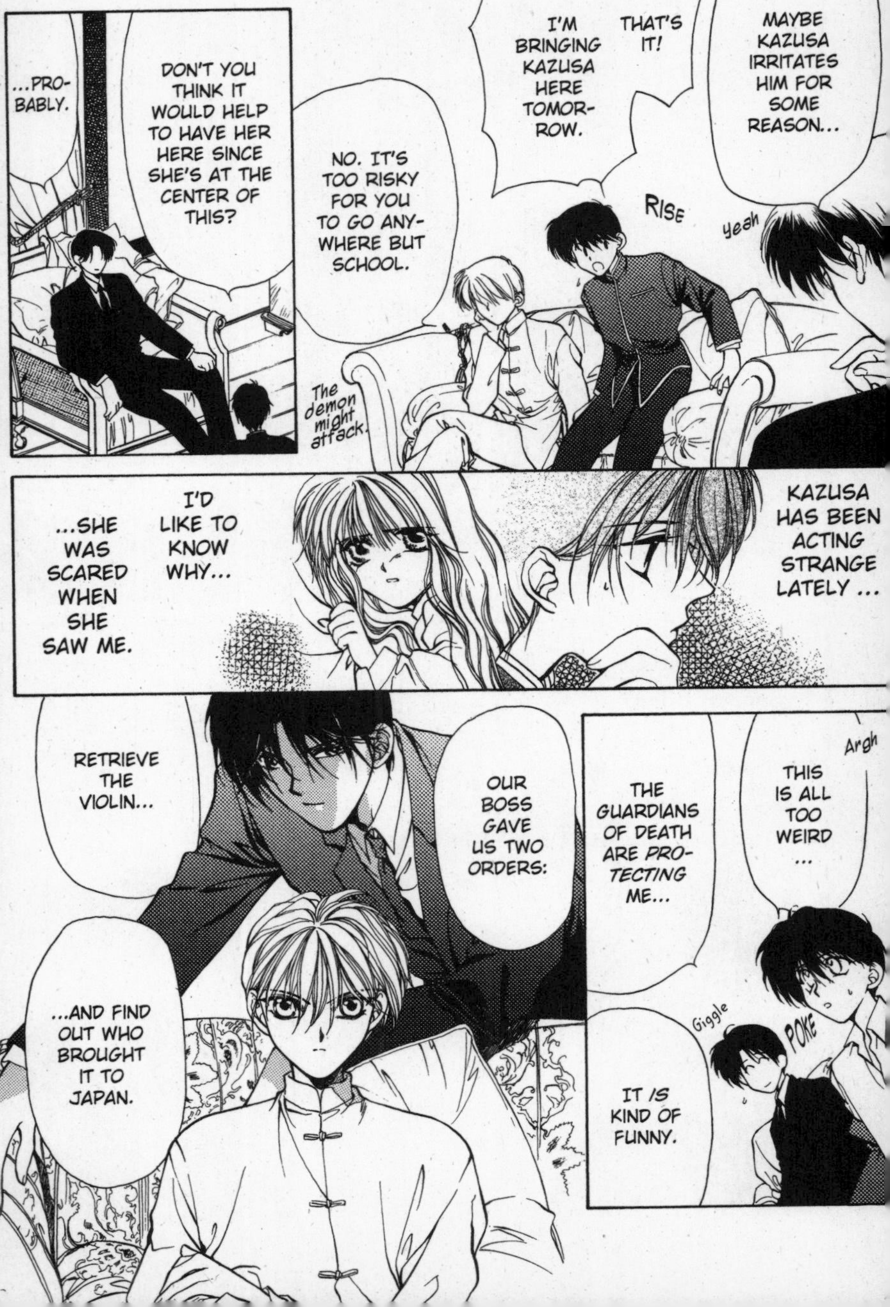
MAYBE KAZUSA IRRITATES HIM FOR SOME REASON...
yeah
THAT'S IT!
I'M BRINGING KAZUSA HERE TOMORROW.
RISE
NO. IT'S TOO RISKY FOR YOU TO GO ANYWHERE BUT SCHOOL.
The demon might attack.
DON'T YOU THINK IT WOULD HELP TO HAVE HER HERE SINCE SHE'S AT THE CENTER OF THIS?
...PROBABLY.
KAZUSA HAS BEEN ACTING STRANGE LATELY ...
I'D LIKE TO KNOW WHY...
...SHE WAS SCARED WHEN SHE SAW ME.
Argh
THIS IS ALL TOO WEIRD ...
THE GUARDIANS OF DEATH ARE *PROTECTING* ME...
POKE
Giggle
IT *IS* KIND OF FUNNY.
OUR BOSS GAVE US TWO ORDERS:
RETRIEVE THE VIOLIN...
...AND FIND OUT WHO BROUGHT IT TO JAPAN.

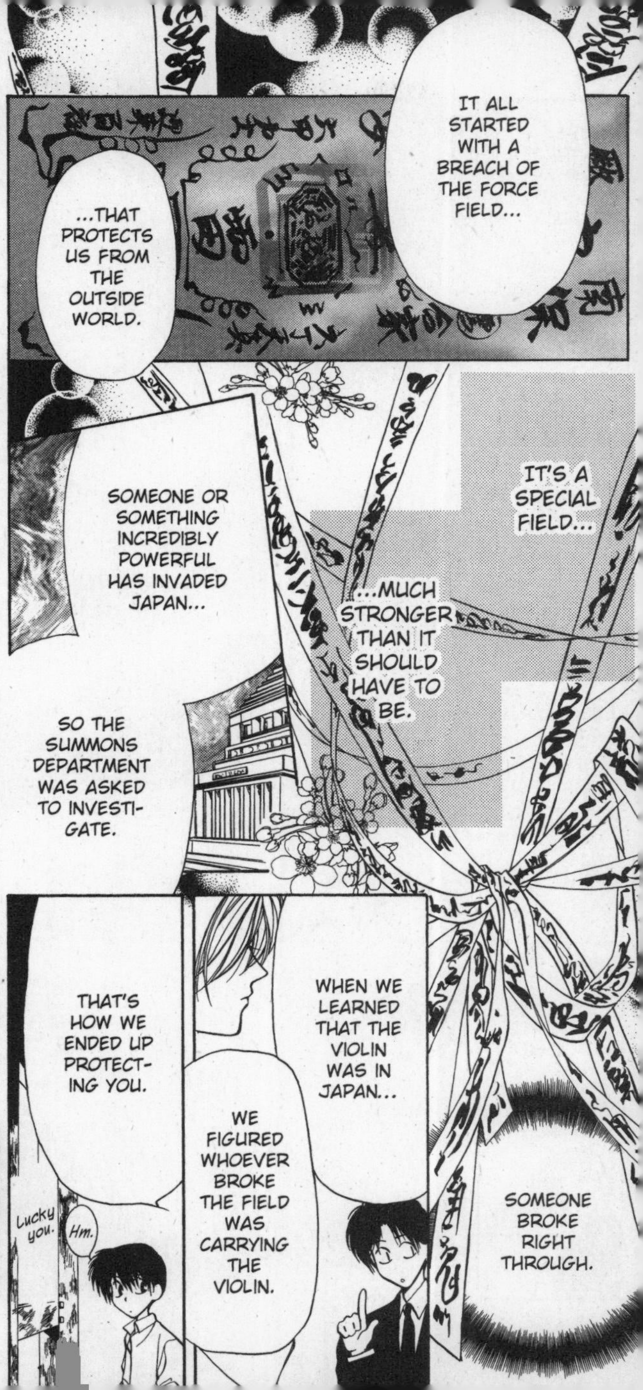
IT ALL STARTED WITH A BREACH OF THE FORCE FIELD...
...THAT PROTECTS US FROM THE OUTSIDE WORLD.
IT'S A SPECIAL FIELD...
...MUCH STRONGER THAN IT SHOULD HAVE TO BE.
SOMEONE OR SOMETHING INCREDIBLY POWERFUL HAS INVADED JAPAN...
SO THE SUMMONS DEPARTMENT WAS ASKED TO INVESTI-GATE.
SOMEONE BROKE RIGHT THROUGH.
WHEN WE LEARNED THAT THE VIOLIN WAS IN JAPAN...
WE FIGURED WHOEVER BROKE THE FIELD WAS CARRYING THE VIOLIN.
THAT'S HOW WE ENDED UP PROTECT-ING YOU.
Hm.
Lucky you.

In this story, we meet Hijiri, who looks very much like Hisoka. He's actually based on my original Hisoka prototype. He was, like, a test print. Yeah, it's confusing, but I thought it would be a waste just to toss him, so I made him a guest! If I get a chance, I'd like to have him stir up trouble again.

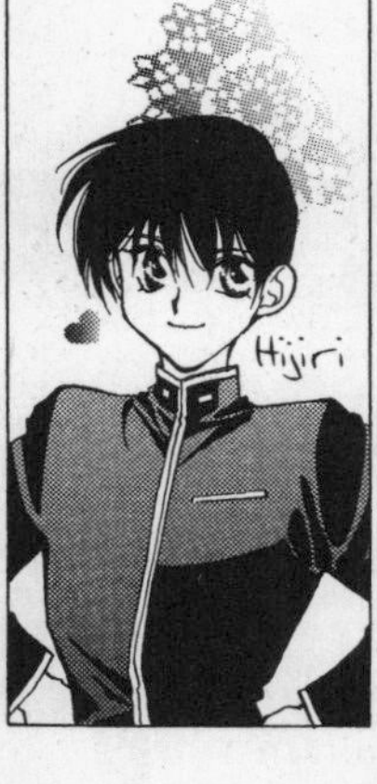
Hijiri

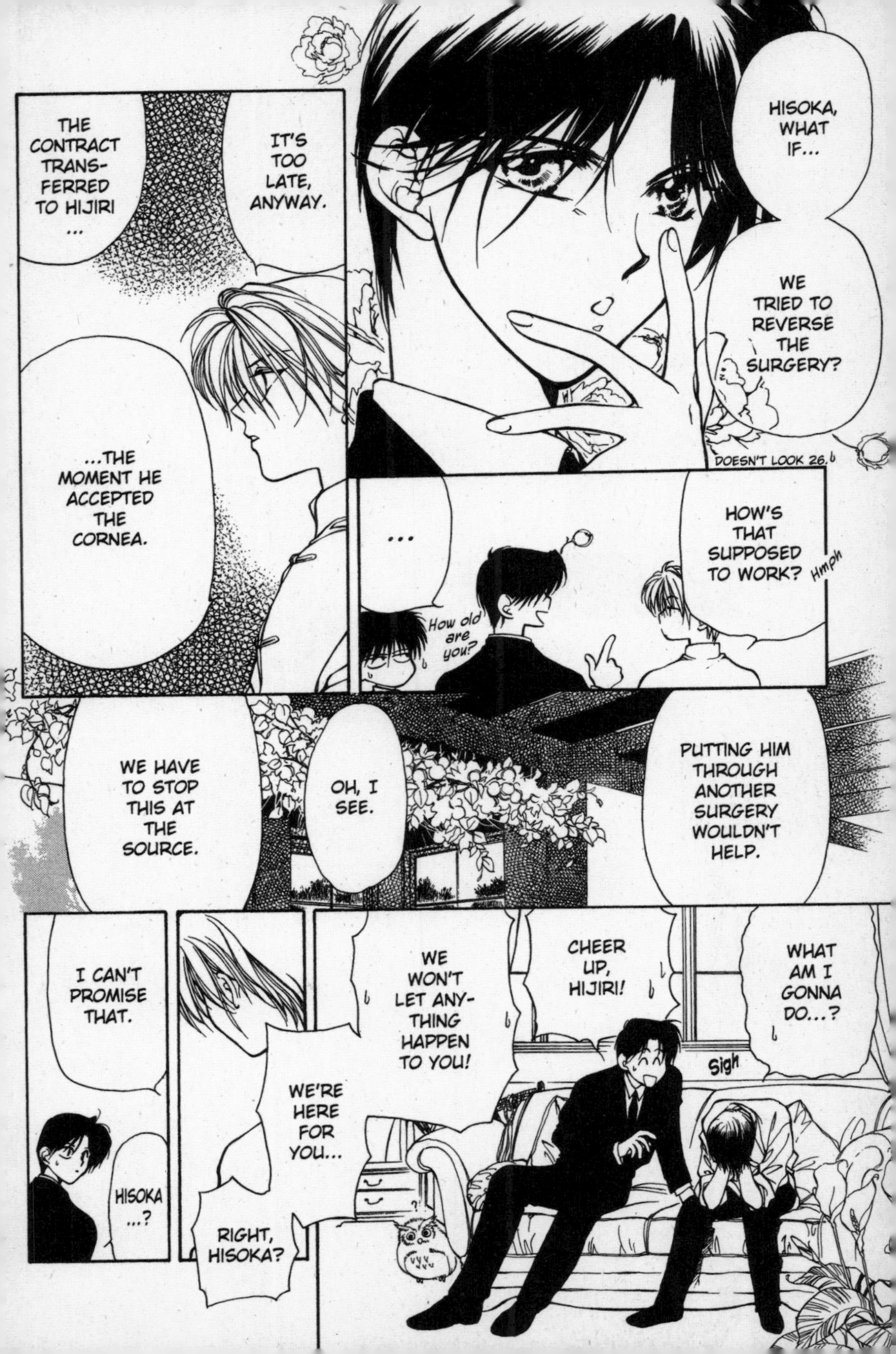
HISOKA, WHAT IF...
WE TRIED TO REVERSE THE SURGERY?
DOESN'T LOOK 26.
HOW'S THAT SUPPOSED TO WORK?
Hmph
How old are you?
...
IT'S TOO LATE, ANYWAY.
THE CONTRACT TRANS-FERRED TO HIJIRI ...
...THE MOMENT HE ACCEPTED THE CORNEA.
PUTTING HIM THROUGH ANOTHER SURGERY WOULDN'T HELP.
OH, I SEE.
WE HAVE TO STOP THIS AT THE SOURCE.
WHAT AM I GONNA DO...?
Sigh
CHEER UP, HIJIRI!
WE WON'T LET ANY-THING HAPPEN TO YOU!
WE'RE HERE FOR YOU...
RIGHT, HISOKA?
I CAN'T PROMISE THAT.
HISOKA ...?

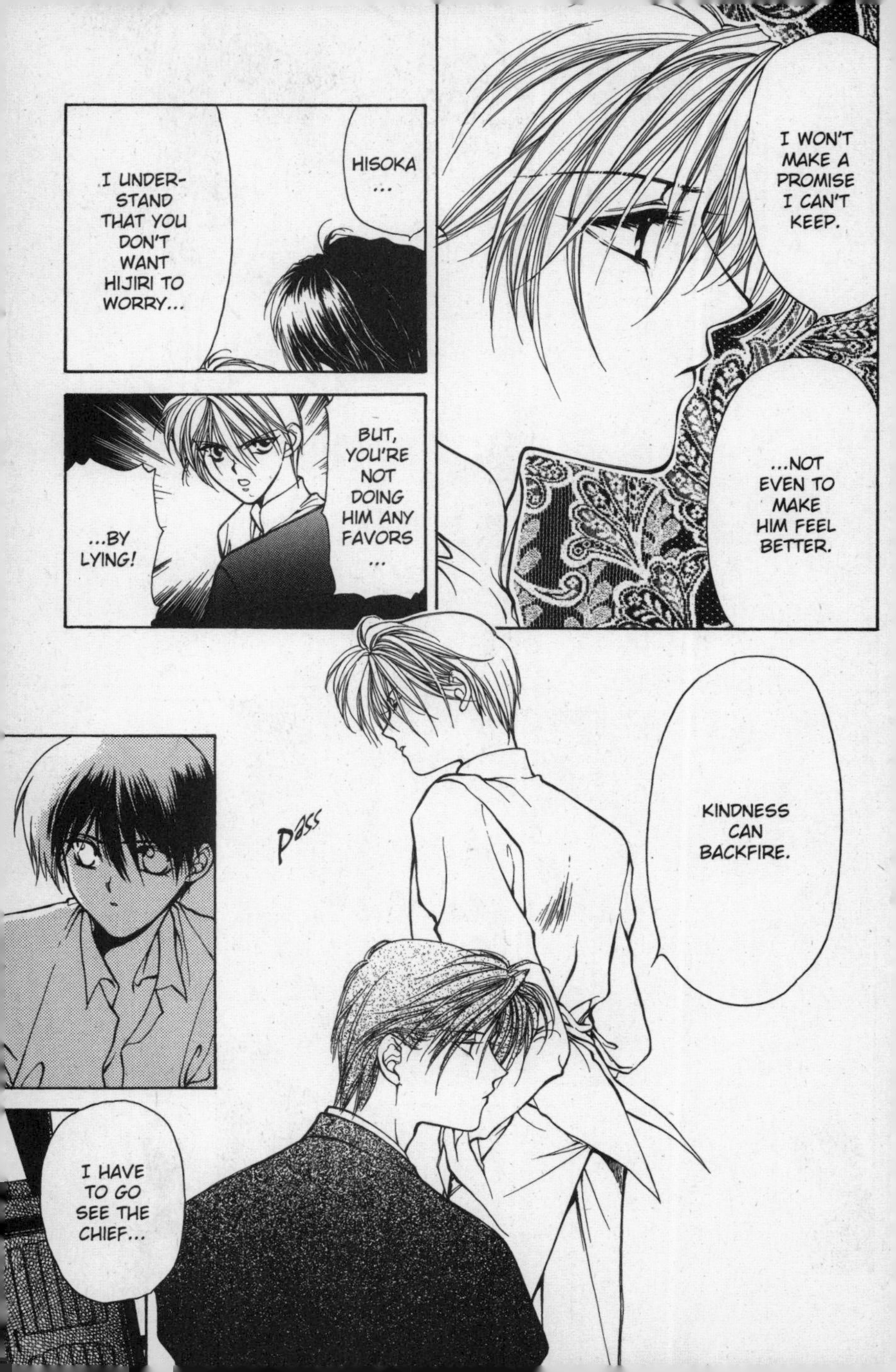
I WON'T MAKE A PROMISE I CAN'T KEEP.
...NOT EVEN TO MAKE HIM FEEL BETTER.
HISOKA ...
I UNDER-STAND THAT YOU DON'T WANT HIJIRI TO WORRY...
BUT, YOU'RE NOT DOING HIM ANY FAVORS ...
...BY LYING!
KINDNESS CAN BACKFIRE.
PASS
I HAVE TO GO SEE THE CHIEF...

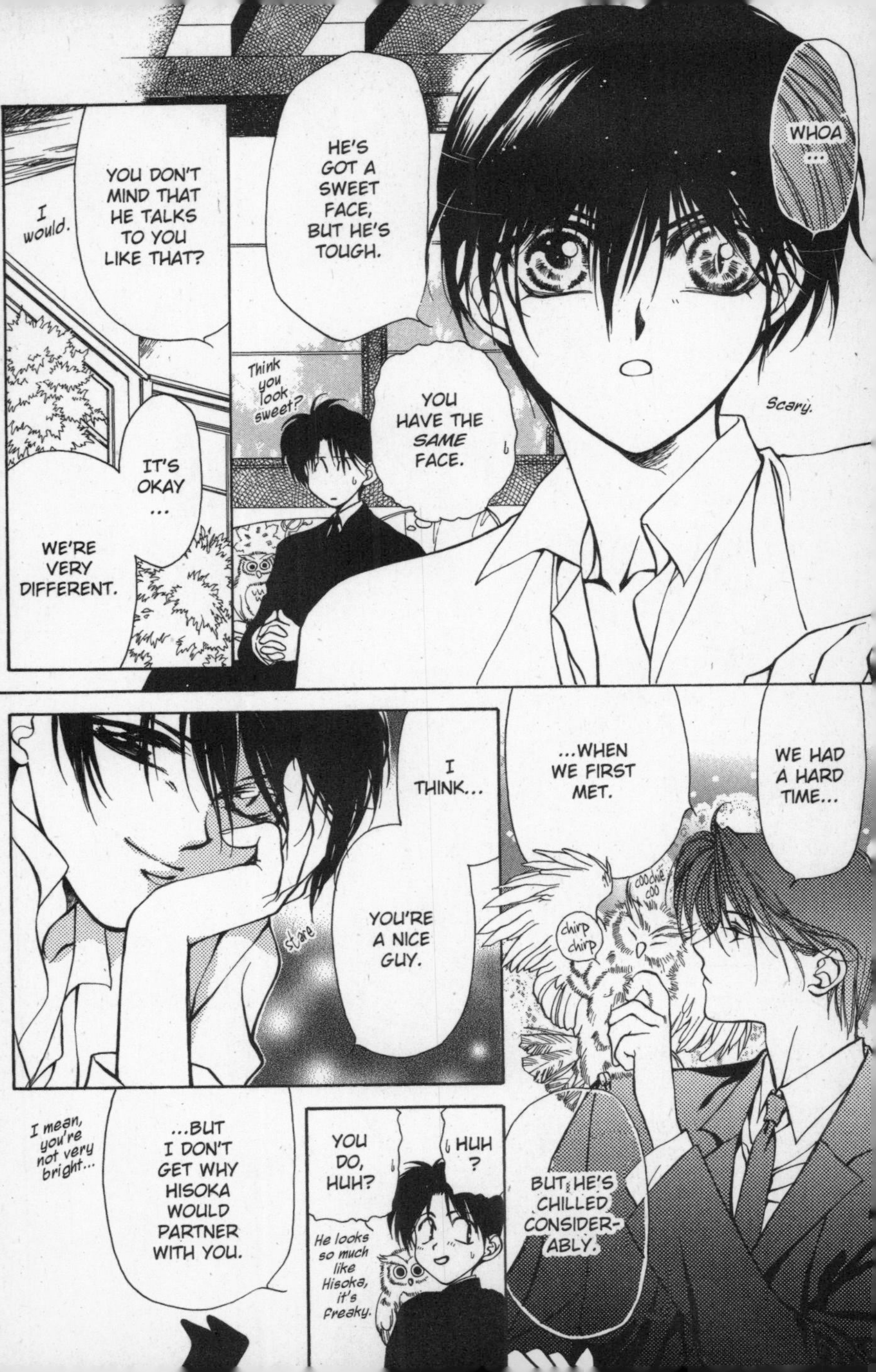
WHOA ...
HE'S GOT A SWEET FACE, BUT HE'S TOUGH.
Scary.
YOU HAVE THE *SAME* FACE.
Think you look sweet?
YOU DON'T MIND THAT HE TALKS TO YOU LIKE THAT?
I would.
IT'S OKAY ...
WE'RE VERY DIFFERENT.
WE HAD A HARD TIME...
...WHEN WE FIRST MET.
coochie coo
chirp chirp
I THINK...
YOU'RE A NICE GUY.
stare
BUT HE'S CHILLED CONSIDERABLY.
HUH?
YOU DO, HUH?
He looks so much like Hisoka, it's freaky.
...BUT I DON'T GET WHY HISOKA WOULD PARTNER WITH YOU.
I mean, you're not very bright...

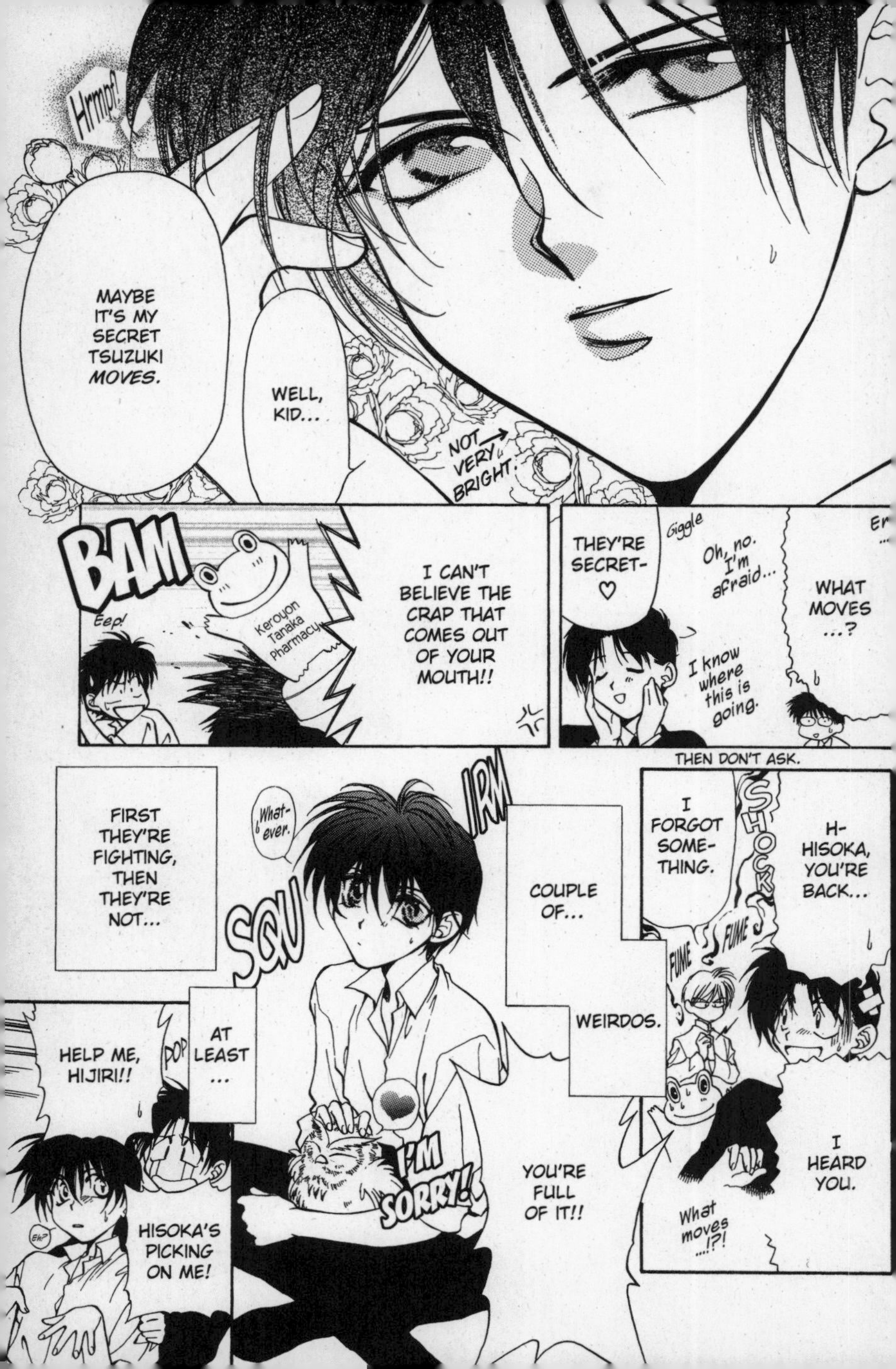
Hrmpf!
WELL, KID...
MAYBE IT'S MY SECRET TSUZUKI MOVES.
NOT VERY BRIGHT.
Er...
WHAT MOVES ...?
Giggle
THEY'RE SECRET- ♡
Oh, no. I'm afraid...
I know where this is going.
I CAN'T BELIEVE THE CRAP THAT COMES OUT OF YOUR MOUTH!!
BAM
Eep!
Keroyon Tanaka Pharmacy
THEN DON'T ASK.
H-HISOKA, YOU'RE BACK...
SHOCK
I FORGOT SOMETHING.
FUME
FUME
I HEARD YOU.
What moves ...!?!
COUPLE OF...
WEIRDOS.
IRM
What-ever.
SQU
YOU'RE FULL OF IT!!
I'M SORRY!!
FIRST THEY'RE FIGHTING, THEN THEY'RE NOT...
AT LEAST ...
POP
HELP ME, HIJIRI!!
HISOKA'S PICKING ON ME!
Eh?

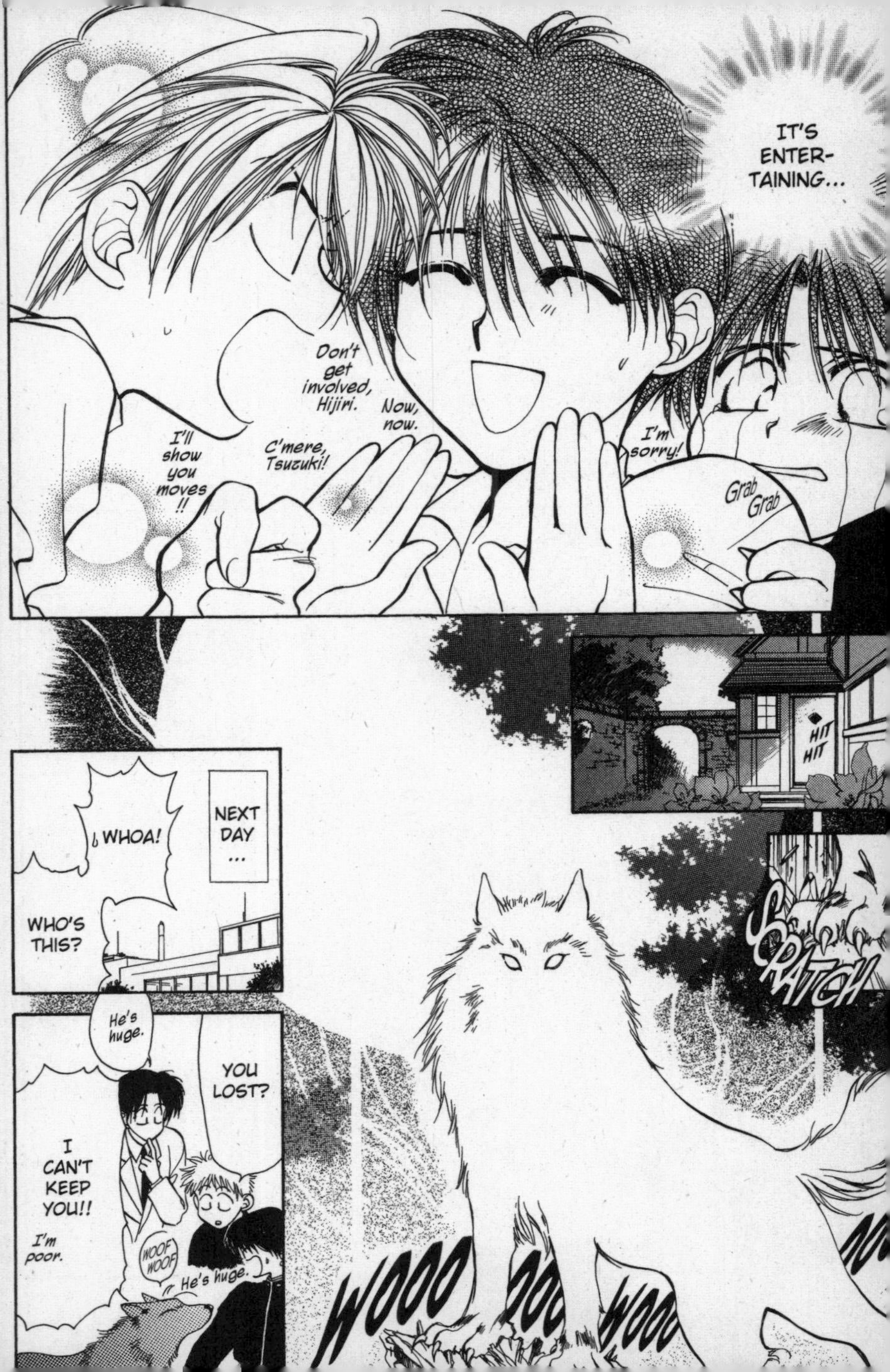
IT'S ENTER-TAINING...
I'm sorry!
Grab Grab
Now, now.
Don't get involved, Hijiri.
C'mere, Tsuzuki!
I'll show you moves !!
HIT HIT
SCRATCH
WOOO WOOO WOOO
NEXT DAY ...
¿WHOA!
WHO'S THIS?
He's huge.
YOU LOST?
I CAN'T KEEP YOU!!
I'm poor.
WOOF WOOF
He's huge.

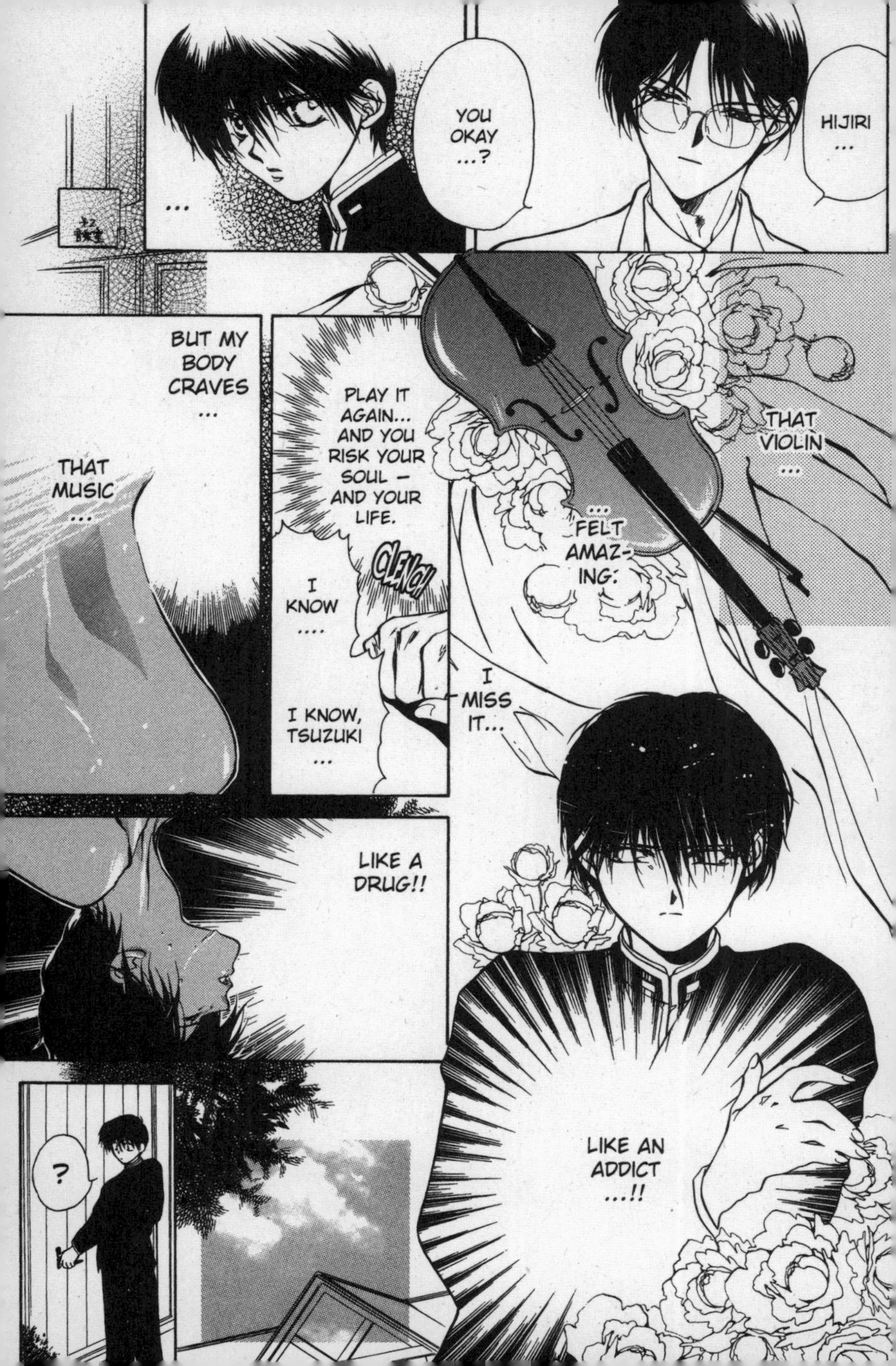
HIJIRI ...
YOU OKAY ...?
...
THAT VIOLIN ...
... FELT AMAZ-ING.
I MISS IT...
PLAY IT AGAIN... AND YOU RISK YOUR SOUL – AND YOUR LIFE.
CLENCH
I KNOW ....
I KNOW, TSUZUKI ...
BUT MY BODY CRAVES ...
THAT MUSIC ...
LIKE AN ADDICT ....!!
LIKE A DRUG!!
?

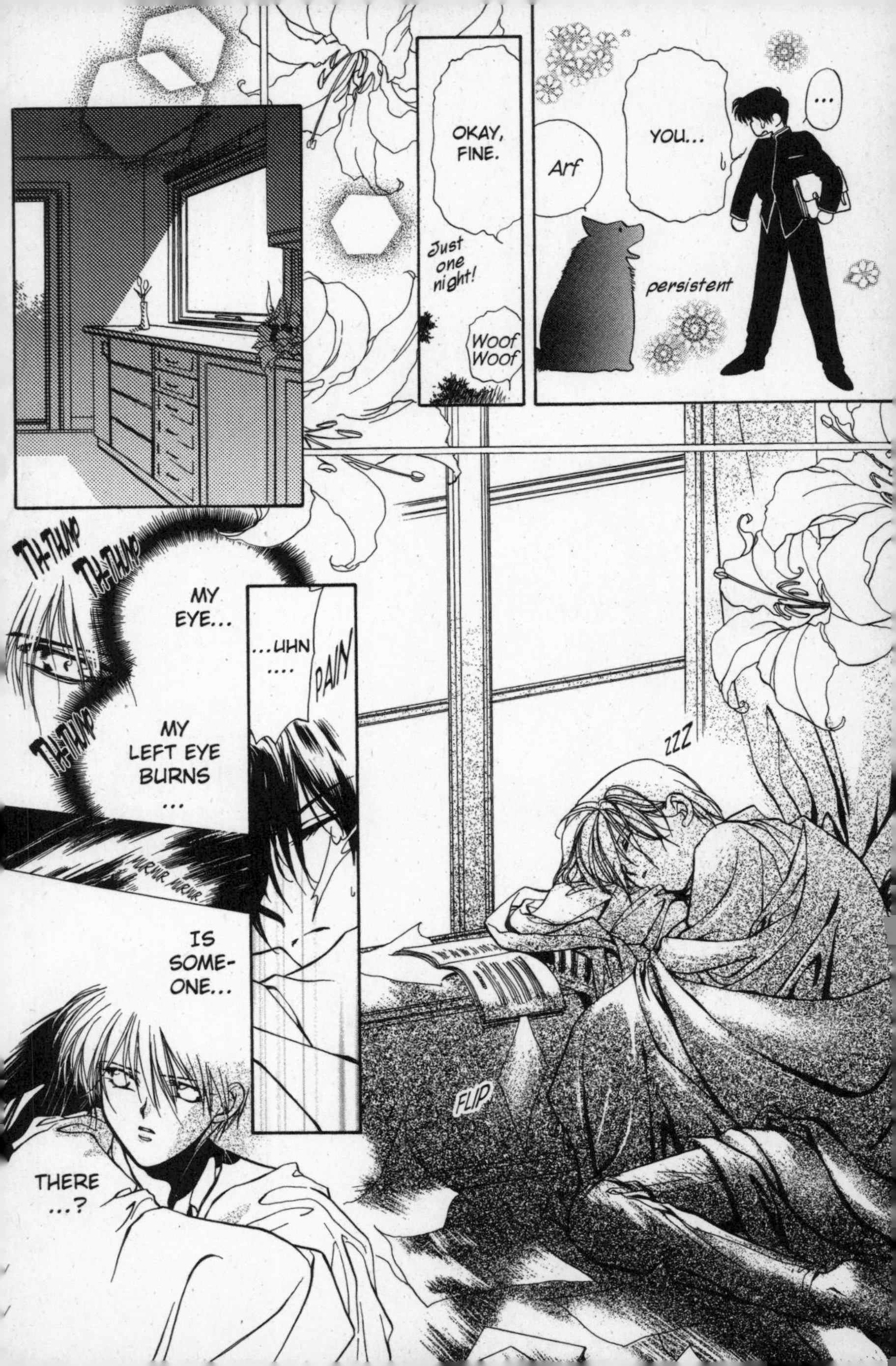
...
YOU...
persistent
Arf
OKAY, FINE.
Just one night!
Woof Woof
ZZZ
FLIP
...UHN ....
PAIN
TH-THUMP TH-THUMP
MY EYE...
TH-THUMP
MY LEFT EYE BURNS ...
MURMUR MURMUR
IS SOME-ONE...
THERE ...?

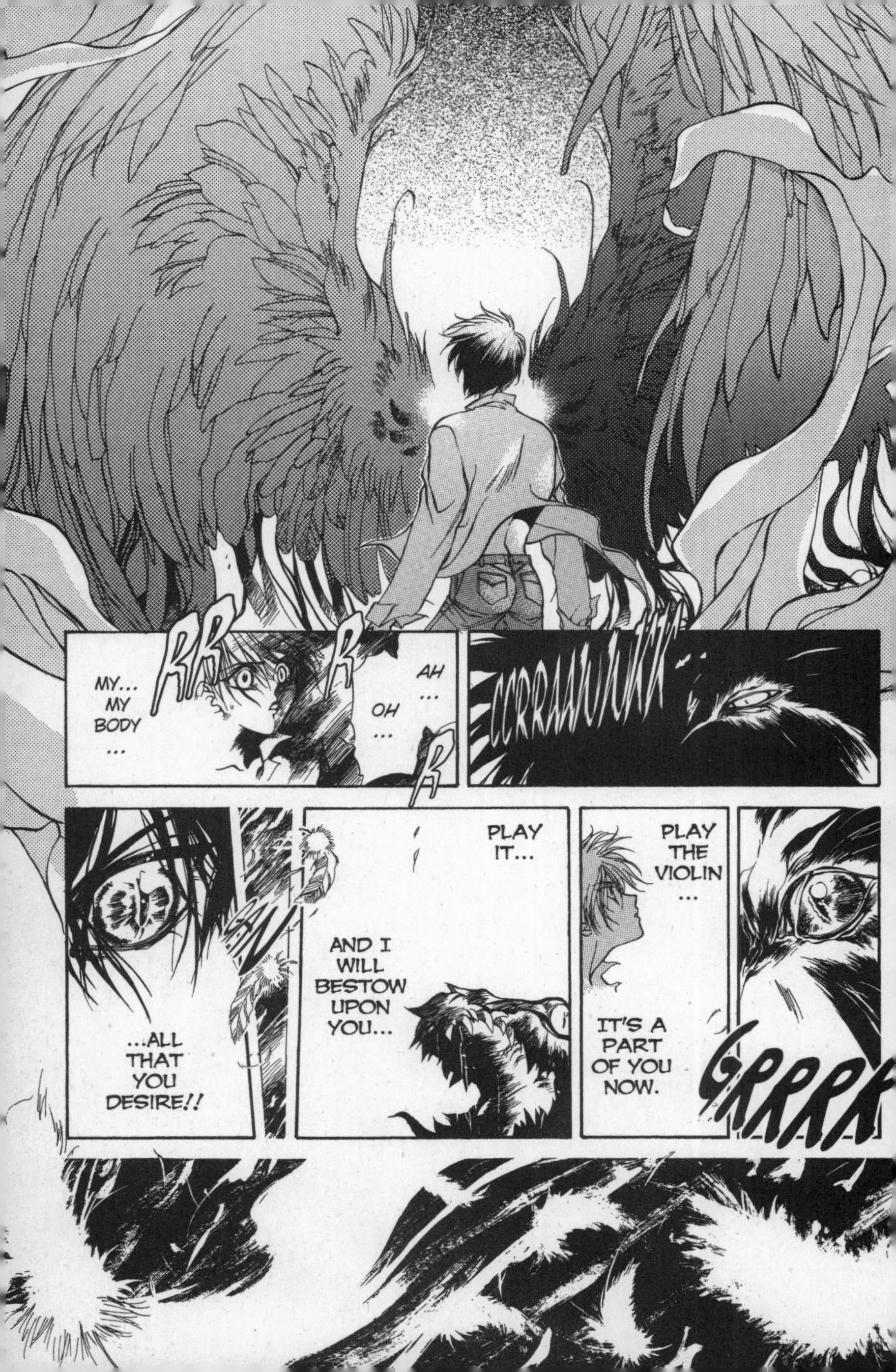
AH ... OH ...
MY... MY BODY ...
GRRRK
PLAY THE VIOLIN ...
IT'S A PART OF YOU NOW.
PLAY IT...
AND I WILL BESTOW UPON YOU...
...ALL THAT YOU DESIRE!!

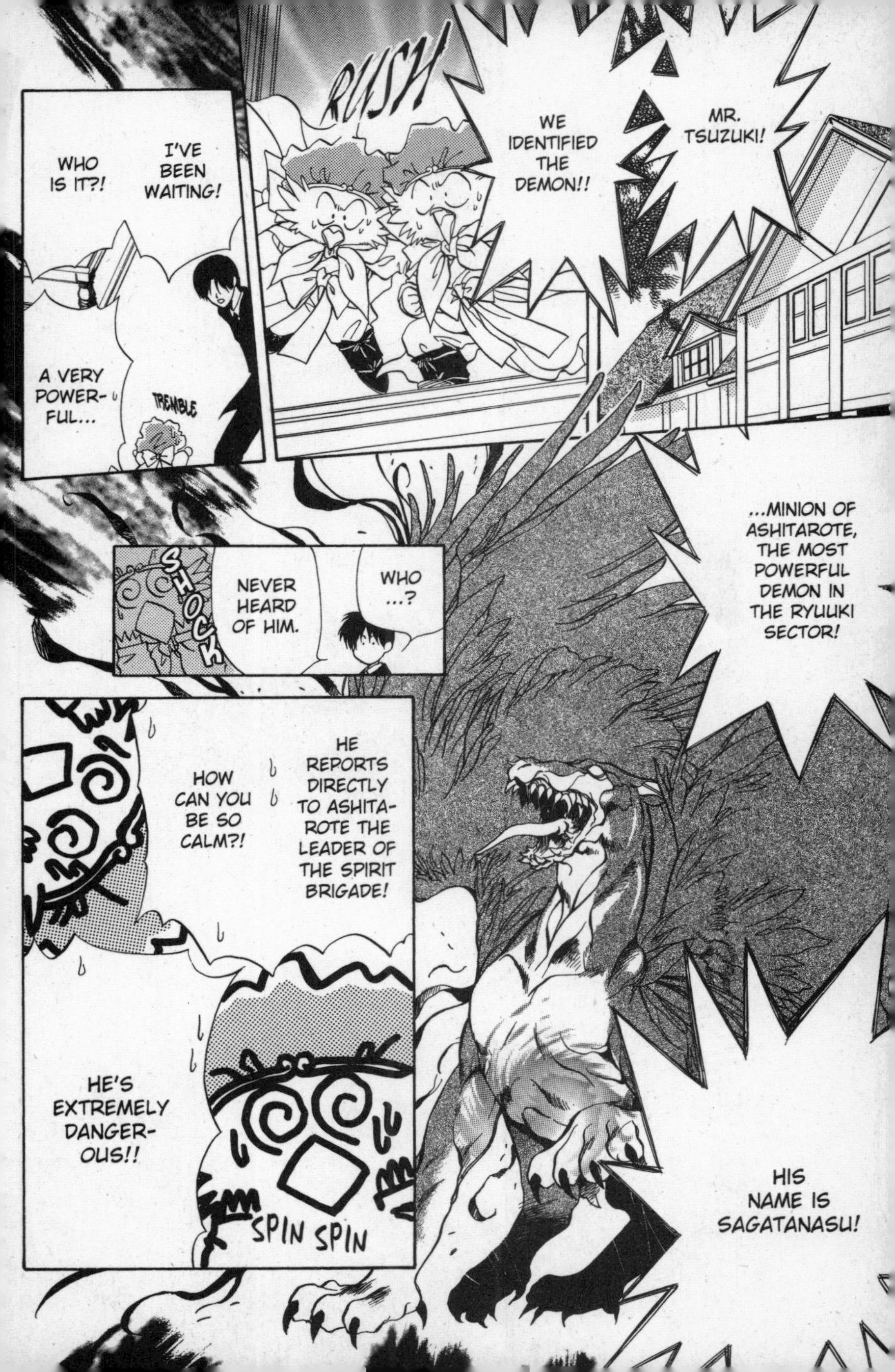
MR. TSUZUKI!
WE IDENTIFIED THE DEMON!!
RUSH
I'VE BEEN WAITING!
WHO IS IT?!
A VERY POWER-FUL...
TREMBLE
...MINION OF ASHITAROTE, THE MOST POWERFUL DEMON IN THE RYUUKI SECTOR!
HIS NAME IS SAGATANASU!
WHO ...?
NEVER HEARD OF HIM.
SHOCK
HE REPORTS DIRECTLY TO ASHITA-ROTE THE LEADER OF THE SPIRIT BRIGADE!
HOW CAN YOU BE SO CALM?!
HE'S EXTREMELY DANGER-OUS!!
SPIN SPIN

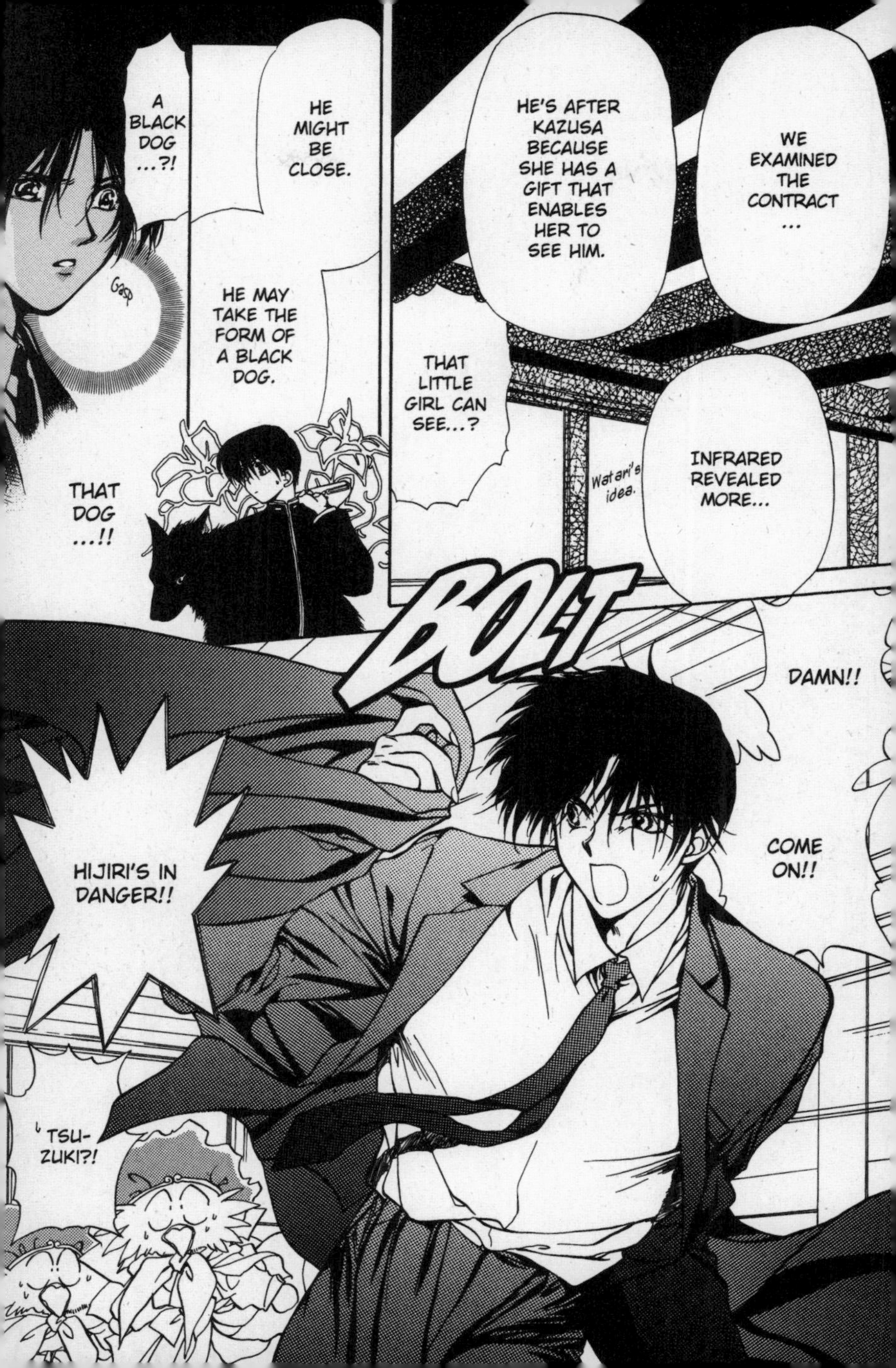
WE EXAMINED THE CONTRACT...
HE'S AFTER KAZUSA BECAUSE SHE HAS A GIFT THAT ENABLES HER TO SEE HIM.
INFRARED REVEALED MORE...
Watari's idea.
THAT LITTLE GIRL CAN SEE...?
HE MIGHT BE CLOSE.
A BLACK DOG...?!
Gasp
HE MAY TAKE THE FORM OF A BLACK DOG.
THAT DOG...!!
BOLT
DAMN!!
COME ON!!
HIJIRI'S IN DANGER!!
TSU-ZUKI?!

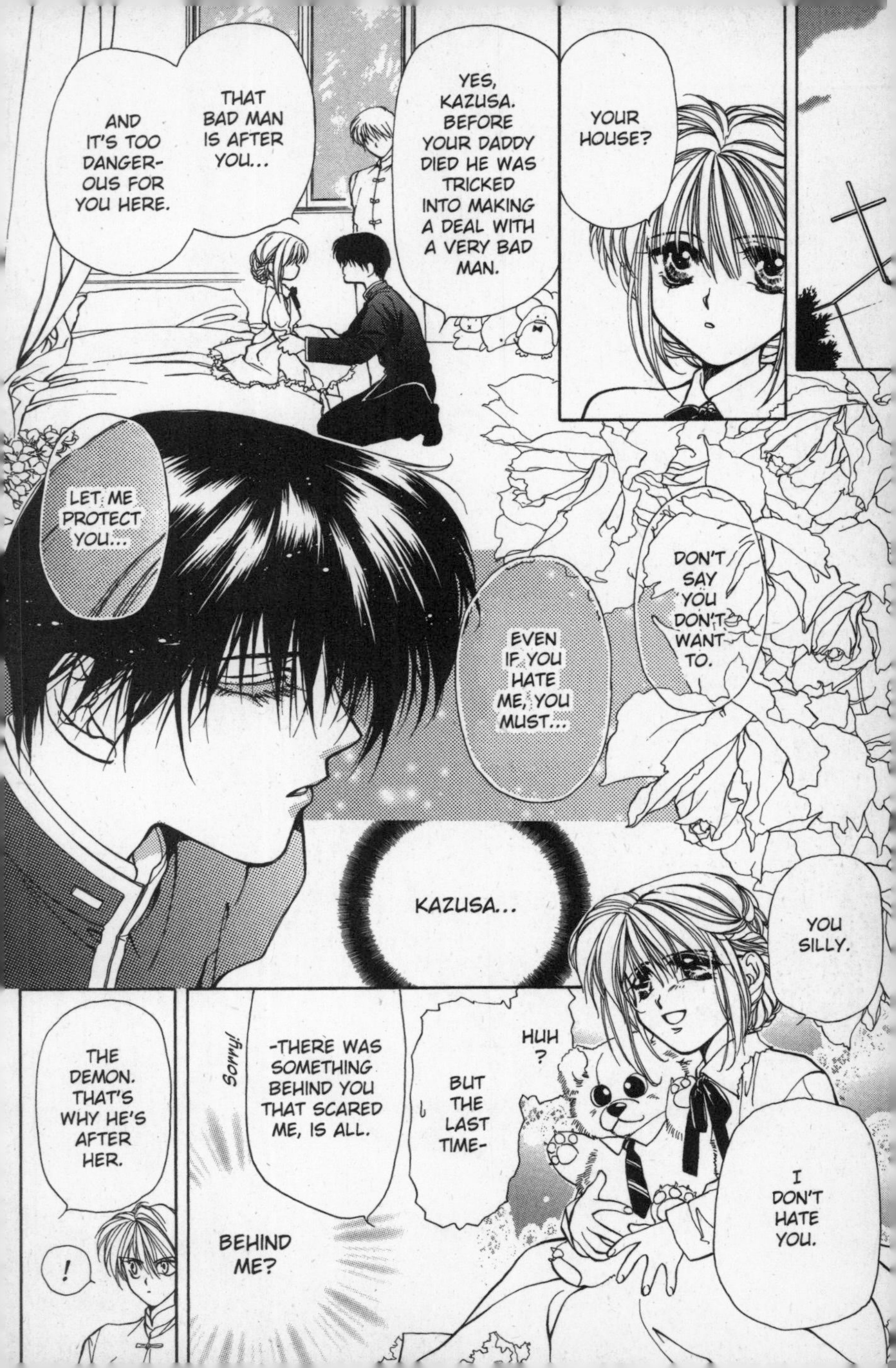

YOUR HOUSE?
YES, KAZUSA. BEFORE YOUR DADDY DIED HE WAS TRICKED INTO MAKING A DEAL WITH A VERY BAD MAN.
THAT BAD MAN IS AFTER YOU...
AND IT'S TOO DANGER-OUS FOR YOU HERE.
LET ME PROTECT YOU...
EVEN IF YOU HATE ME, YOU MUST...
DON'T SAY YOU DON'T WANT TO.
KAZUSA...
YOU SILLY.
I DON'T HATE YOU.
HUH?
BUT THE LAST TIME-
Sorry!
-THERE WAS SOMETHING BEHIND YOU THAT SCARED ME, IS ALL.
BEHIND ME?
THE DEMON. THAT'S WHY HE'S AFTER HER.
!

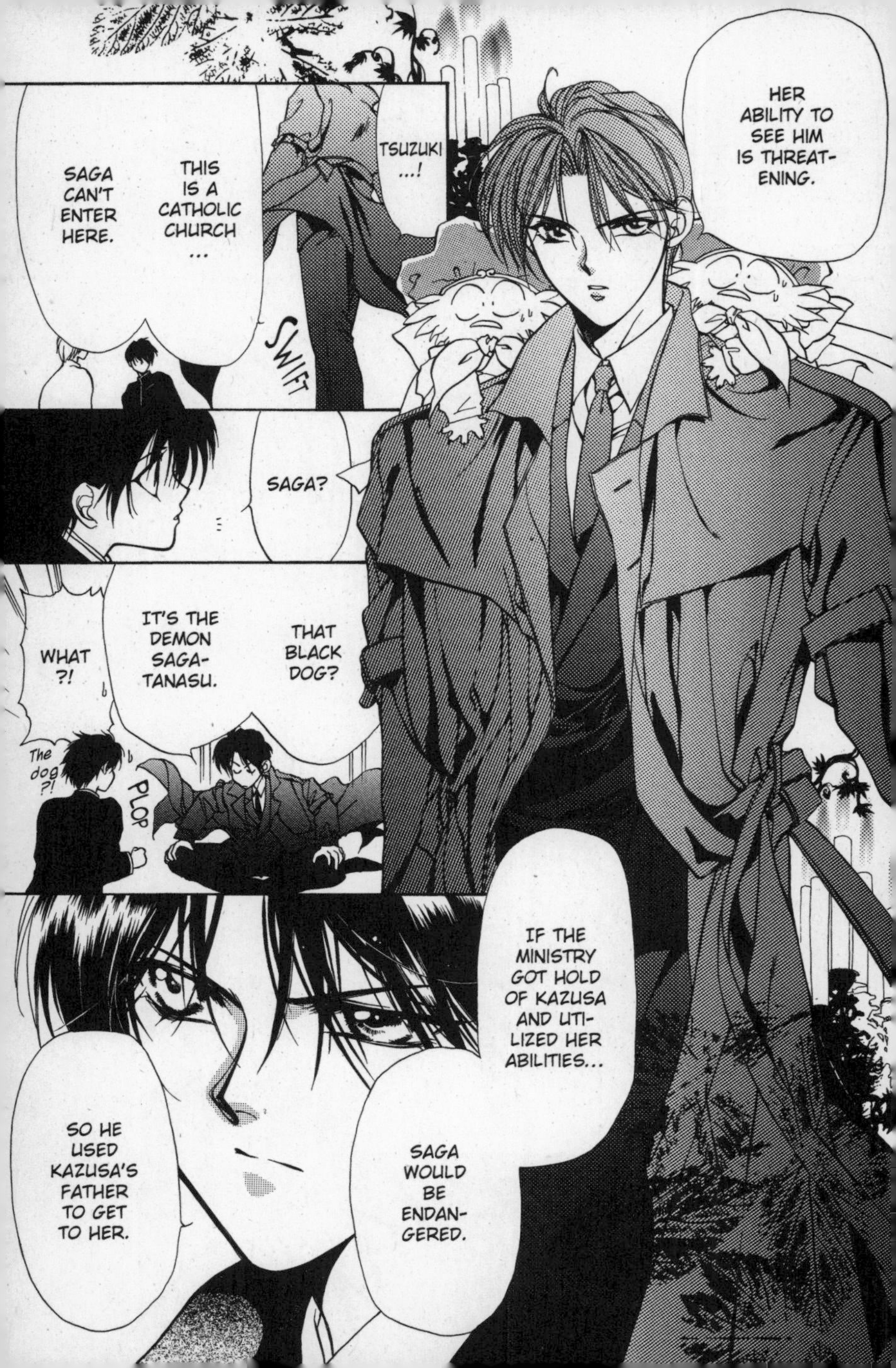
TSUZUKI ...!
THIS IS A CATHOLIC CHURCH ...
SAGA CAN'T ENTER HERE.
SWIFT
SAGA?
THAT BLACK DOG?
IT'S THE DEMON SAGATANASU.
WHAT ?!
The dog ?!
PLOP
HER ABILITY TO SEE HIM IS THREAT-ENING.
IF THE MINISTRY GOT HOLD OF KAZUSA AND UTI-LIZED HER ABILITIES...
SAGA WOULD BE ENDAN-GERED.
SO HE USED KAZUSA'S FATHER TO GET TO HER.

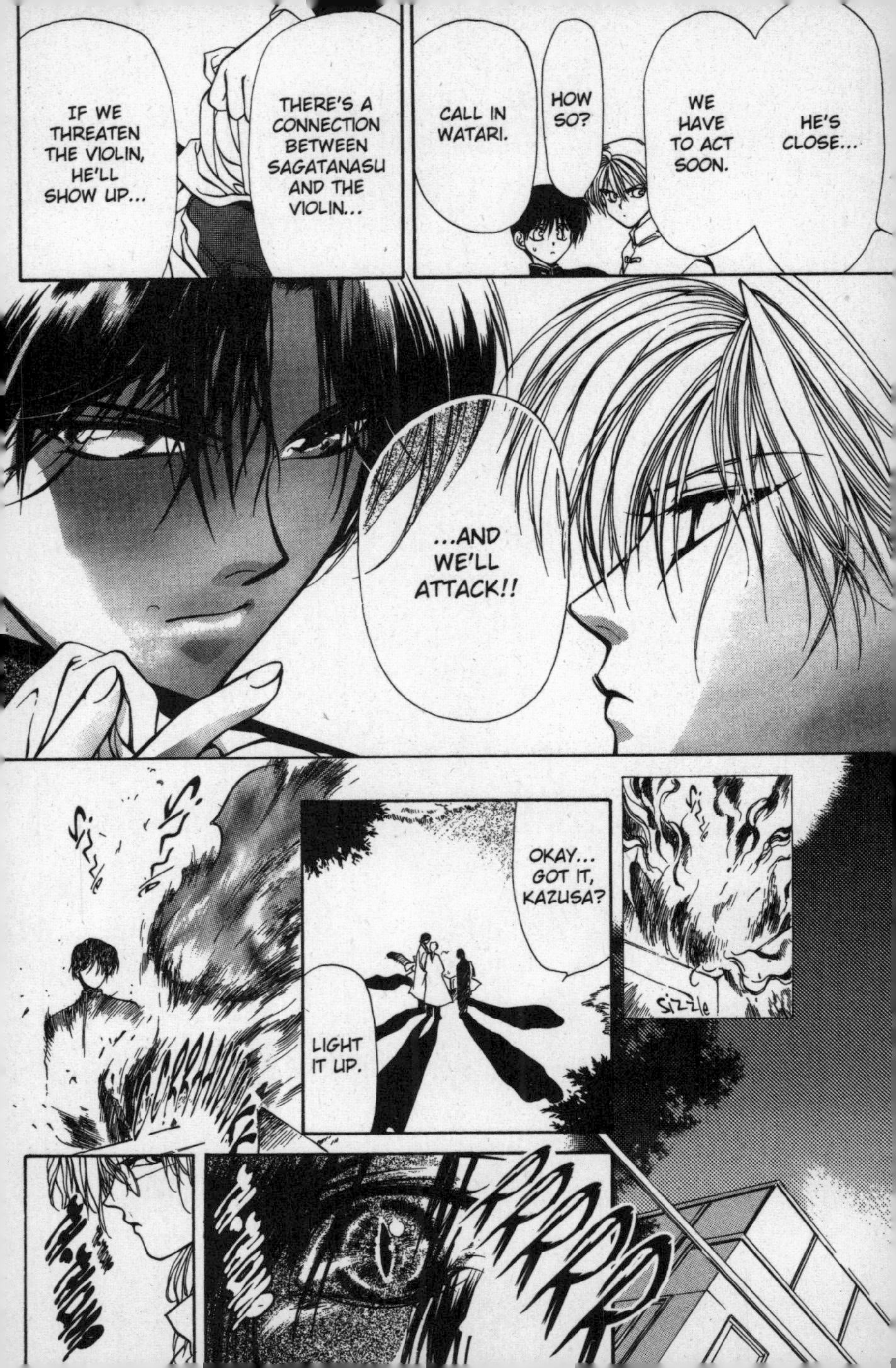
HE'S CLOSE...
WE HAVE TO ACT SOON.
HOW SO?
CALL IN WATARI.
THERE'S A CONNECTION BETWEEN SAGATANASU AND THE VIOLIN...
IF WE THREATEN THE VIOLIN, HE'LL SHOW UP...
...AND WE'LL ATTACK!!
Sizzle
Sizzle
OKAY... GOT IT, KAZUSA?
LIGHT IT UP.
Sizzle

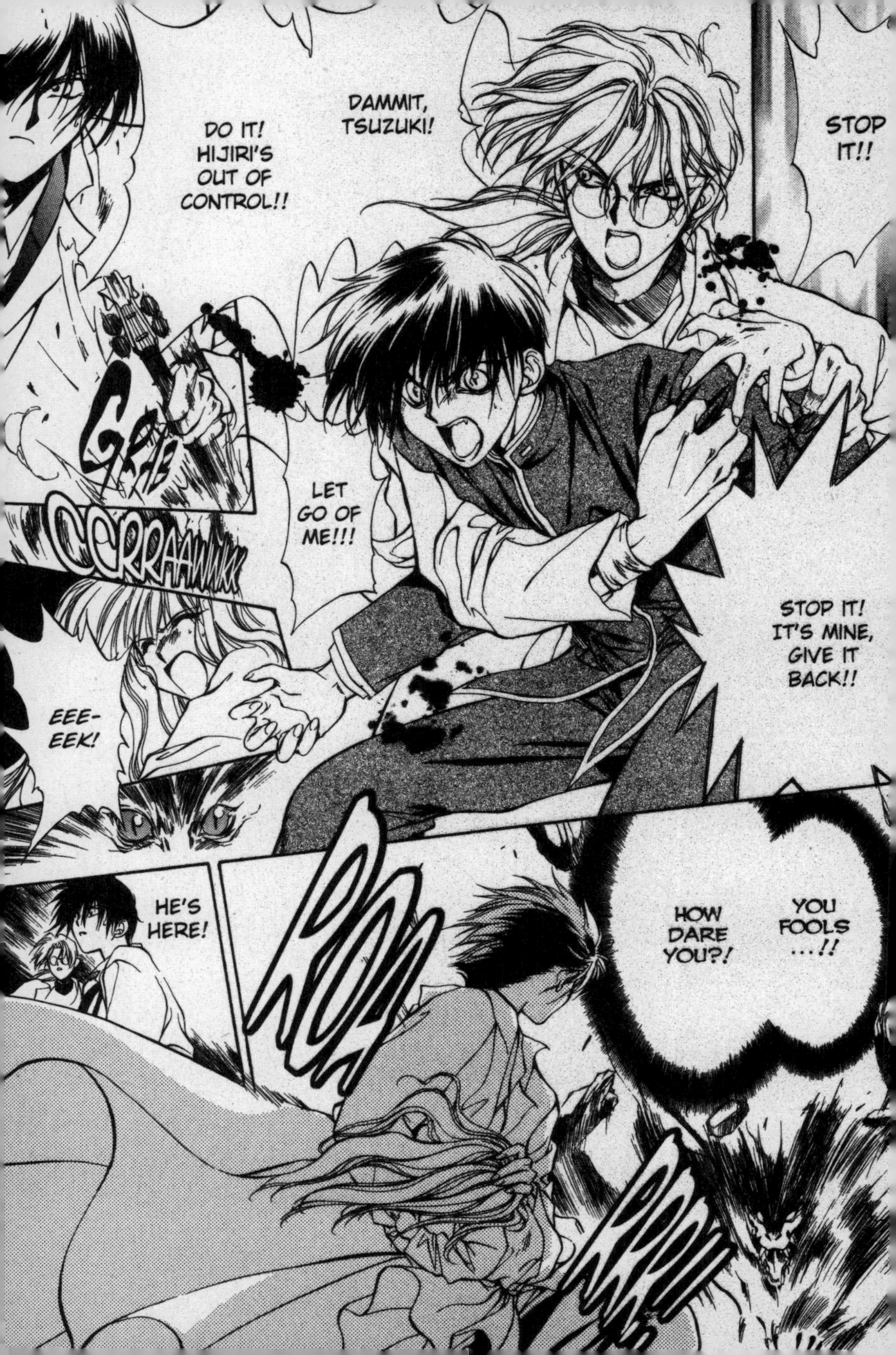
STOP IT!!
DAMMIT, TSUZUKI!
DO IT! HIJIRI'S OUT OF CONTROL!!
LET GO OF ME!!!
GRAB
STOP IT! IT'S MINE, GIVE IT BACK!!
CCRRAAWKK
EEE-EEK!
YOU FOOLS ...!!
HOW DARE YOU?!
HE'S HERE!

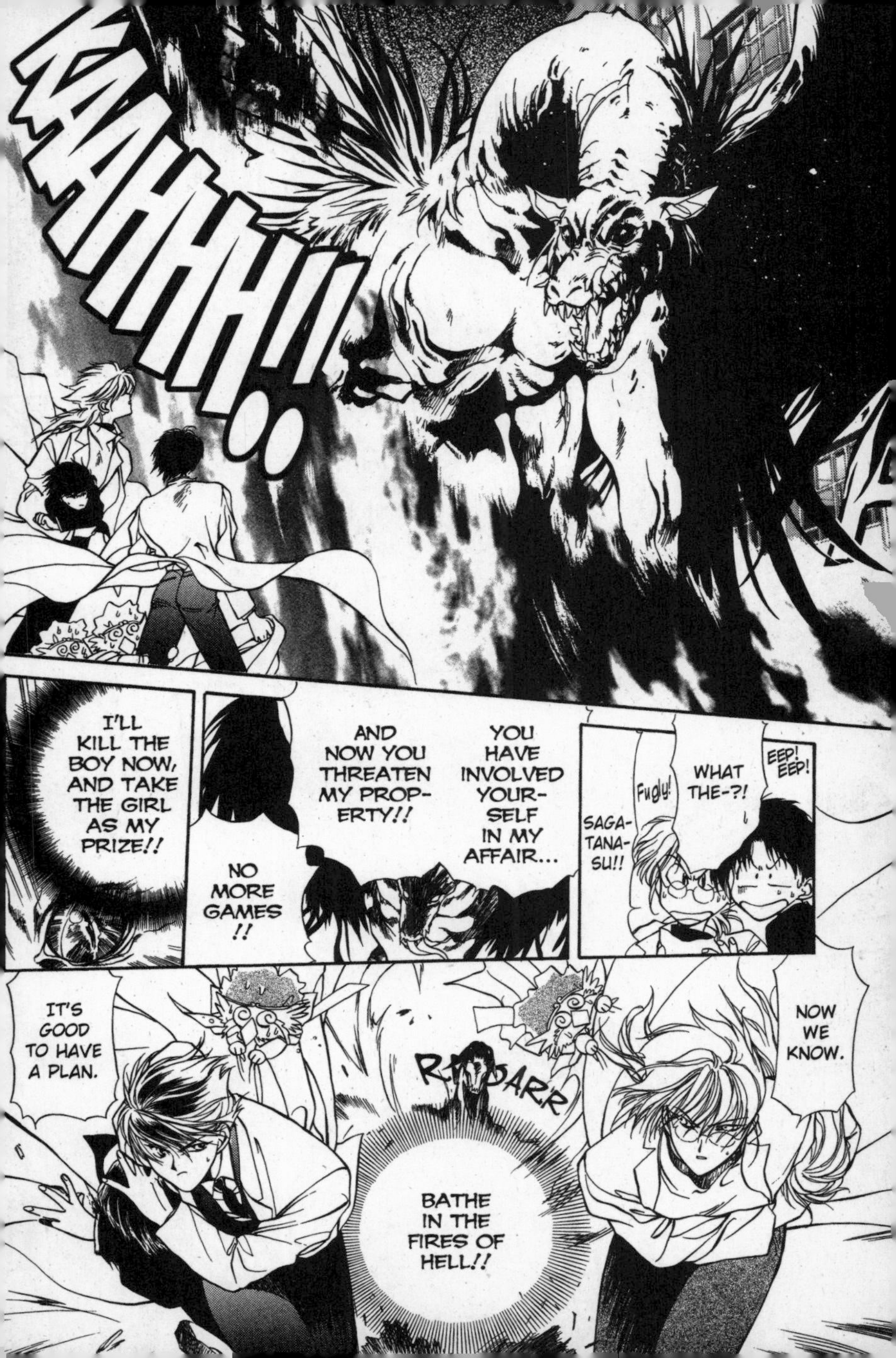
KAAHHH!!..
EEP! EEP!
WHAT THE-?!
Fugly!
SAGA-TANA-SU!!
YOU HAVE INVOLVED YOUR-SELF IN MY AFFAIR...
AND NOW YOU THREATEN MY PROP-ERTY!!
NO MORE GAMES!!
I'LL KILL THE BOY NOW, AND TAKE THE GIRL AS MY PRIZE!!
NOW WE KNOW.
BATHE IN THE FIRES OF HELL!!
IT'S GOOD TO HAVE A PLAN.

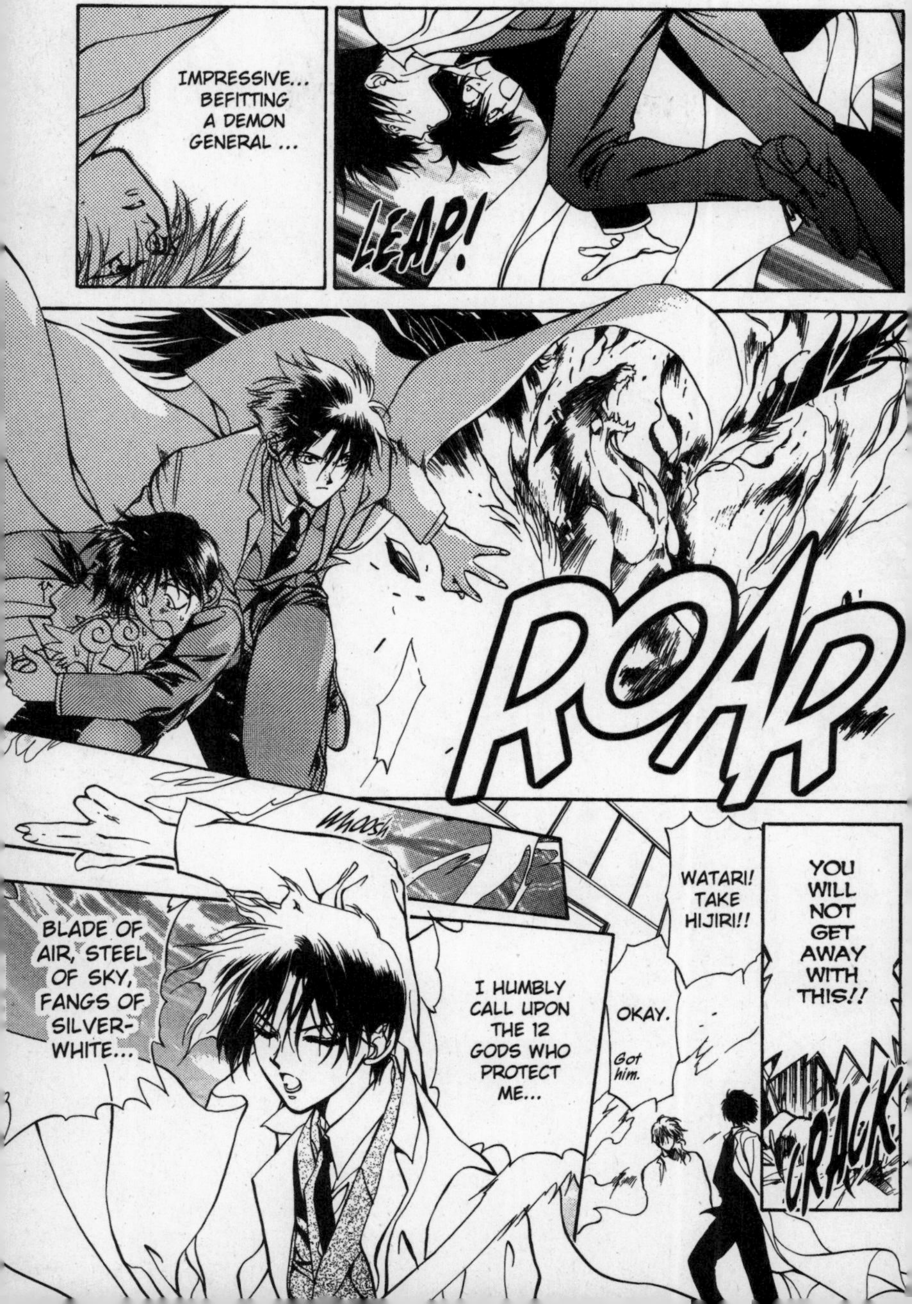

LEAP!
IMPRESSIVE... BEFITTING A DEMON GENERAL ...
ROAR
YOU WILL NOT GET AWAY WITH THIS!!
CRACK
WHOOSH
WATARI! TAKE HIJIRI!!
OKAY.
Got him.
I HUMBLY CALL UPON THE 12 GODS WHO PROTECT ME...
BLADE OF AIR, STEEL OF SKY, FANGS OF SILVER-WHITE...

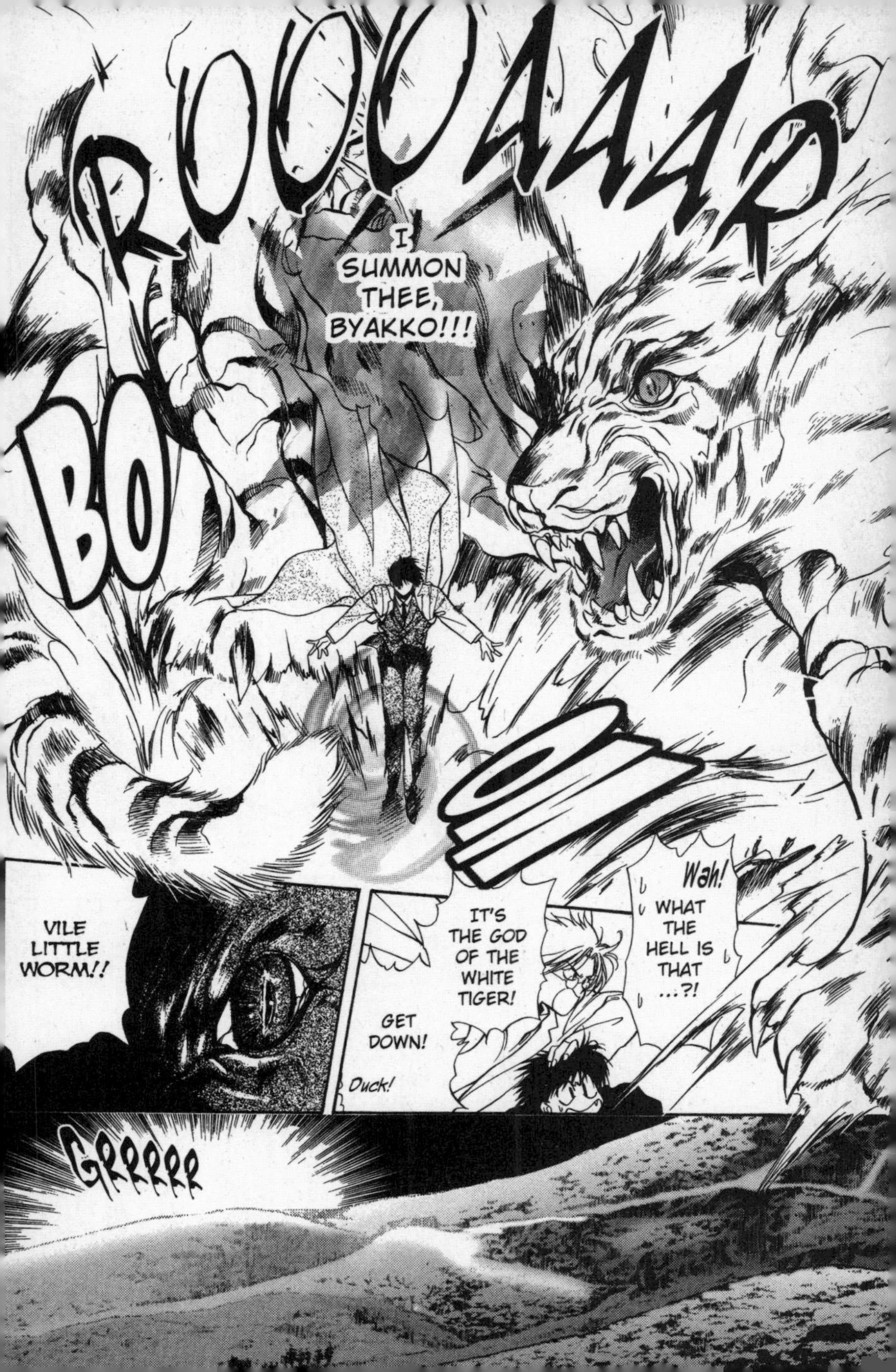

ROOOAAAR
I SUMMON THEE, BYAKKO!!!
BO
O
Wah!
WHAT THE HELL IS THAT ...?!
IT'S THE GOD OF THE WHITE TIGER!
GET DOWN!
Duck!
VILE LITTLE WORM!!
GRRRRR

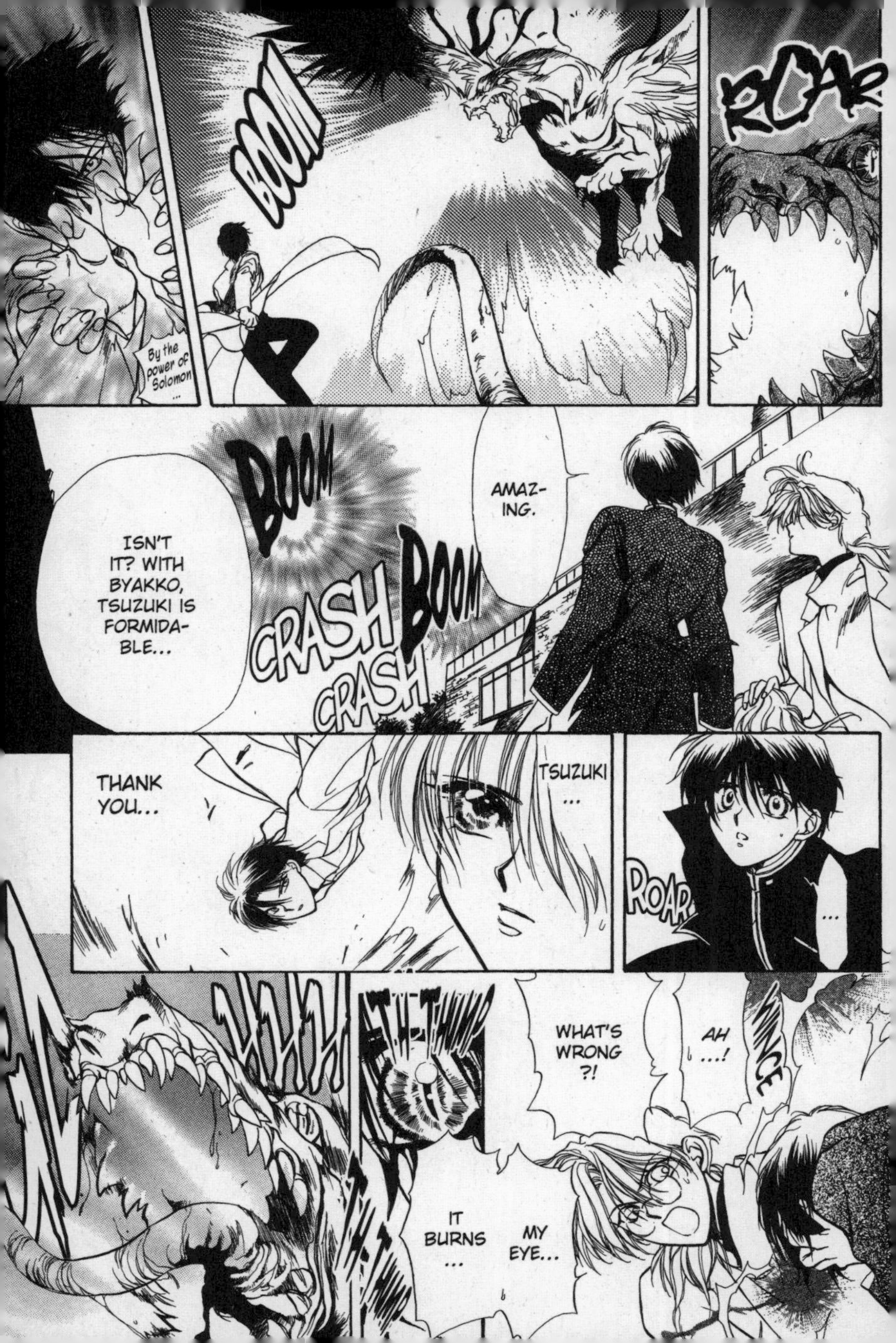

ROAR
BOOM
By the power of Solomon ...
AMAZ-ING.
BOOM
ISN'T IT? WITH BYAKKO, TSUZUKI IS FORMIDA-BLE...
BOOM
CRASH
CRASH
ROAR
...
TSUZUKI ...
THANK YOU...
AH ...!
WINCE
WHAT'S WRONG ?!
MY EYE...
IT BURNS ...

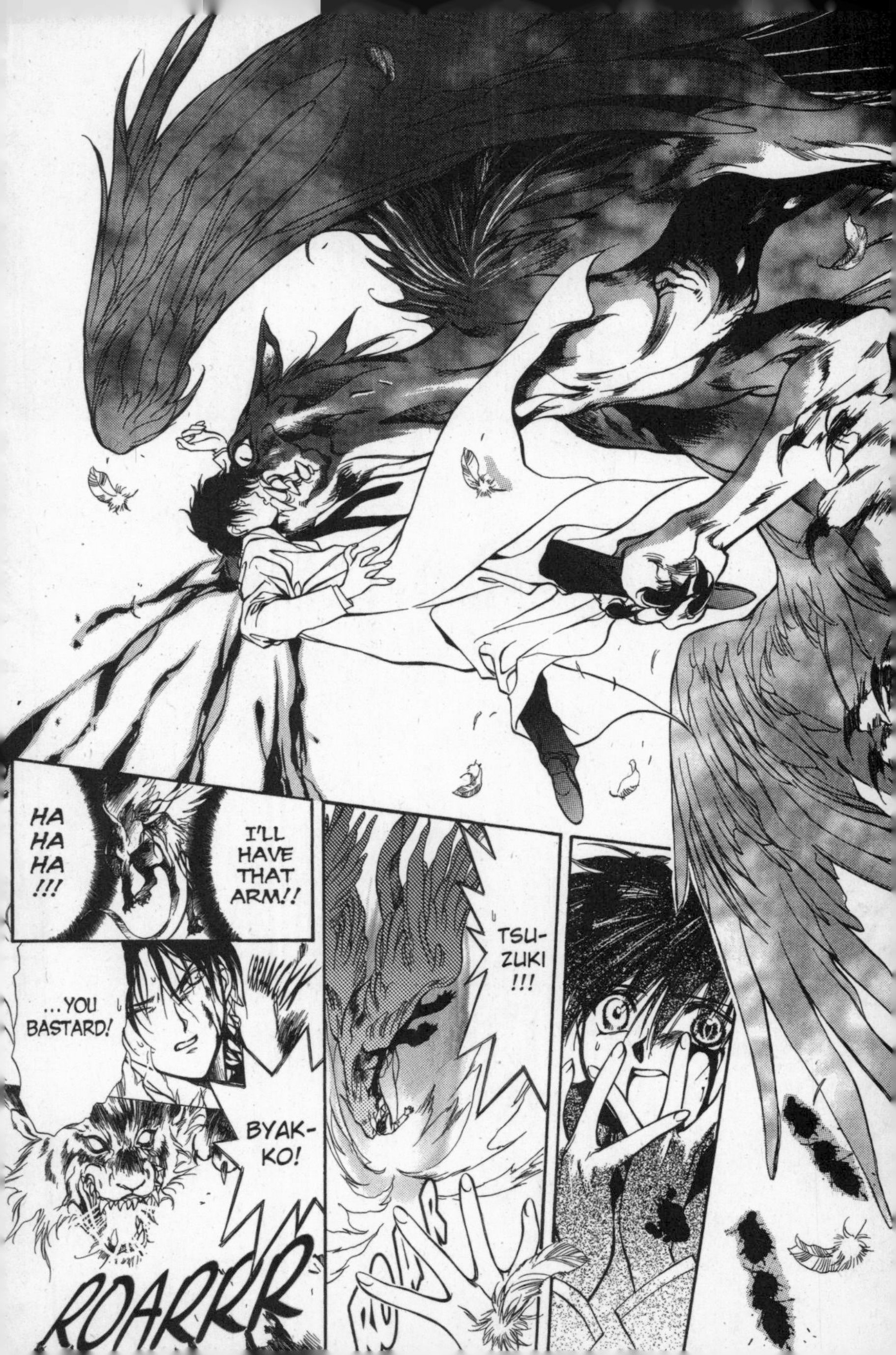

TSU-ZUKI!!!
HA HA HA!!!
I'LL HAVE THAT ARM!!
...YOU BASTARD!
BYAK-KO!
ROARRR

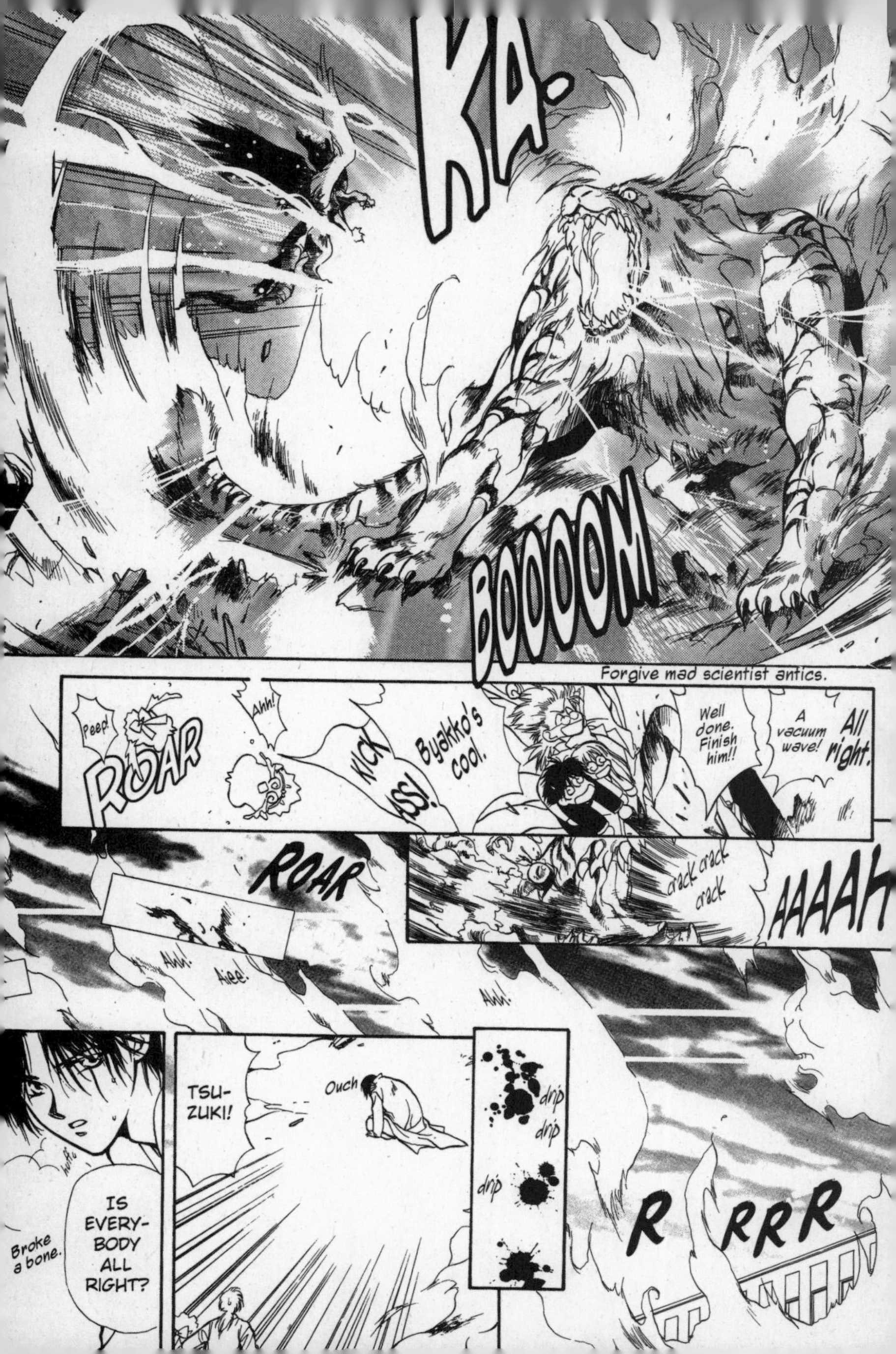
KA.
BOOOOM
Forgive mad scientist antics.
All right.
A vacuum wave!
Well done. Finish him!!
Byakko's cool.
KICK ASS!
Ahh!
Peep!
ROAR
AAAAH
crack crack crack
ROAR
Ahh!
Aiee!
Ahh!
R RRR
drip drip drip
Ouch
TSU-ZUKI!
IS EVERY-BODY ALL RIGHT?
Broke a bone.

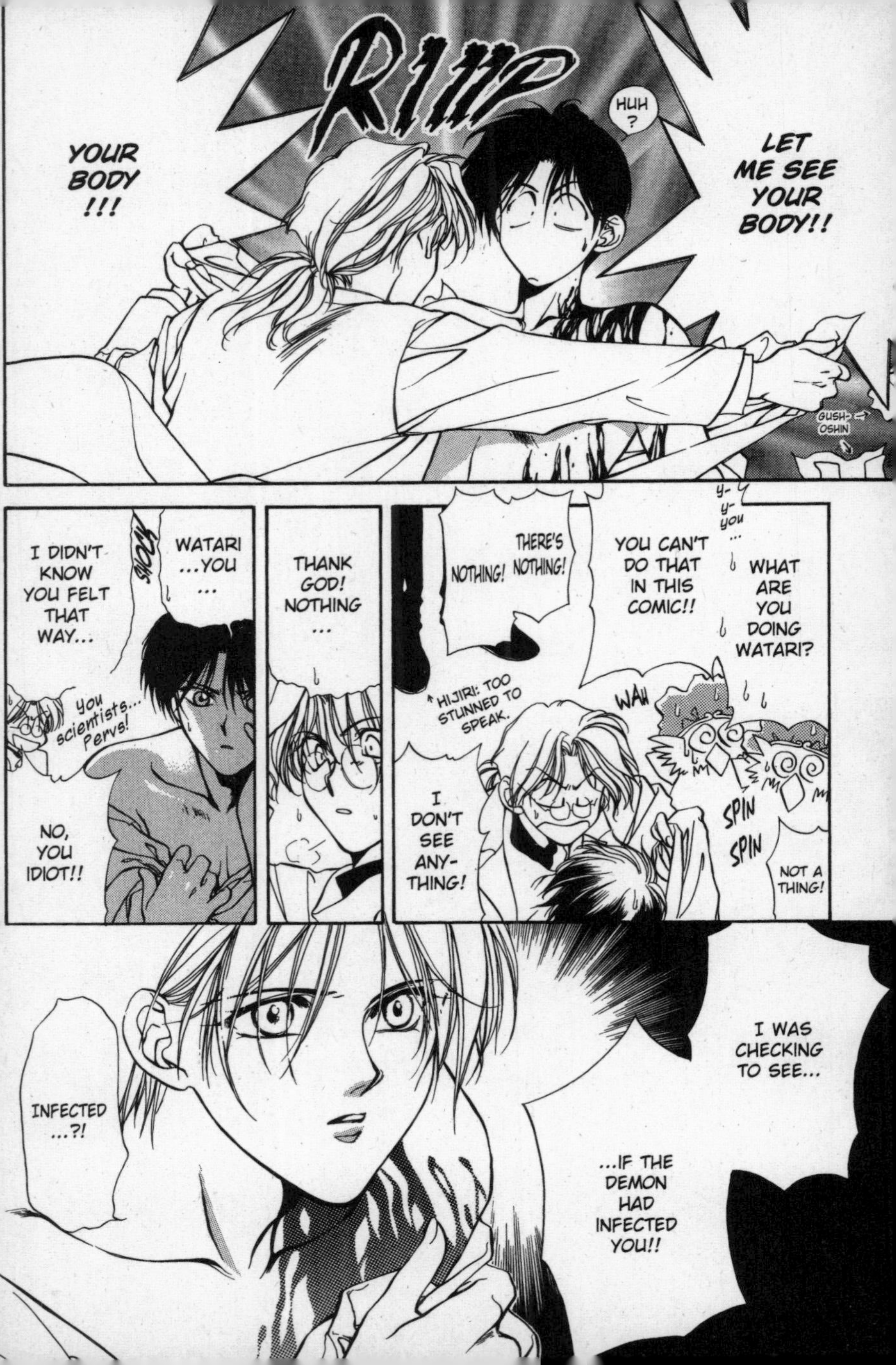
RIIIP
LET ME SEE YOUR BODY!!
HUH ?
YOUR BODY !!!
GUSH- OSHIN
y- y- you ...
WHAT ARE YOU DOING WATARI?
YOU CAN'T DO THAT IN THIS COMIC!!
THERE'S NOTHING!
NOTHING!
HIJIRI: TOO STUNNED TO SPEAK.
WAH
SPIN
SPIN
NOT A THING!
I DON'T SEE ANY- THING!
THANK GOD! NOTHING ...
WATARI ...YOU ...
I DIDN'T KNOW YOU FELT THAT WAY...
you scientists... Pervs!
NO, YOU IDIOT!!
I WAS CHECKING TO SEE...
...IF THE DEMON HAD INFECTED YOU!!
INFECTED ...?!

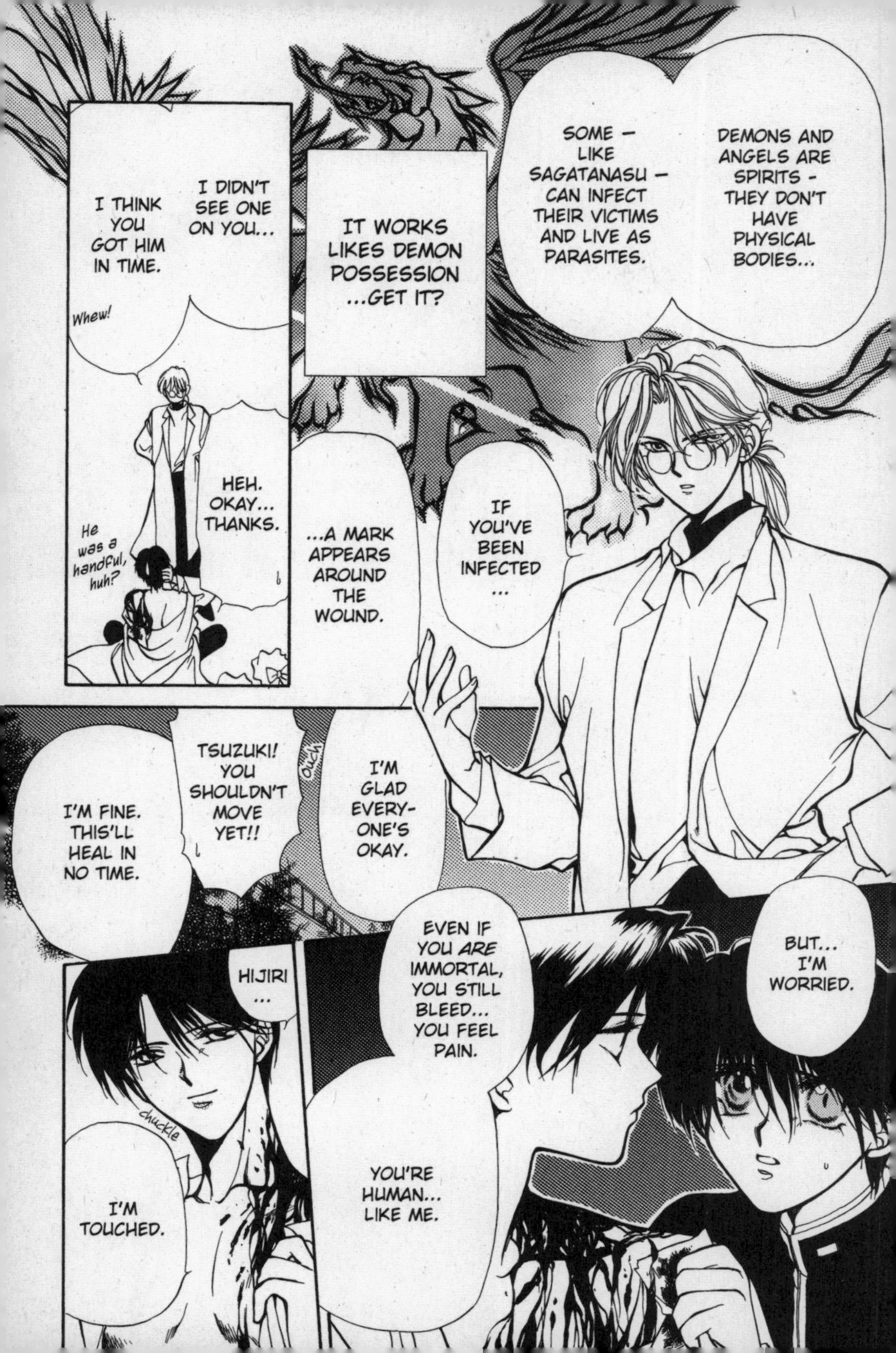
DEMONS AND ANGELS ARE SPIRITS - THEY DON'T HAVE PHYSICAL BODIES...
SOME – LIKE SAGATANASU – CAN INFECT THEIR VICTIMS AND LIVE AS PARASITES.
IT WORKS LIKES DEMON POSSESSION ...GET IT?
IF YOU'VE BEEN INFECTED ...
...A MARK APPEARS AROUND THE WOUND.
I DIDN'T SEE ONE ON YOU...
I THINK YOU GOT HIM IN TIME.
Whew!
HEH. OKAY... THANKS.
He was a handful, huh?
I'M GLAD EVERY-ONE'S OKAY.
Ouch
TSUZUKI! YOU SHOULDN'T MOVE YET!!
I'M FINE. THIS'LL HEAL IN NO TIME.
BUT... I'M WORRIED.
EVEN IF YOU *ARE* IMMORTAL, YOU STILL BLEED... YOU FEEL PAIN.
YOU'RE HUMAN... LIKE ME.
HIJIRI ...
chuckle
I'M TOUCHED.

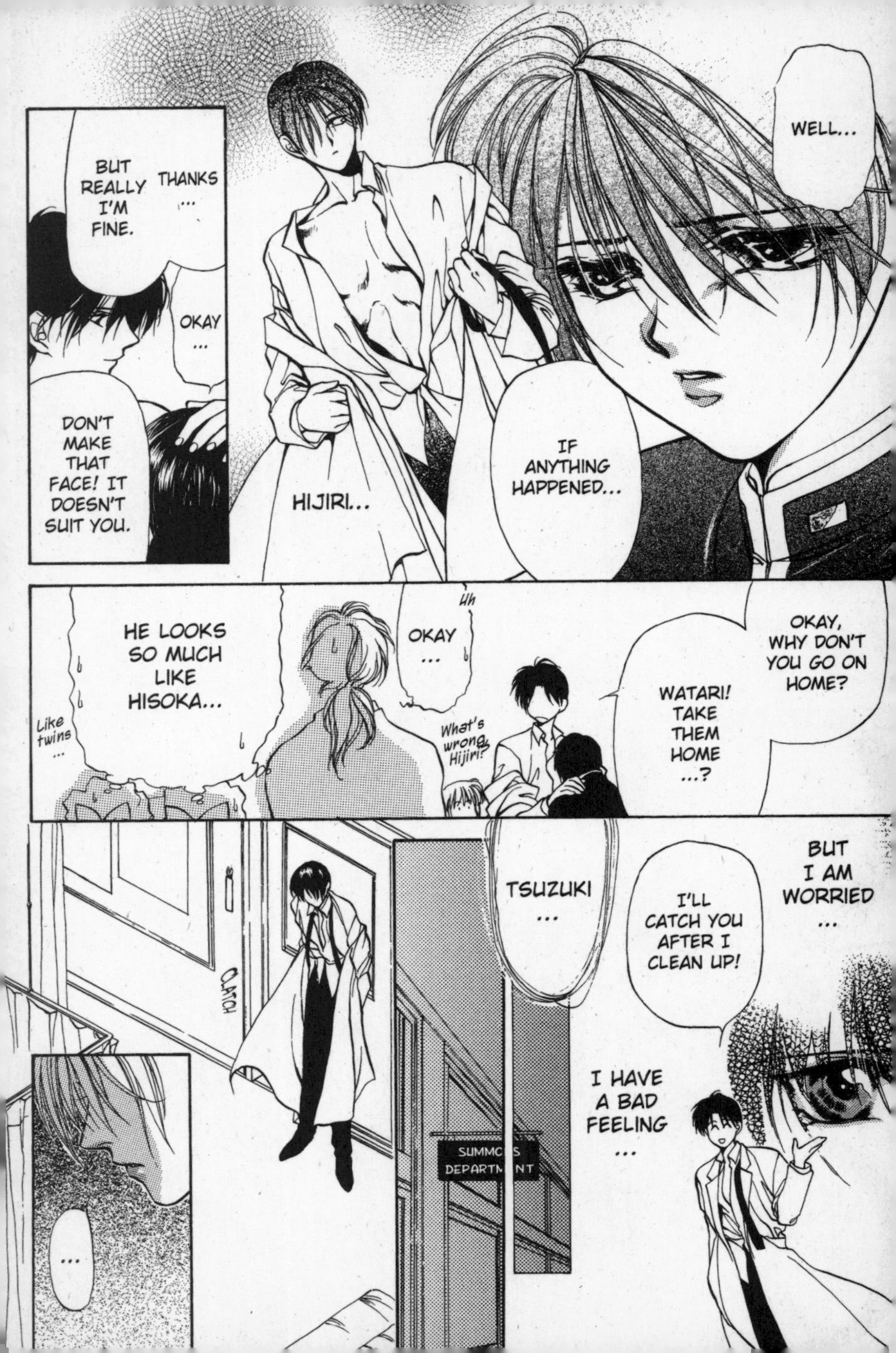
WELL...
IF ANYTHING HAPPENED...
HIJIRI...
THANKS ...
BUT REALLY I'M FINE.
OKAY ...
DON'T MAKE THAT FACE! IT DOESN'T SUIT YOU.
OKAY, WHY DON'T YOU GO ON HOME?
WATARI! TAKE THEM HOME ...?
What's wrong Hijiri?
Uh
OKAY ...
HE LOOKS SO MUCH LIKE HISOKA...
Like twins ...
BUT I AM WORRIED ...
I'LL CATCH YOU AFTER I CLEAN UP!
I HAVE A BAD FEELING ...
TSUZUKI ...
SUMMO S
DEPARTM NT
CLATCH
...

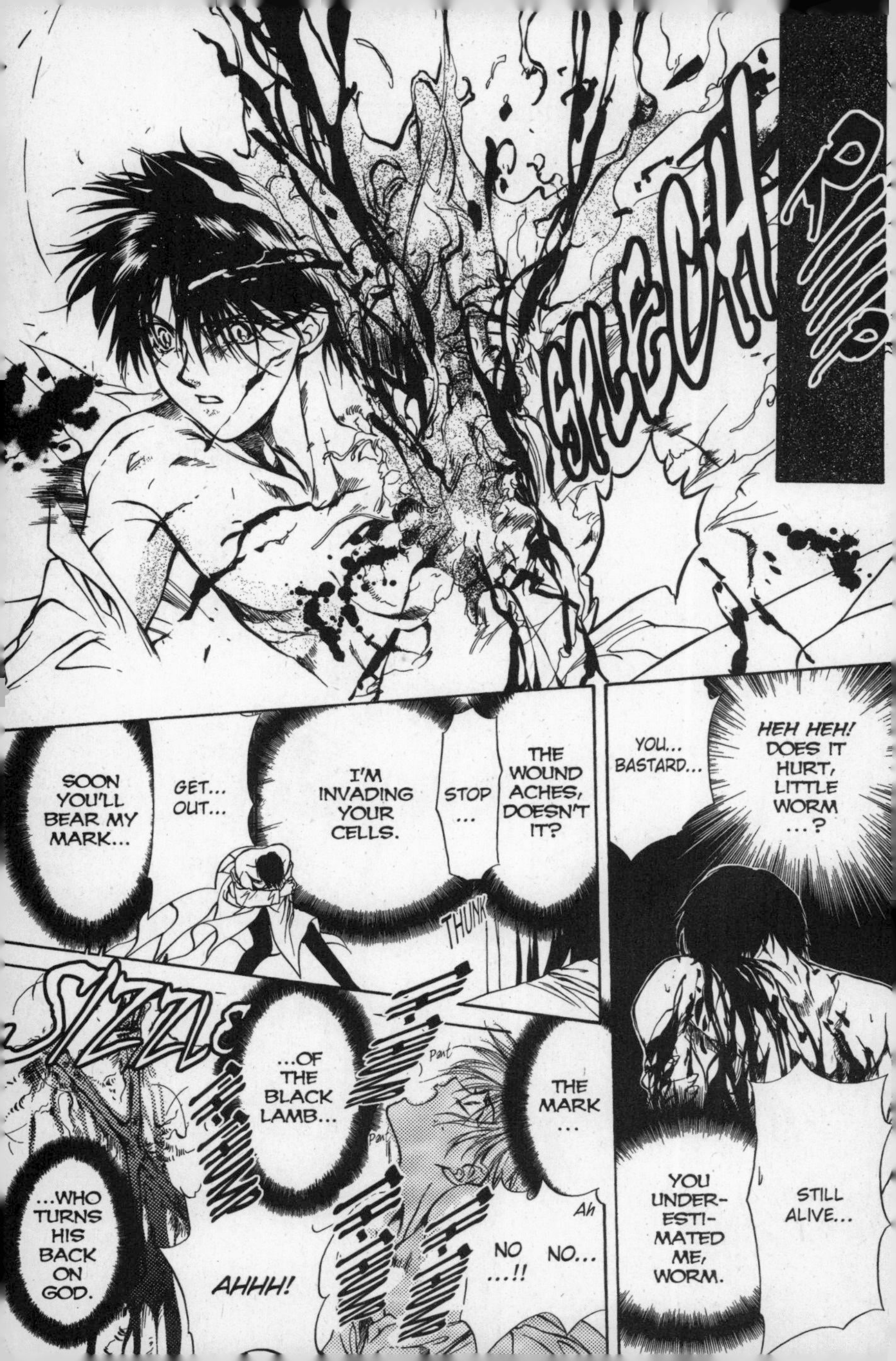
HEH HEH! DOES IT HURT, LITTLE WORM ...?
YOU... BASTARD...
STILL ALIVE...
YOU UNDER-ESTI-MATED ME, WORM.
THE WOUND ACHES, DOESN'T IT?
STOP ...
I'M INVADING YOUR CELLS.
GET... OUT...
SOON YOU'LL BEAR MY MARK...
THUNK
THE MARK ...
Ah
NO...
NO ...!!
Pant
Pant
...OF THE BLACK LAMB...
SIZZLE
...WHO TURNS HIS BACK ON GOD.
AHHH!

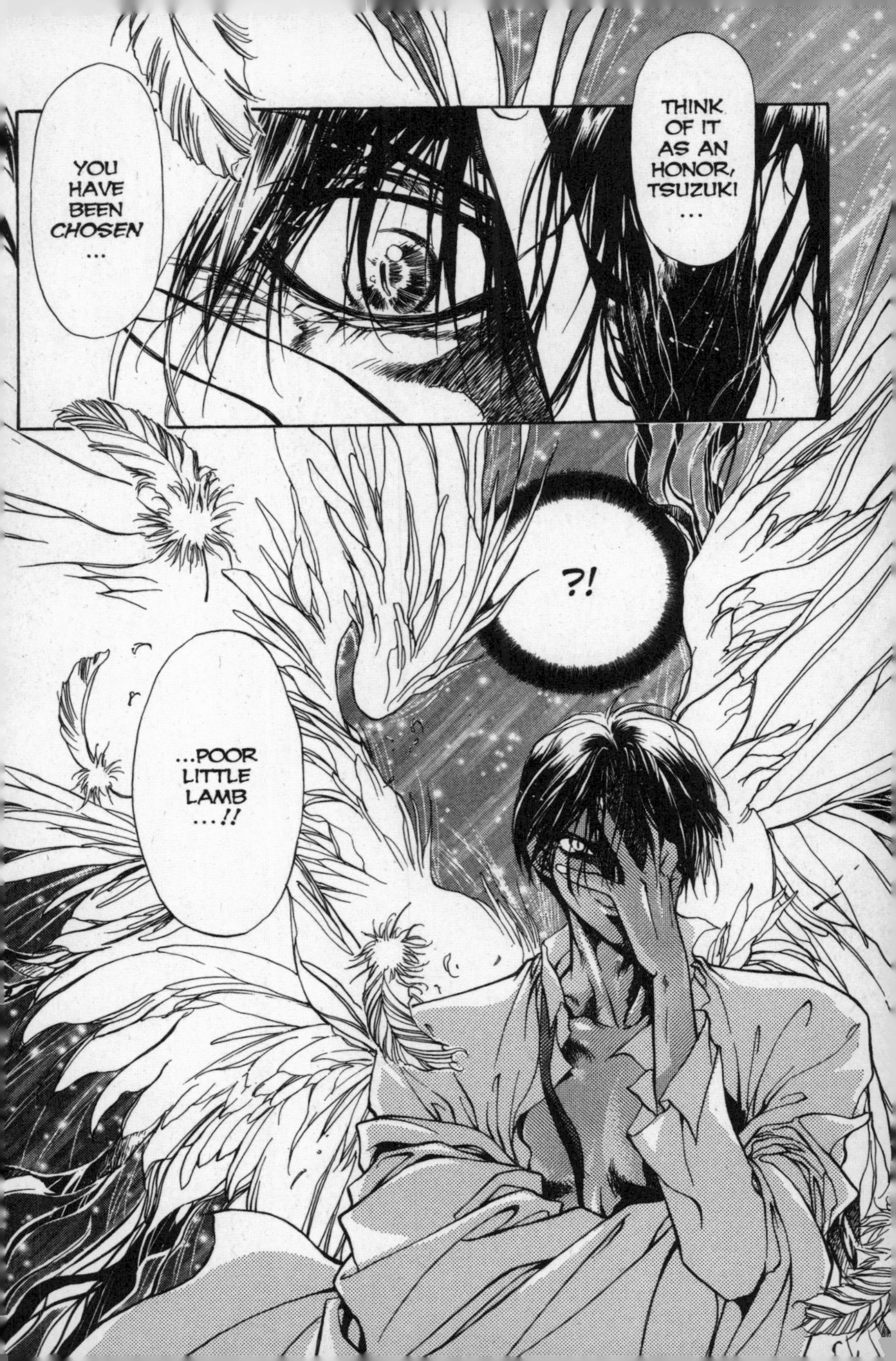
THINK OF IT AS AN HONOR, TSUZUKI ...
YOU HAVE BEEN CHOSEN ...
?!
...POOR LITTLE LAMB ...!!

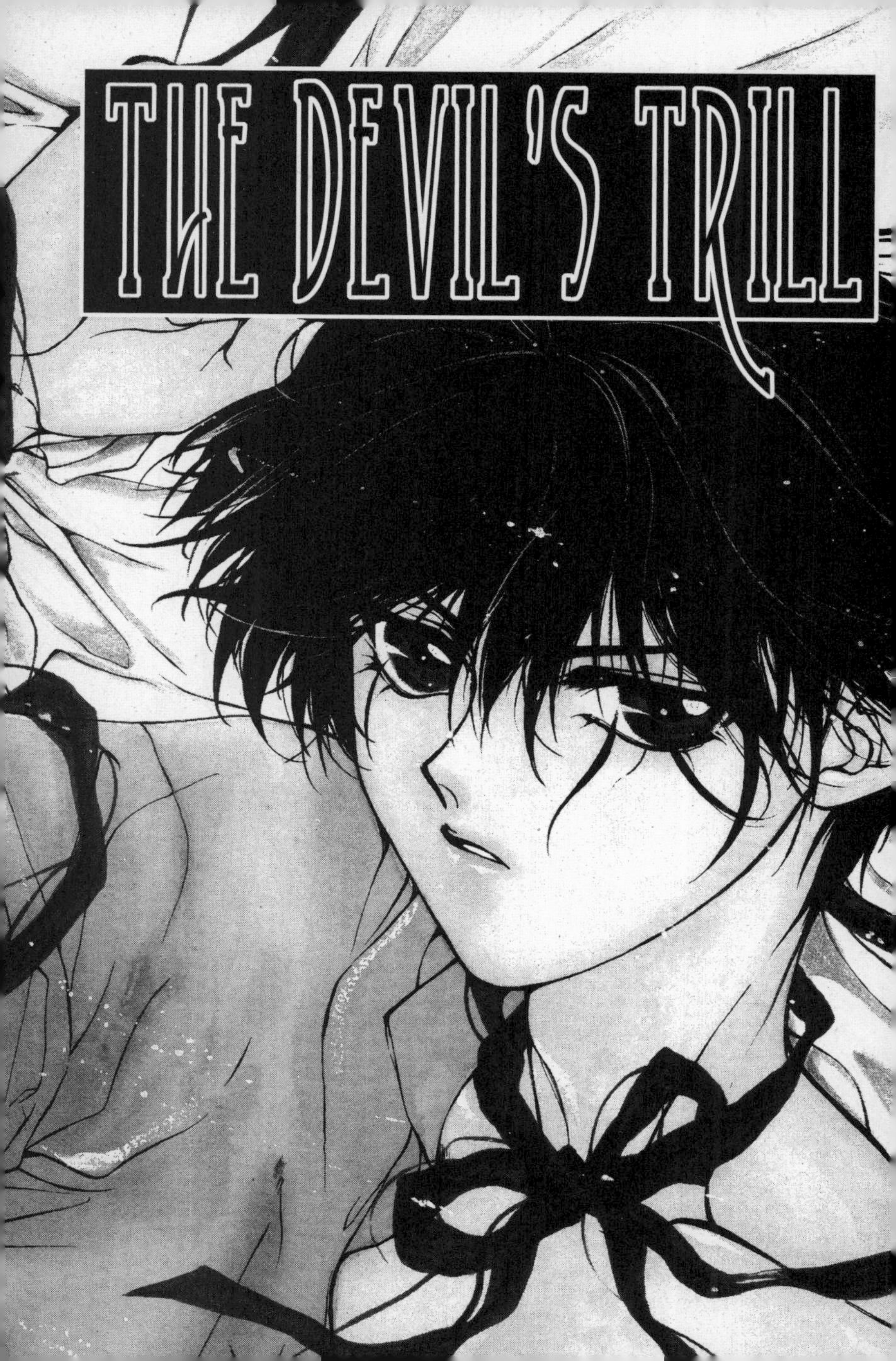
THE DEVIL'S TRILL

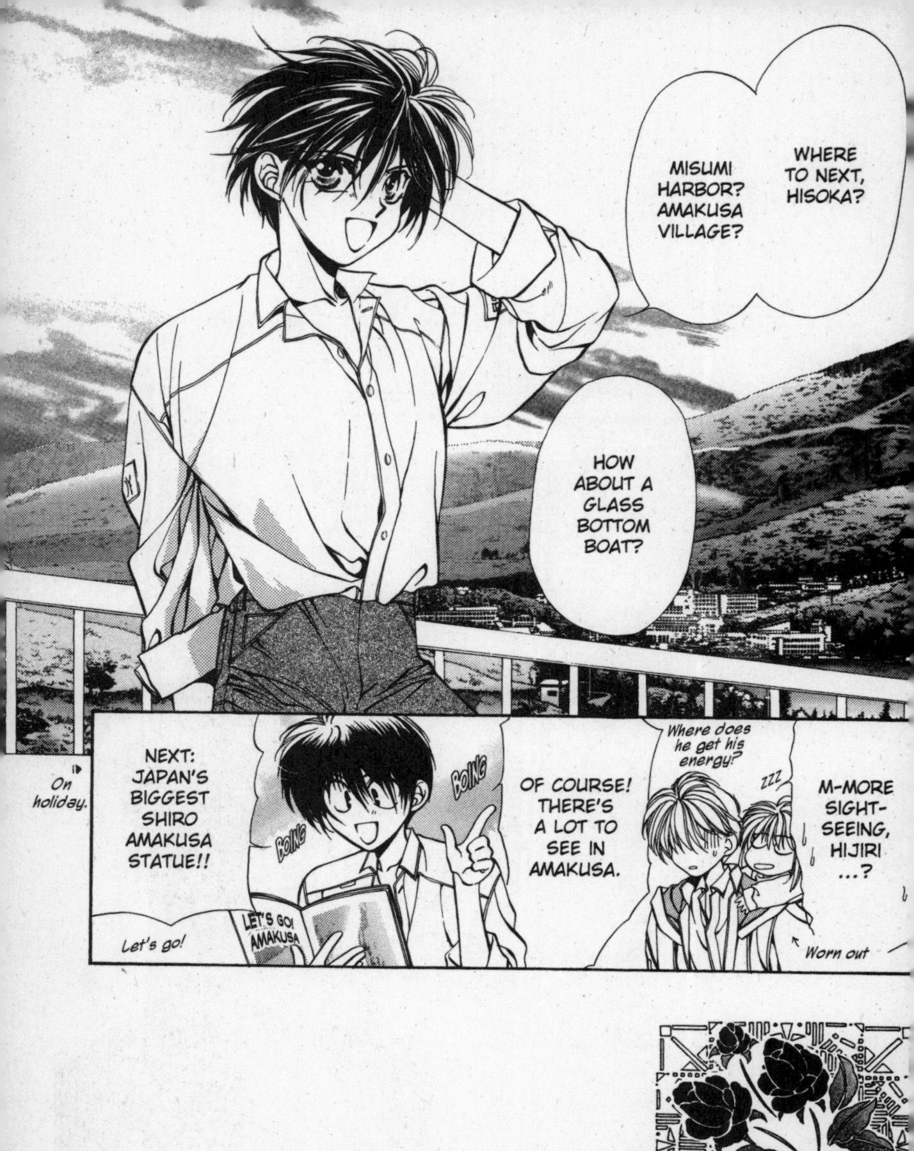
WHERE TO NEXT, HISOKA?
MISUMI HARBOR? AMAKUSA VILLAGE?
HOW ABOUT A GLASS BOTTOM BOAT?
M-MORE SIGHT-SEEING, HIJIRI ...?
Where does he get his energy?
ZZZ
Worn out
OF COURSE! THERE'S A LOT TO SEE IN AMAKUSA.
BOING
BOING
NEXT: JAPAN'S BIGGEST SHIRO AMAKUSA STATUE!!
LET'S GO! AMAKUSA
Let's go!
On holiday.

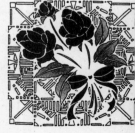

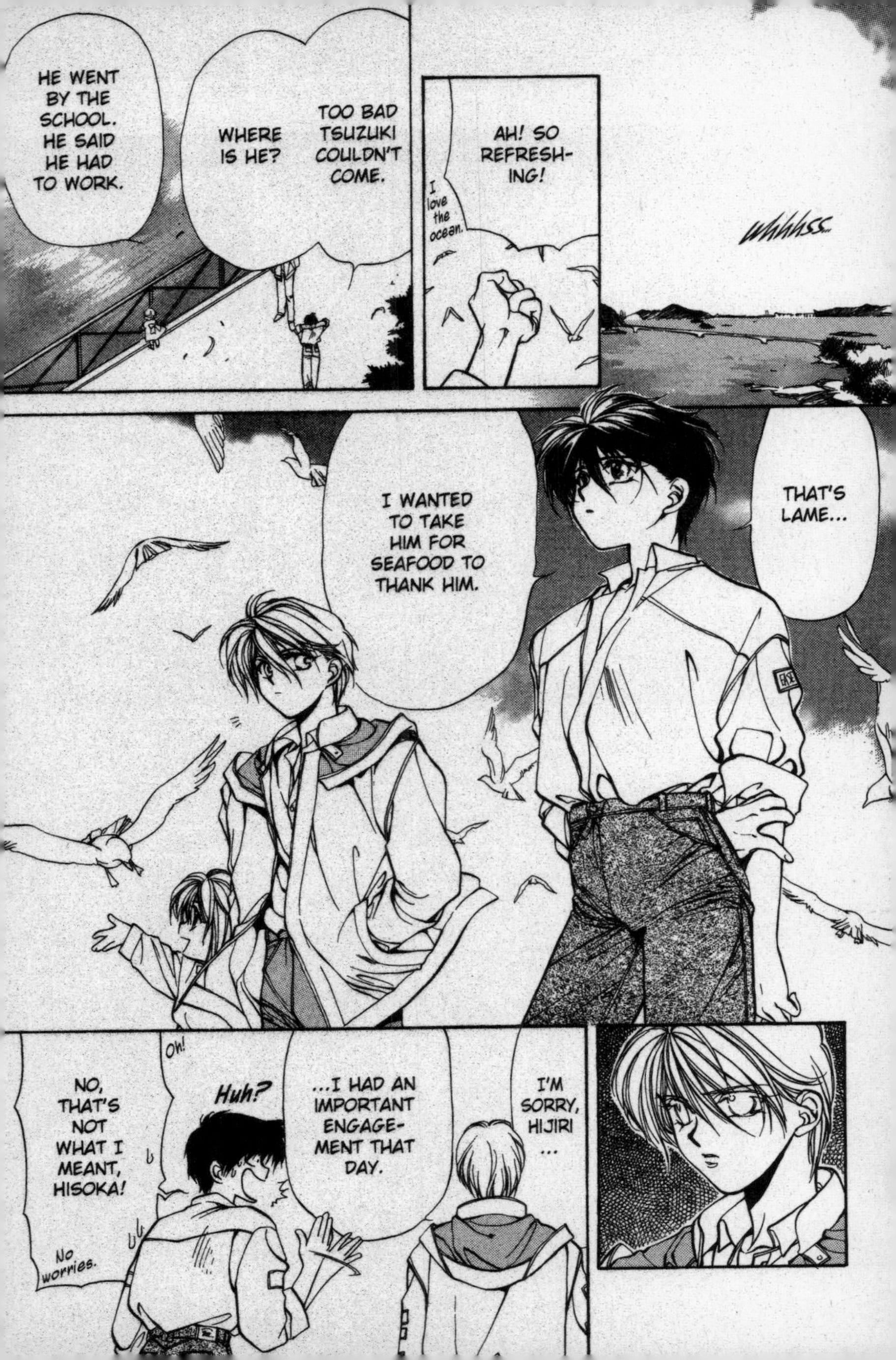
whhhss...
AH! SO REFRESHING!
I love the ocean.
TOO BAD TSUZUKI COULDN'T COME.
WHERE IS HE?
HE WENT BY THE SCHOOL. HE SAID HE HAD TO WORK.
THAT'S LAME...
I WANTED TO TAKE HIM FOR SEAFOOD TO THANK HIM.
I'M SORRY, HIJIRI...
...I HAD AN IMPORTANT ENGAGEMENT THAT DAY.
Oh!
Huh?
NO, THAT'S NOT WHAT I MEANT, HISOKA!
No worries.

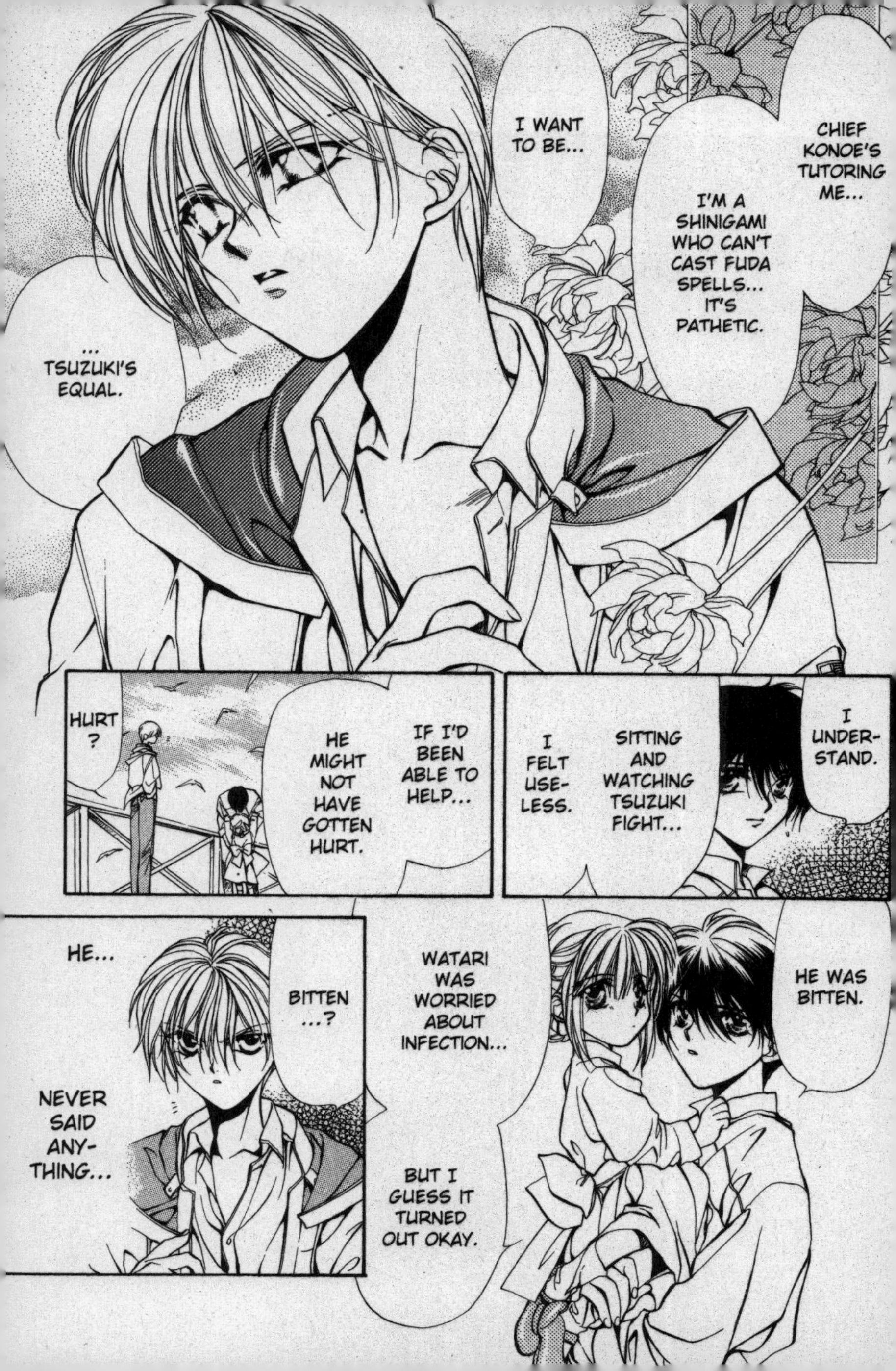
CHIEF KONOE'S TUTORING ME...
I'M A SHINIGAMI WHO CAN'T CAST FUDA SPELLS... IT'S PATHETIC.
I WANT TO BE...
... TSUZUKI'S EQUAL.
I UNDER-STAND.
SITTING AND WATCHING TSUZUKI FIGHT...
I FELT USE-LESS.
IF I'D BEEN ABLE TO HELP...
HE MIGHT NOT HAVE GOTTEN HURT.
HURT?
HE WAS BITTEN.
WATARI WAS WORRIED ABOUT INFECTION...
BUT I GUESS IT TURNED OUT OKAY.
BITTEN ...?
HE...
NEVER SAID ANY-THING...

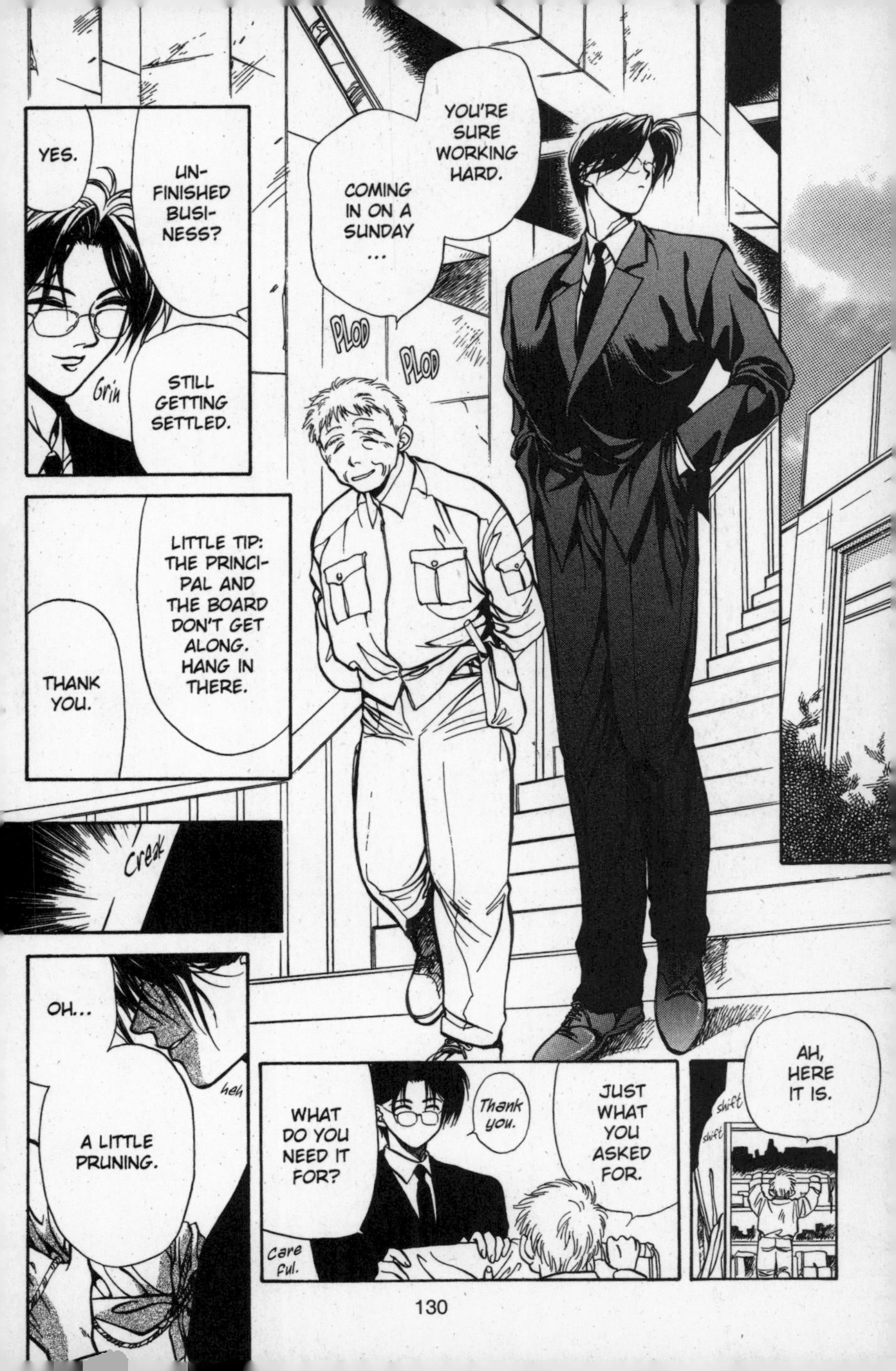
YOU'RE SURE WORKING HARD.
COMING IN ON A SUNDAY ...
PLOD
PLOD
UN-FINISHED BUSI-NESS?
YES.
Grin
STILL GETTING SETTLED.
LITTLE TIP: THE PRINCI-PAL AND THE BOARD DON'T GET ALONG. HANG IN THERE.
THANK YOU.
Creak
AH, HERE IT IS.
shift
shift
JUST WHAT YOU ASKED FOR.
Thank you.
WHAT DO YOU NEED IT FOR?
Care ful.
OH...
heh
A LITTLE PRUNING.

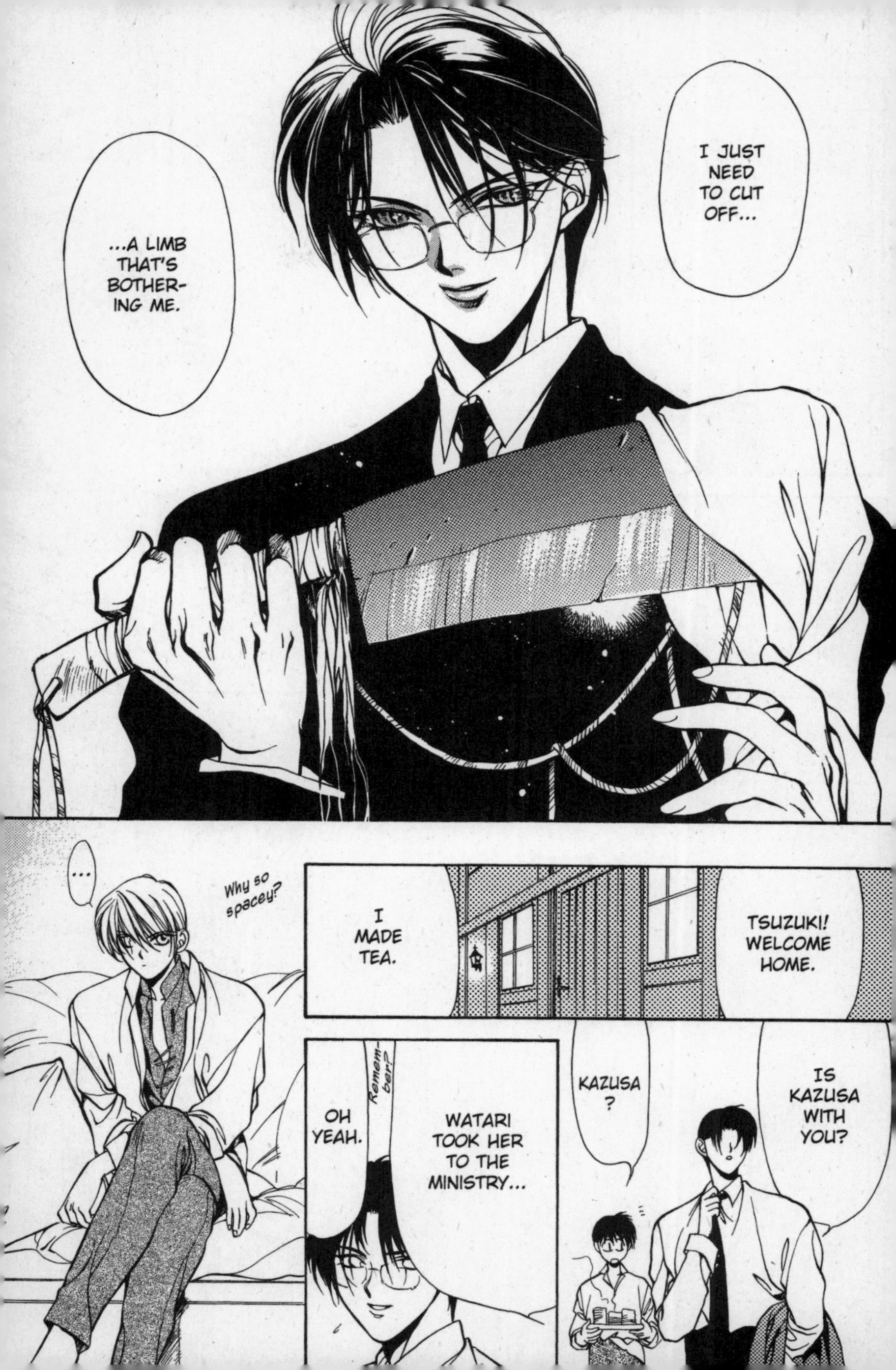
I JUST NEED TO CUT OFF...
...A LIMB THAT'S BOTHER-ING ME.
TSUZUKI! WELCOME HOME.
I MADE TEA.
IS KAZUSA WITH YOU?
KAZUSA?
WATARI TOOK HER TO THE MINISTRY...
Remem-ber?
OH YEAH.
...
Why so spacey?

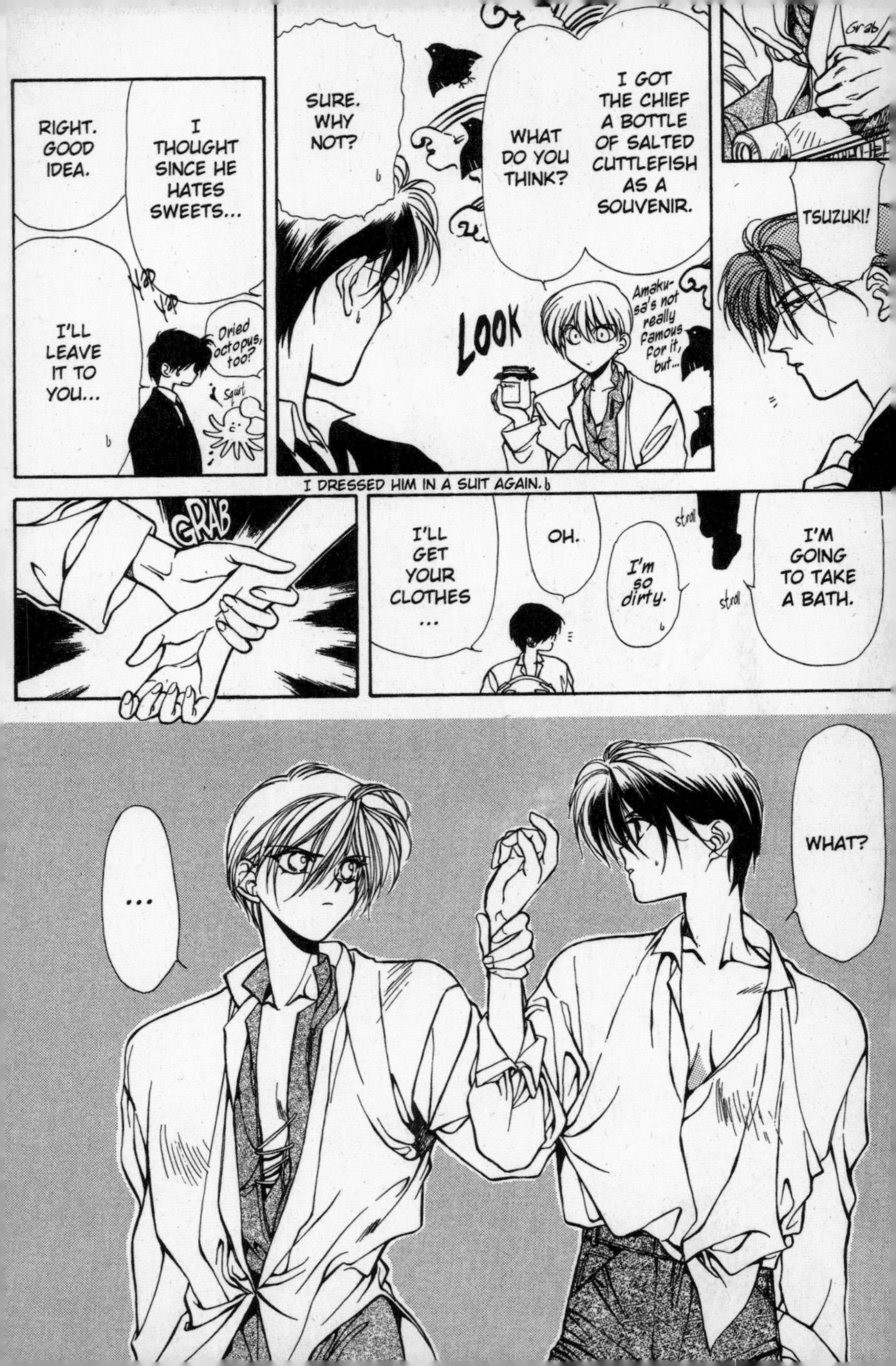
Grab
TSUZUKI!
I GOT THE CHIEF A BOTTLE OF SALTED CUTTLEFISH AS A SOUVENIR.
WHAT DO YOU THINK?
Amakusa's not really famous for it, but...
LOOK
SURE. WHY NOT?
I THOUGHT SINCE HE HATES SWEETS...
RIGHT. GOOD IDEA.
Yap yap
Dried octopus, too?
Squirt
I'LL LEAVE IT TO YOU...
I DRESSED HIM IN A SUIT AGAIN.
I'M GOING TO TAKE A BATH.
stroll
stroll
I'm so dirty.
OH.
I'LL GET YOUR CLOTHES ...
GRAB
WHAT?
...

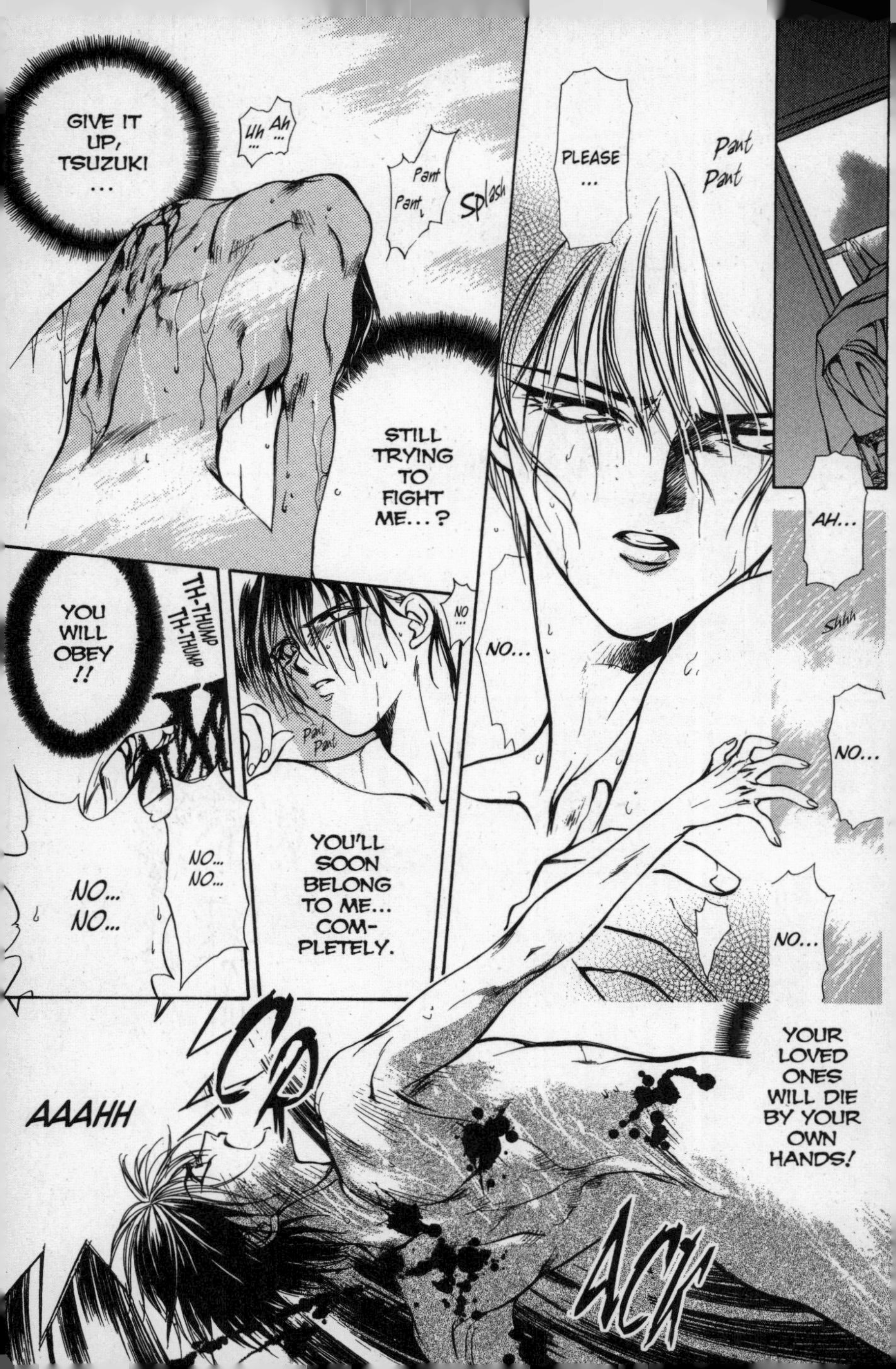
PLEASE ...
Pant Pant
GIVE IT UP, TSUZUKI ...
Uh ... Ah ...
Pant Pant
Splash
STILL TRYING TO FIGHT ME...?
AH...
Shhh
NO...
NO...
NO...
NO ...
Pant Pant
YOU'LL SOON BELONG TO ME... COMPLETELY.
YOU WILL OBEY !!
TH-THUMP TH-THUMP
NO... NO...
NO... NO...
YOUR LOVED ONES WILL DIE BY YOUR OWN HANDS!
CR
ACK
AAAHH

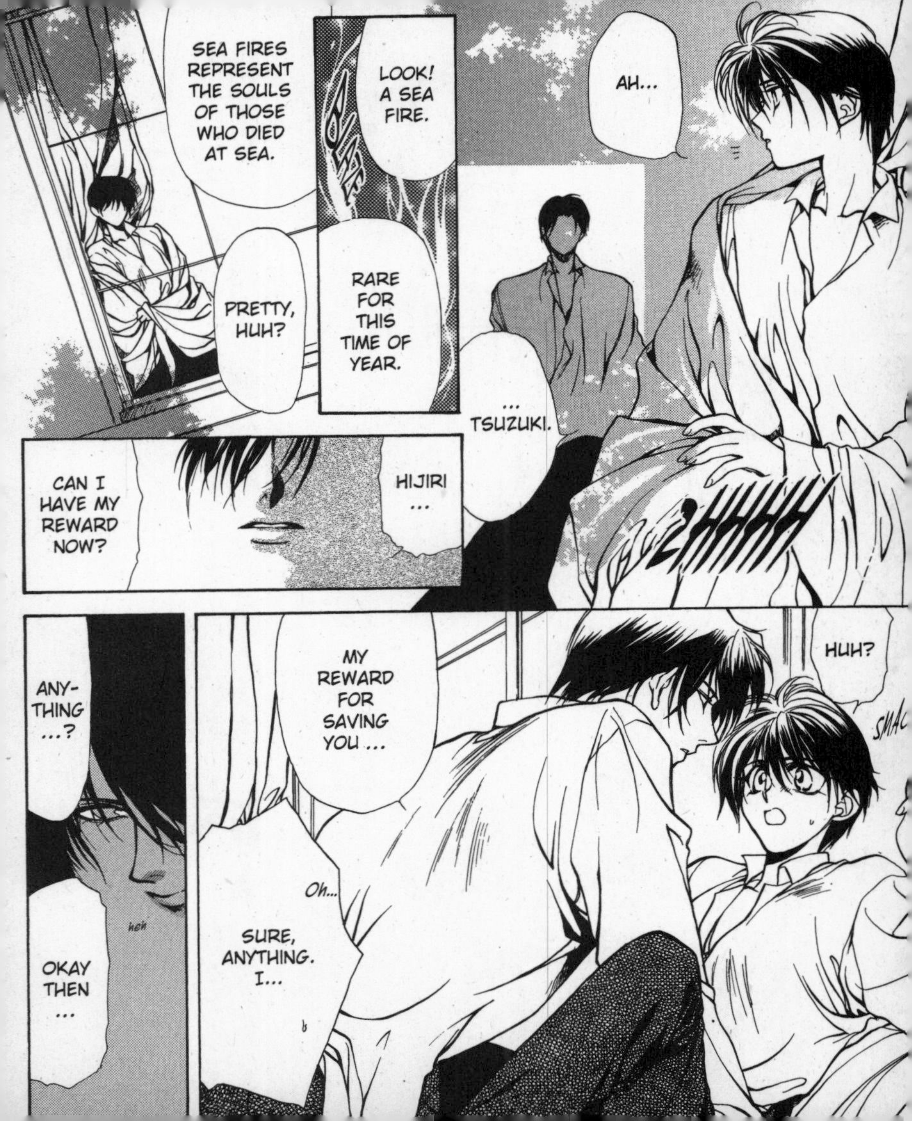
AH...
... TSUZUKI.
LOOK! A SEA FIRE.
RARE FOR THIS TIME OF YEAR.
SEA FIRES REPRESENT THE SOULS OF THOSE WHO DIED AT SEA.
PRETTY, HUH?
HIJIRI ...
CAN I HAVE MY REWARD NOW?
HUH?
SMAC
MY REWARD FOR SAVING YOU ...
Oh...
SURE, ANYTHING. I...
ANY-THING ...?
heh
OKAY THEN ...

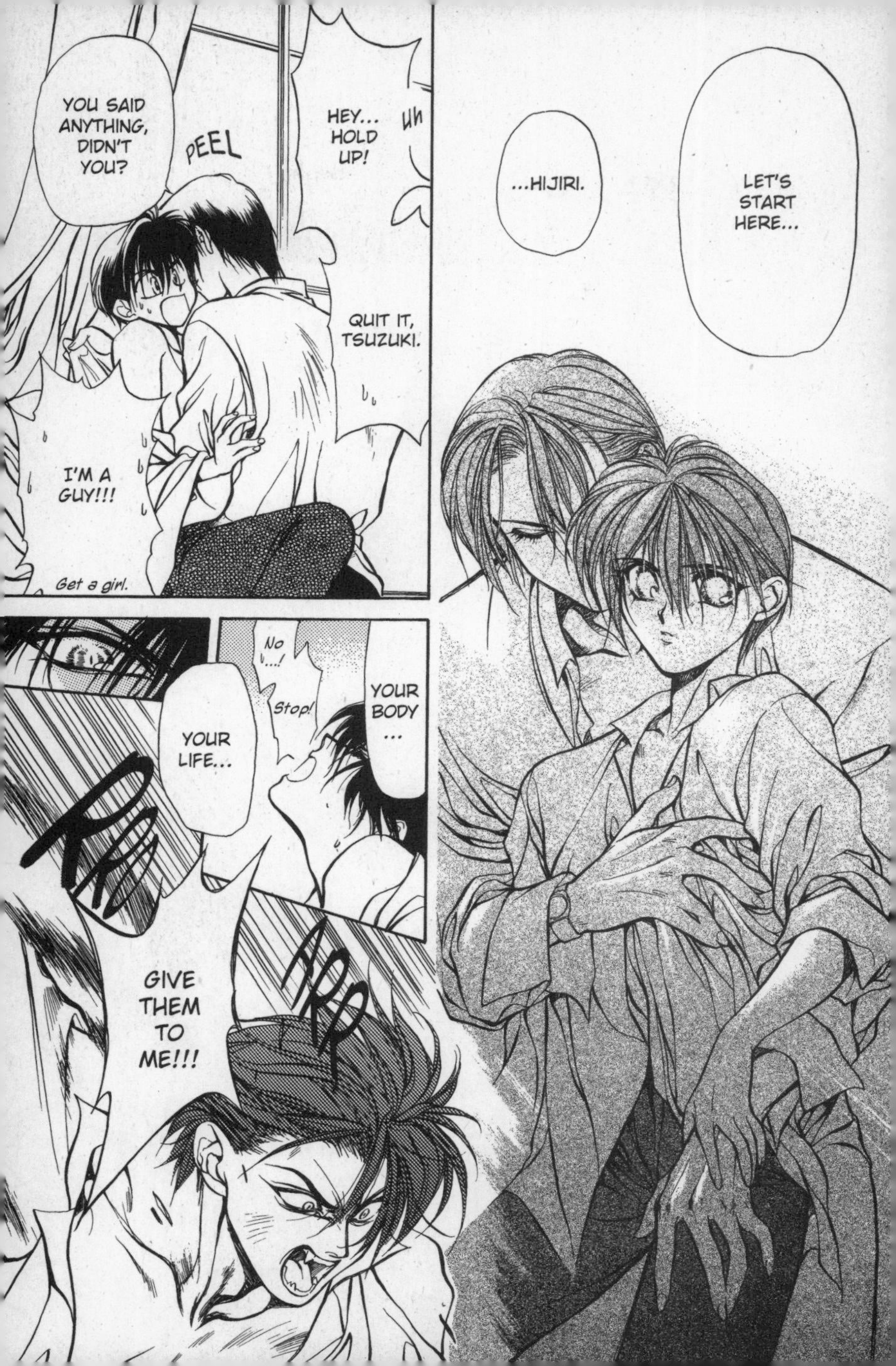
LET'S START HERE...
...HIJIRI.
UH
HEY... HOLD UP!
YOU SAID ANYTHING, DIDN'T YOU?
PEEL
QUIT IT, TSUZUKI.
I'M A GUY!!!
Get a girl.
YOUR BODY ...
No ...!
Stop!
YOUR LIFE...
GIVE THEM TO ME!!!

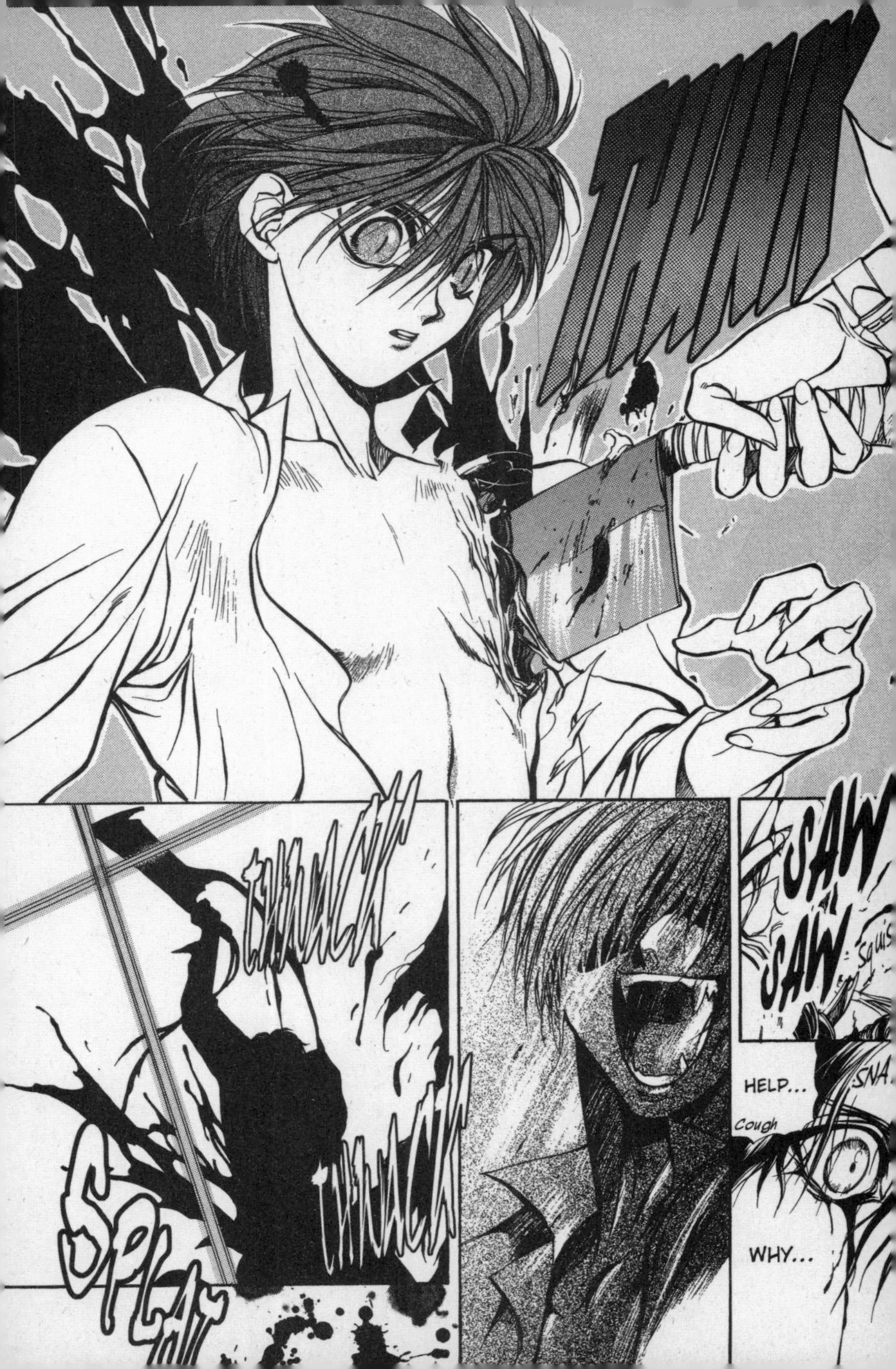
SAW
SAW
Squis
HELP...
SNA
Cough
WHY...
THWACK
THWACK
SPLAT

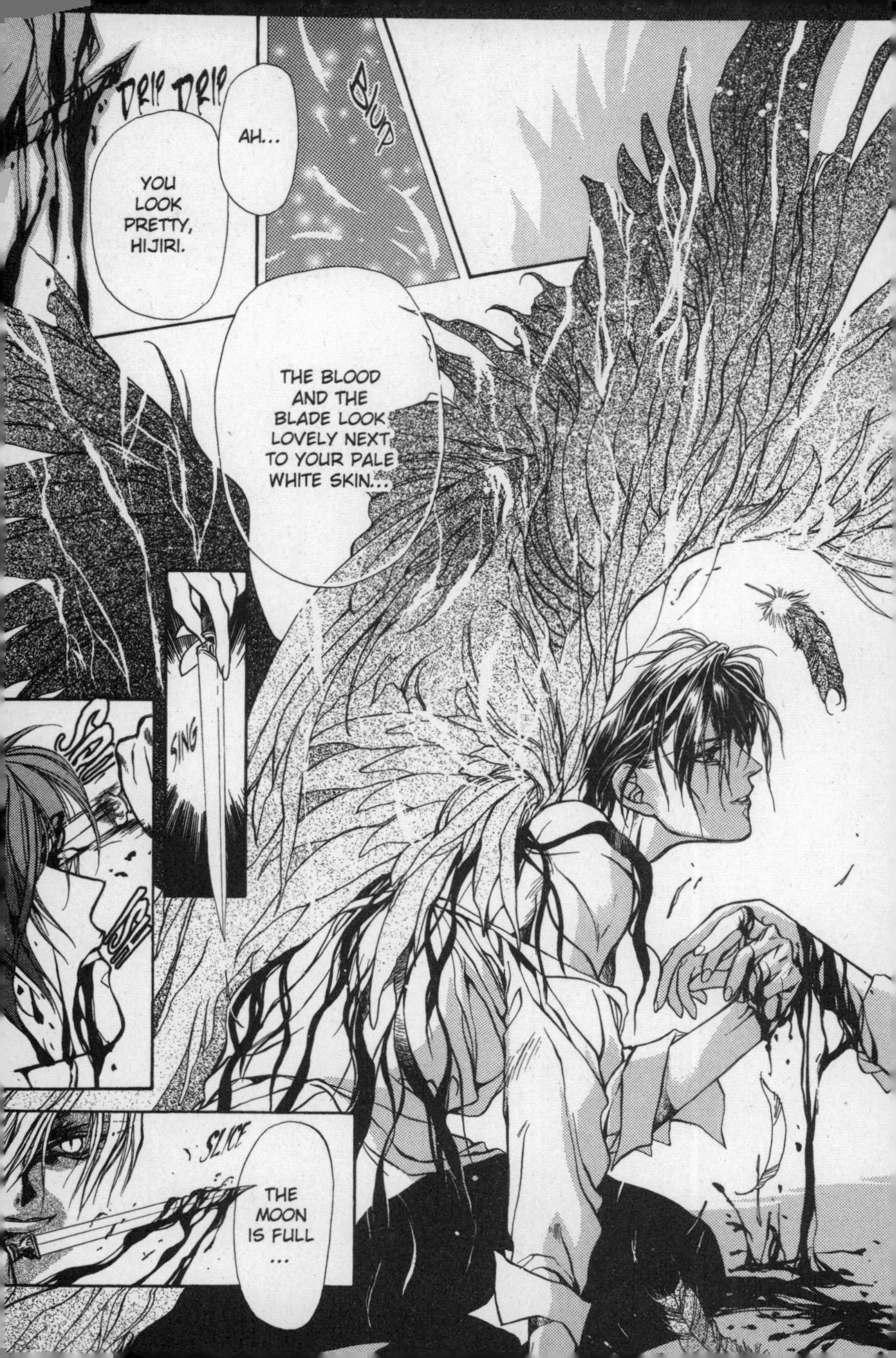
BLUP
DRIP DRIP
AH...
YOU LOOK PRETTY, HIJIRI.
THE BLOOD AND THE BLADE LOOK LOVELY NEXT TO YOUR PALE WHITE SKIN...
SING
SLICE
THE MOON IS FULL ...

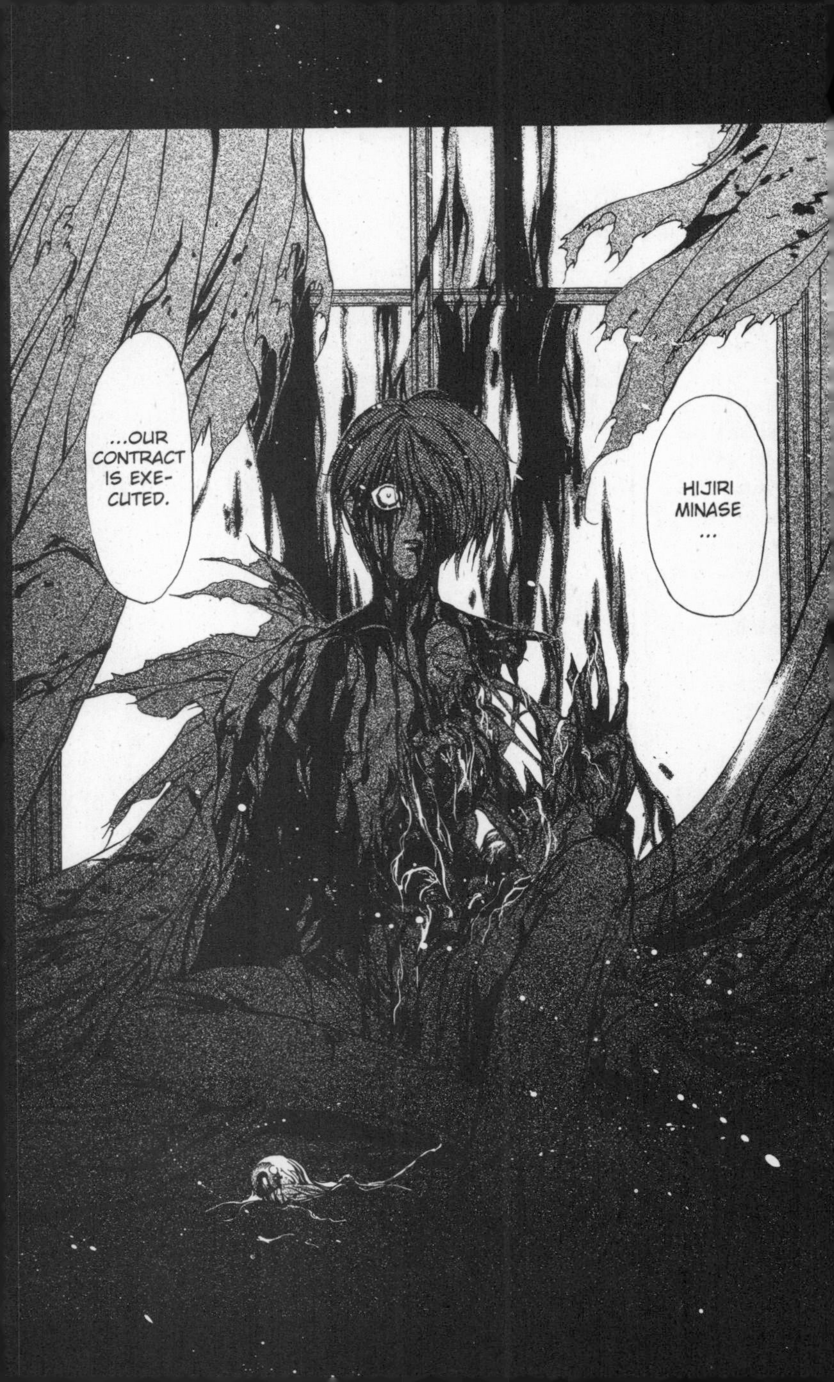
HIJIRI MINASE ...
...OUR CONTRACT IS EXE-CUTED.

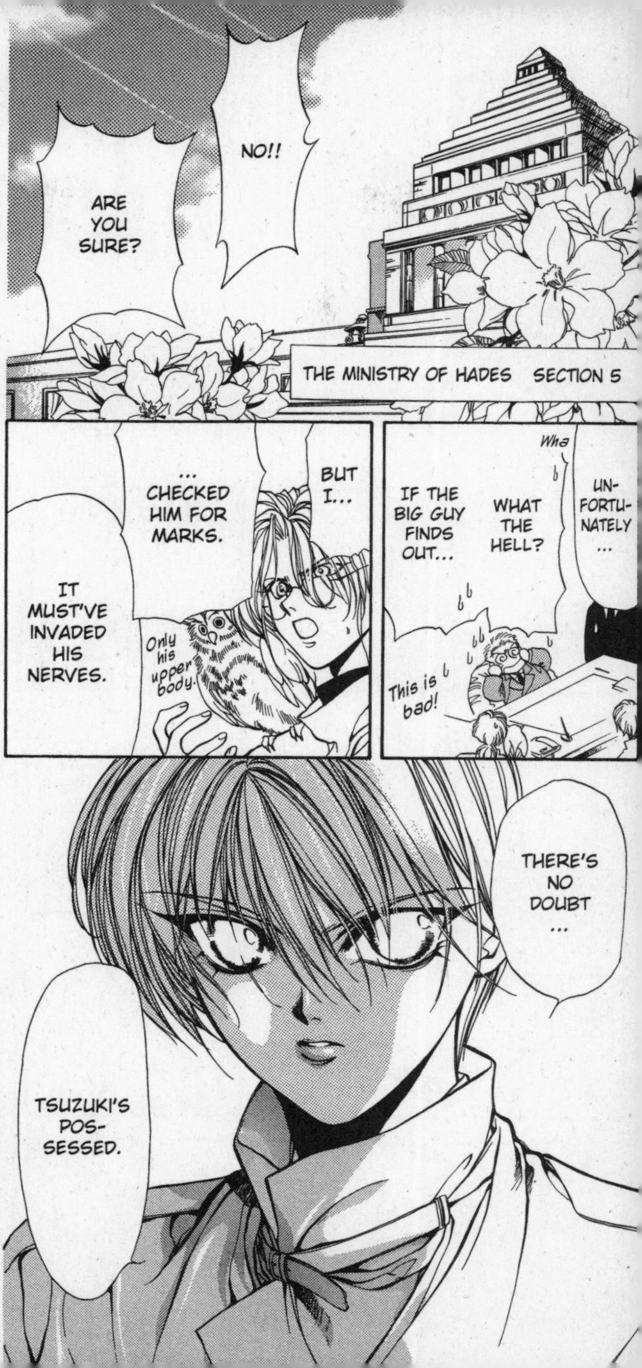
NO!!
ARE YOU SURE?
THE MINISTRY OF HADES SECTION 5
UN-FORTU-NATELY ...
Wha
WHAT THE HELL?
IF THE BIG GUY FINDS OUT...
This is bad!
BUT I...
... CHECKED HIM FOR MARKS.
IT MUST'VE INVADED HIS NERVES.
Only his upper body.
THERE'S NO DOUBT ...
TSUZUKI'S POS-SESSED.

In this arc, we meet Watari, the guy in the glasses, again. (He also made a brief appearance in the Nagasaki story, remember?) He was originally supposed to help Tsuzuki and Hisoka reconcile, but that part was cut. (Poor Doctor Watari!) He appears a lot in this story, though. I like him. He's the kind of character I can forgive no matter what he does. He's also easy for me to maneuver and I appreciate that. Is he close to becoming a regular? Maybe...

Hang in there Watari!!

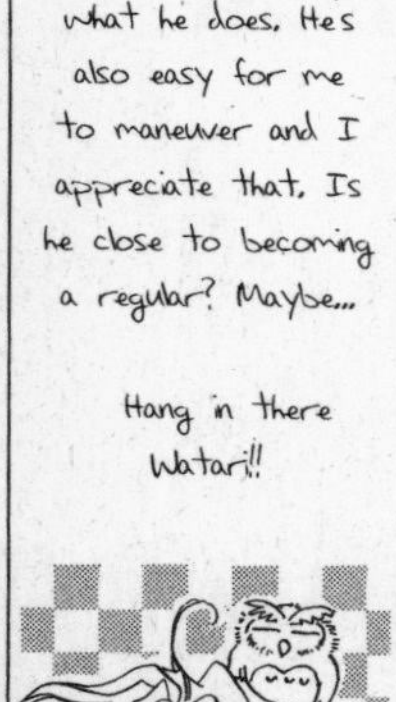
Huh ?

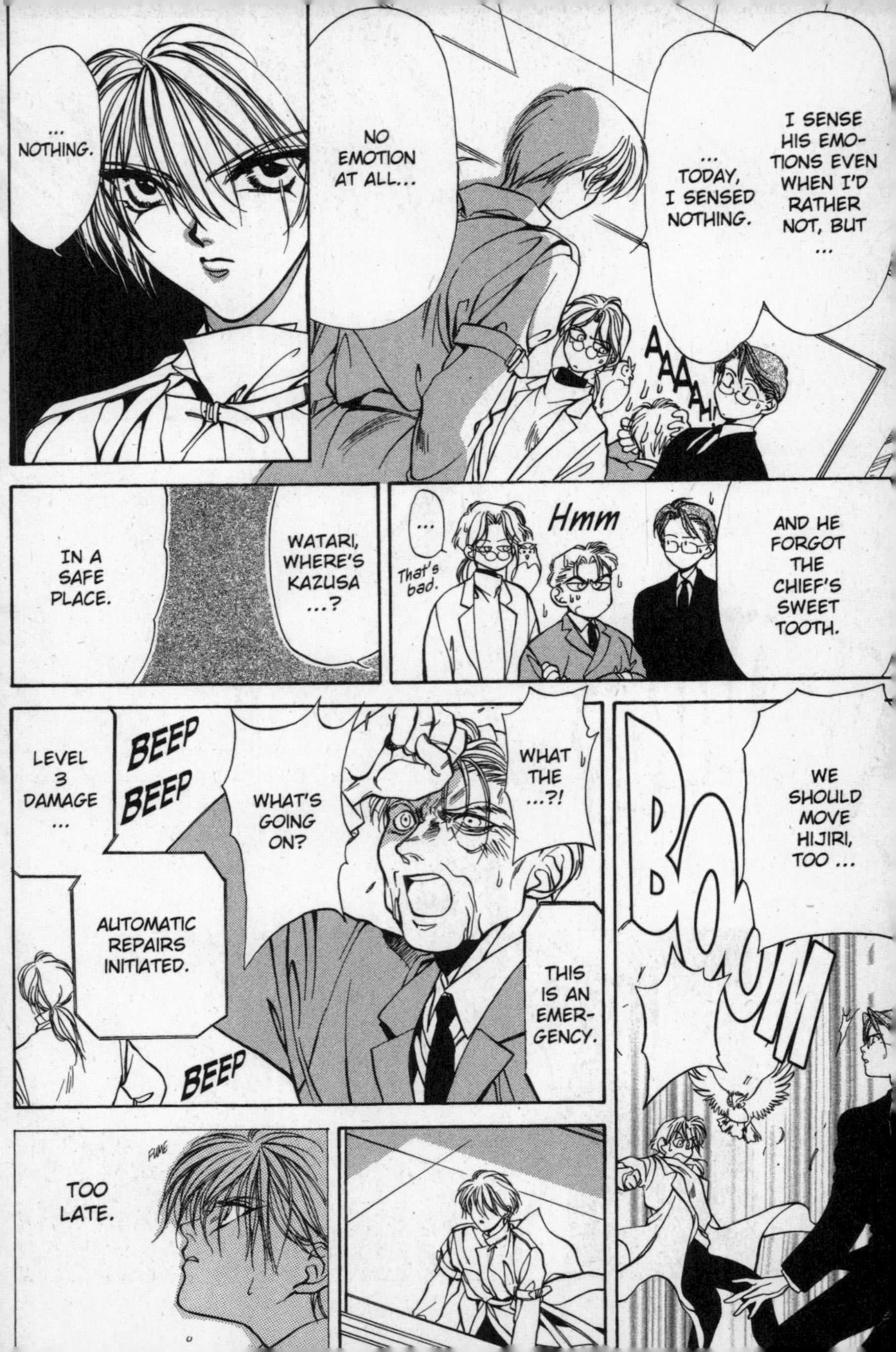
I SENSE HIS EMOTIONS EVEN WHEN I'D RATHER NOT, BUT ...
... TODAY, I SENSED NOTHING.
AAAAH!
NO EMOTION AT ALL...
... NOTHING.
AND HE FORGOT THE CHIEF'S SWEET TOOTH.
Hmm
...
That's bad.
WATARI, WHERE'S KAZUSA ...?
IN A SAFE PLACE.
WE SHOULD MOVE HIJIRI, TOO ...
BOOM
WHAT THE ...?!
WHAT'S GOING ON?
THIS IS AN EMERGENCY.
BEEP BEEP
LEVEL 3 DAMAGE ...
AUTOMATIC REPAIRS INITIATED.
BEEP
FUME
TOO LATE.

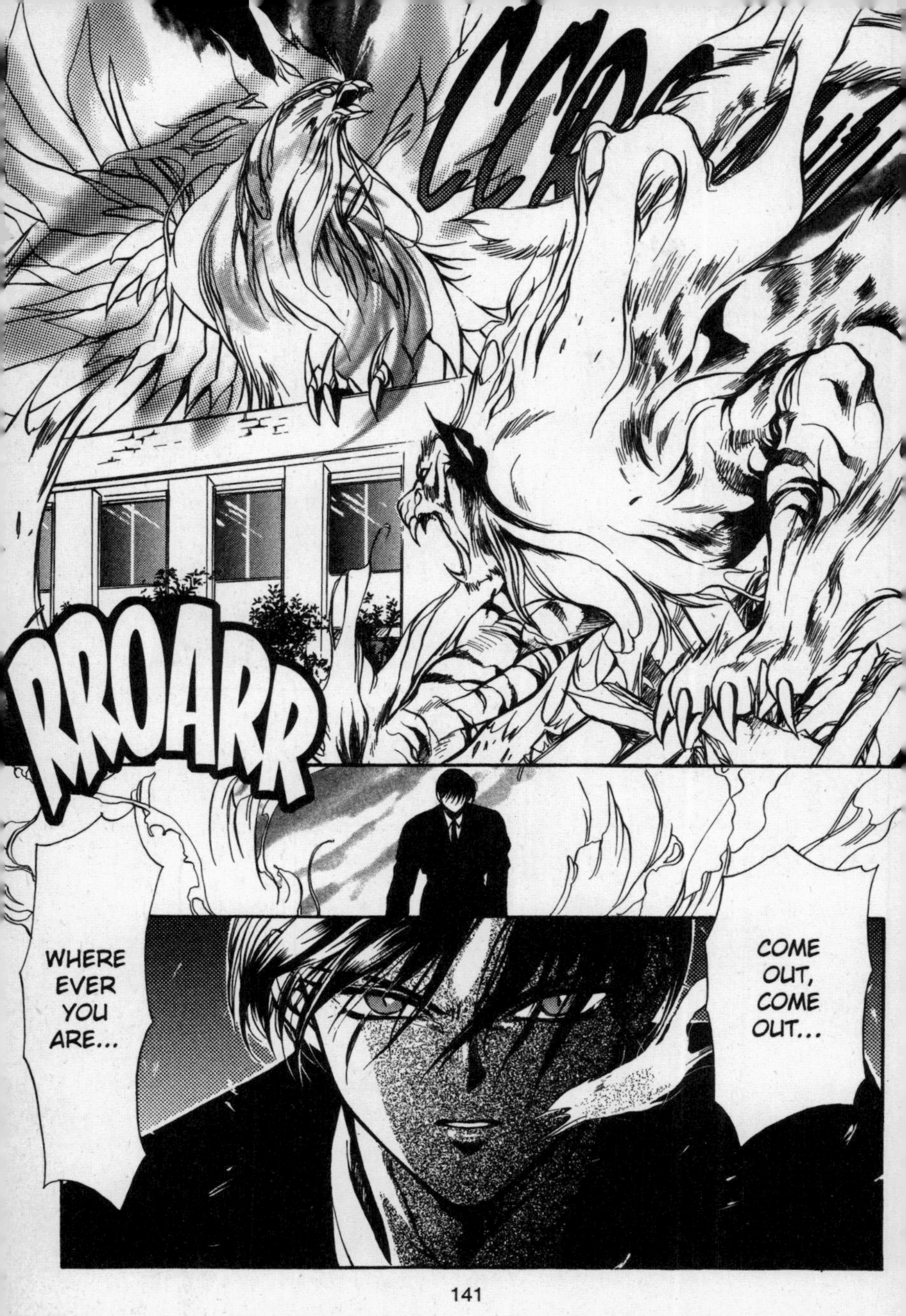
RROARR
COME OUT, COME OUT...
WHERE EVER YOU ARE...

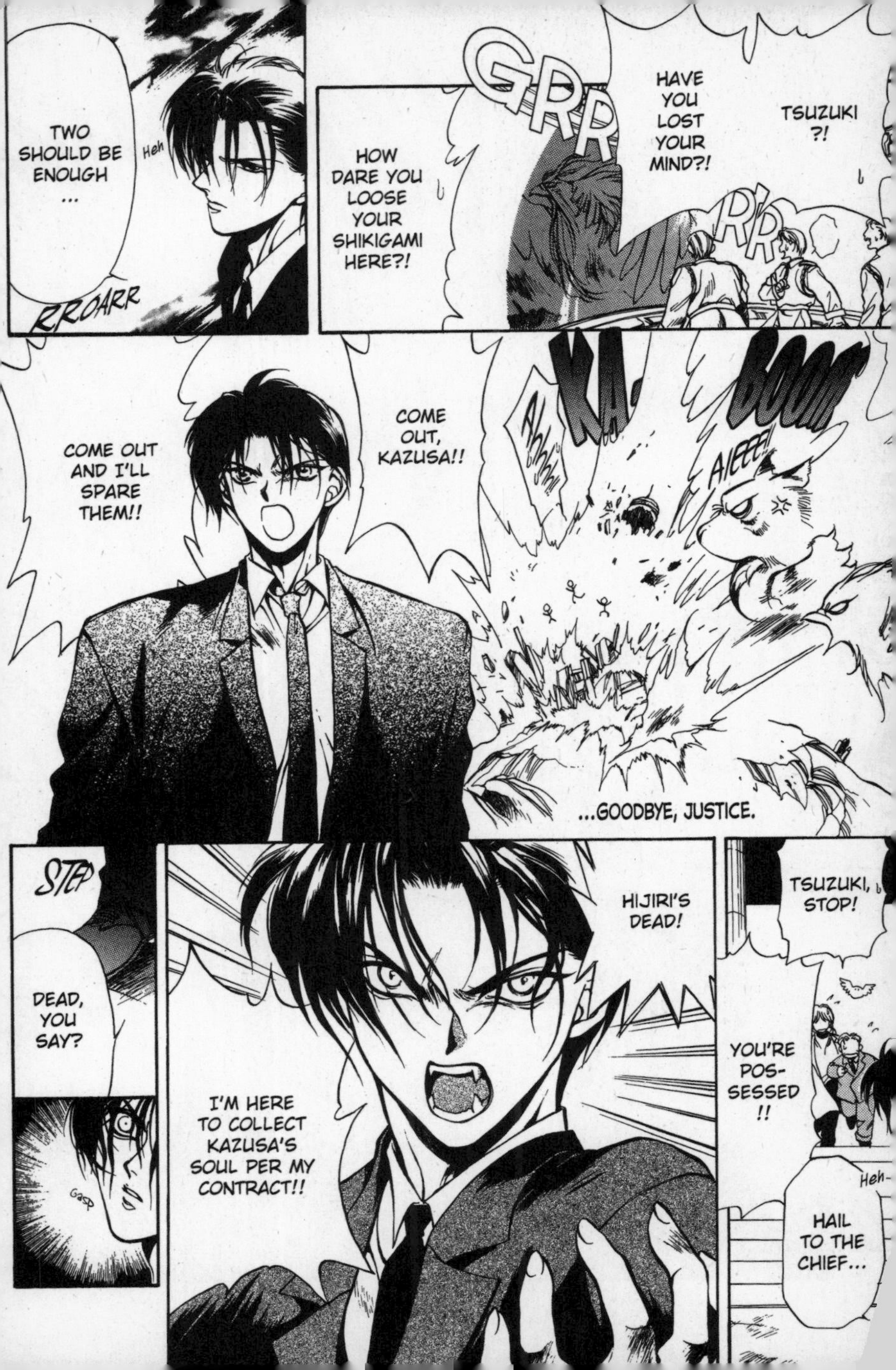
TSUZUKI ?!
HAVE YOU LOST YOUR MIND?!
GRR
RRR
HOW DARE YOU LOOSE YOUR SHIKIGAMI HERE?!
Heh
TWO SHOULD BE ENOUGH ...
RROARR
KA-
BOOM
AIEEE!!
...GOODBYE, JUSTICE.
COME OUT, KAZUSA!!
COME OUT AND I'LL SPARE THEM!!
TSUZUKI, STOP!
YOU'RE POS-SESSED !!
Heh-
HAIL TO THE CHIEF...
HIJIRI'S DEAD!
I'M HERE TO COLLECT KAZUSA'S SOUL PER MY CONTRACT!!
STEP
DEAD, YOU SAY?
Gasp

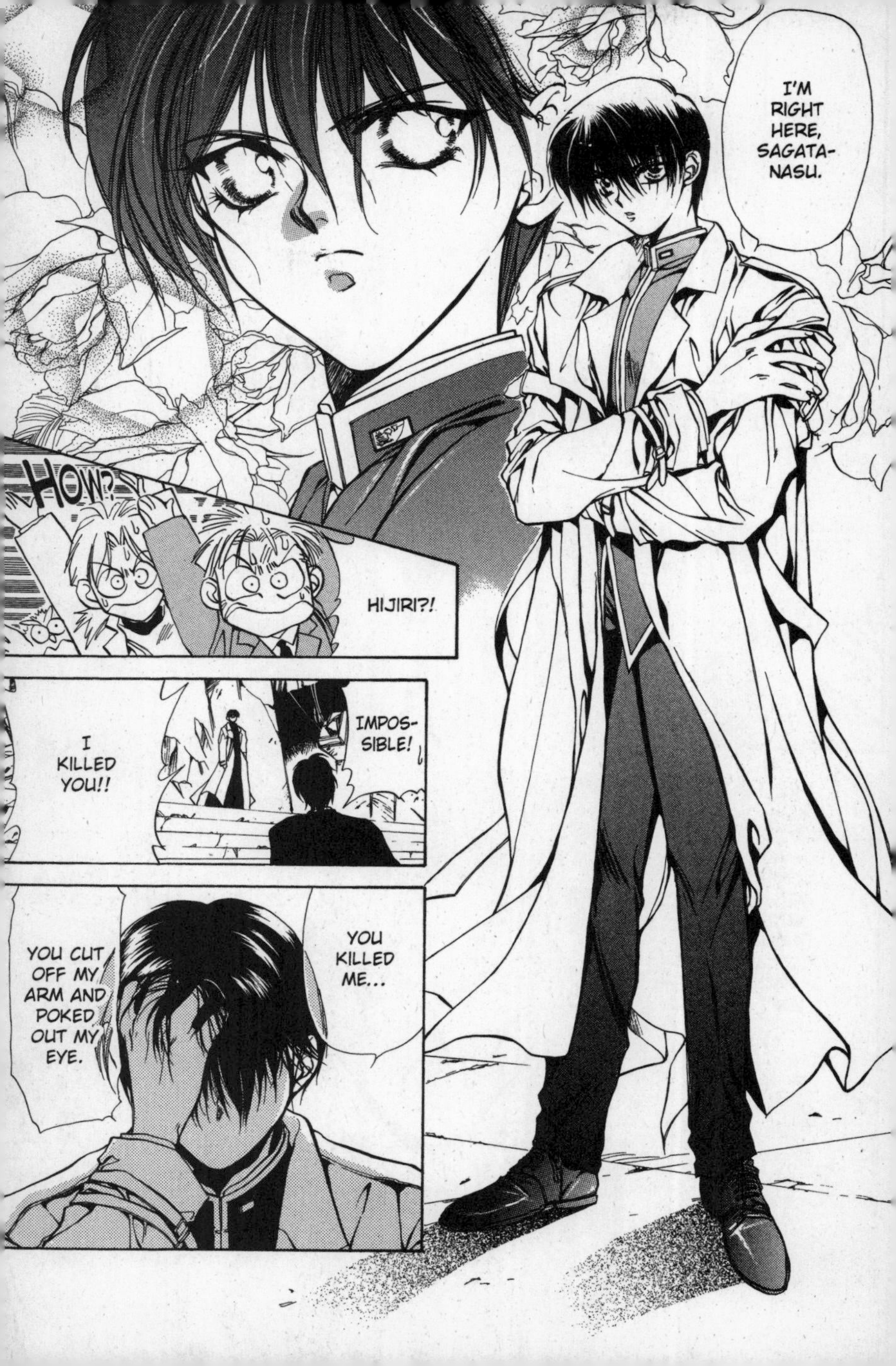
I'M RIGHT HERE, SAGATA-NASU.
HOW?
HIJIRI?!
IMPOS-SIBLE!
I KILLED YOU!!
YOU KILLED ME...
YOU CUT OFF MY ARM AND POKED OUT MY EYE.

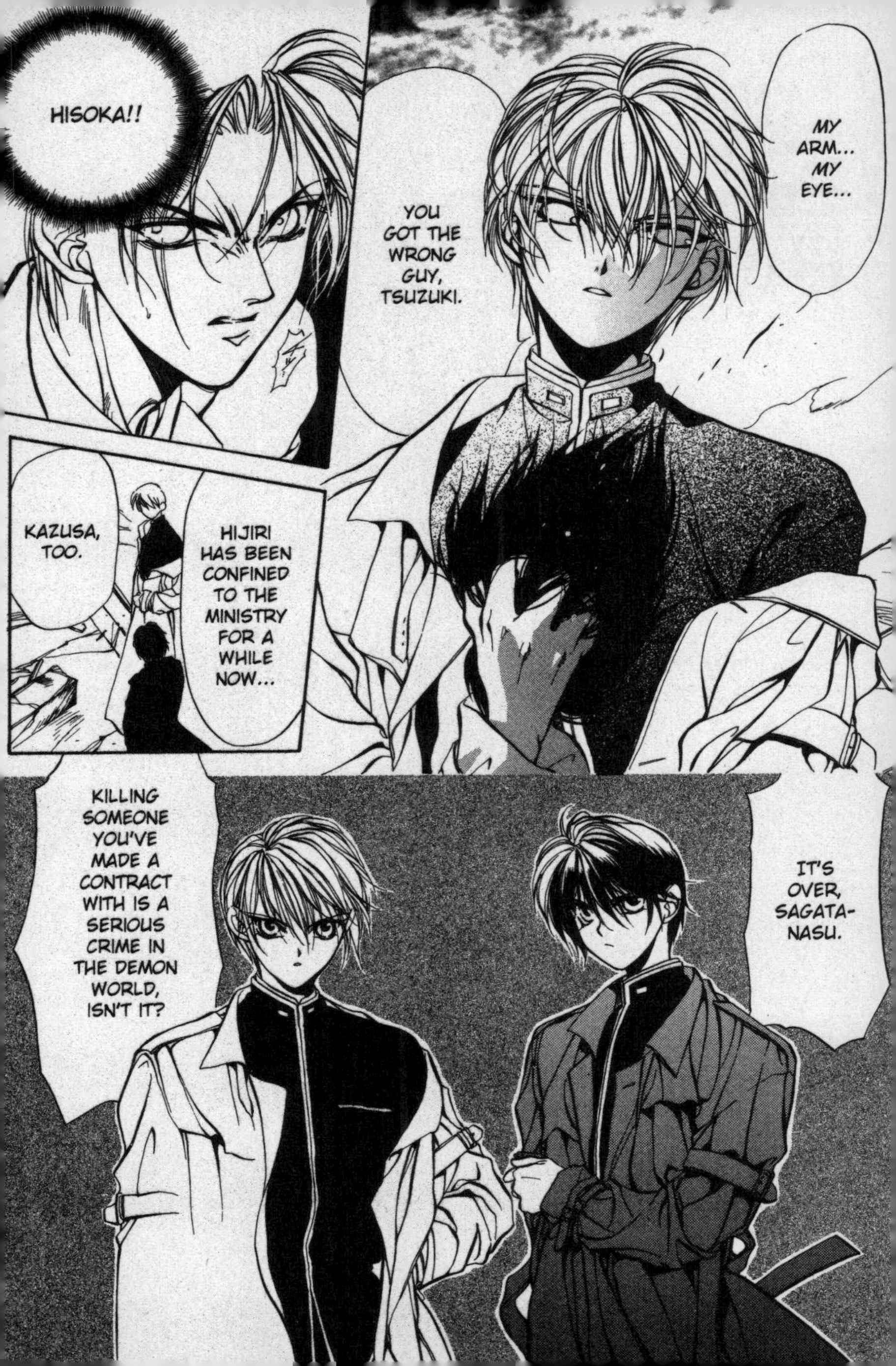
MY ARM... MY EYE...
YOU GOT THE WRONG GUY, TSUZUKI.
HISOKA!!
HIJIRI HAS BEEN CONFINED TO THE MINISTRY FOR A WHILE NOW...
KAZUSA, TOO.
IT'S OVER, SAGATA-NASU.
KILLING SOMEONE YOU'VE MADE A CONTRACT WITH IS A SERIOUS CRIME IN THE DEMON WORLD, ISN'T IT?

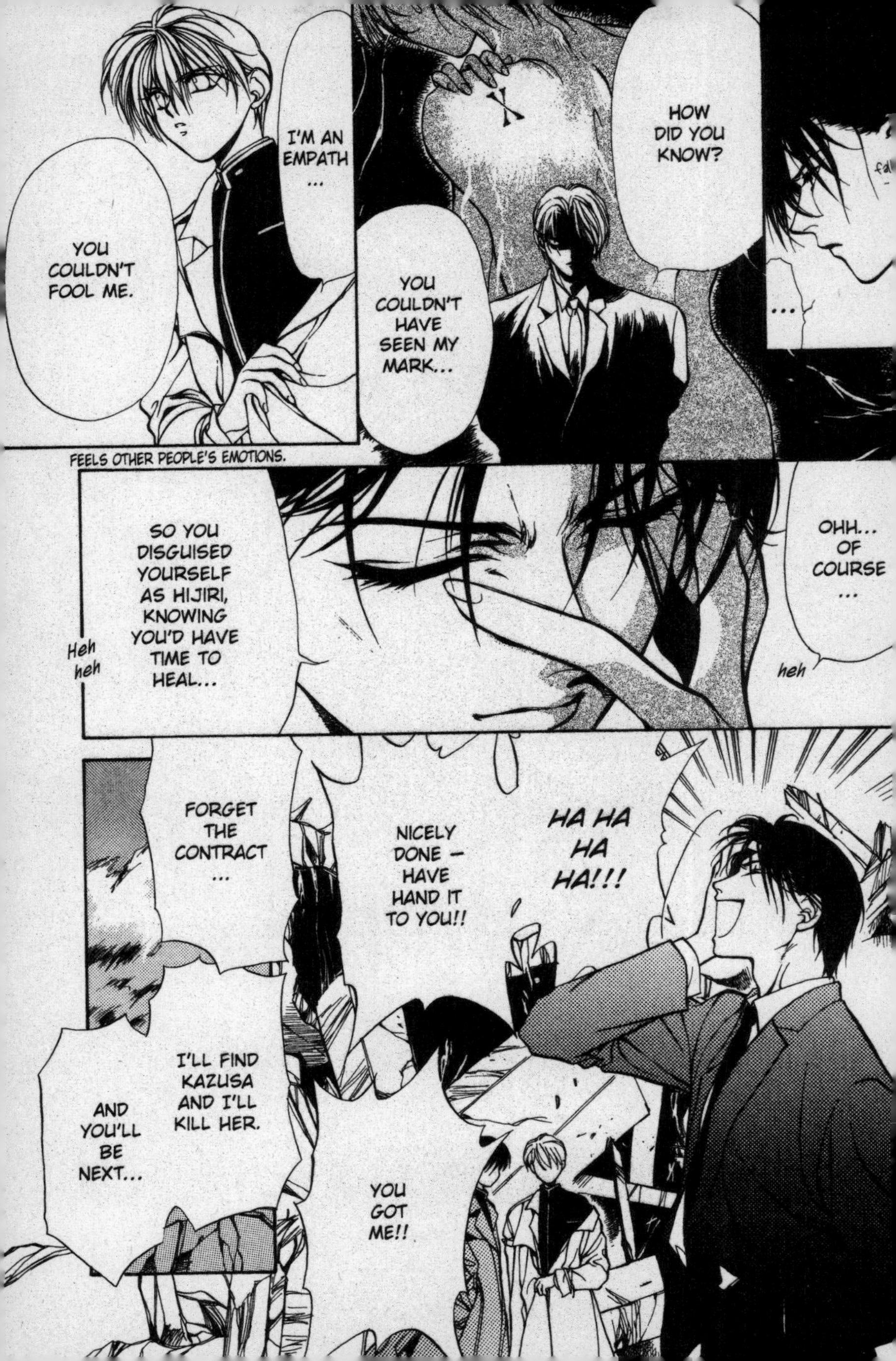
...
HOW DID YOU KNOW?
YOU COULDN'T HAVE SEEN MY MARK...
I'M AN EMPATH ...
YOU COULDN'T FOOL ME.
FEELS OTHER PEOPLE'S EMOTIONS.
OHH... OF COURSE ...
heh
SO YOU DISGUISED YOURSELF AS HIJIRI, KNOWING YOU'D HAVE TIME TO HEAL...
Heh heh
HA HA HA HA!!!
NICELY DONE — HAVE HAND IT TO YOU!!
YOU GOT ME!!
FORGET THE CONTRACT ...
I'LL FIND KAZUSA AND I'LL KILL HER.
AND YOU'LL BE NEXT...

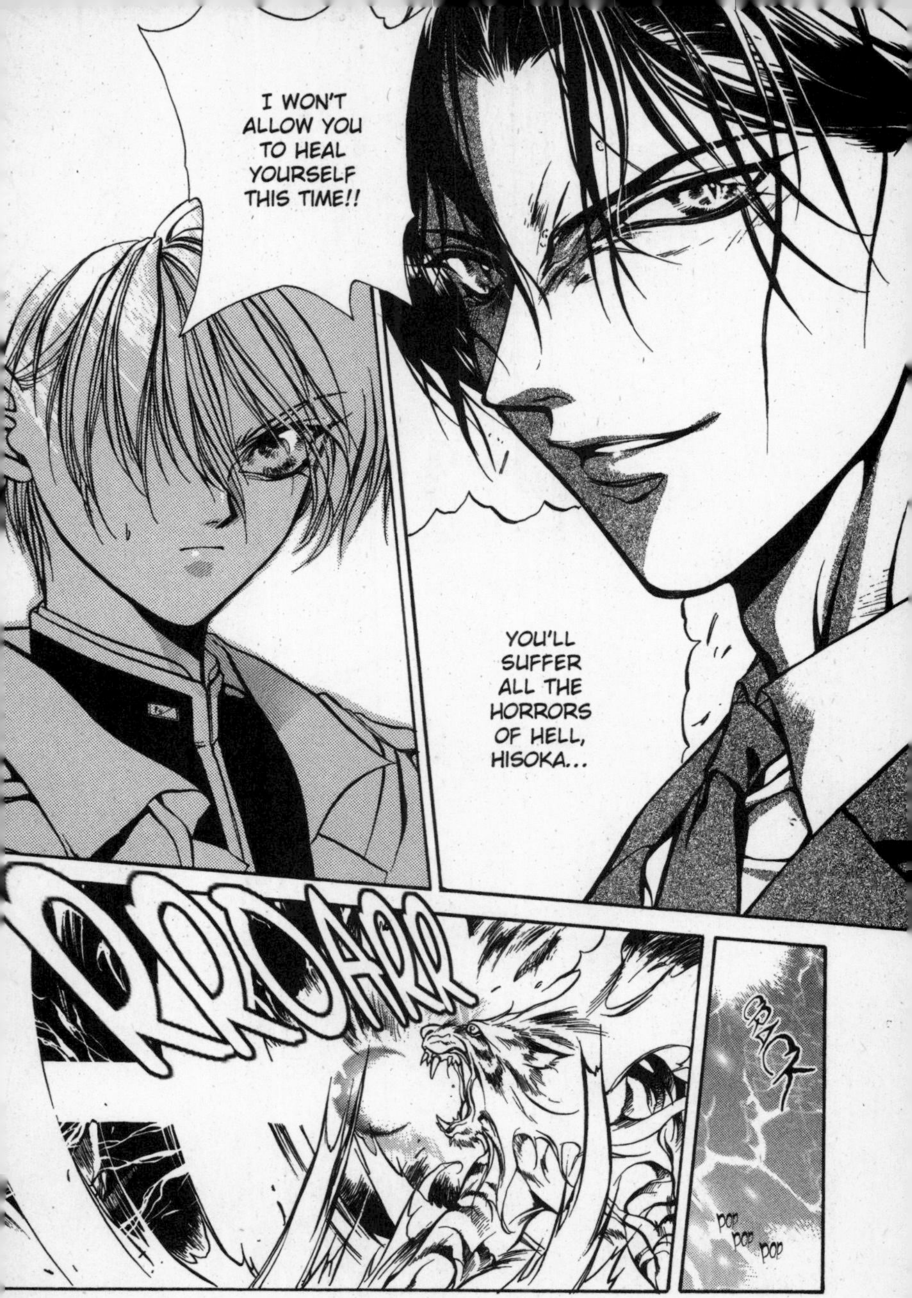
I WON'T ALLOW YOU TO HEAL YOURSELF THIS TIME!!
YOU'LL SUFFER ALL THE HORRORS OF HELL, HISOKA...
CRACK
pop pop pop
DODOARR

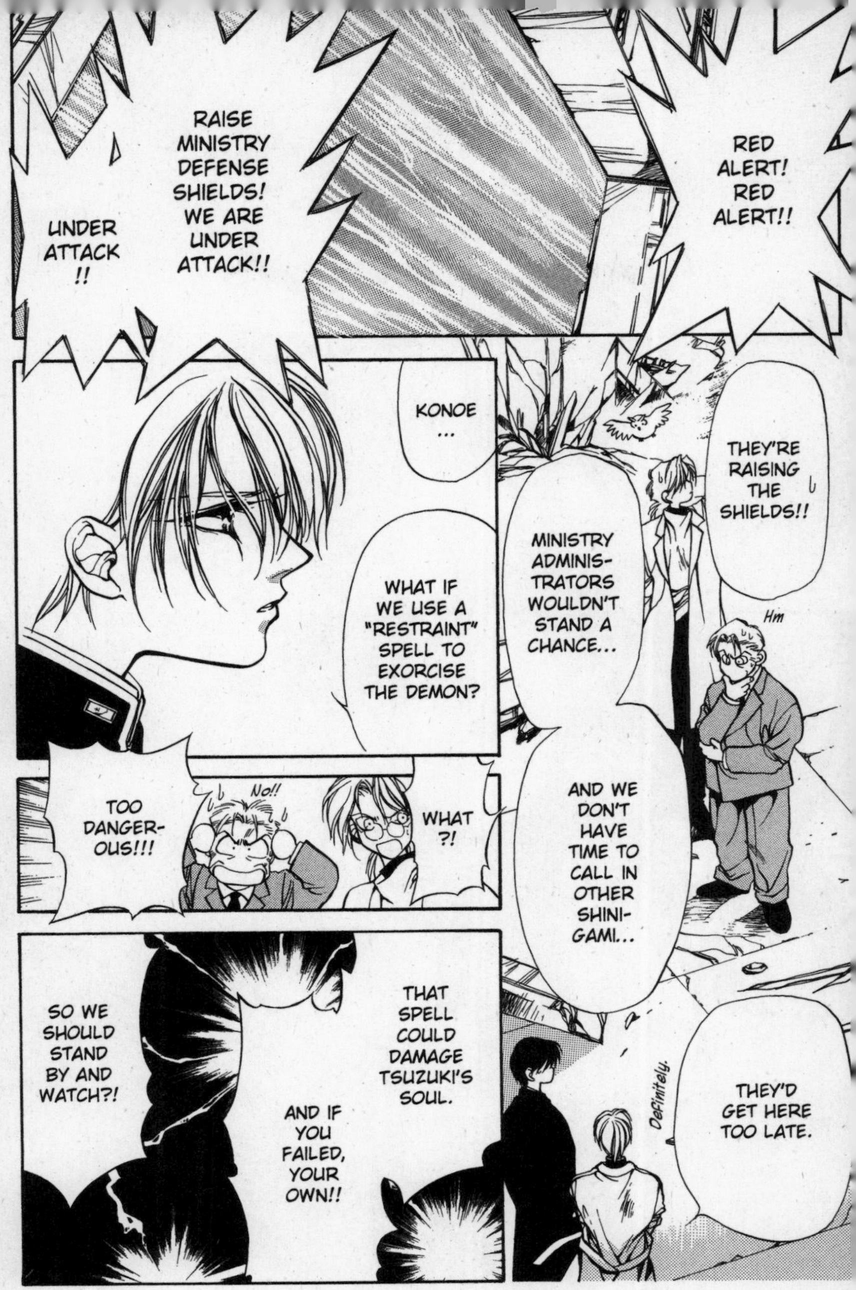
RED ALERT! RED ALERT!!
RAISE MINISTRY DEFENSE SHIELDS! WE ARE UNDER ATTACK!!
UNDER ATTACK!!
THEY'RE RAISING THE SHIELDS!!
MINISTRY ADMINIS-TRATORS WOULDN'T STAND A CHANCE...
Hm
AND WE DON'T HAVE TIME TO CALL IN OTHER SHINI-GAMI...
THEY'D GET HERE TOO LATE.
Definitely.
KONOE ...
WHAT IF WE USE A "RESTRAINT" SPELL TO EXORCISE THE DEMON?
WHAT ?!
No!!
TOO DANGER-OUS!!!
THAT SPELL COULD DAMAGE TSUZUKI'S SOUL.
AND IF YOU FAILED, YOUR OWN!!
SO WE SHOULD STAND BY AND WATCH?!

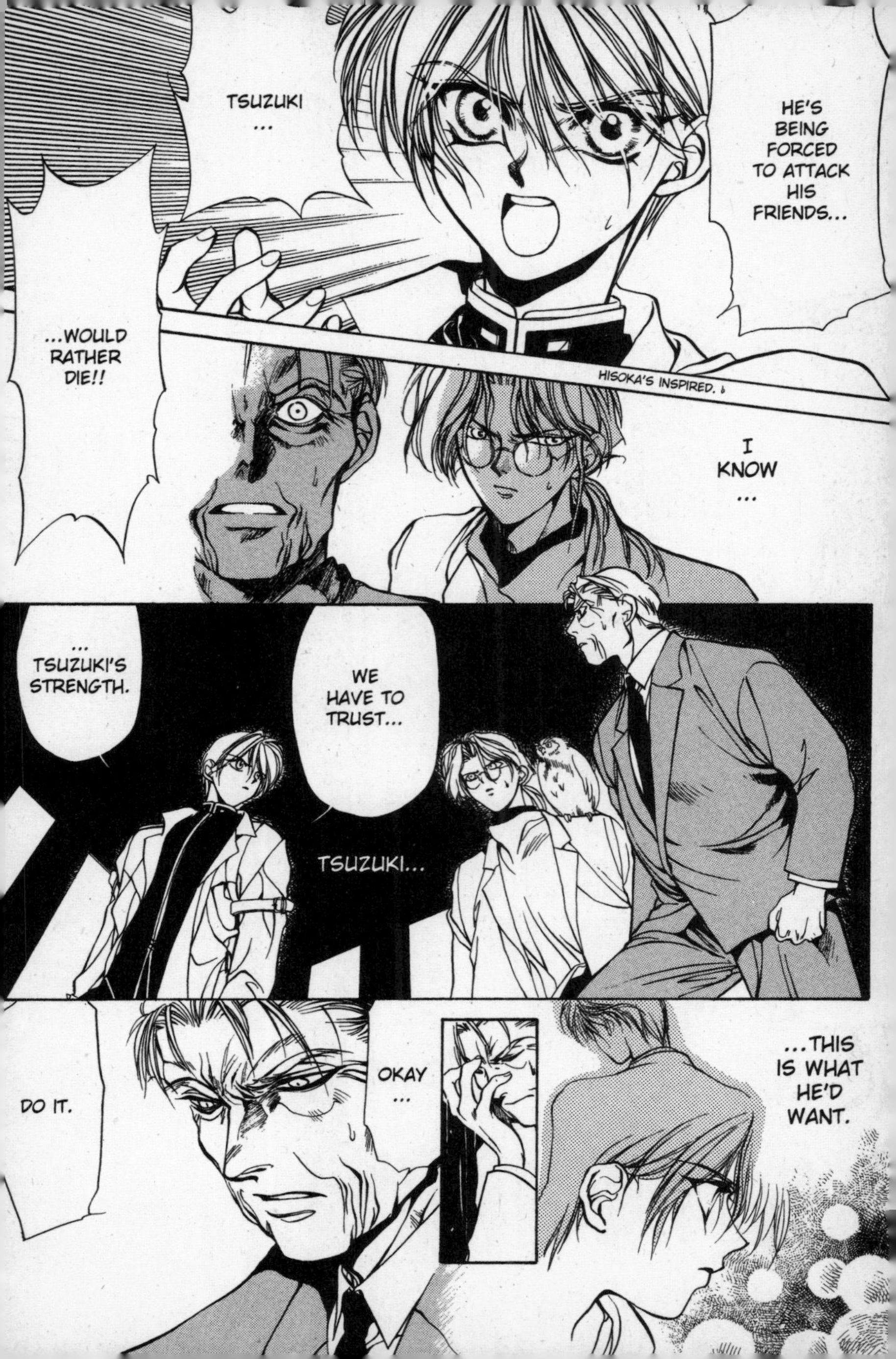
HE'S BEING FORCED TO ATTACK HIS FRIENDS...
TSUZUKI ...
...WOULD RATHER DIE!!
HISOKA'S INSPIRED.
I KNOW ...
WE HAVE TO TRUST...
... TSUZUKI'S STRENGTH.
TSUZUKI...
...THIS IS WHAT HE'D WANT.
OKAY ...
DO IT.

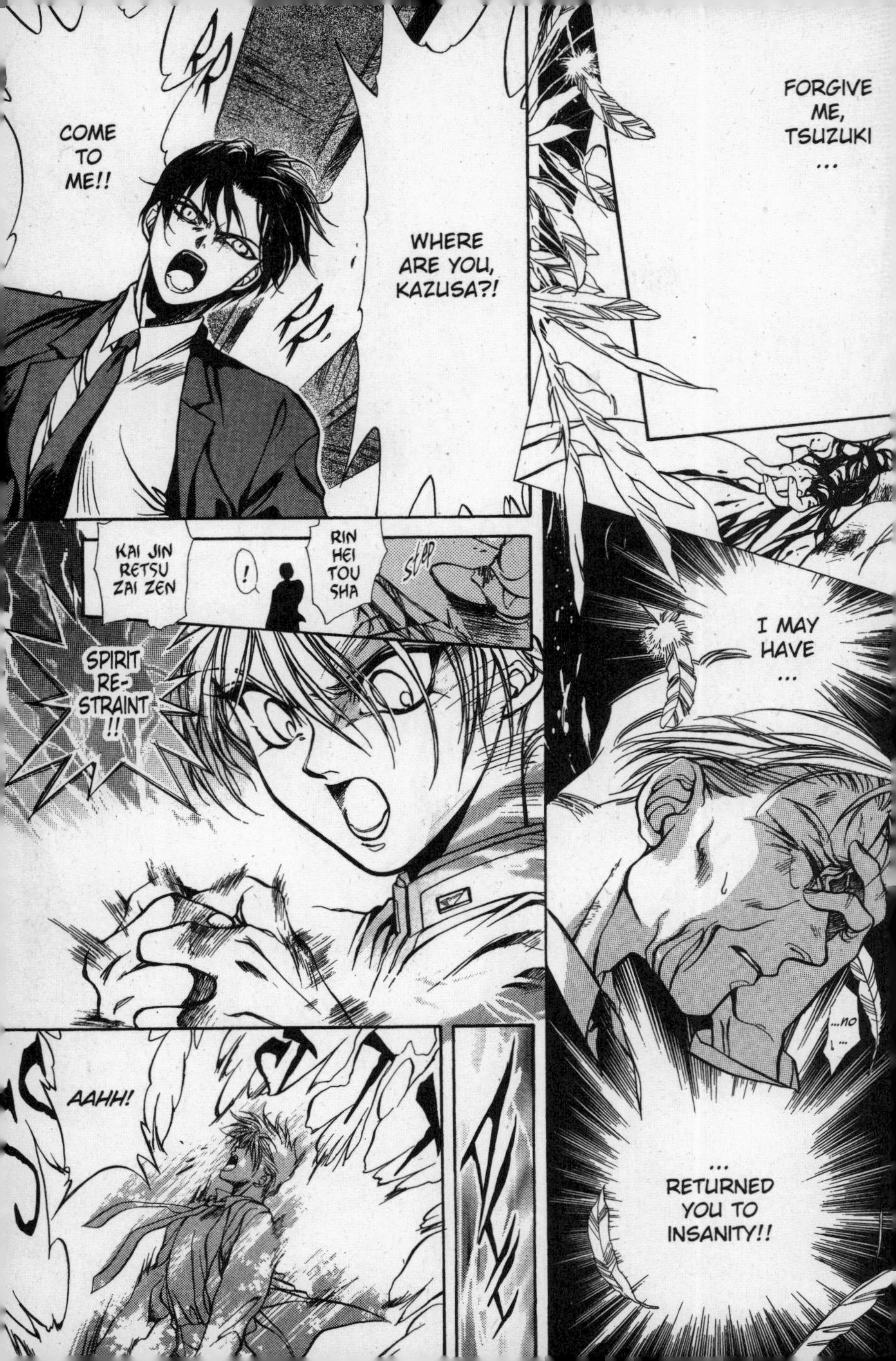
FORGIVE ME, TSUZUKI ...
I MAY HAVE ...
...no ...
... RETURNED YOU TO INSANITY!!
WHERE ARE YOU, KAZUSA?!
COME TO ME!!
RR
RR
RIN HEI TOU SHA
KAI JIN RETSU ZAI ZEN
!
SPIRIT RE-STRAINT!!
AAHH!

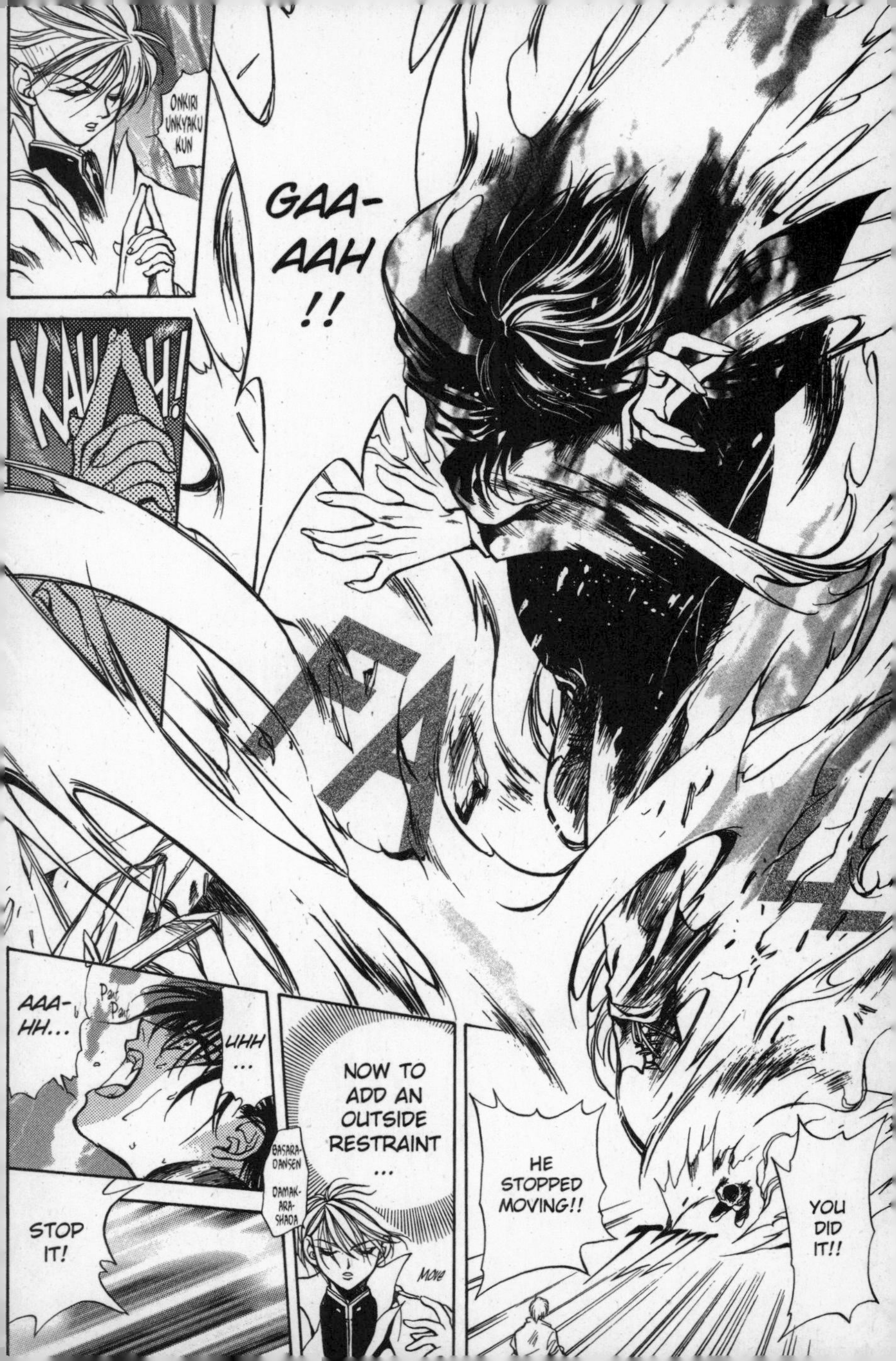
GAA-AAH!!
FA
ONKIRI UNKYAKU KUN
KAWAH!
YOU DID IT!!
HE STOPPED MOVING!!
NOW TO ADD AN OUTSIDE RESTRAINT ...
BASARA-DANSEN DAMAK-ARA-SHADA
Move
Pant Pant
UHH ...
AAA-HH...
STOP IT!

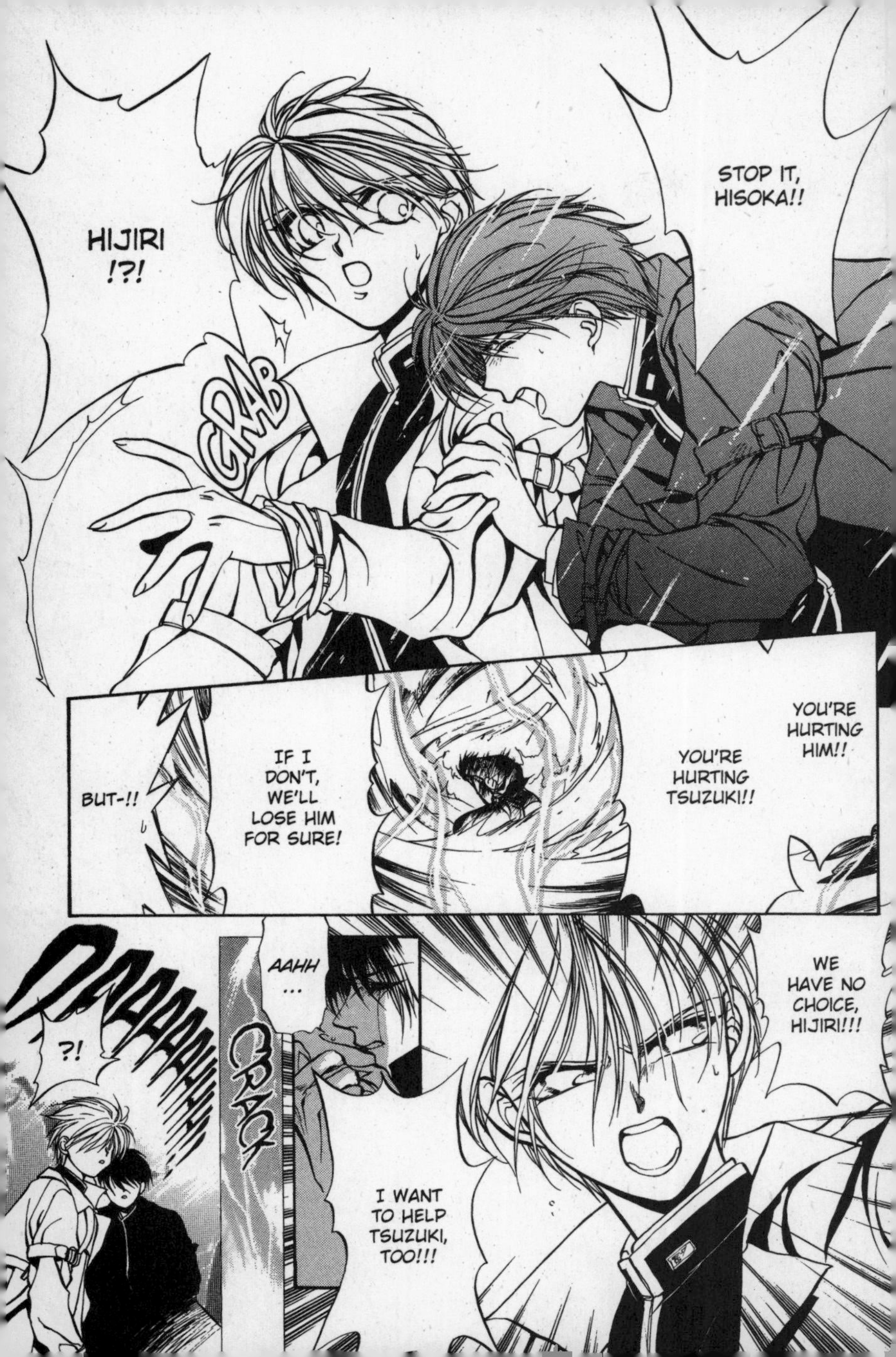
STOP IT, HISOKA!!
HIJIRI !?!
GRAB
YOU'RE HURTING HIM!!
YOU'RE HURTING TSUZUKI!!
IF I DON'T, WE'LL LOSE HIM FOR SURE!
BUT-!!
WE HAVE NO CHOICE, HIJIRI!!!
I WANT TO HELP TSUZUKI, TOO!!!
AAHH ...
CRACK
?!

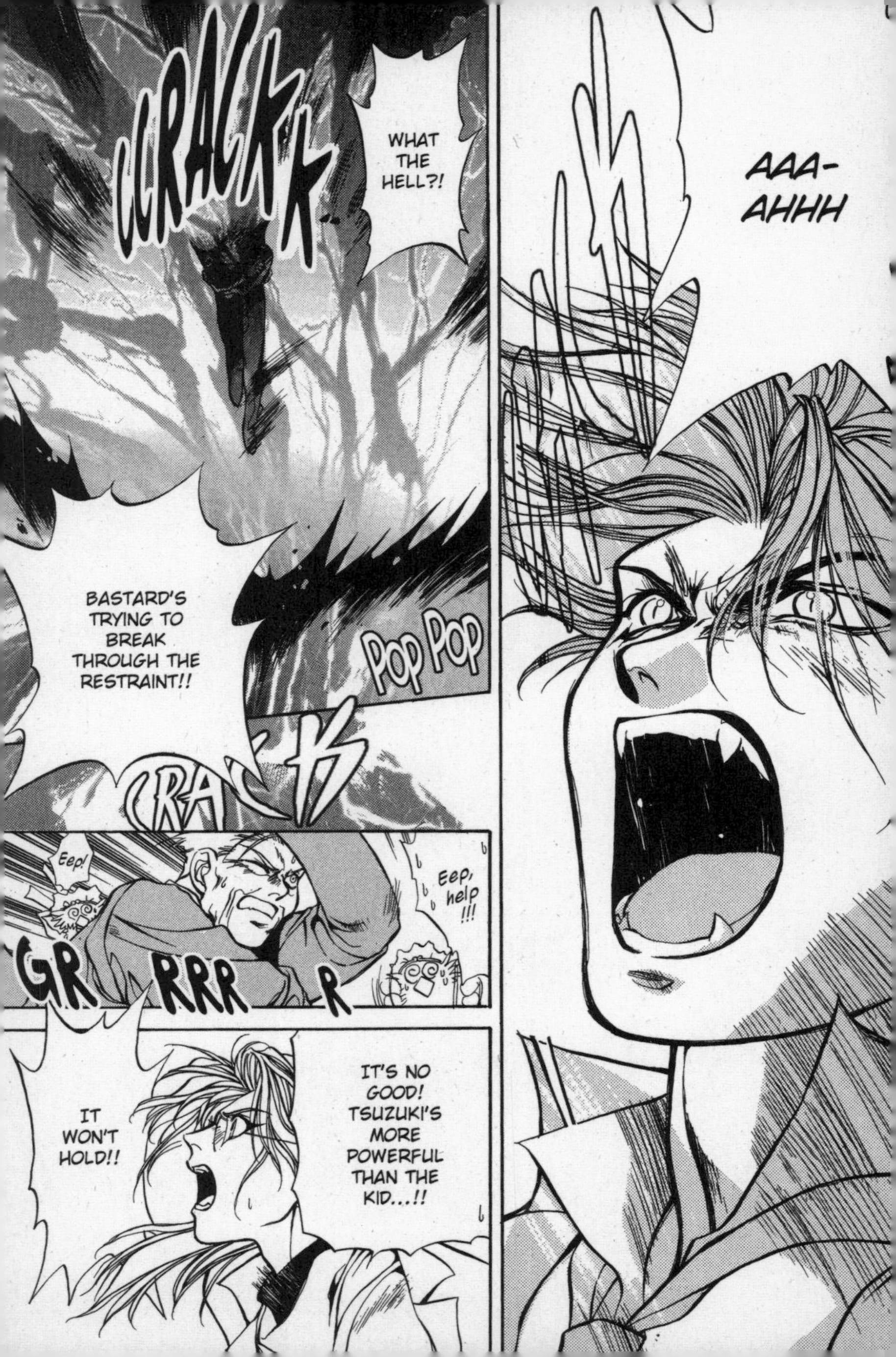
AAA-
AHHH
WHAT THE HELL?!
CRACKK
BASTARD'S TRYING TO BREAK THROUGH THE RESTRAINT!!
Pop Pop
CRA K
Eep, help!!!
Eep!
GR RRR R
IT'S NO GOOD! TSUZUKI'S MORE POWERFUL THAN THE KID...!!
IT WON'T HOLD!!

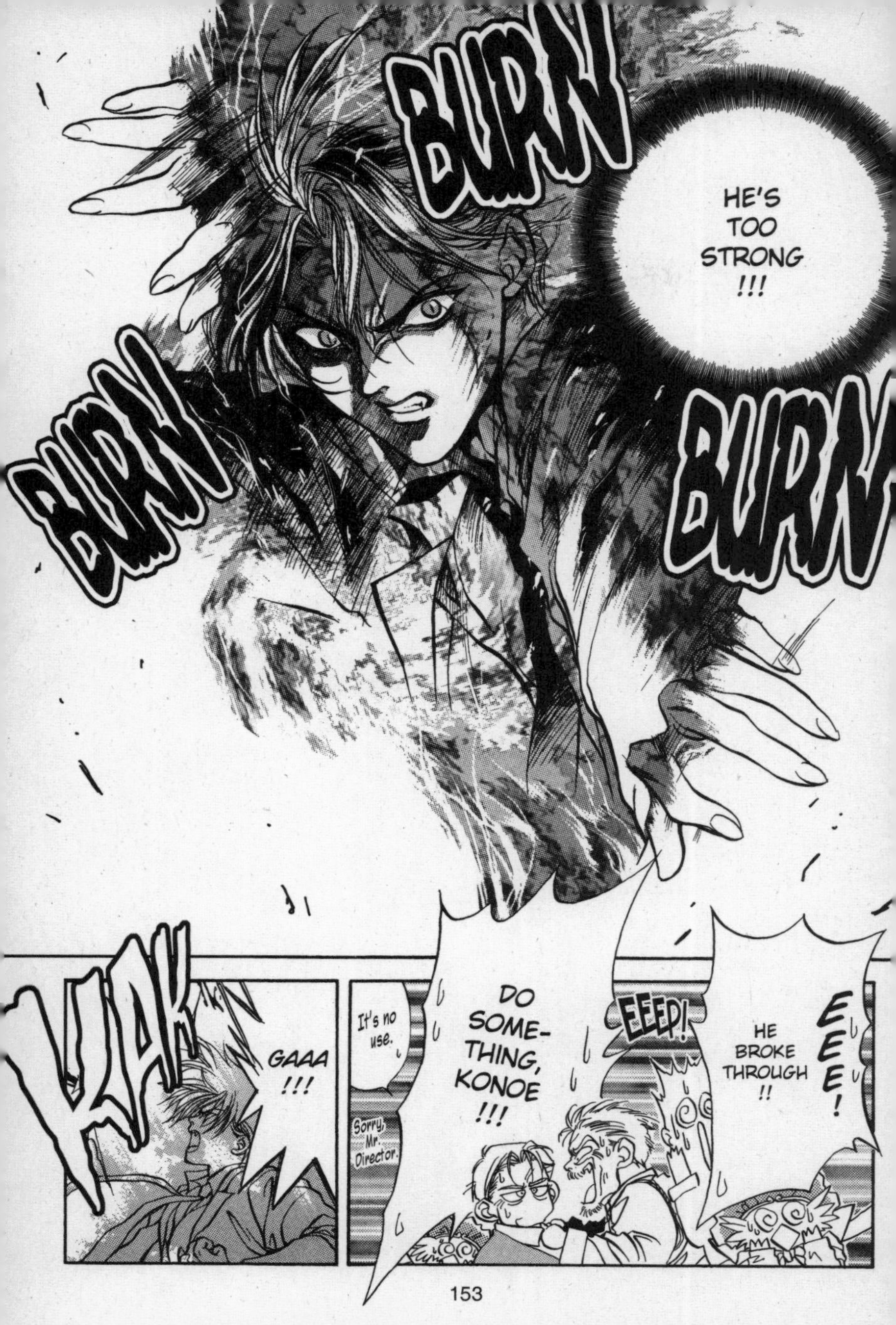
BURN
HE'S TOO STRONG !!!
BURN
BURN
EEE!
HE BROKE THROUGH !!
EEEP!
DO SOME-THING, KONOE !!!
It's no use.
Sorry, Mr. Director.
KRAK
GAAA !!!

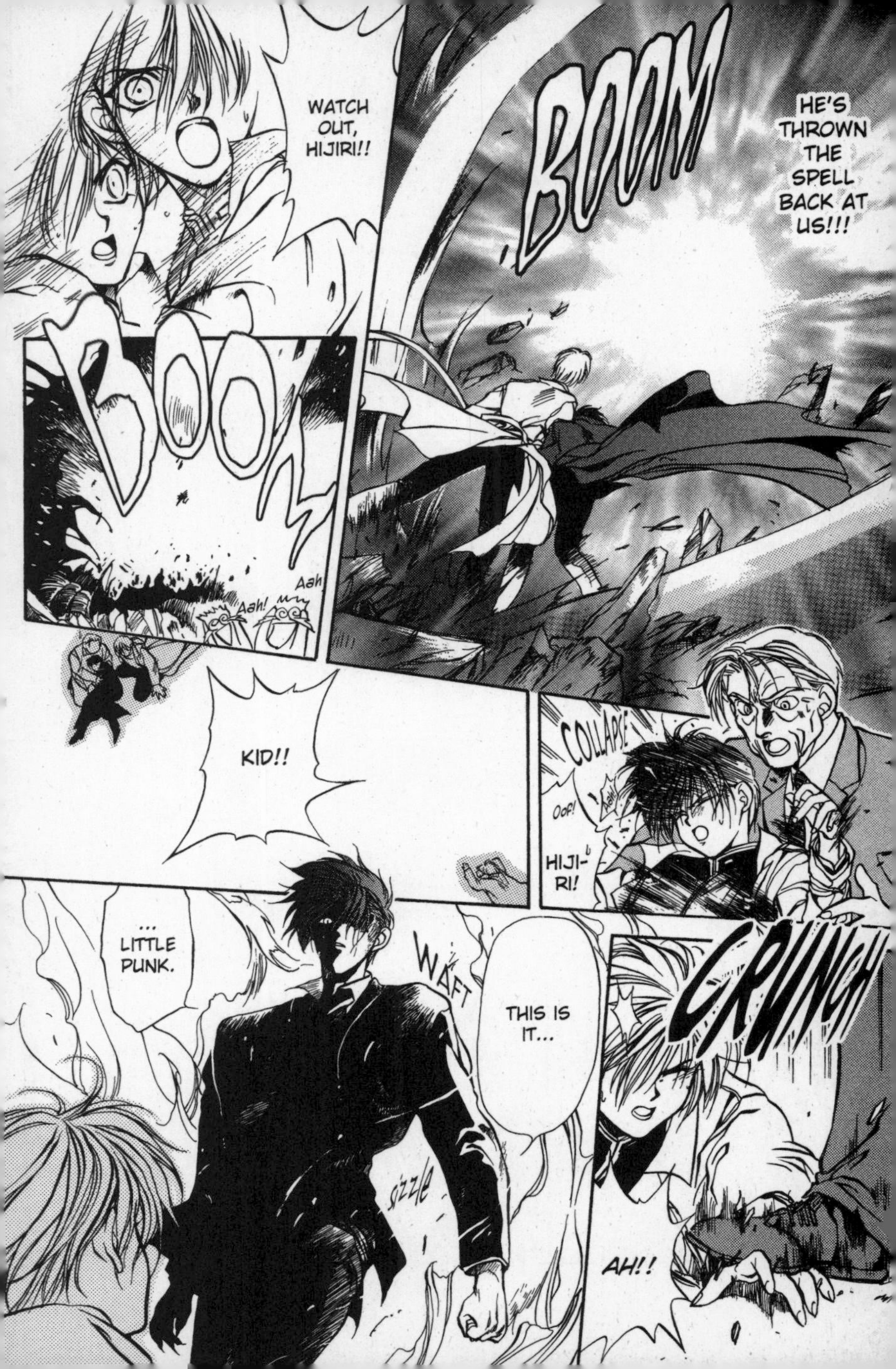
BOOM
HE'S THROWN THE SPELL BACK AT US!!!
WATCH OUT, HIJIRI!!
BOOM
Aah
Aah!
COLLAPSE
Aah!
Oof!
HIJI-RI!
KID!!
CRUNCH
AH!!
WAFT
THIS IS IT...
... LITTLE PUNK.
sizzle

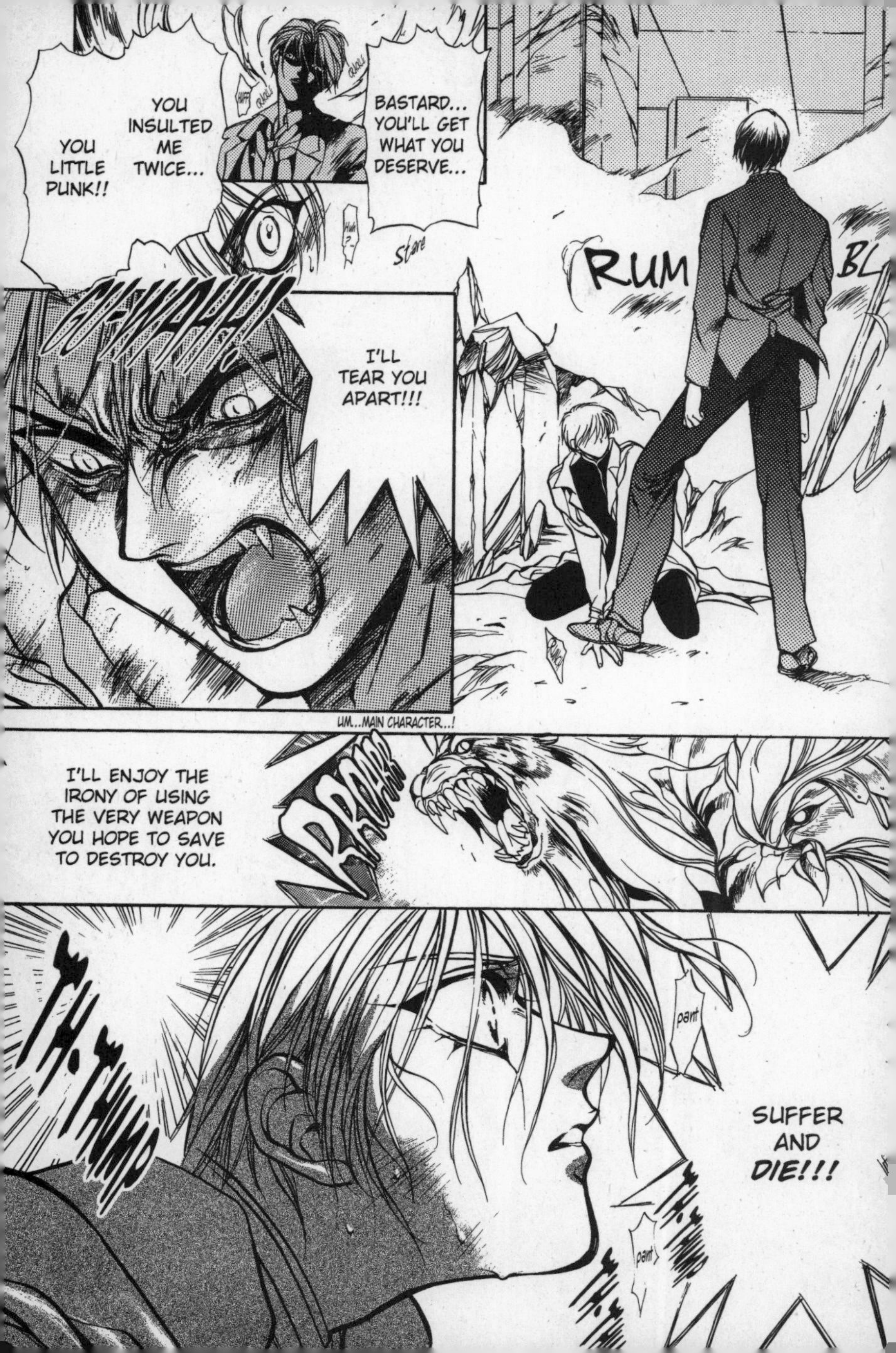
RUM
BL
BASTARD... YOU'LL GET WHAT YOU DESERVE...
YOU INSULTED ME TWICE...
YOU LITTLE PUNK!!
Huh?
Stare
I'LL TEAR YOU APART!!!
UM...MAIN CHARACTER...!
I'LL ENJOY THE IRONY OF USING THE VERY WEAPON YOU HOPE TO SAVE TO DESTROY YOU.
SUFFER AND DIE!!!
pant
TH-THUMP
pant

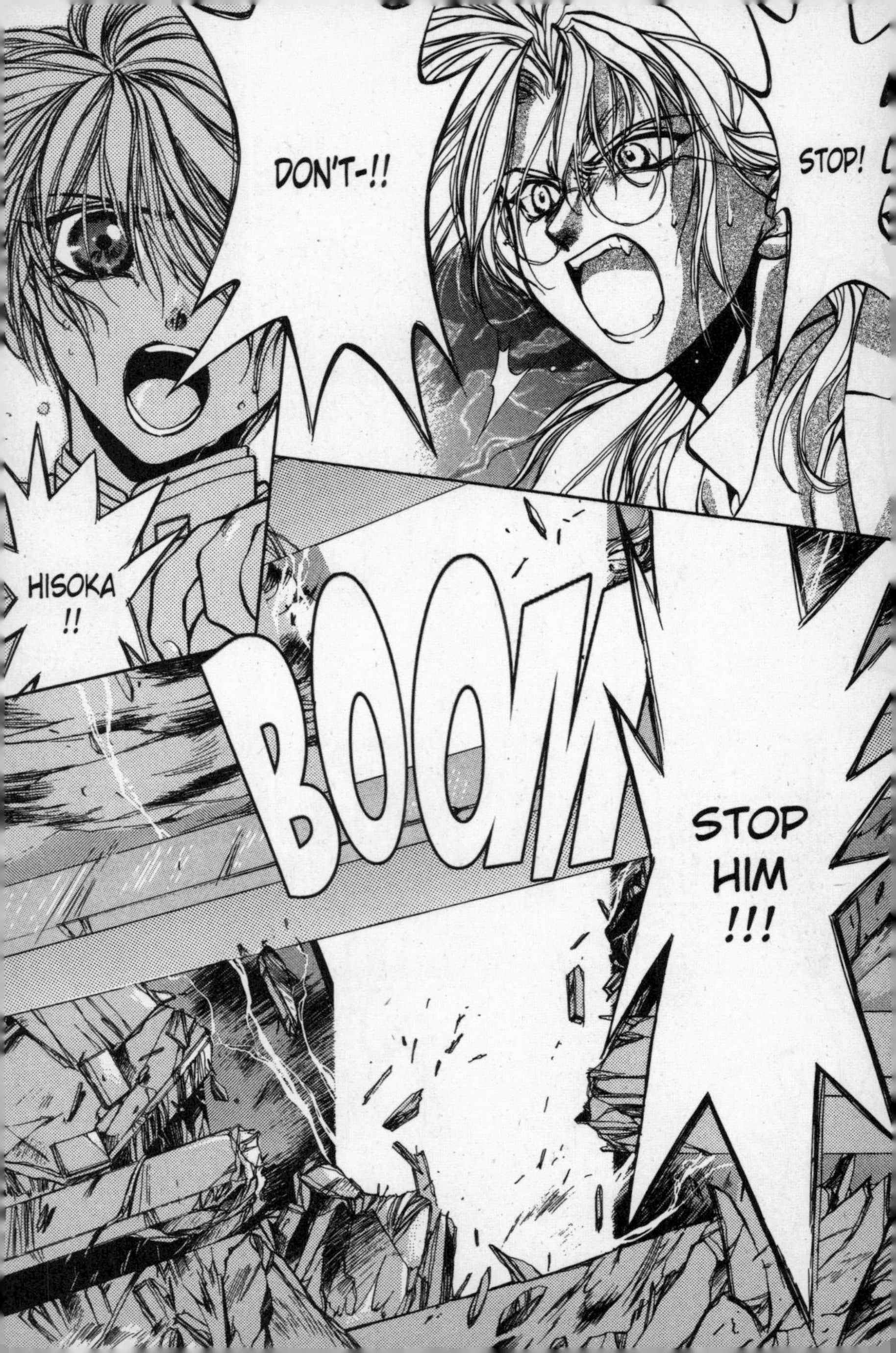
STOP!
DON'T-!!
HISOKA !!
BOOM
STOP HIM !!!

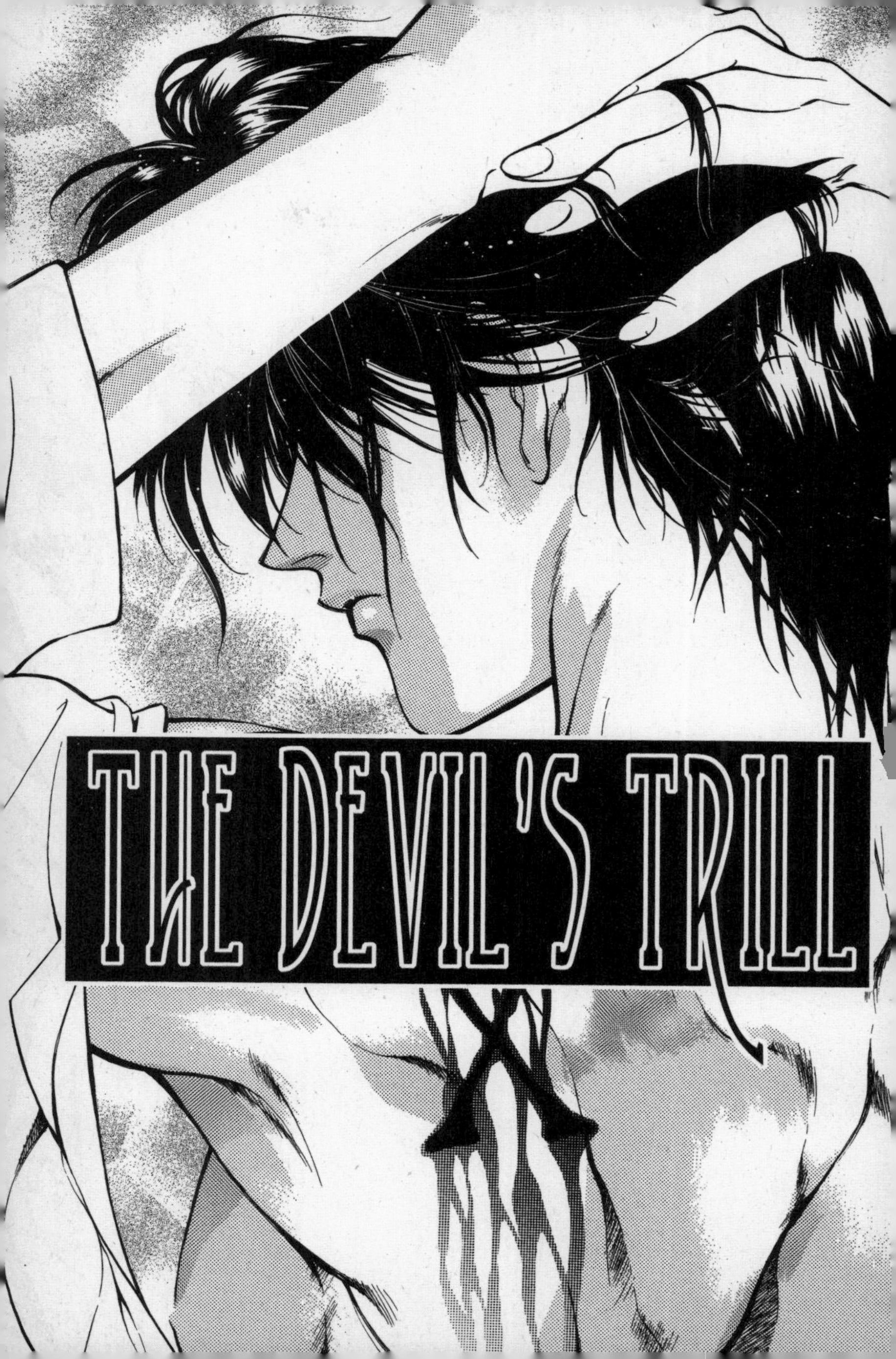
THE DEVIL'S TRILL

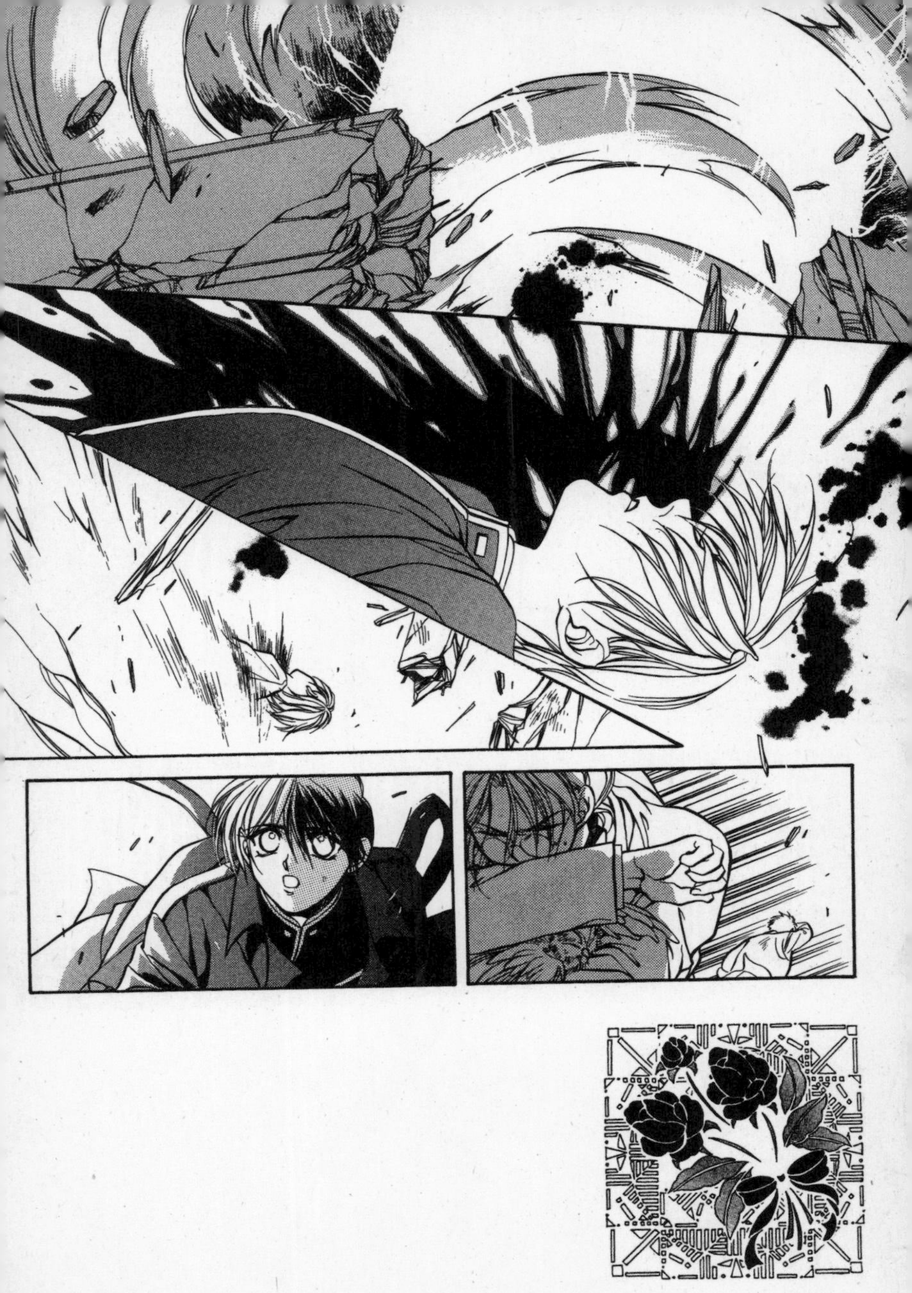

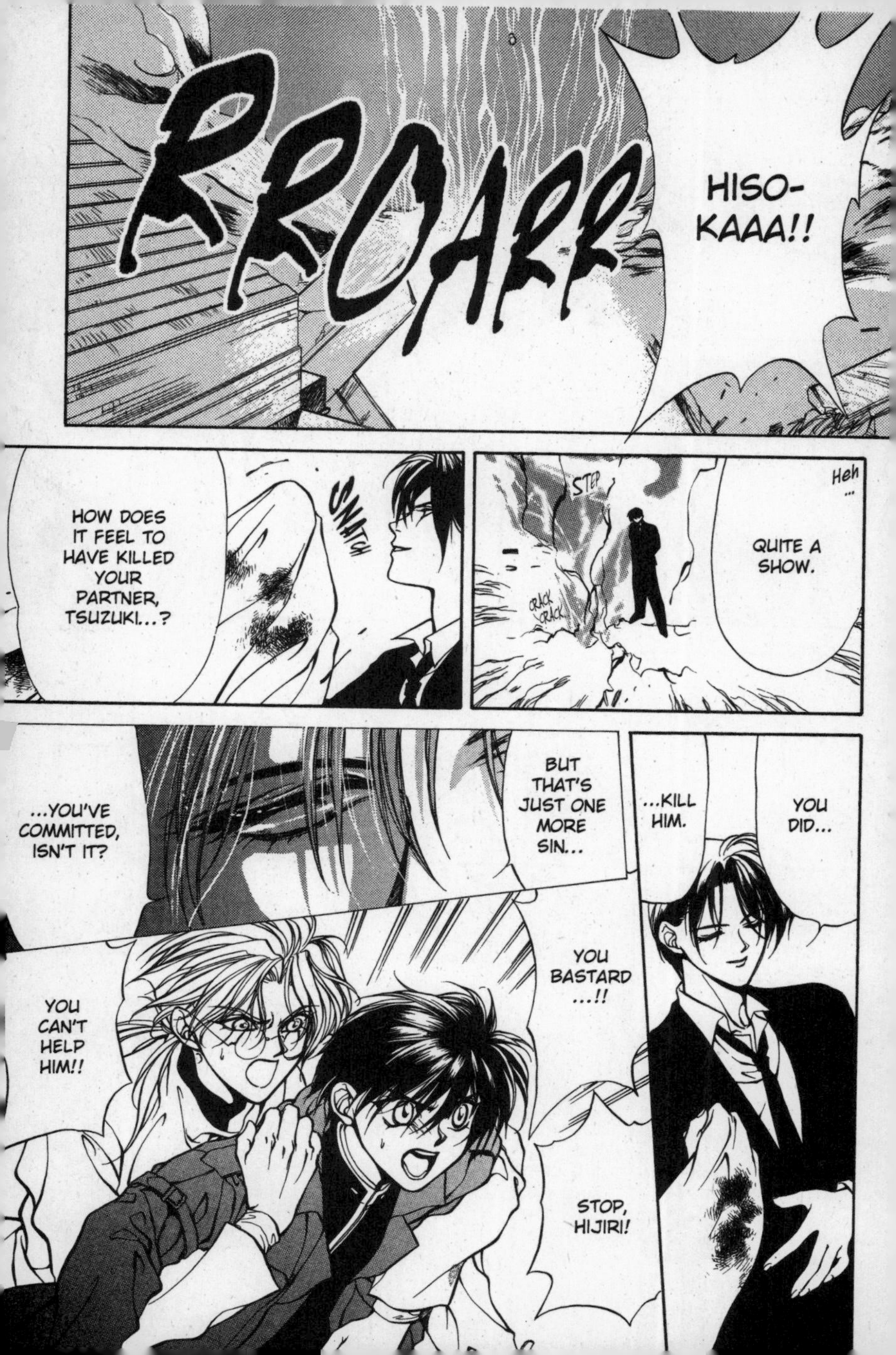
HISO-KAAA!!
RROARR
Heh...
QUITE A SHOW.
STEP
CRACK CRACK
SNATCH
HOW DOES IT FEEL TO HAVE KILLED YOUR PARTNER, TSUZUKI...?
YOU DID...
...KILL HIM.
BUT THAT'S JUST ONE MORE SIN...
...YOU'VE COMMITTED, ISN'T IT?
YOU BASTARD...!!
STOP, HIJIRI!
YOU CAN'T HELP HIM!!

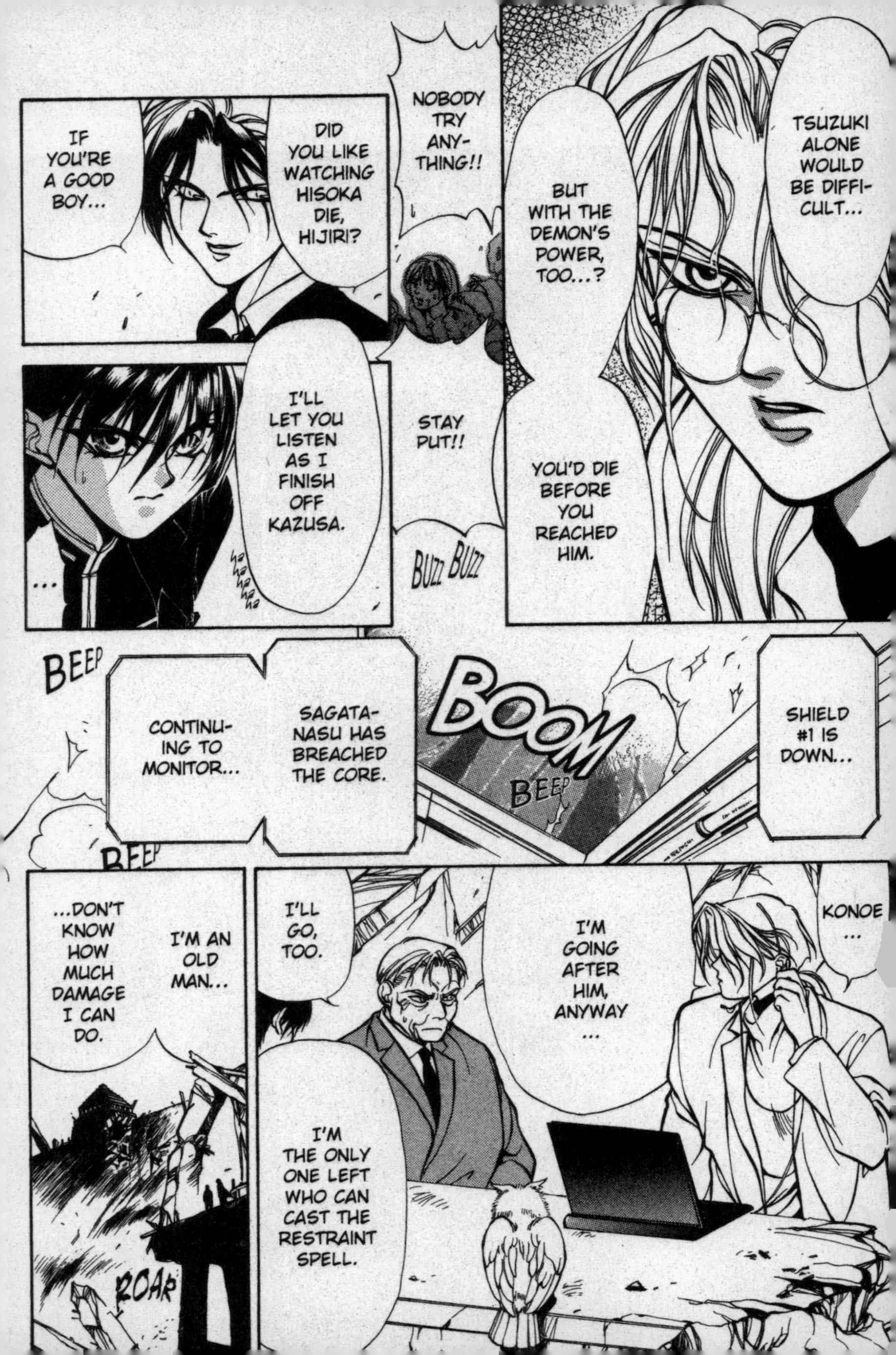

TSUZUKI ALONE WOULD BE DIFFI-CULT...
BUT WITH THE DEMON'S POWER, TOO...?
YOU'D DIE BEFORE YOU REACHED HIM.
NOBODY TRY ANY-THING!!
STAY PUT!!
BUZZ BUZZ
DID YOU LIKE WATCHING HISOKA DIE, HIJIRI?
IF YOU'RE A GOOD BOY...
I'LL LET YOU LISTEN AS I FINISH OFF KAZUSA.
...
SHIELD #1 IS DOWN...
BOOM
BEEP
SAGATA-NASU HAS BREACHED THE CORE.
CONTINU-ING TO MONITOR...
BEEP
BEEP
KONOE ...
I'M GOING AFTER HIM, ANYWAY ...
I'LL GO, TOO.
I'M THE ONLY ONE LEFT WHO CAN CAST THE RESTRAINT SPELL.
I'M AN OLD MAN...
...DON'T KNOW HOW MUCH DAMAGE I CAN DO.
ROAR

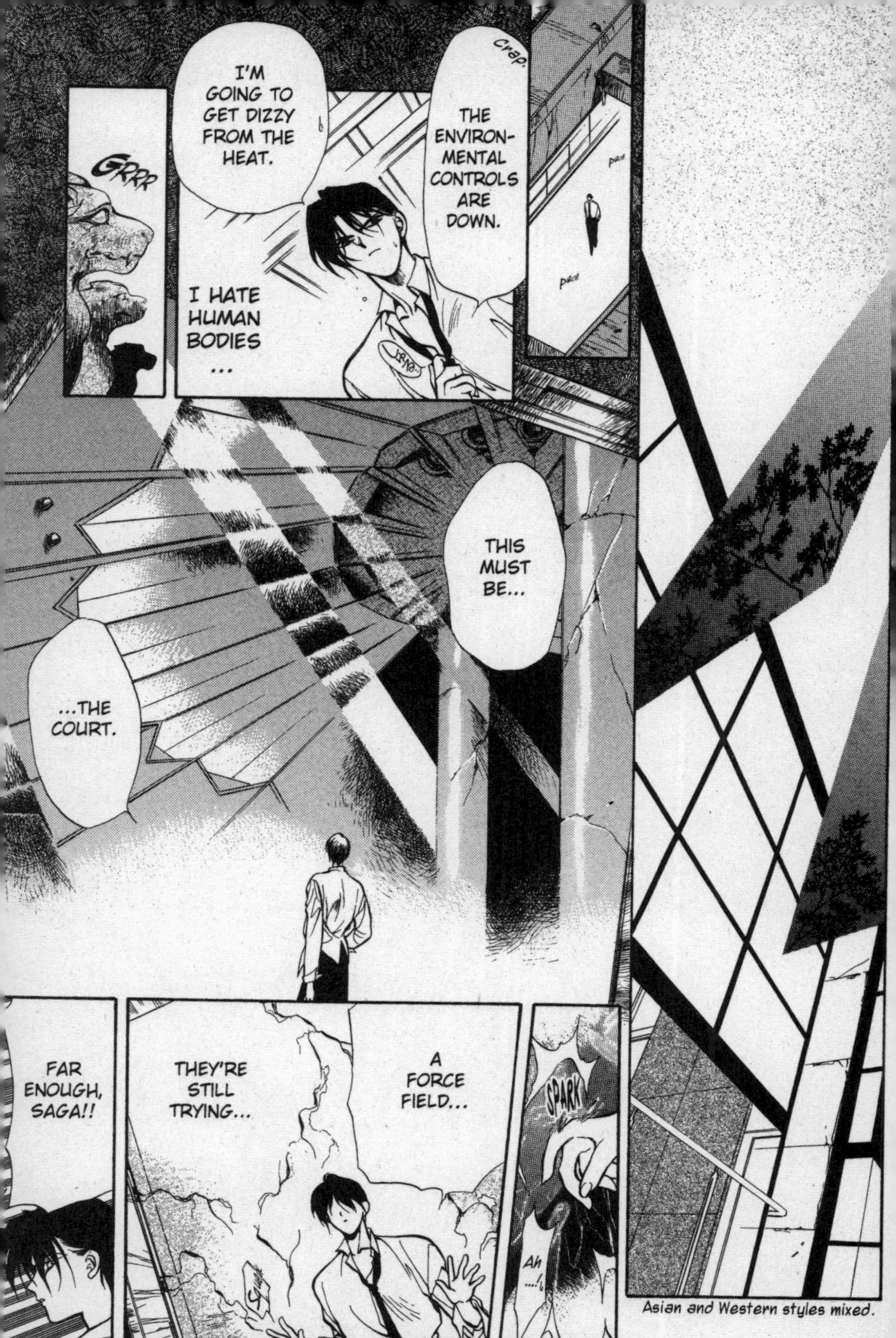
pace
pace
Crap.
THE ENVIRON-MENTAL CONTROLS ARE DOWN.
I'M GOING TO GET DIZZY FROM THE HEAT.
I HATE HUMAN BODIES ...
GRRR
THIS MUST BE...
...THE COURT.
SPARK
Ah ...!
A FORCE FIELD...
THEY'RE STILL TRYING...
FAR ENOUGH, SAGA!!

Asian and Western styles mixed.

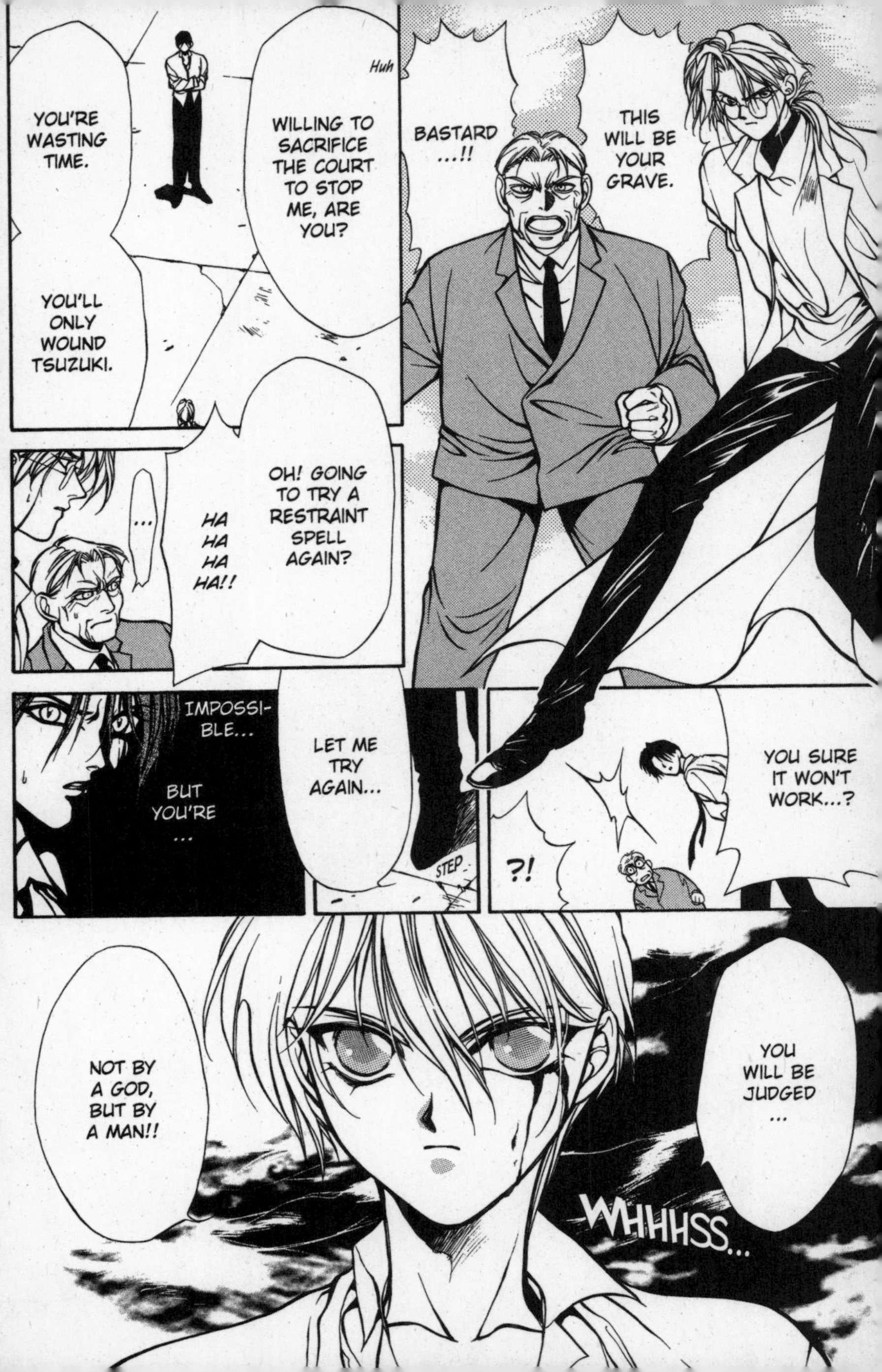
THIS WILL BE YOUR GRAVE.
BASTARD ...!!
Huh
WILLING TO SACRIFICE THE COURT TO STOP ME, ARE YOU?
YOU'RE WASTING TIME.
YOU'LL ONLY WOUND TSUZUKI.
OH! GOING TO TRY A RESTRAINT SPELL AGAIN?
HA HA HA HA!!
...
YOU SURE IT WON'T WORK...?
?!
STEP
LET ME TRY AGAIN...
IMPOSSIBLE...
BUT YOU'RE ...
YOU WILL BE JUDGED ...
WHHHSS...
NOT BY A GOD, BUT BY A MAN!!

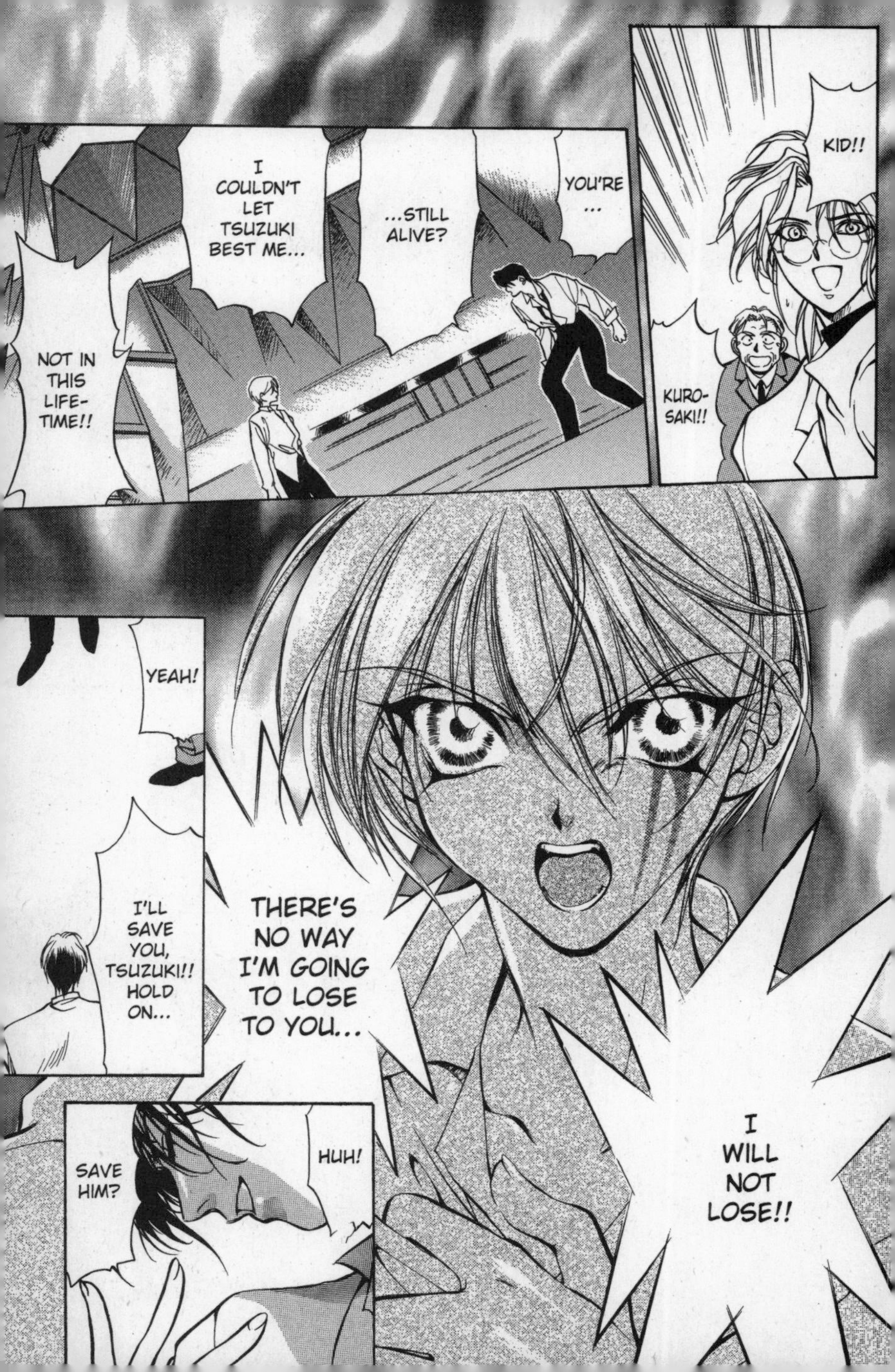
KID!!
KURO-SAKI!!
YOU'RE ...
...STILL ALIVE?
I COULDN'T LET TSUZUKI BEST ME...
NOT IN THIS LIFE-TIME!!
THERE'S NO WAY I'M GOING TO LOSE TO YOU...
I WILL NOT LOSE!!
YEAH!
I'LL SAVE YOU, TSUZUKI!! HOLD ON...
HUH!
SAVE HIM?

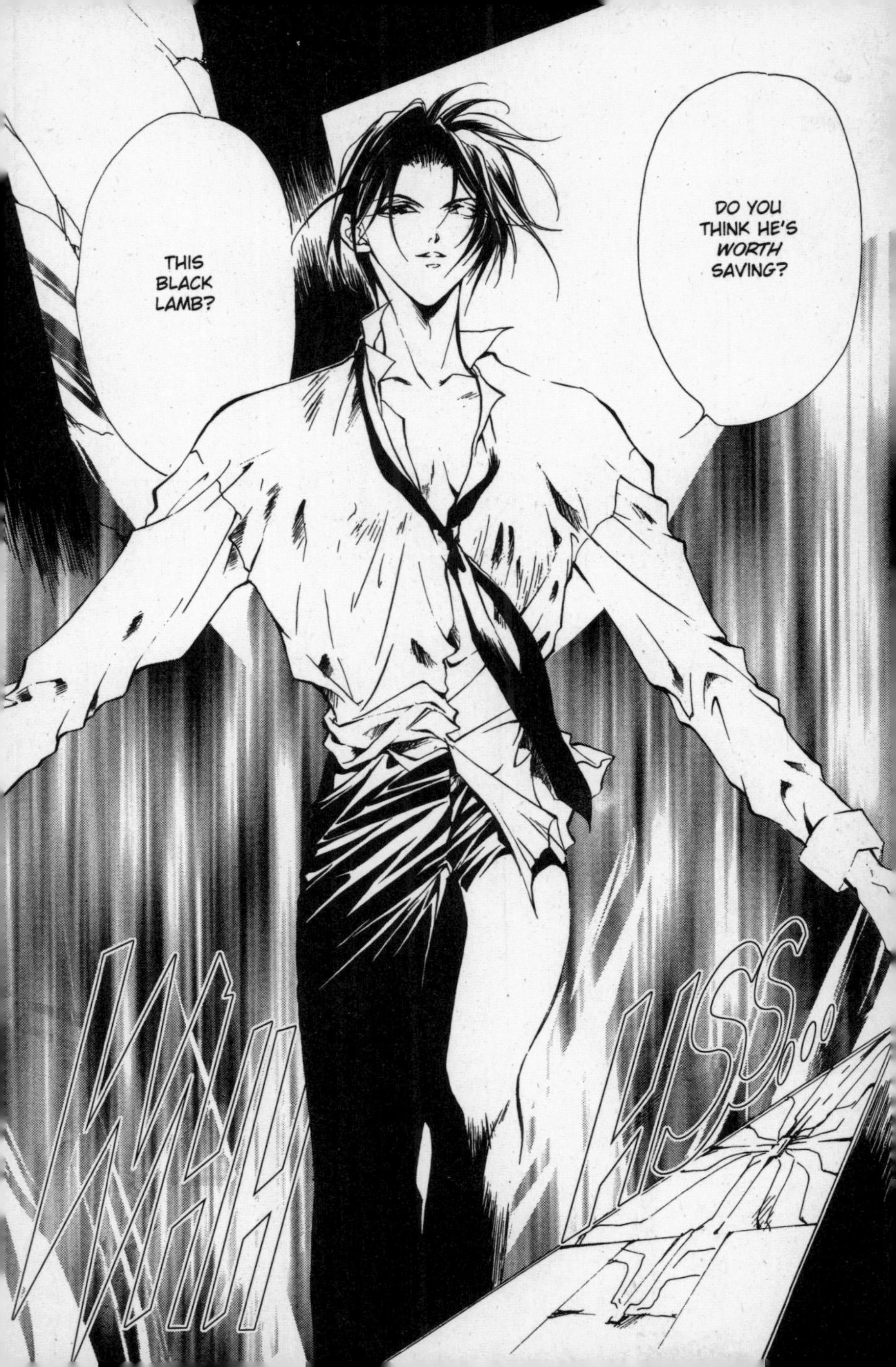
DO YOU THINK HE'S *WORTH* SAVING?
THIS BLACK LAMB?
HISS...

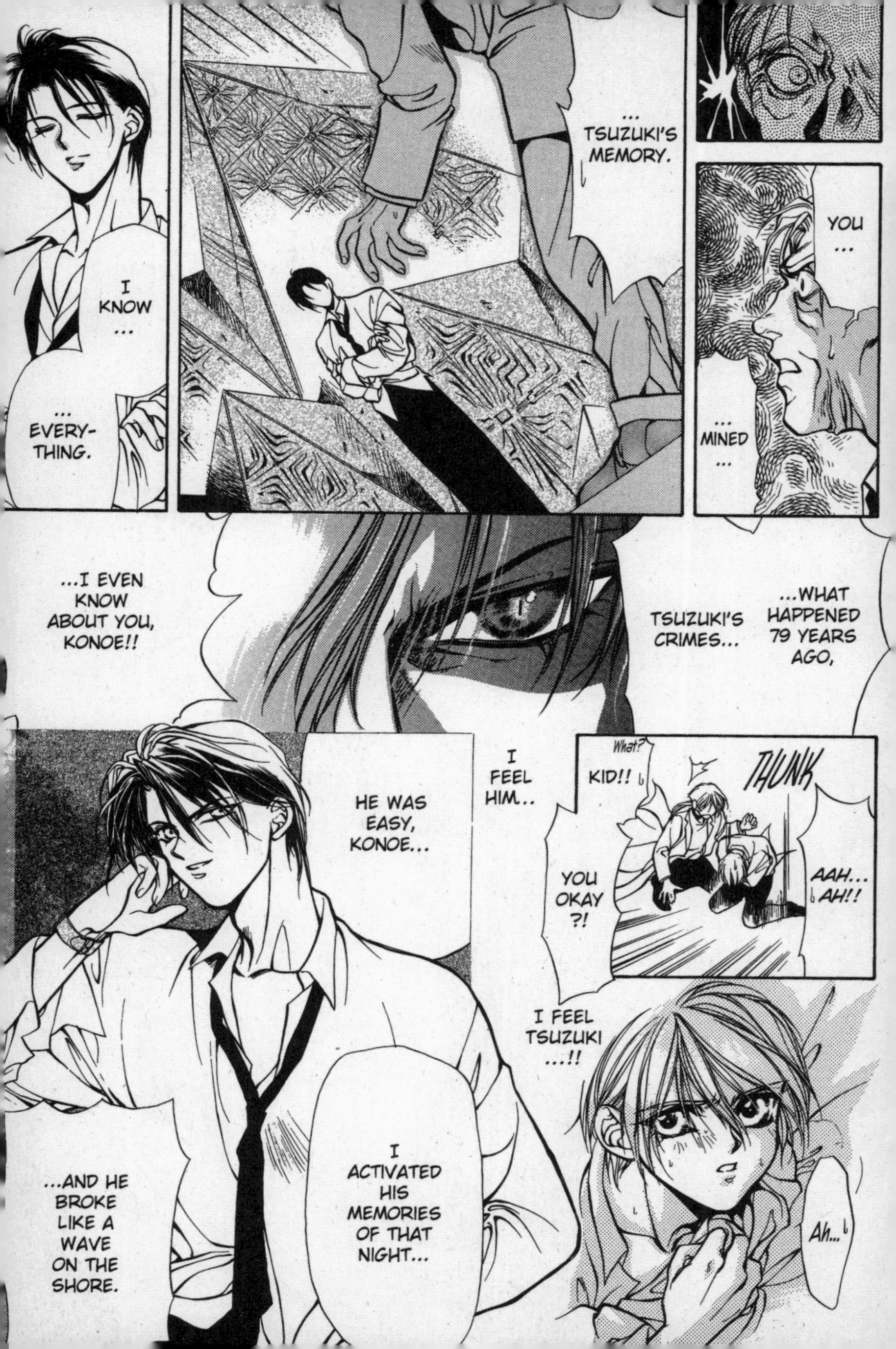
YOU ...
... MINED ...
... TSUZUKI'S MEMORY.
I KNOW ...
... EVERYTHING.
...WHAT HAPPENED 79 YEARS AGO,
TSUZUKI'S CRIMES...
...I EVEN KNOW ABOUT YOU, KONOE!!
THUNK
What?
KID!!
AAH... AH!!
YOU OKAY ?!
I FEEL HIM..
I FEEL TSUZUKI ...!!
Ah...
HE WAS EASY, KONOE...
I ACTIVATED HIS MEMORIES OF THAT NIGHT...
...AND HE BROKE LIKE A WAVE ON THE SHORE.

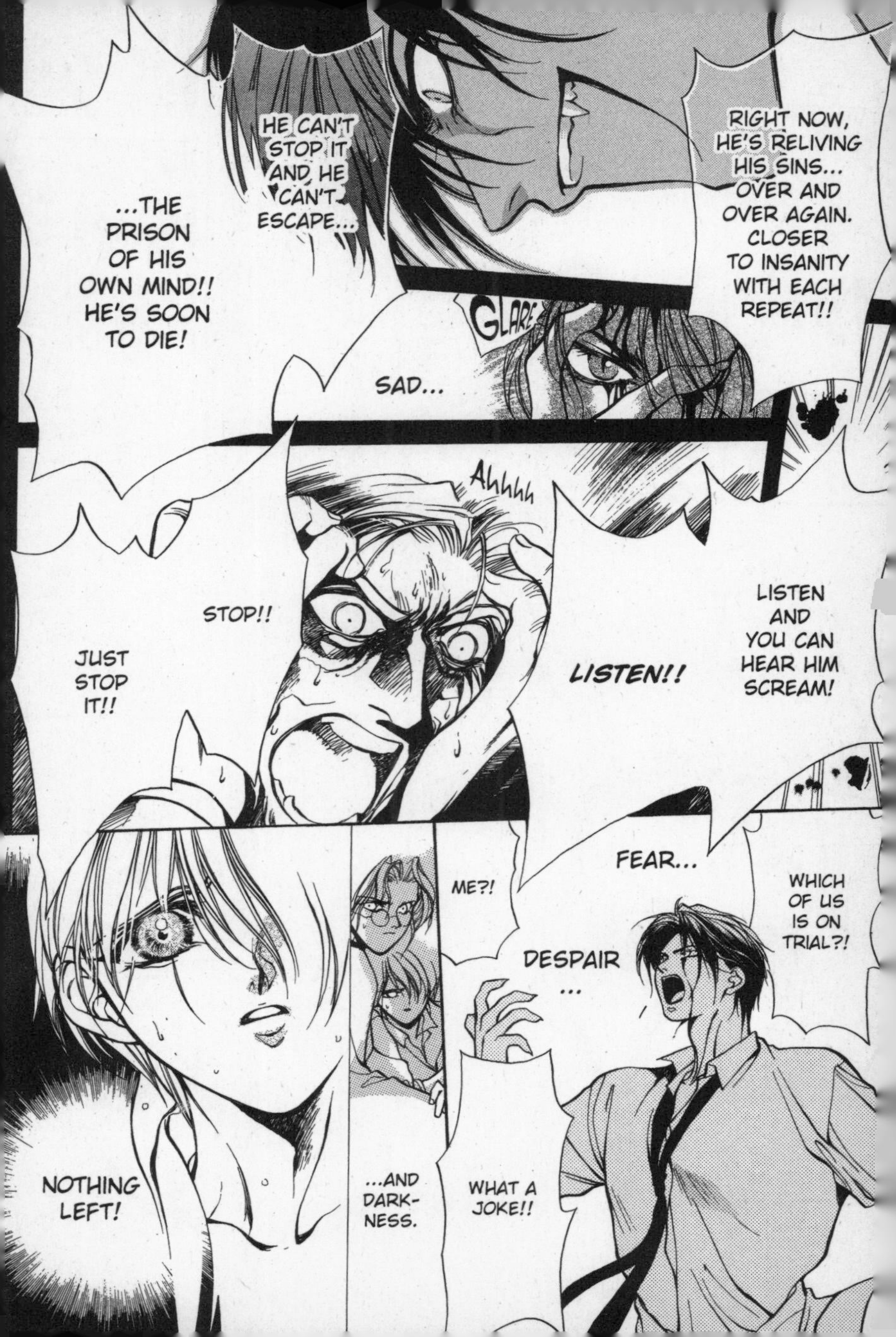
RIGHT NOW, HE'S RELIVING HIS SINS... OVER AND OVER AGAIN. CLOSER TO INSANITY WITH EACH REPEAT!!
HE CAN'T STOP IT AND HE CAN'T ESCAPE...
...THE PRISON OF HIS OWN MIND!! HE'S SOON TO DIE!
GLARE
SAD...
Ahhhh
LISTEN AND YOU CAN HEAR HIM SCREAM!
LISTEN!!
STOP!!
JUST STOP IT!!
WHICH OF US IS ON TRIAL?!
FEAR...
ME?!
DESPAIR ...
WHAT A JOKE!!
...AND DARK-NESS.
NOTHING LEFT!

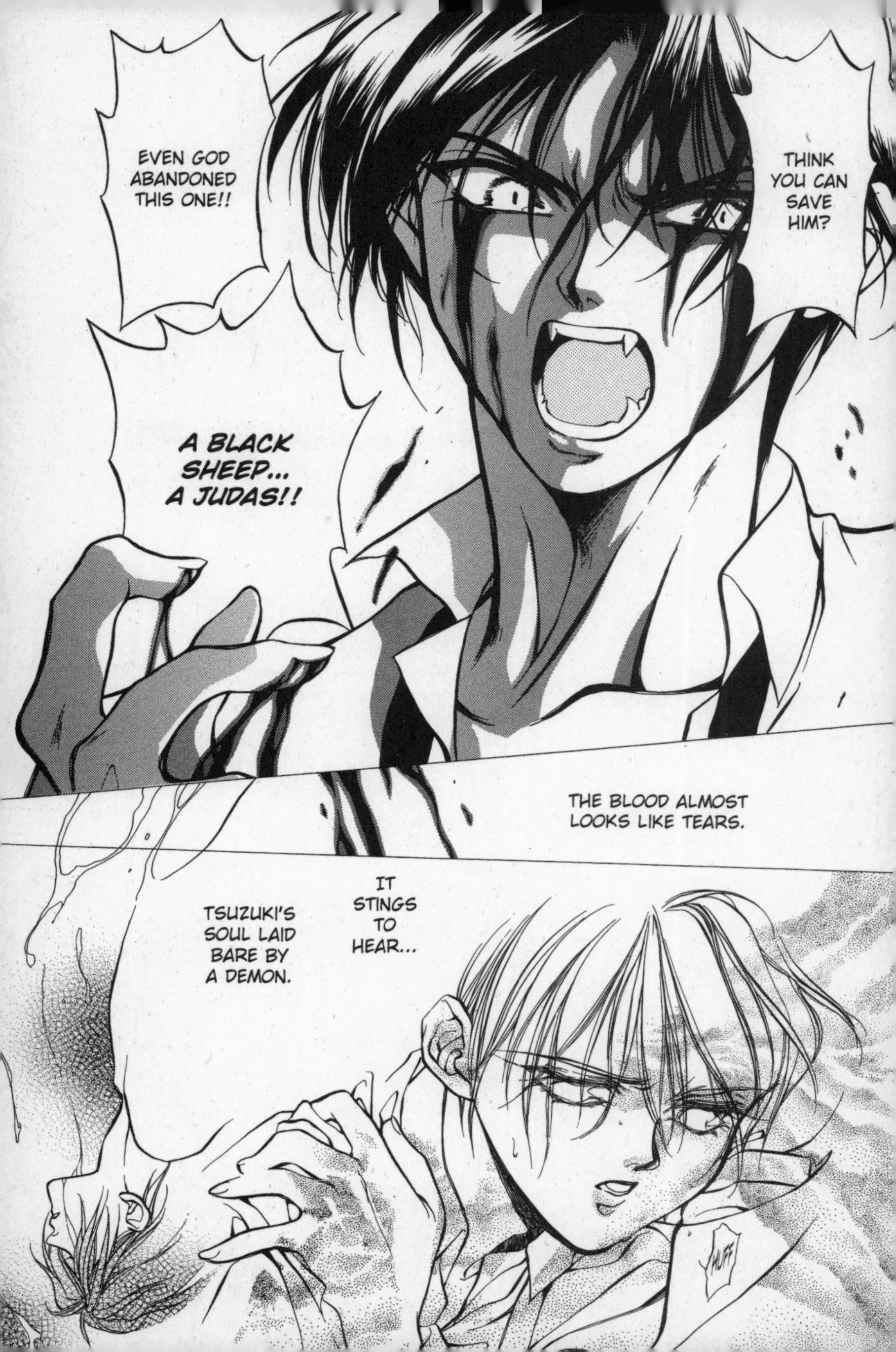
THINK YOU CAN SAVE HIM?
EVEN GOD ABANDONED THIS ONE!!
A BLACK SHEEP... A JUDAS!!
THE BLOOD ALMOST LOOKS LIKE TEARS.
IT STINGS TO HEAR...
TSUZUKI'S SOUL LAID BARE BY A DEMON.
HUFF

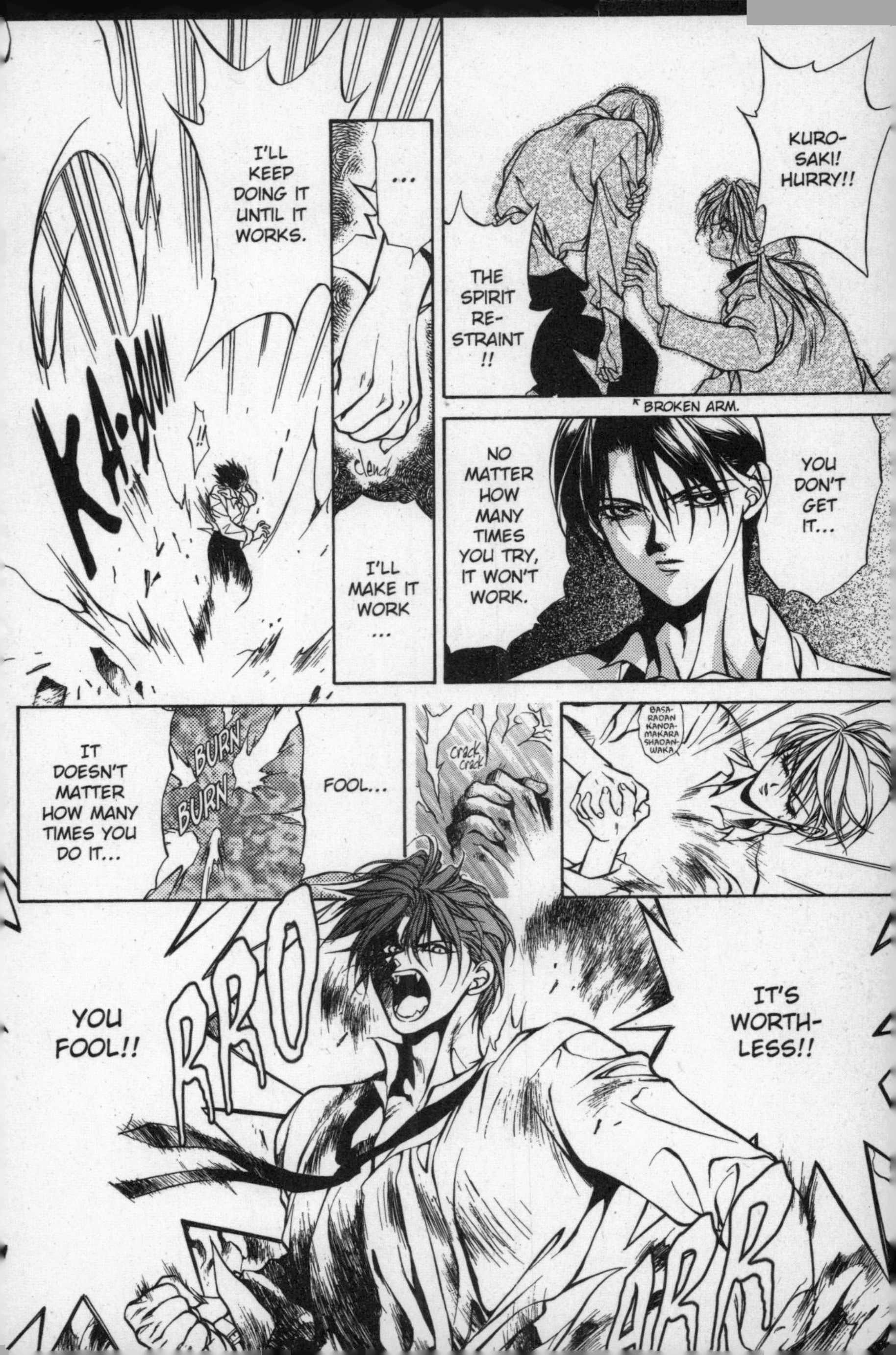
KURO-SAKI! HURRY!!
THE SPIRIT RE-STRAINT !!
BROKEN ARM.
YOU DON'T GET IT...
NO MATTER HOW MANY TIMES YOU TRY, IT WON'T WORK.
...
clench
I'LL MAKE IT WORK ...
I'LL KEEP DOING IT UNTIL IT WORKS.
KA-BOOM
!!
BASA-RADAN KANOA-MAKARA SHADAN-WAKA
crack crack
FOOL...
BURN BURN
IT DOESN'T MATTER HOW MANY TIMES YOU DO IT...
IT'S WORTH-LESS!!
YOU FOOL!!

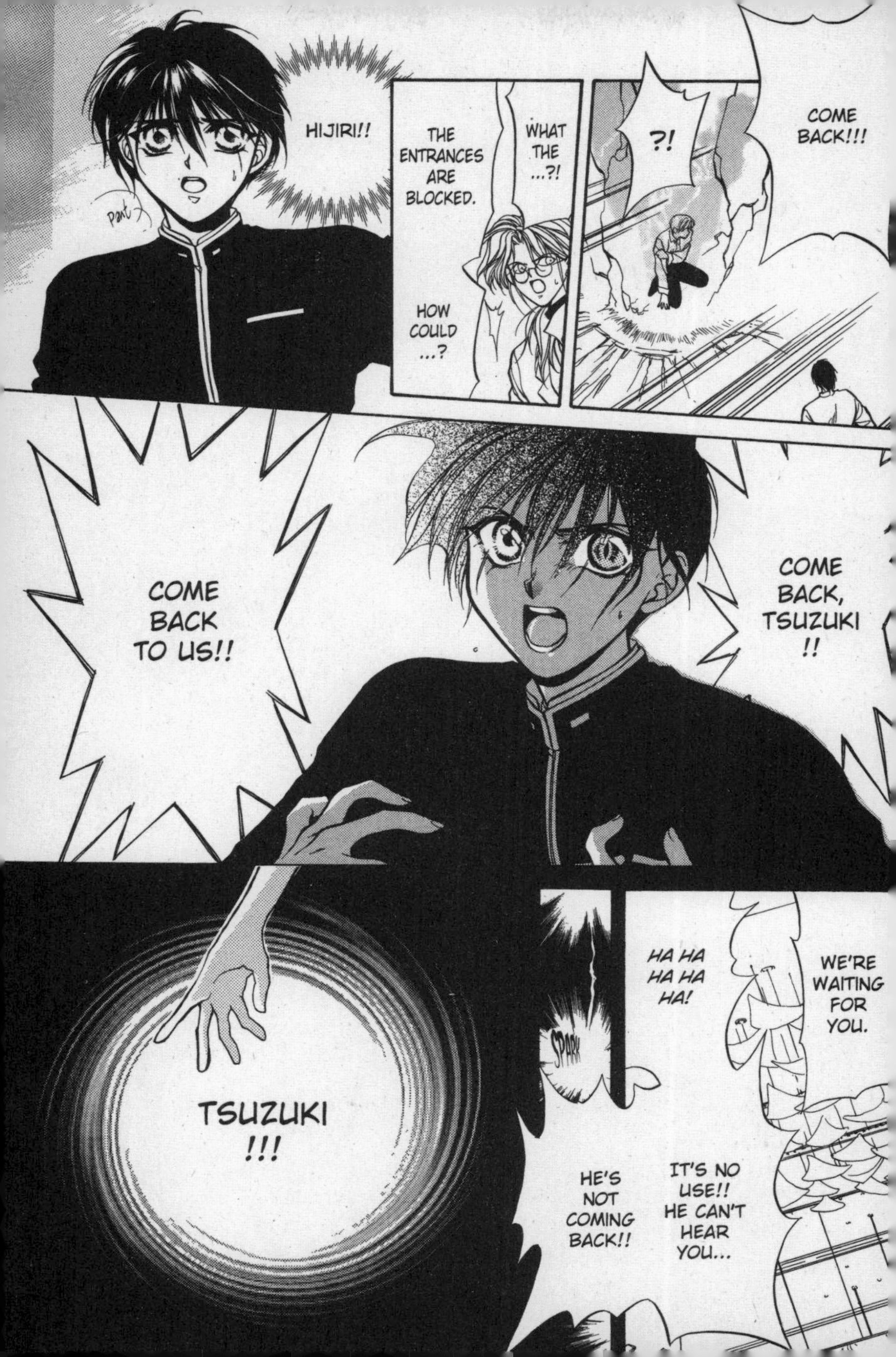
COME BACK!!!
?!
WHAT THE ...?!
THE ENTRANCES ARE BLOCKED.
HOW COULD ...?
HIJIRI!!
pant
COME BACK, TSUZUKI !!
COME BACK TO US!!
WE'RE WAITING FOR YOU.
HA HA HA HA HA!
SPARK
IT'S NO USE!! HE CAN'T HEAR YOU...
HE'S NOT COMING BACK!!
TSUZUKI !!!

SCRAPE
SCRAPE
step
RROARR
I'M SORRY...
I'M SORRY...
I'M SORRY...
FORGIVE ME...
I DIDN'T KNOW ...I DIDN'T KNOW.
I...
THAT'S WHY I...!!
Haaa
Haaa
Haaa
WHERE ARE YOU GOING TO HIDE?
YOU BEAR MY MARK ON YOUR FOREHEAD.

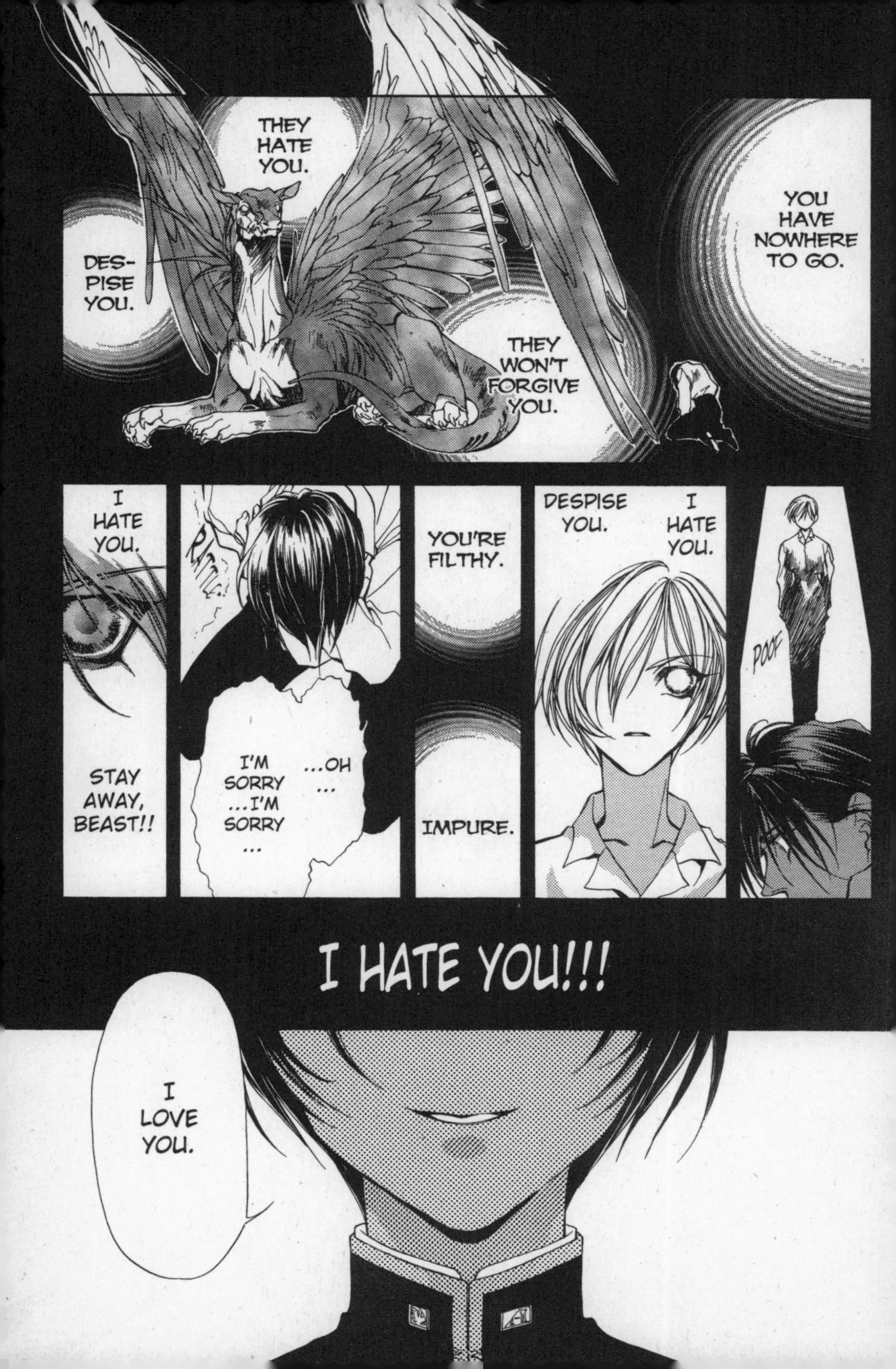
YOU HAVE NOWHERE TO GO.
THEY HATE YOU.
THEY WON'T FORGIVE YOU.
DESPISE YOU.
POOF
I HATE YOU.
DESPISE YOU.
YOU'RE FILTHY.
IMPURE.
RATTLE..!
...OH ...
I'M SORRY ...I'M SORRY ...
I HATE YOU.
STAY AWAY, BEAST!!
I HATE YOU!!!
I LOVE YOU.

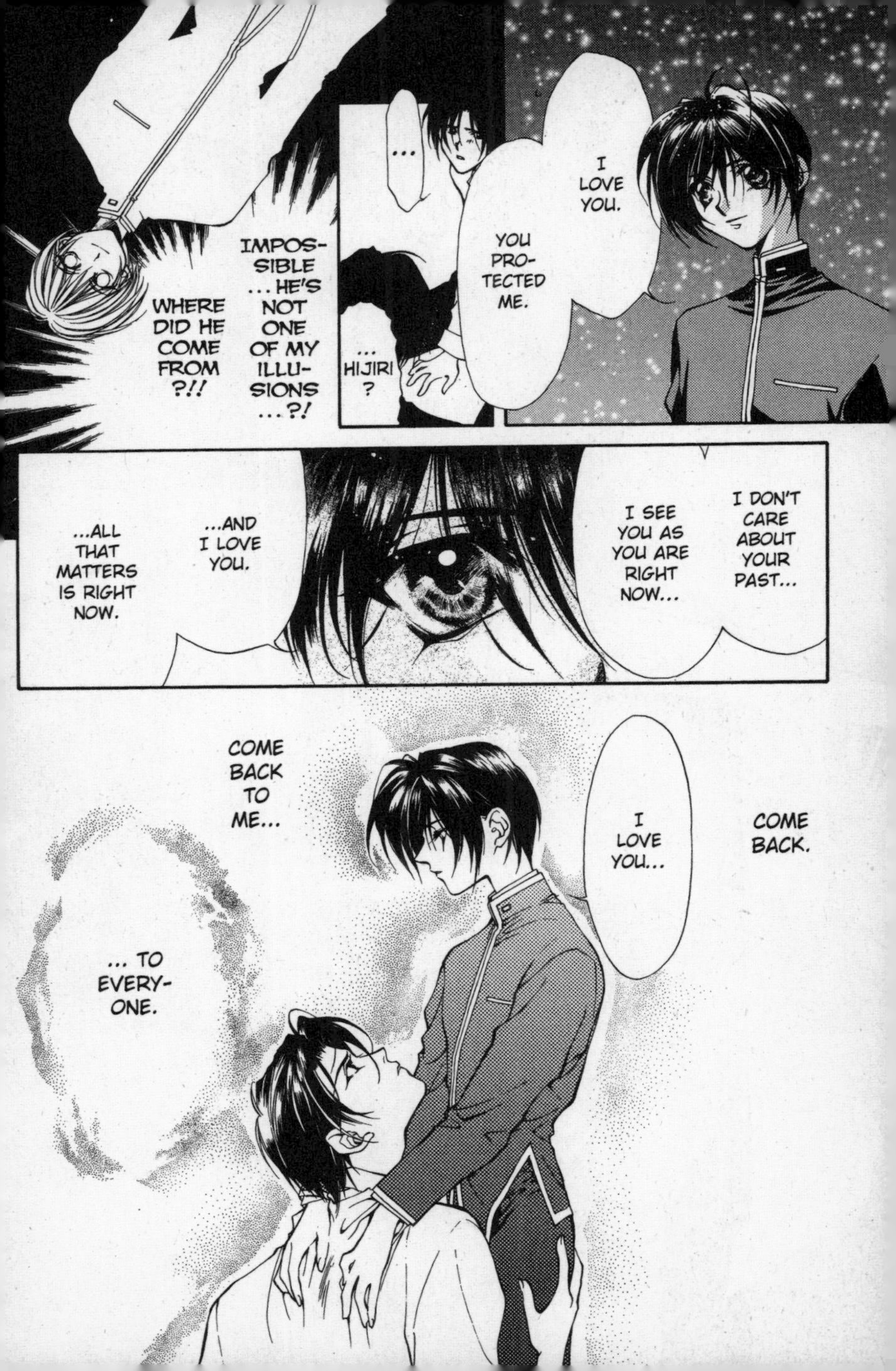
I LOVE YOU.
YOU PROTECTED ME.
...
...HIJIRI?
IMPOSSIBLE ...HE'S NOT ONE OF MY ILLUSIONS ...?!
WHERE DID HE COME FROM ?!!
I DON'T CARE ABOUT YOUR PAST...
I SEE YOU AS YOU ARE RIGHT NOW...
...AND I LOVE YOU.
...ALL THAT MATTERS IS RIGHT NOW.
COME BACK.
I LOVE YOU...
COME BACK TO ME...
... TO EVERYONE.

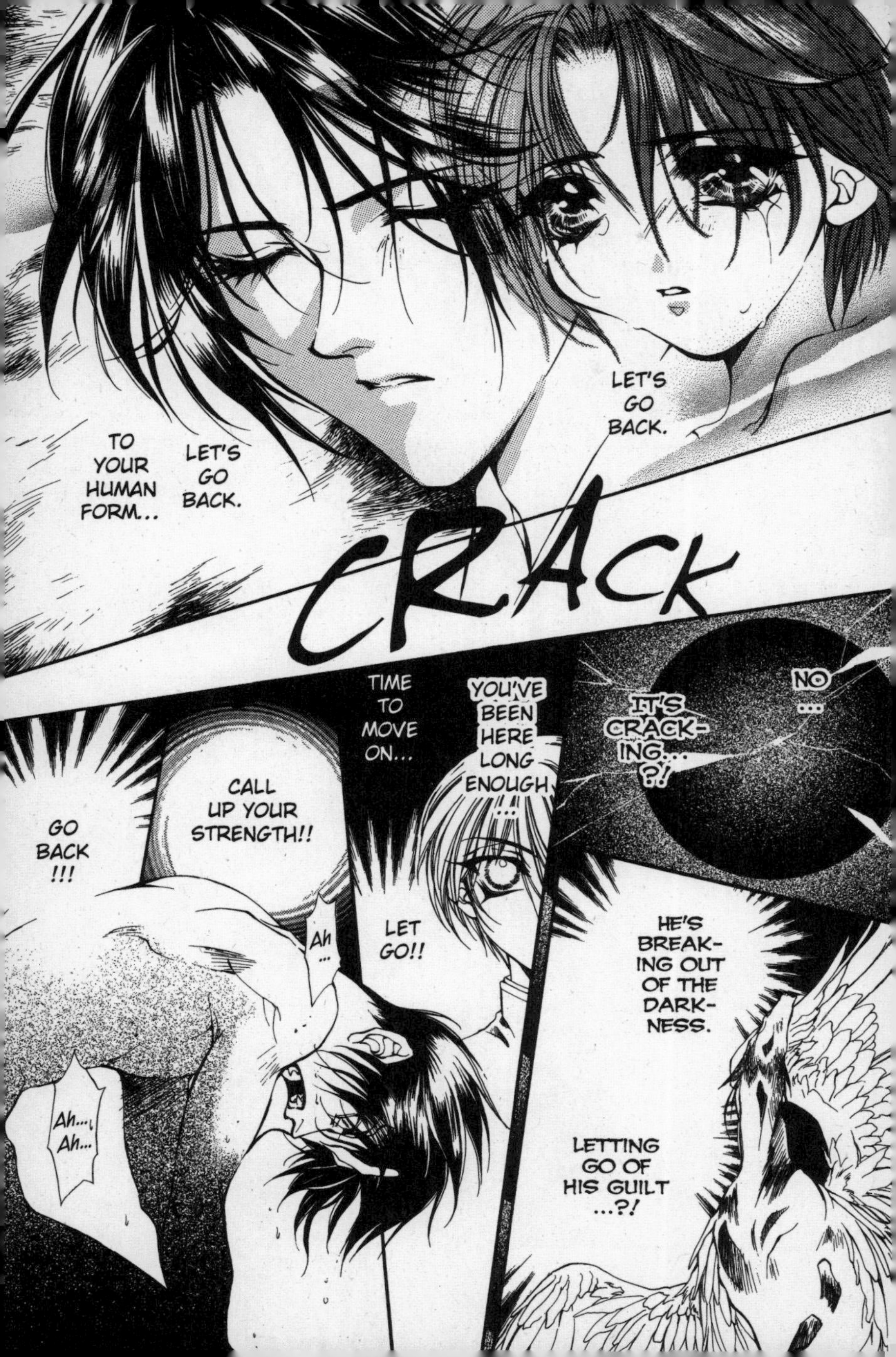
LET'S GO BACK.
LET'S GO BACK.
TO YOUR HUMAN FORM...
CRACK
NO ...
IT'S CRACKING... ?!
HE'S BREAKING OUT OF THE DARKNESS.
LETTING GO OF HIS GUILT ...?!
YOU'VE BEEN HERE LONG ENOUGH ...
TIME TO MOVE ON...
LET GO!!
CALL UP YOUR STRENGTH!!
Ah ...
GO BACK !!!
Ah... Ah...

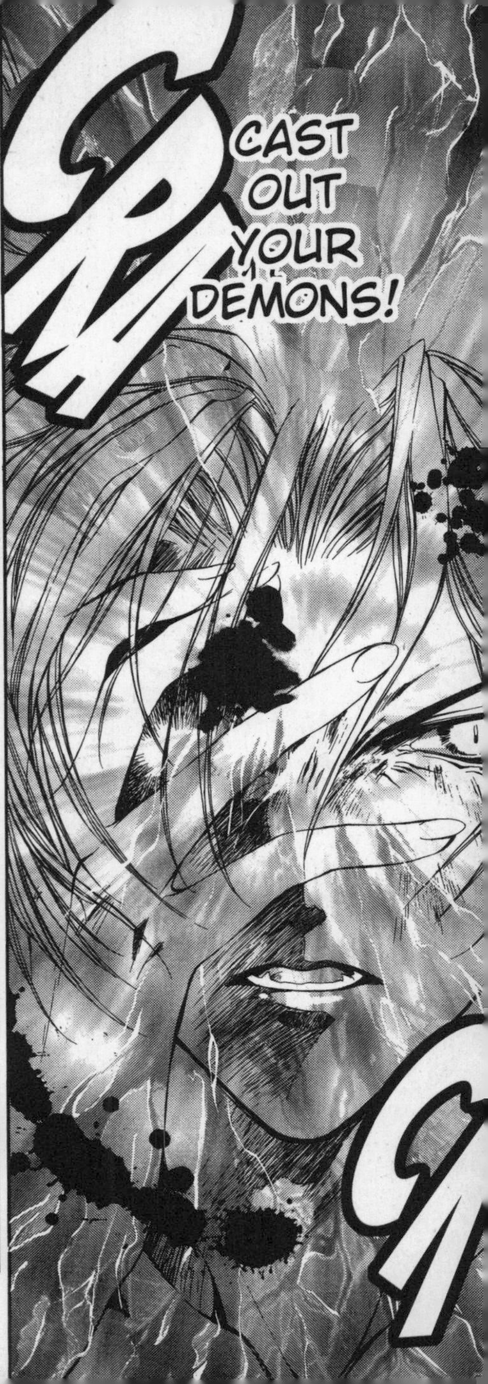
CAST OUT YOUR DEMONS!

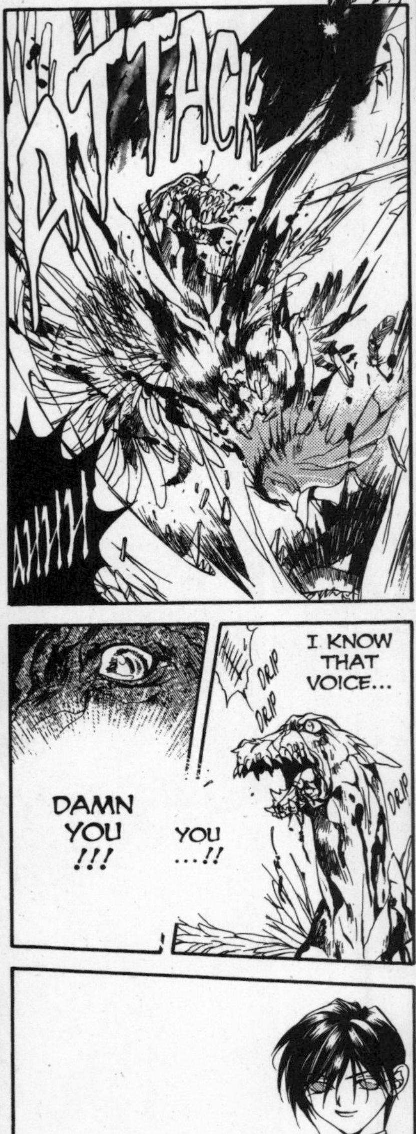
ATTACK
I KNOW THAT VOICE...
DRIP
DRIP
DRIP
YOU ...!!
DAMN YOU !!!

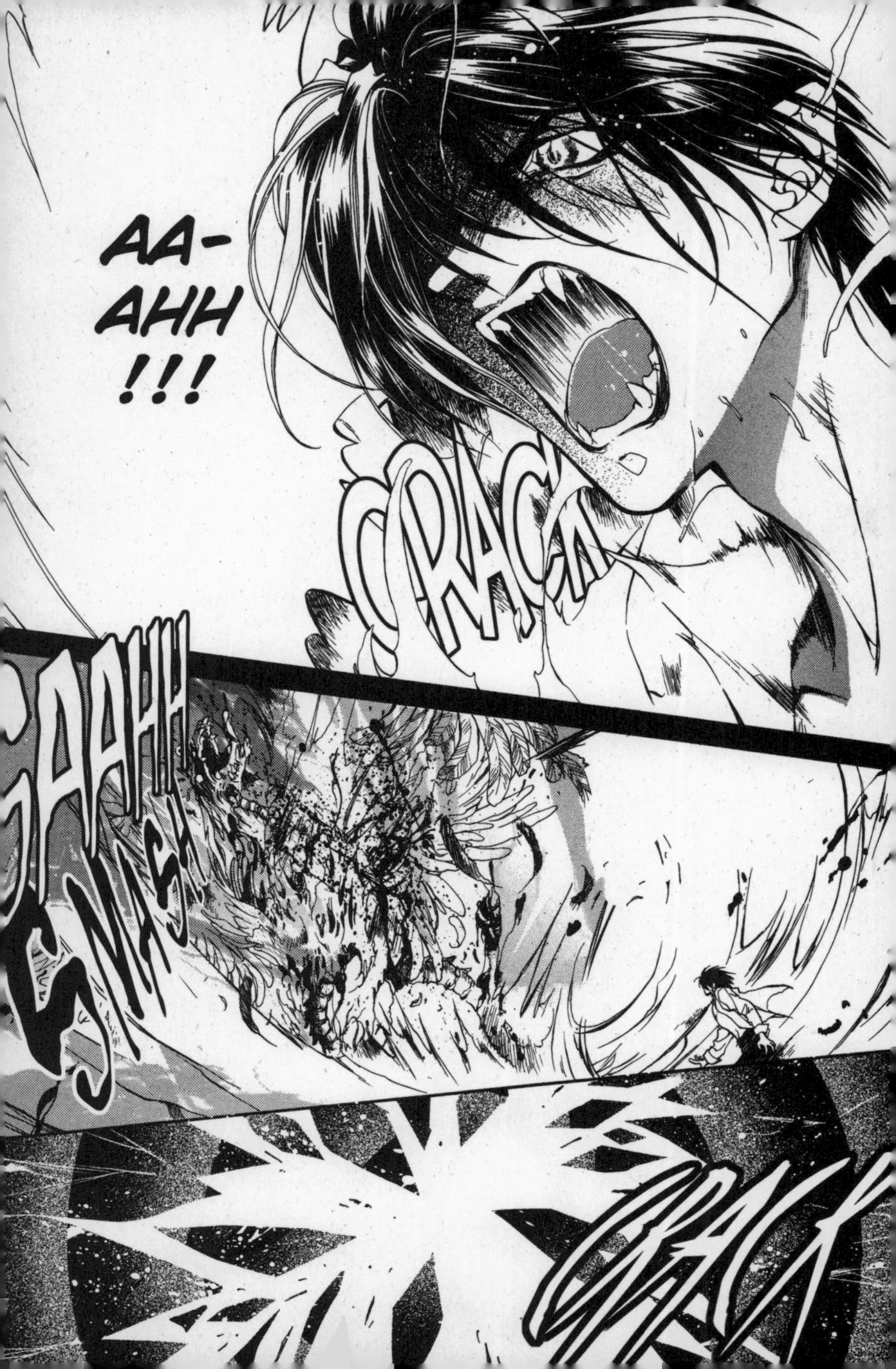
AA-
AHH
!!!
CRACK

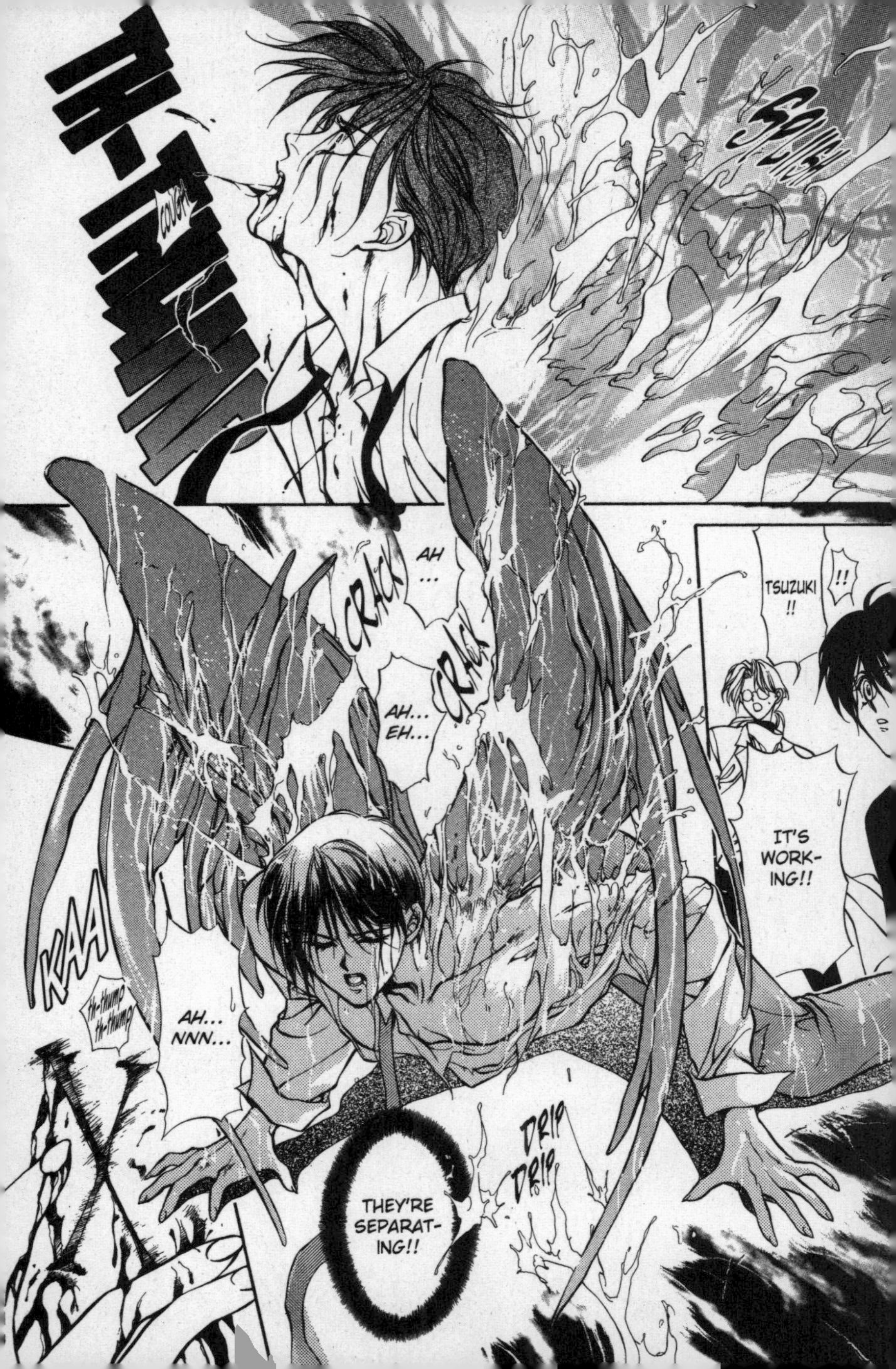
SPLISH
COUGH
TH-THUMP
TSUZUKI !!
!!
IT'S WORK-ING!!
AH ...
CRACK
CRACK
AH... EH...
KAA
th-thump th-thump
AH... NNN...
DRIP DRIP
THEY'RE SEPARAT-ING!!

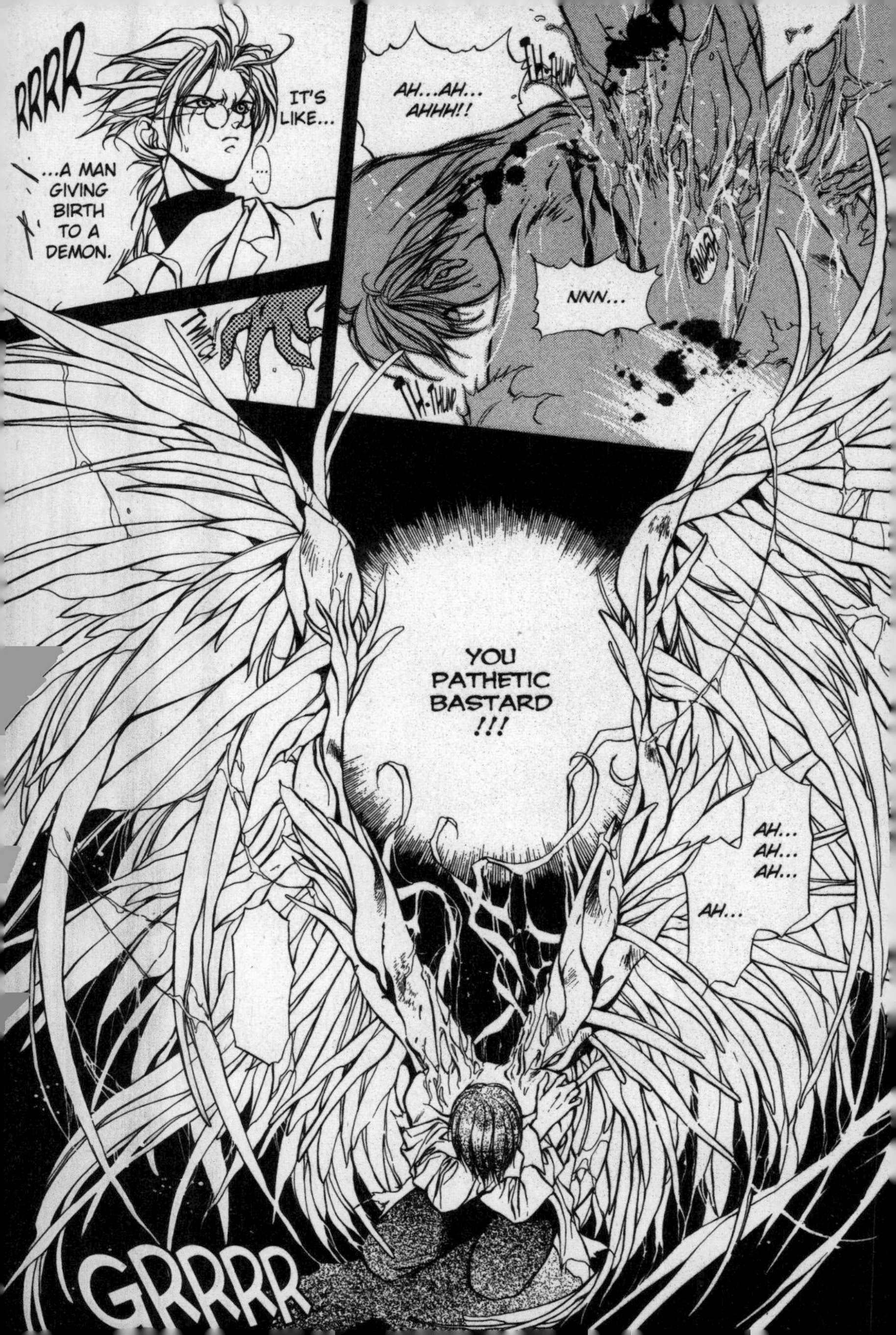
TH-THUMP
AH...AH... AHHH!!
NNN...
TH-THUMP
RRRR
IT'S LIKE...
...
...A MAN GIVING BIRTH TO A DEMON.
TWITCH
YOU PATHETIC BASTARD !!!
AH... AH... AH...
AH...
GRRRR

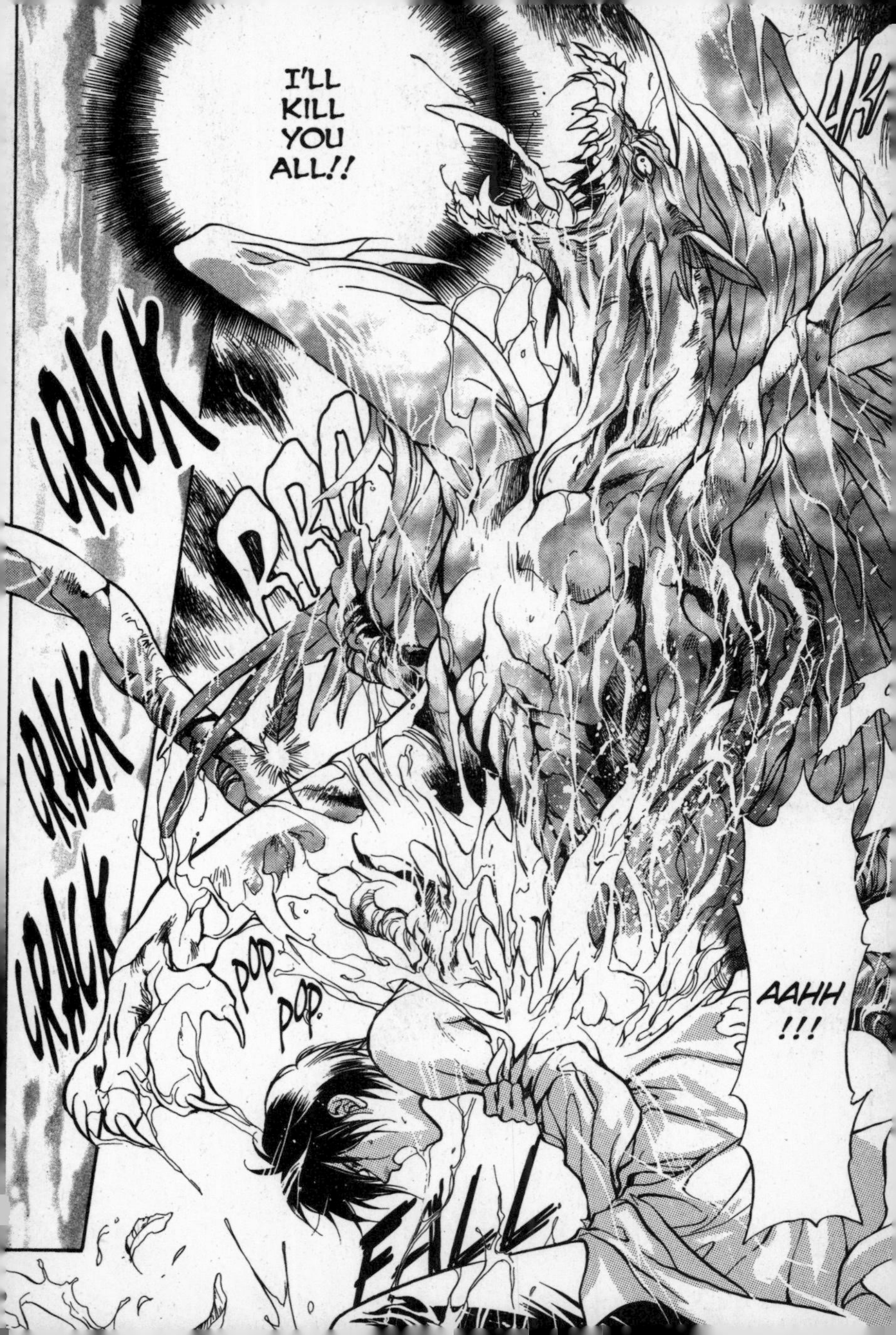
I'LL KILL YOU ALL!!
AAHH !!!
CRACK
CRACK
CRACK
POP POP.
FALL

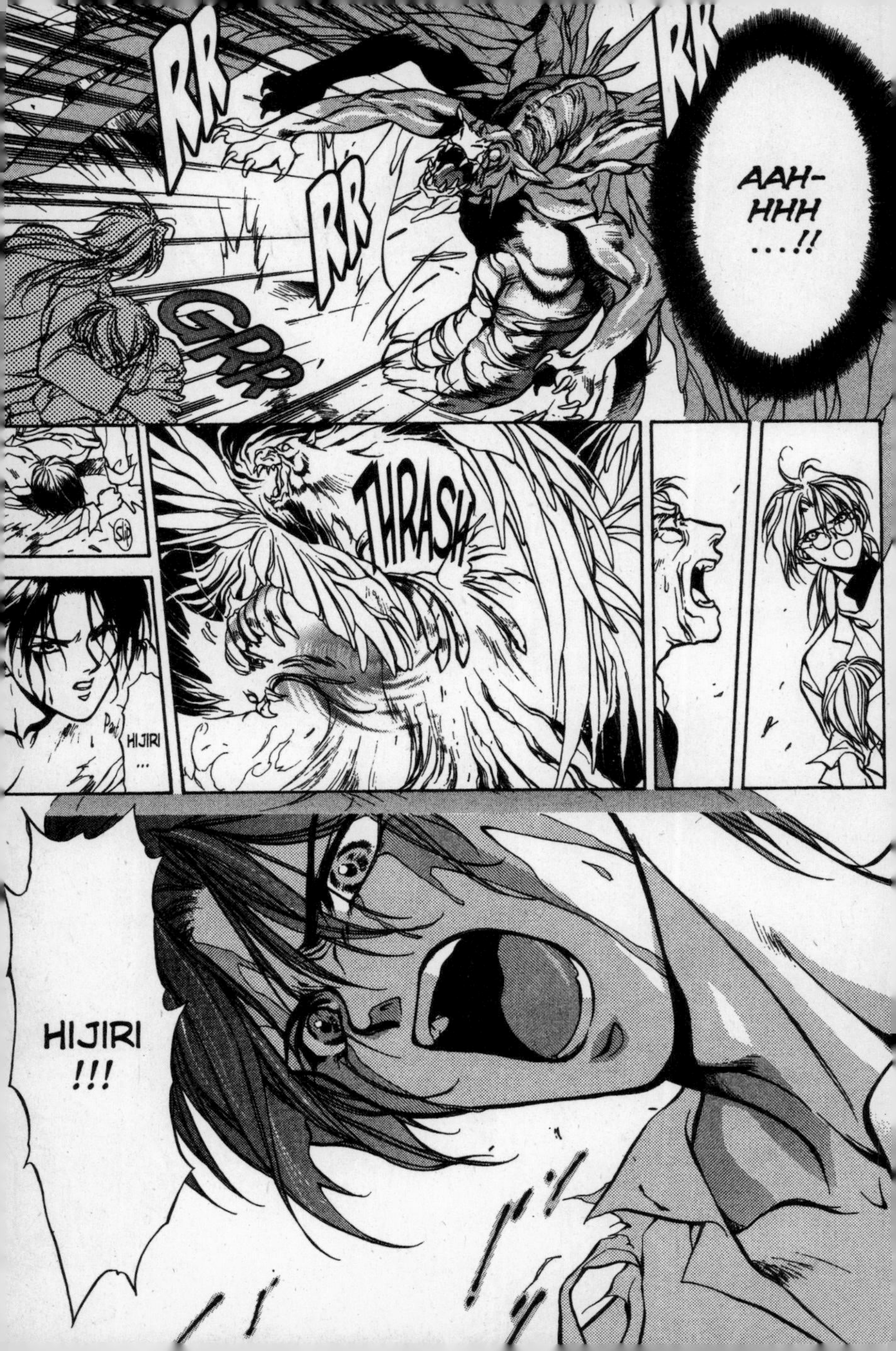
RR
AAH-HHH ...!!
RR
RR
GRR
THRASH
Slip
Pant
HIJIRI ...
HIJIRI !!!

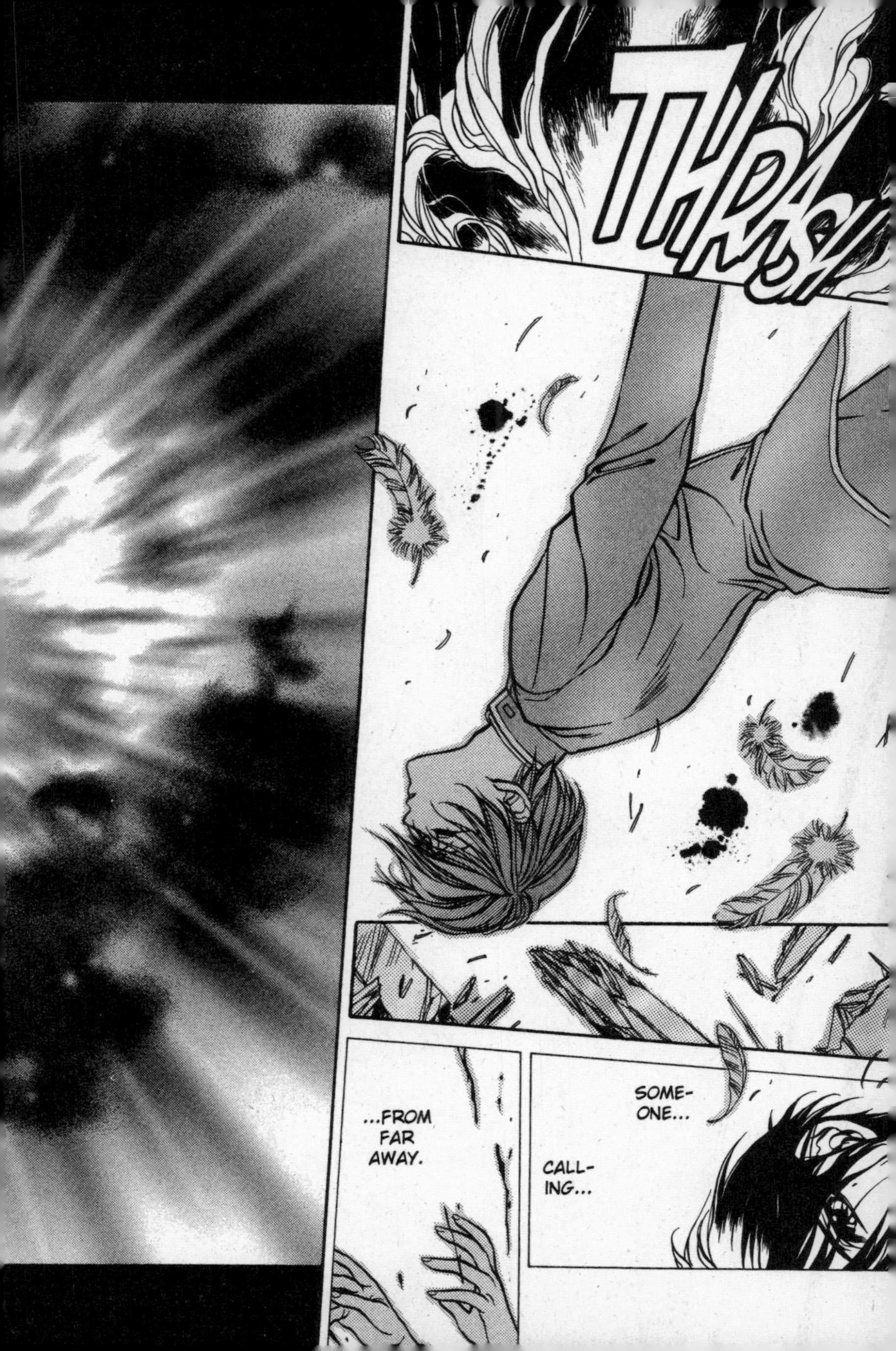
SOME-ONE...
CALL-ING...
...FROM FAR AWAY.

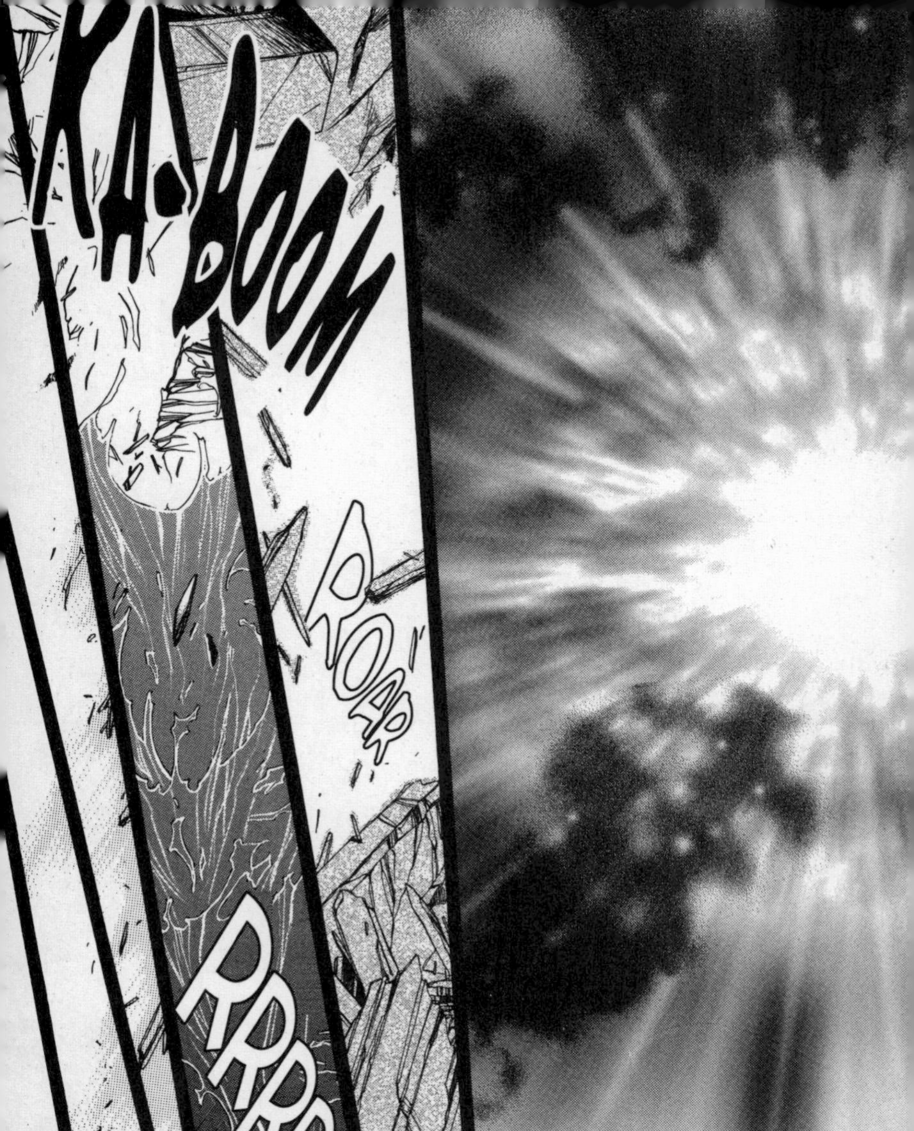
KA-BOOM
ROAR
RRRR

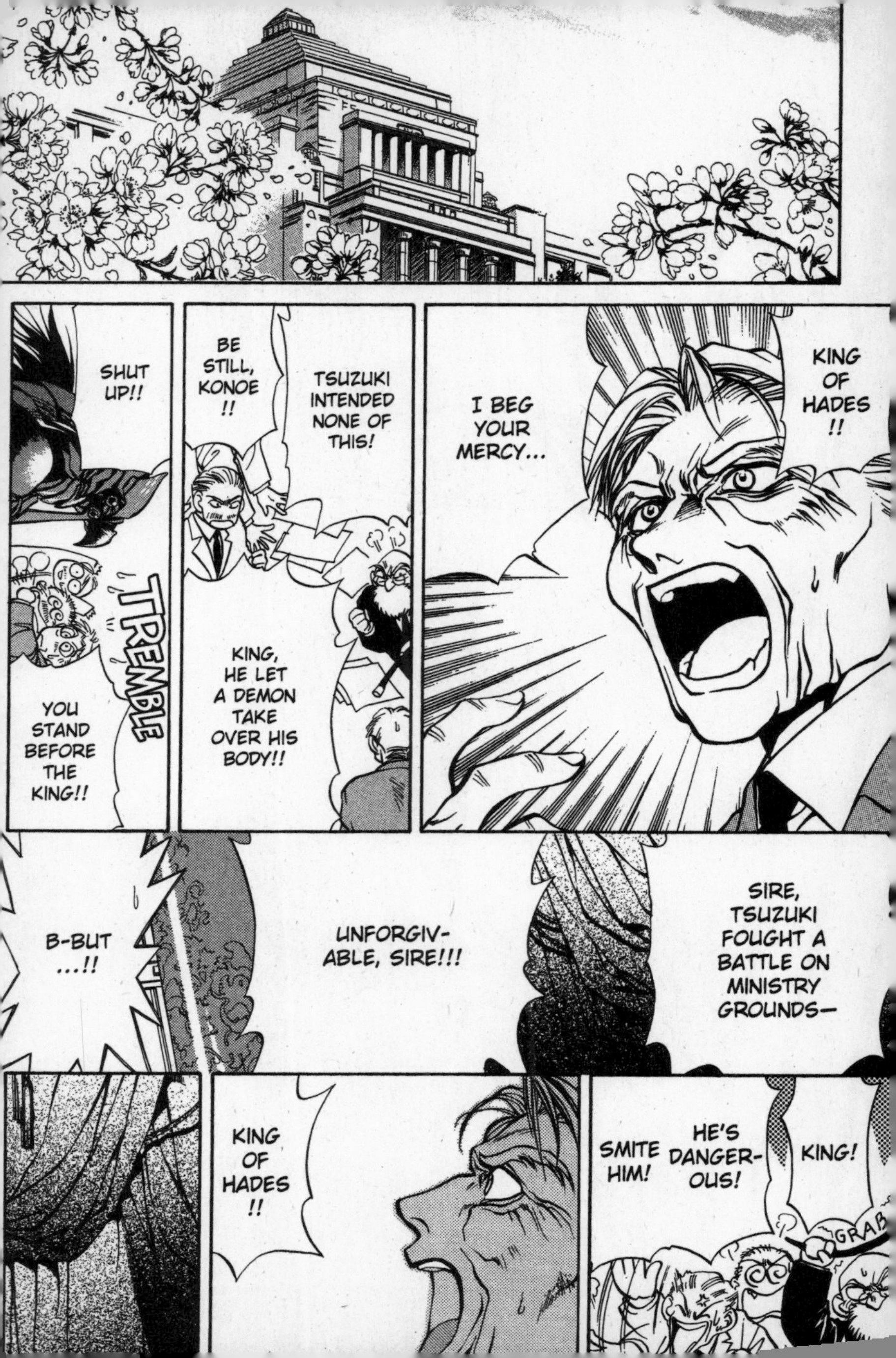
KING OF HADES !!
I BEG YOUR MERCY...
TSUZUKI INTENDED NONE OF THIS!
BE STILL, KONOE !!
KING, HE LET A DEMON TAKE OVER HIS BODY!!
SHUT UP!!
TREMBLE
YOU STAND BEFORE THE KING!!
SIRE, TSUZUKI FOUGHT A BATTLE ON MINISTRY GROUNDS—
UNFORGIV-ABLE, SIRE!!!
B-BUT ...!!
KING!
HE'S DANGER-OUS!
SMITE HIM!
GRAB
KING OF HADES !!

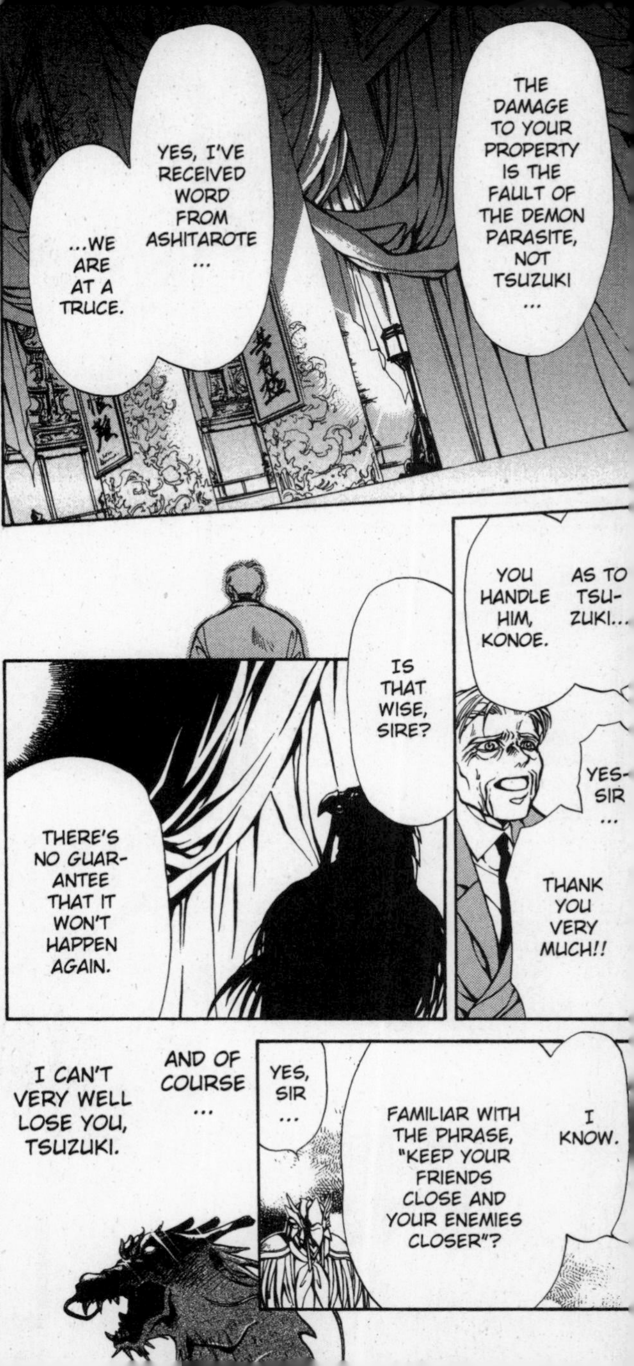
THE DAMAGE TO YOUR PROPERTY IS THE FAULT OF THE DEMON PARASITE, NOT TSUZUKI ...
YES, I'VE RECEIVED WORD FROM ASHITAROTE ...
...WE ARE AT A TRUCE.
AS TO TSU-ZUKI...
YOU HANDLE HIM, KONOE.
YES-SIR ...
THANK YOU VERY MUCH!!
IS THAT WISE, SIRE?
THERE'S NO GUAR-ANTEE THAT IT WON'T HAPPEN AGAIN.
I KNOW.
FAMILIAR WITH THE PHRASE, "KEEP YOUR FRIENDS CLOSE AND YOUR ENEMIES CLOSER"?
YES, SIR ...
AND OF COURSE ...
I CAN'T VERY WELL LOSE YOU, TSUZUKI.

Okay, so, I made a lot of additions to this story so it's different from what originally appeared in the magazine. (Well, maybe not that different.)

I figured that the collections would stay around for a long time, and this would be my last chance to restore some of the things I had to cut before. I know you are spending a lot of money on these books and I want to make sure that I give you the best and most complete story possible. Now I kind of feel bad for the people who only got to read the magazine version... Those of you who are not satisfied with this story's ending, well, you're free to imagine your own. Well, until next time...

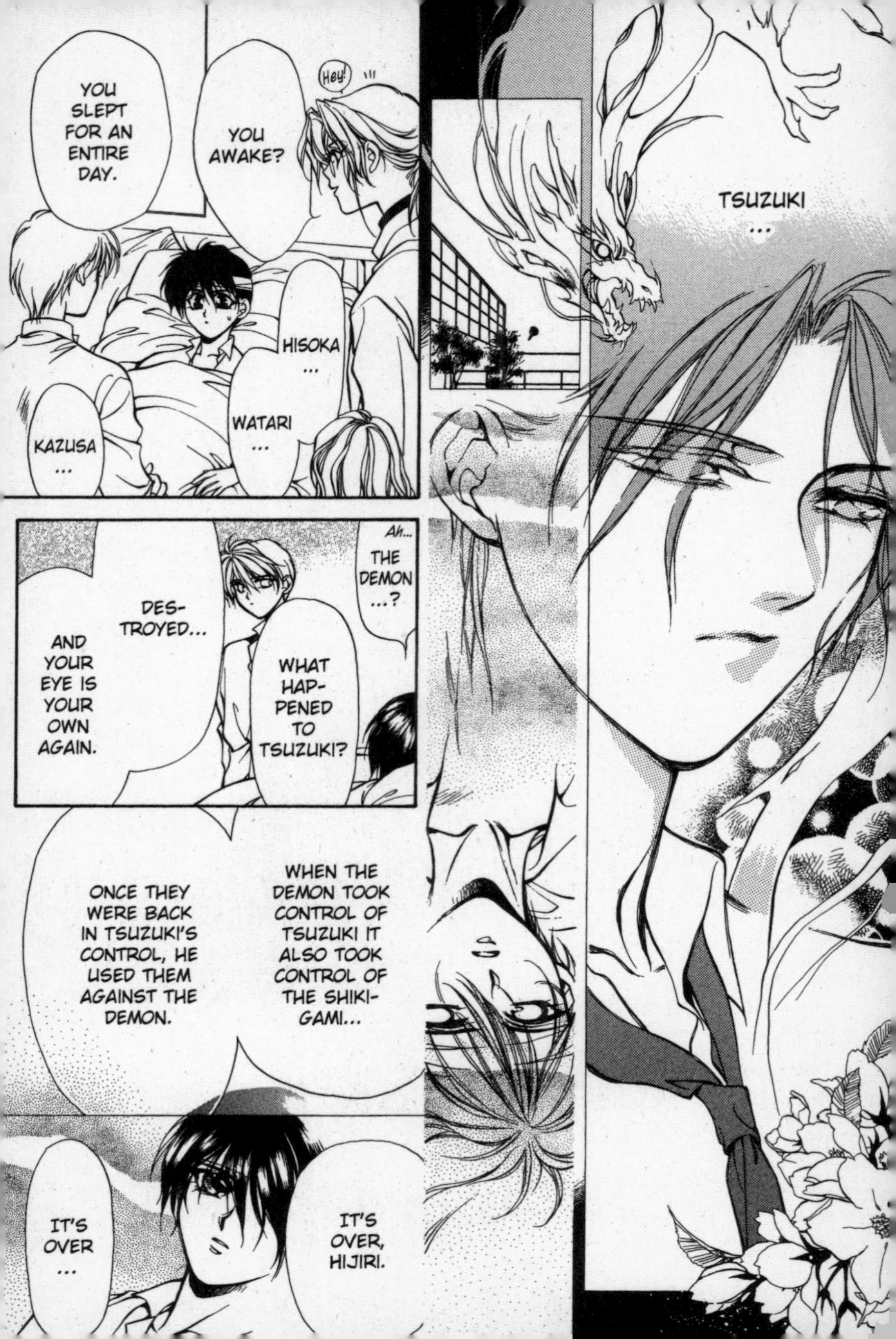
TSUZUKI ...
Hey!
YOU AWAKE?
YOU SLEPT FOR AN ENTIRE DAY.
HISOKA ...
WATARI ...
KAZUSA ...
Ah... THE DEMON ...?
WHAT HAPPENED TO TSUZUKI?
DESTROYED...
AND YOUR EYE IS YOUR OWN AGAIN.
WHEN THE DEMON TOOK CONTROL OF TSUZUKI IT ALSO TOOK CONTROL OF THE SHIKIGAMI...
ONCE THEY WERE BACK IN TSUZUKI'S CONTROL, HE USED THEM AGAINST THE DEMON.
IT'S OVER, HIJIRI.
IT'S OVER ...

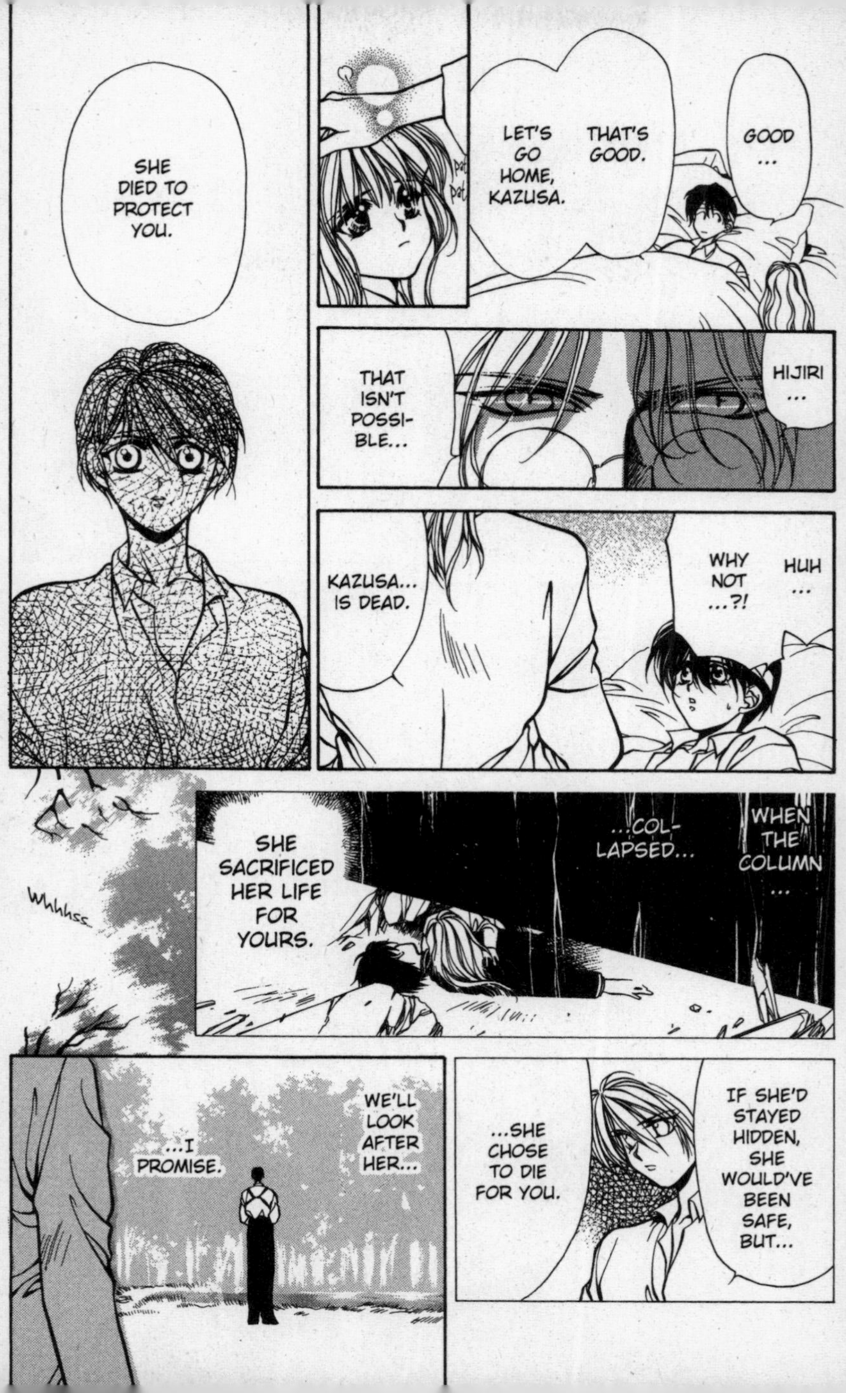
GOOD ...
THAT'S GOOD.
LET'S GO HOME, KAZUSA.
pat pat
HIJIRI ...
THAT ISN'T POSSI-BLE...
HUH ...
WHY NOT ...?!
KAZUSA... IS DEAD.
SHE DIED TO PROTECT YOU.
WHEN THE COLUMN ...
...COL-LAPSED...
SHE SACRIFICED HER LIFE FOR YOURS.
Whhhss
IF SHE'D STAYED HIDDEN, SHE WOULD'VE BEEN SAFE, BUT...
...SHE CHOSE TO DIE FOR YOU.
WE'LL LOOK AFTER HER...
...I PROMISE.

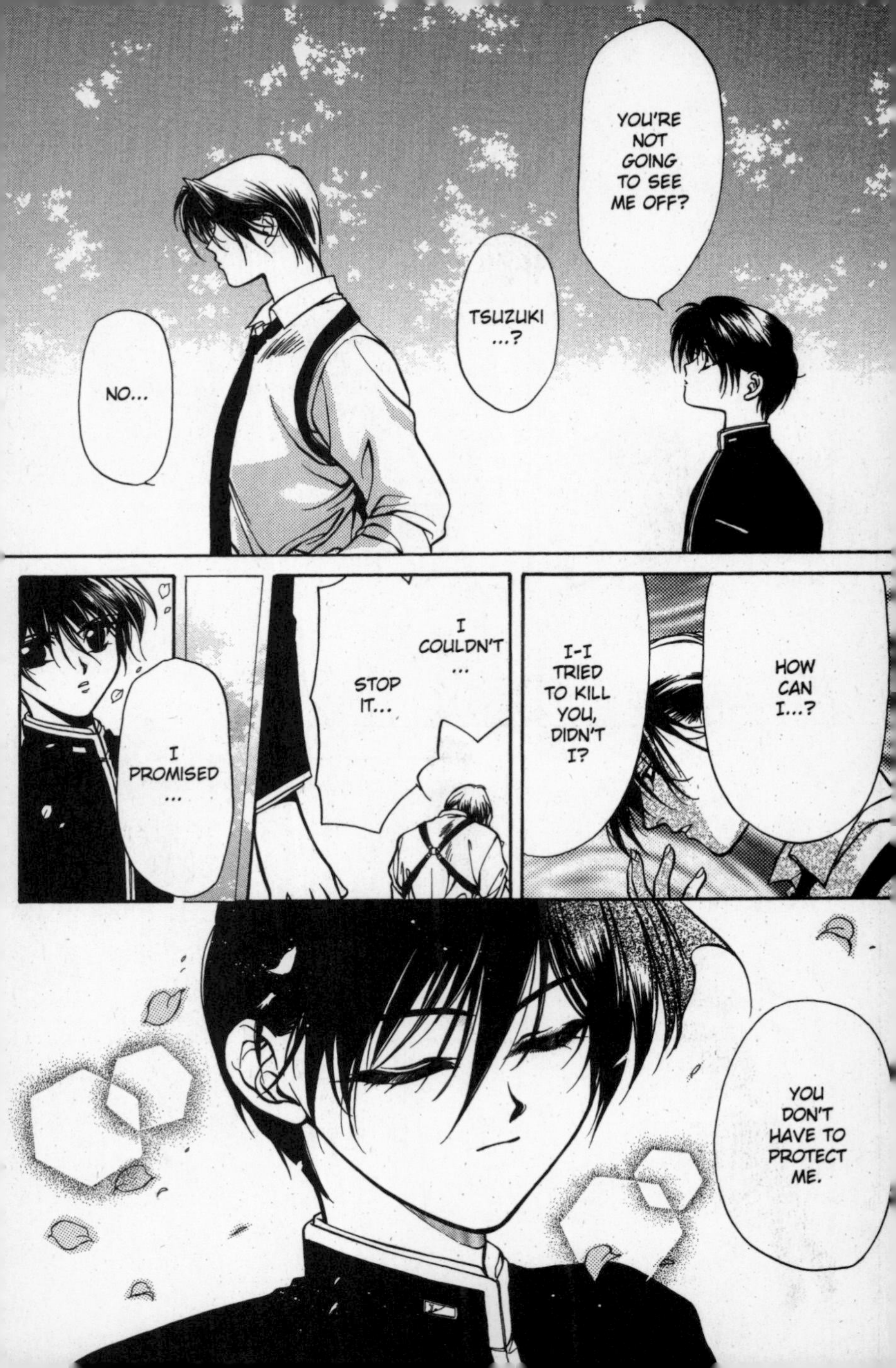
YOU'RE NOT GOING TO SEE ME OFF?
TSUZUKI ...?
NO...
HOW CAN I...?
I-I TRIED TO KILL YOU, DIDN'T I?
I COULDN'T ...
STOP IT...
I PROMISED ...
YOU DON'T HAVE TO PROTECT ME.

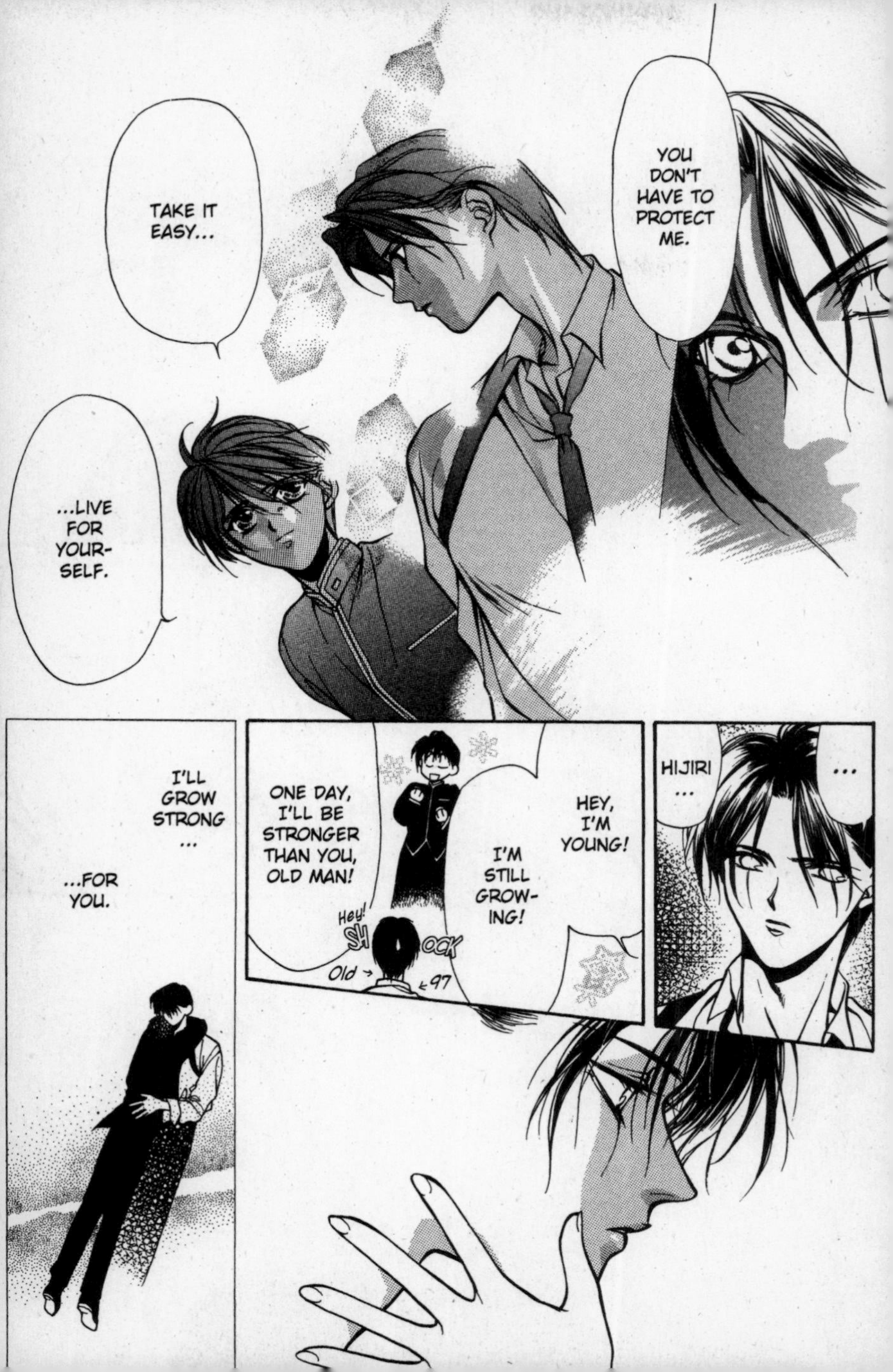
YOU DON'T HAVE TO PROTECT ME.
TAKE IT EASY...
...LIVE FOR YOUR-SELF.
...
HIJIRI ...
HEY, I'M YOUNG!
I'M STILL GROW-ING!
ONE DAY, I'LL BE STRONGER THAN YOU, OLD MAN!
Hey!
SHOCK
Old
97
I'LL GROW STRONG ...
...FOR YOU.

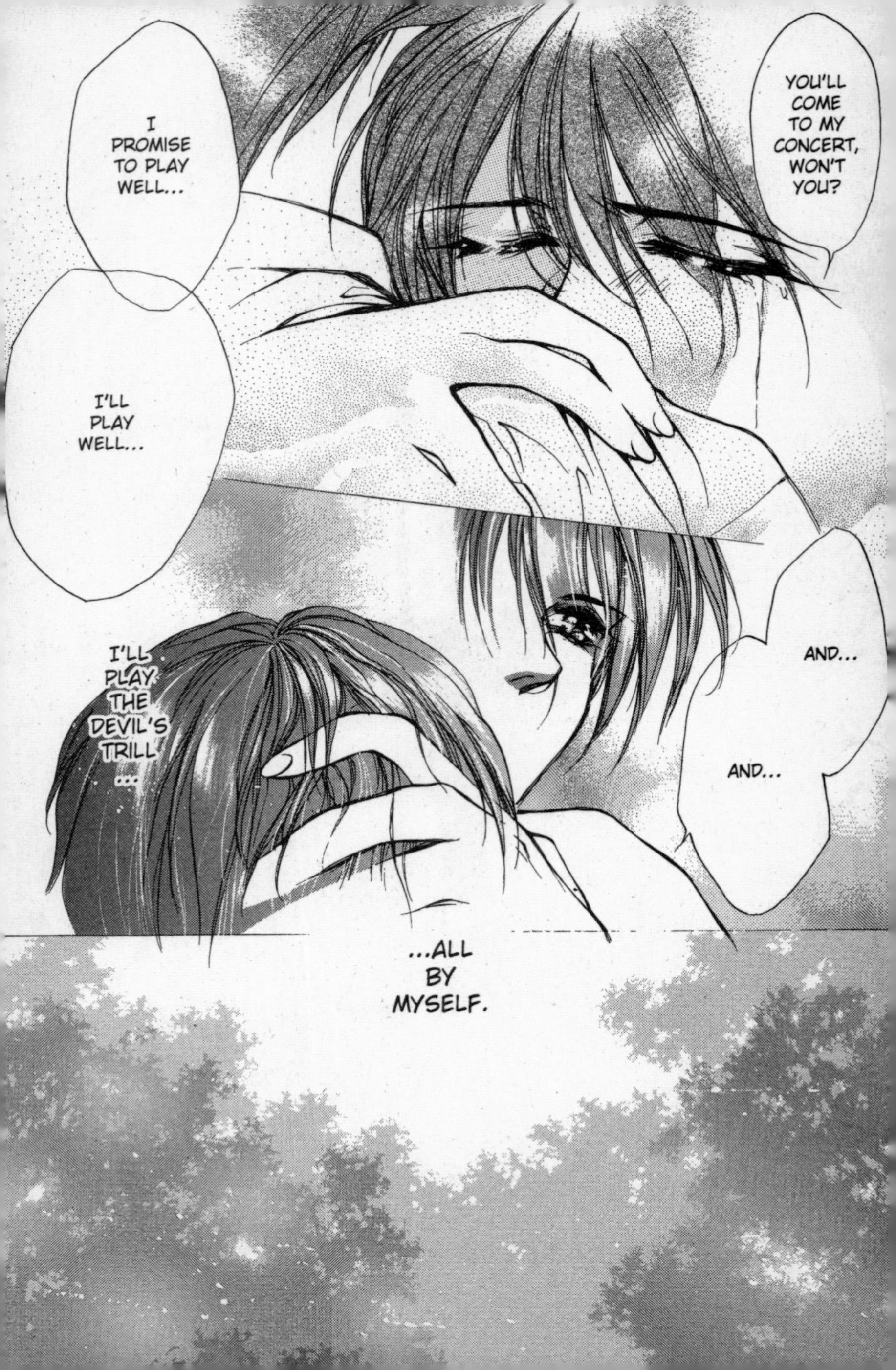
YOU'LL COME TO MY CONCERT, WON'T YOU?
I PROMISE TO PLAY WELL...
I'LL PLAY WELL...
AND...
AND...
I'LL PLAY THE DEVIL'S TRILL...
...ALL BY MYSELF.

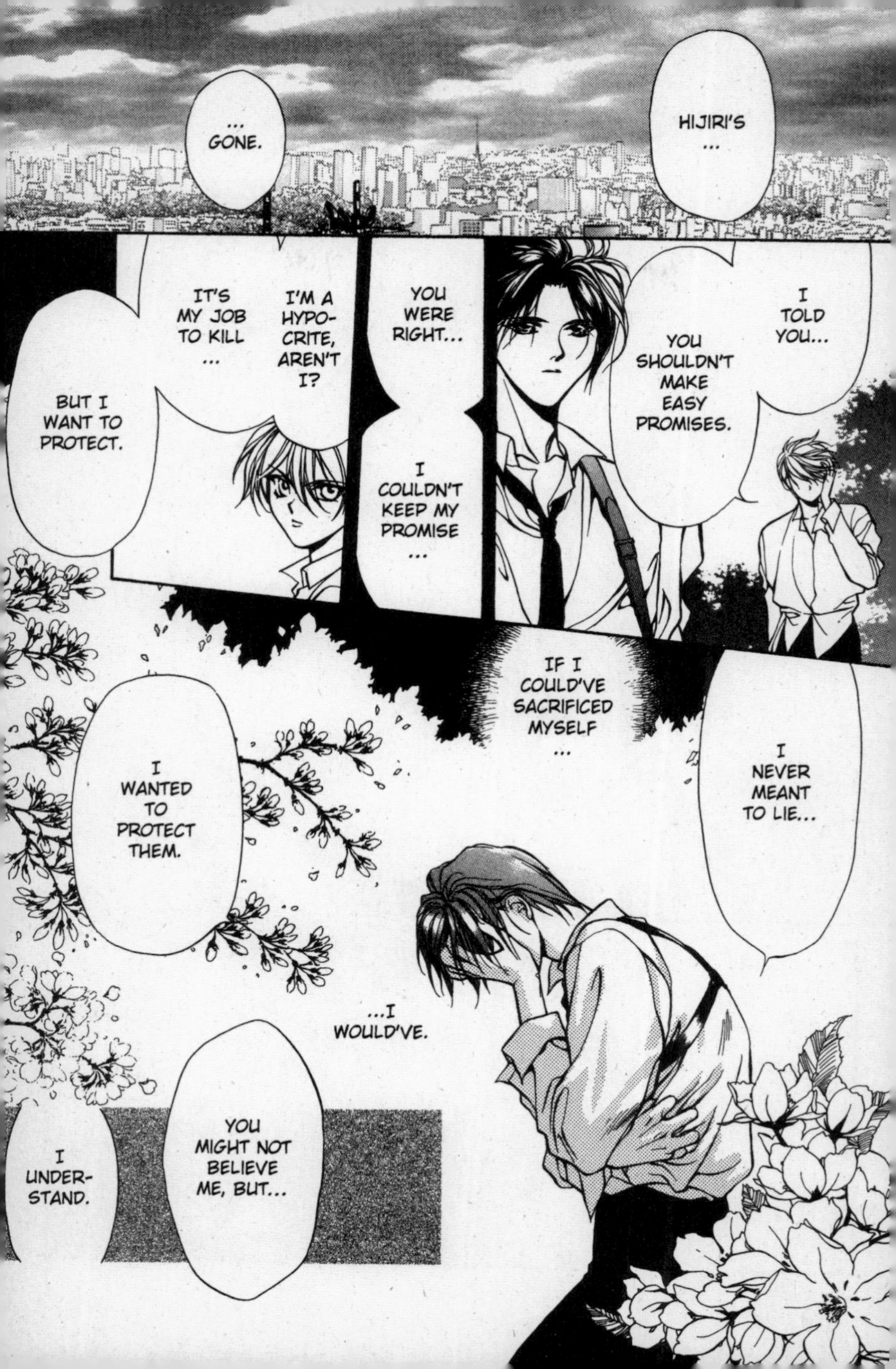

HIJIRI'S ...
... GONE.
I TOLD YOU...
YOU SHOULDN'T MAKE EASY PROMISES.
YOU WERE RIGHT...
I COULDN'T KEEP MY PROMISE ...
I'M A HYPO-CRITE, AREN'T I?
IT'S MY JOB TO KILL ...
BUT I WANT TO PROTECT.
I NEVER MEANT TO LIE...
IF I COULD'VE SACRIFICED MYSELF ...
...I WOULD'VE.
I WANTED TO PROTECT THEM.
YOU MIGHT NOT BELIEVE ME, BUT...
I UNDER-STAND.

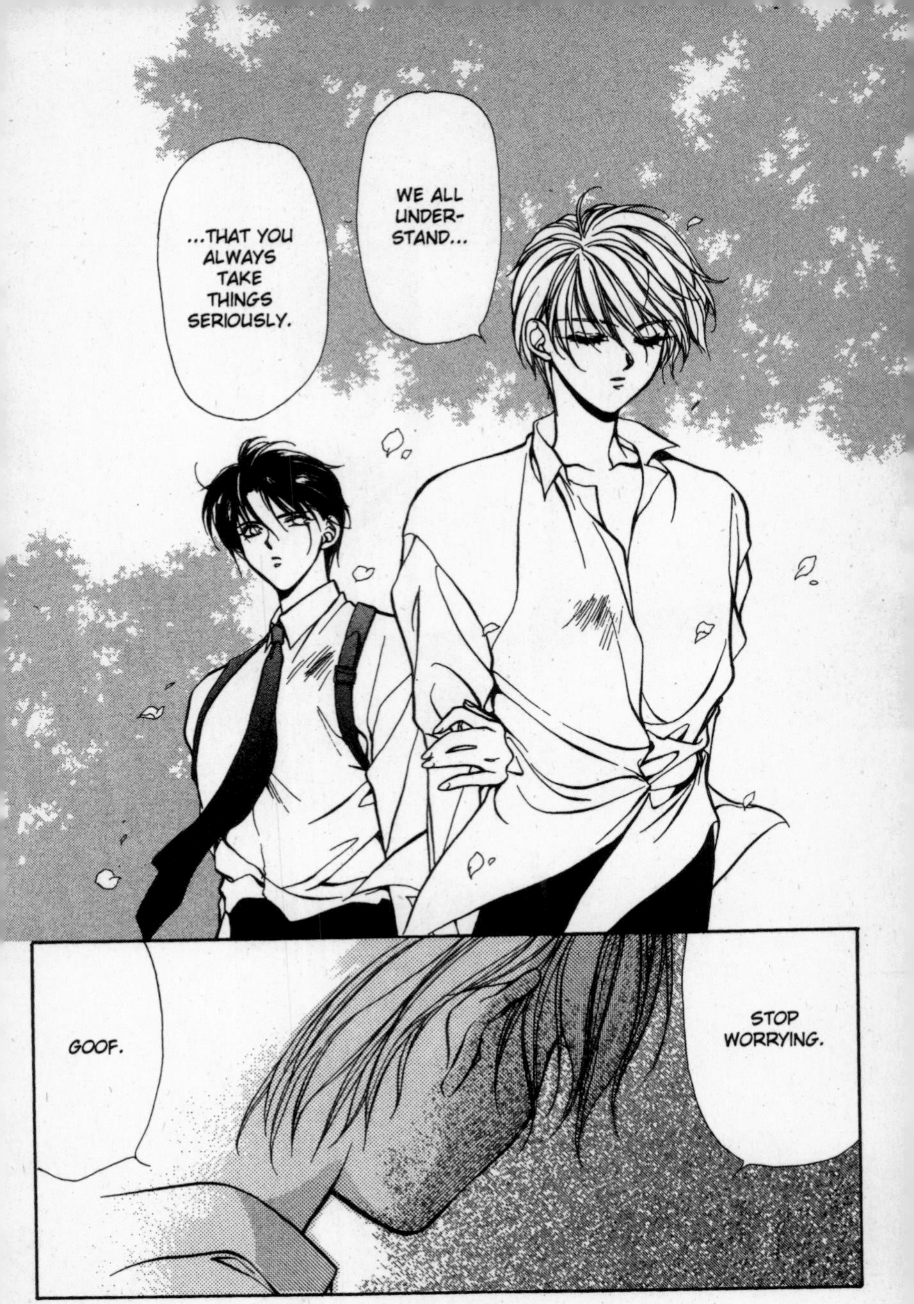
WE ALL UNDER- STAND...
...THAT YOU ALWAYS TAKE THINGS SERIOUSLY.
STOP WORRYING.
GOOF.

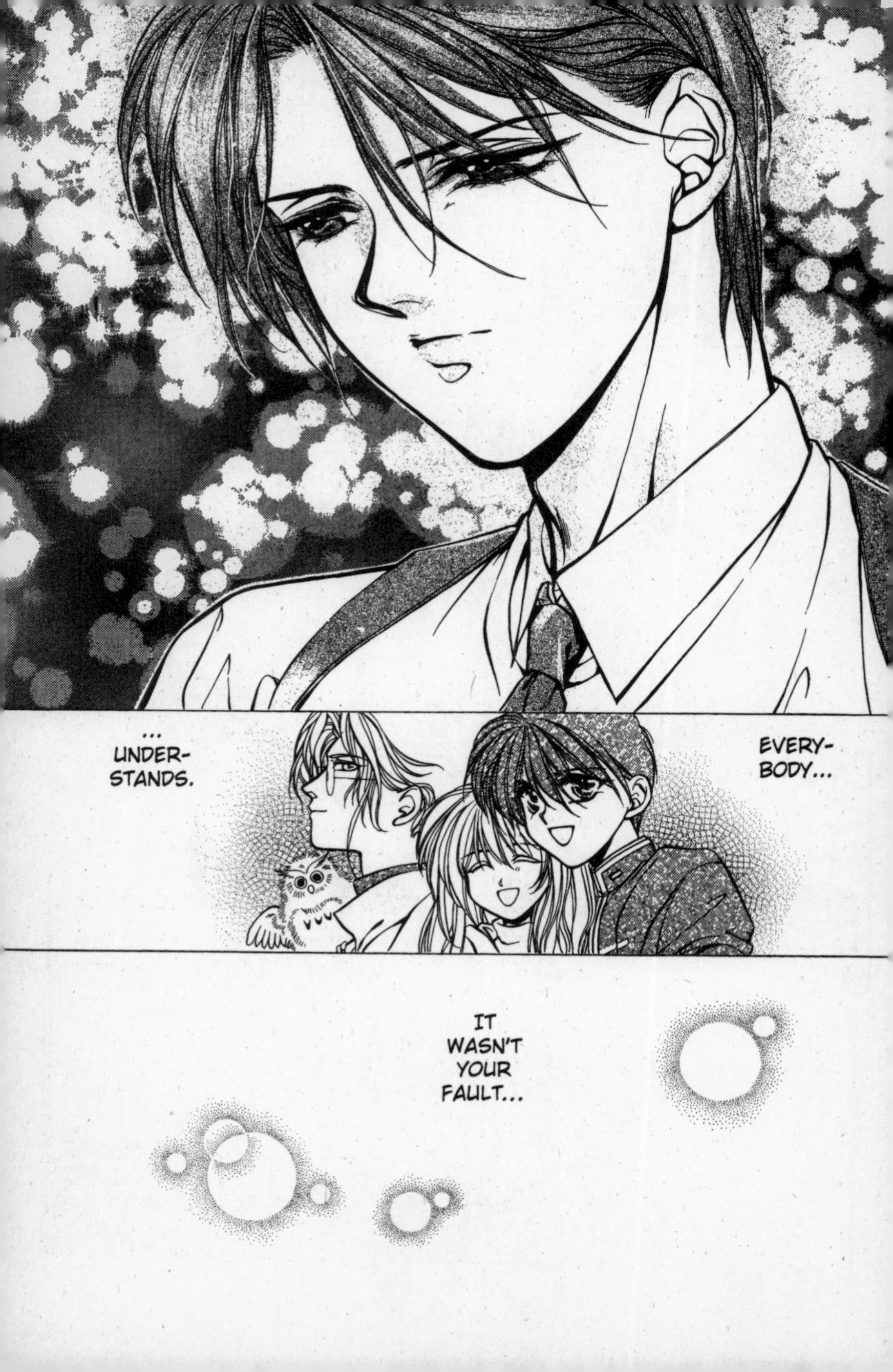
EVERY-BODY...
... UNDER-STANDS.
IT WASN'T YOUR FAULT...

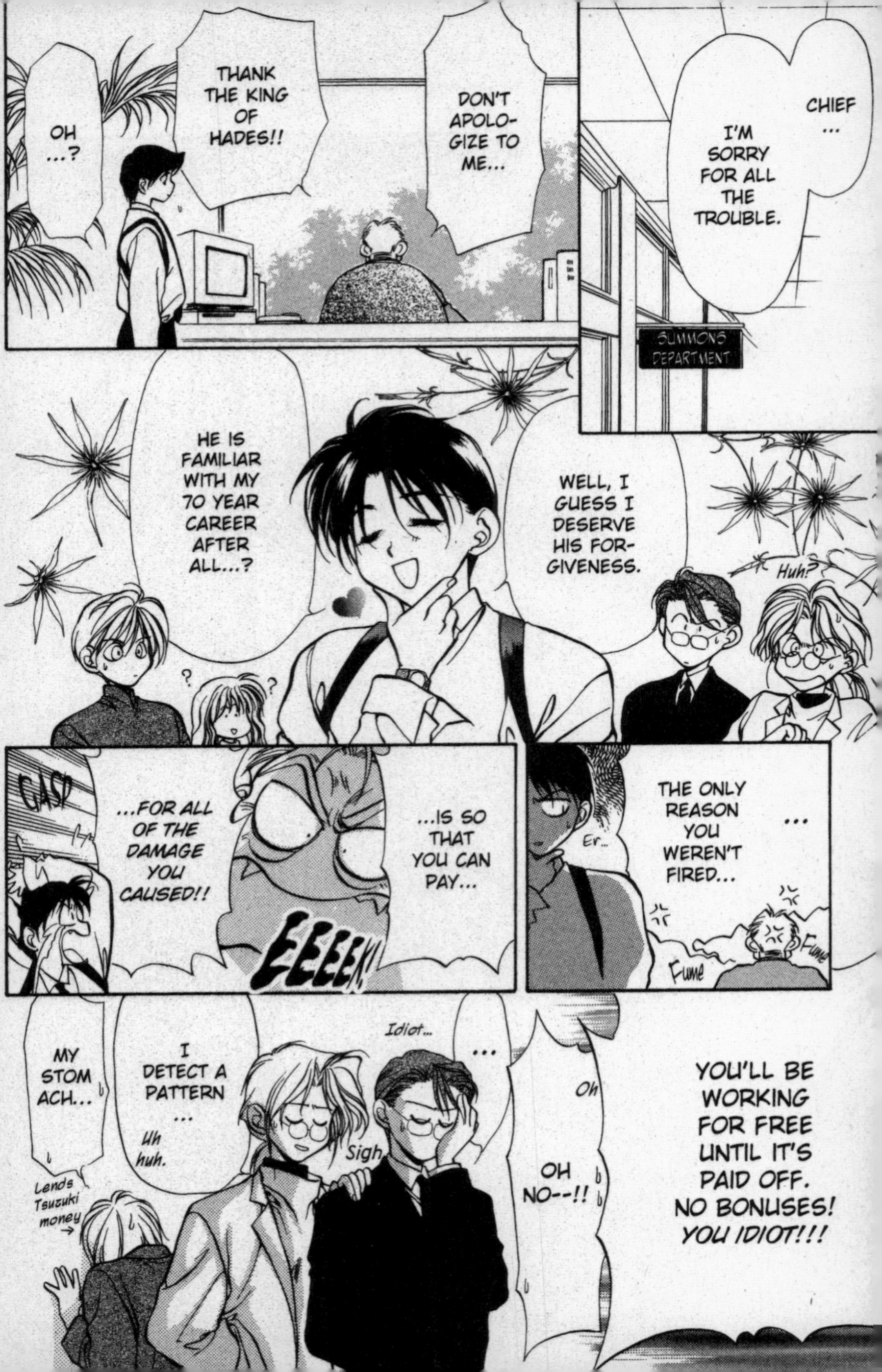
CHIEF ...
I'M SORRY FOR ALL THE TROUBLE.
SUMMONS DEPARTMENT
DON'T APOLOGIZE TO ME...
THANK THE KING OF HADES!!
OH ...?
WELL, I GUESS I DESERVE HIS FORGIVENESS.
Huh?
HE IS FAMILIAR WITH MY 70 YEAR CAREER AFTER ALL...?
...
THE ONLY REASON YOU WEREN'T FIRED...
Er...
Fume
Fume
...IS SO THAT YOU CAN PAY...
...FOR ALL OF THE DAMAGE YOU CAUSED!!
EEEEK!
GASP
YOU'LL BE WORKING FOR FREE UNTIL IT'S PAID OFF. NO BONUSES! YOU IDIOT!!!
Oh
OH NO--!!
...
Idiot...
Sigh
I DETECT A PATTERN ...
Uh huh.
MY STOMACH...
Lends Tsuzuki money →

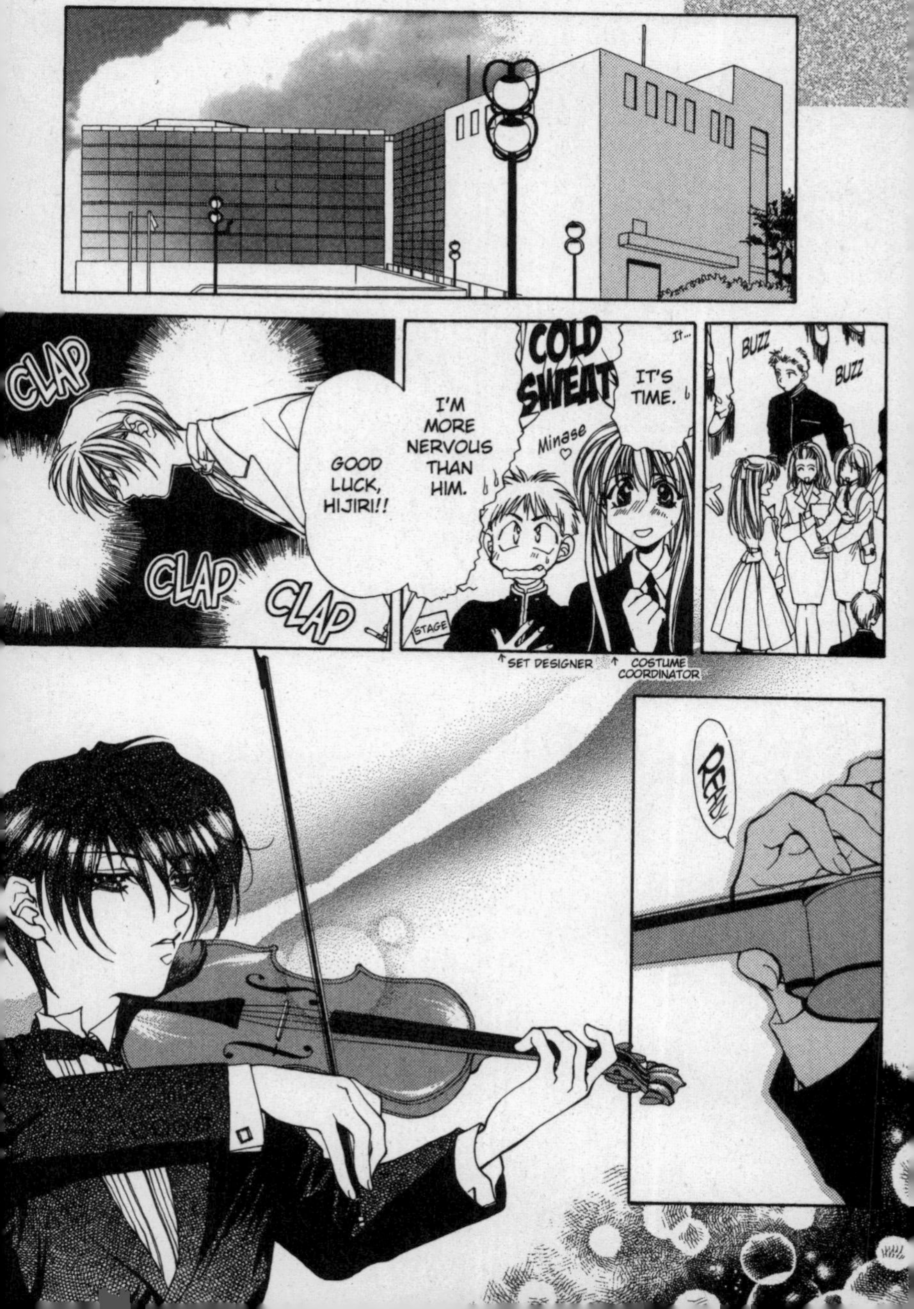
BUZZ
BUZZ
It...
IT'S TIME.
COLD SWEAT
Minase ♡
I'M MORE NERVOUS THAN HIM.
STAGE
SET DESIGNER
COSTUME COORDINATOR
GOOD LUCK, HIJIRI!!
CLAP
CLAP
CLAP
READY

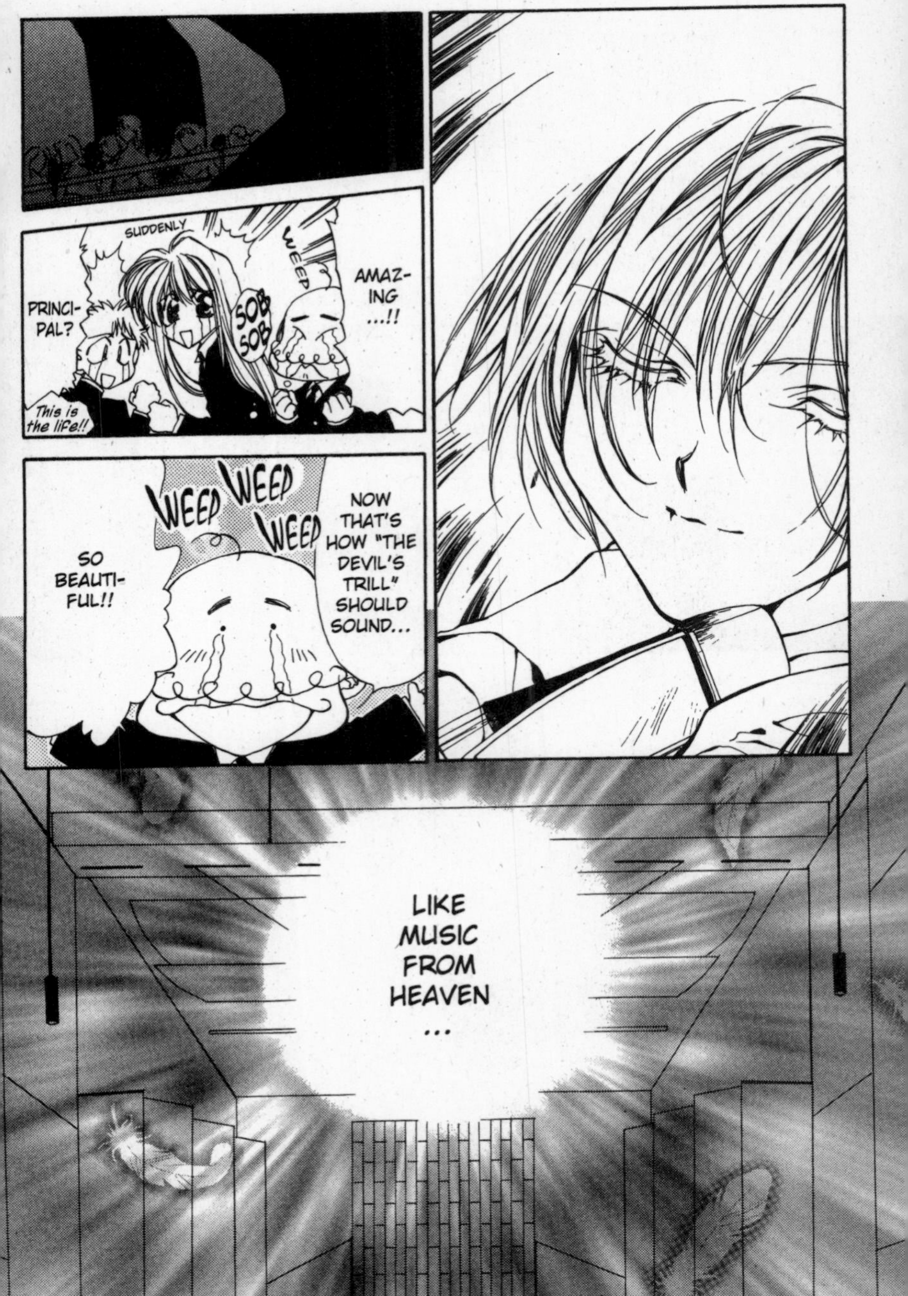
AMAZ-ING ...!!
WEEP
SOB SOB
SUDDENLY
PRINCI-PAL?
This is the life!!
NOW THAT'S HOW "THE DEVIL'S TRILL" SHOULD SOUND...
WEEP WEEP WEEP
SO BEAUTI-FUL!!
LIKE MUSIC FROM HEAVEN ...

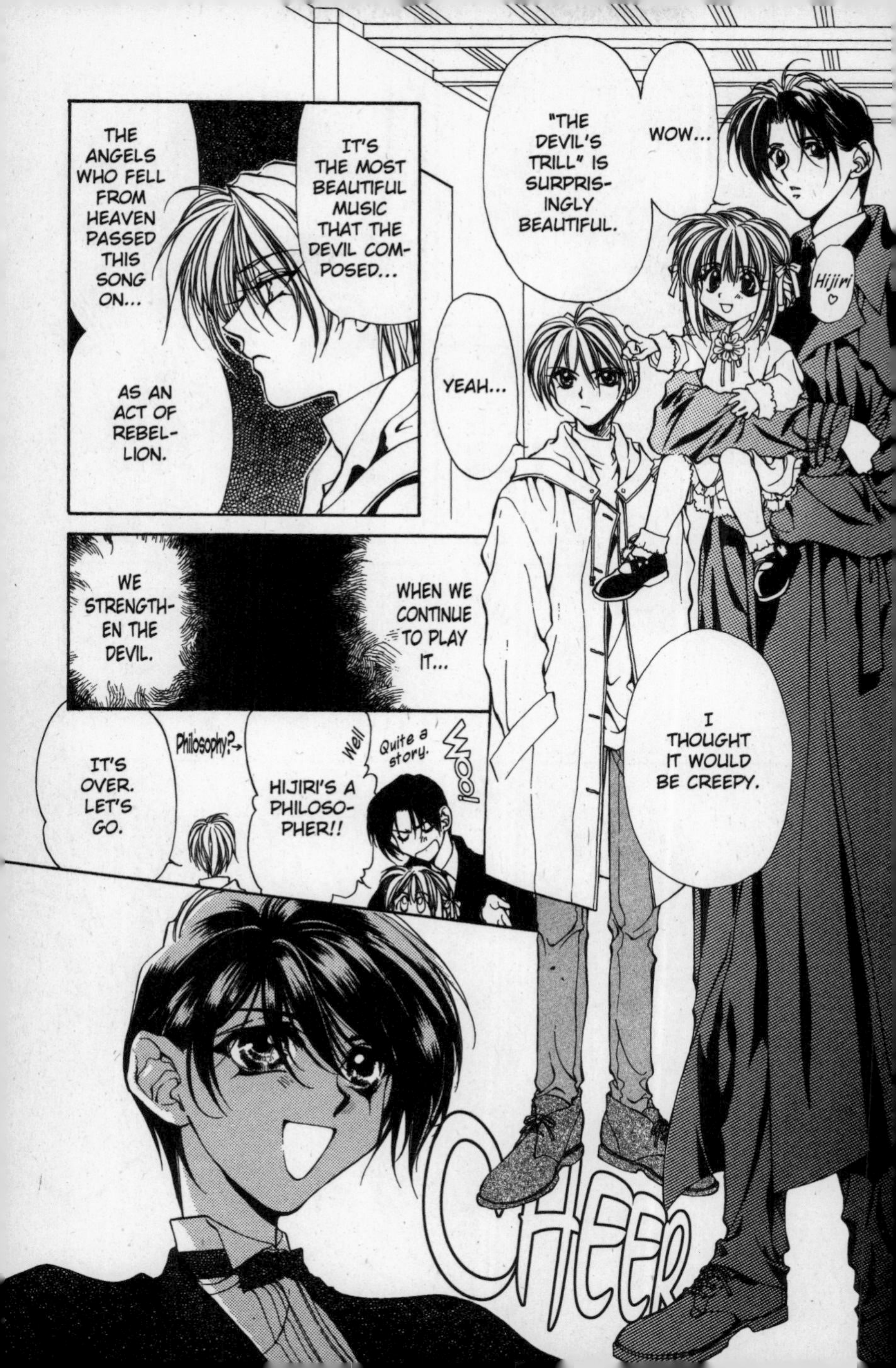

WOW...
"THE DEVIL'S TRILL" IS SURPRISINGLY BEAUTIFUL.
YEAH...
Hijiri ♡
I THOUGHT IT WOULD BE CREEPY.
IT'S THE MOST BEAUTIFUL MUSIC THAT THE DEVIL COMPOSED...
THE ANGELS WHO FELL FROM HEAVEN PASSED THIS SONG ON...
AS AN ACT OF REBELLION.
WHEN WE CONTINUE TO PLAY IT...
WE STRENGTHEN THE DEVIL.
Woo!
Quite a story.
Well
HIJIRI'S A PHILOSOPHER!!
Philosophy?
IT'S OVER. LET'S GO.
CHEER

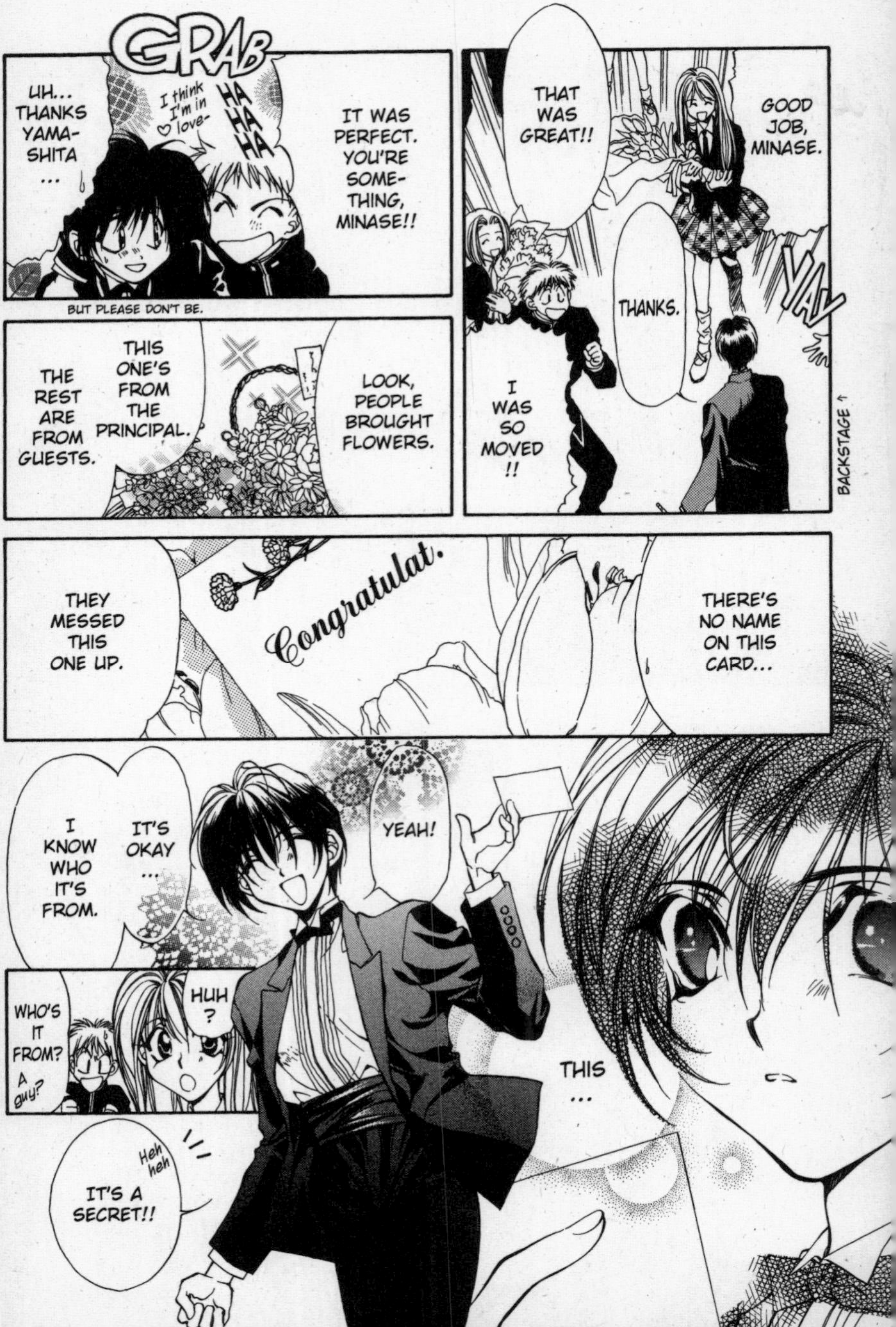
BACKSTAGE
GOOD JOB, MINASE.
THAT WAS GREAT!!
YAY
THANKS.
I WAS SO MOVED!!
GRAB
IT WAS PERFECT. YOU'RE SOME-THING, MINASE!!
HA HA HA
I think I'm in love-
UH... THANKS YAMA-SHITA...
BUT PLEASE DON'T BE.
LOOK, PEOPLE BROUGHT FLOWERS.
THIS ONE'S FROM THE PRINCIPAL.
THE REST ARE FROM GUESTS.
THERE'S NO NAME ON THIS CARD...
Congratulat.
THEY MESSED THIS ONE UP.
THIS...
YEAH!
IT'S OKAY...
I KNOW WHO IT'S FROM.
HUH?
WHO'S IT FROM?
A guy?
Heh heh
IT'S A SECRET!!

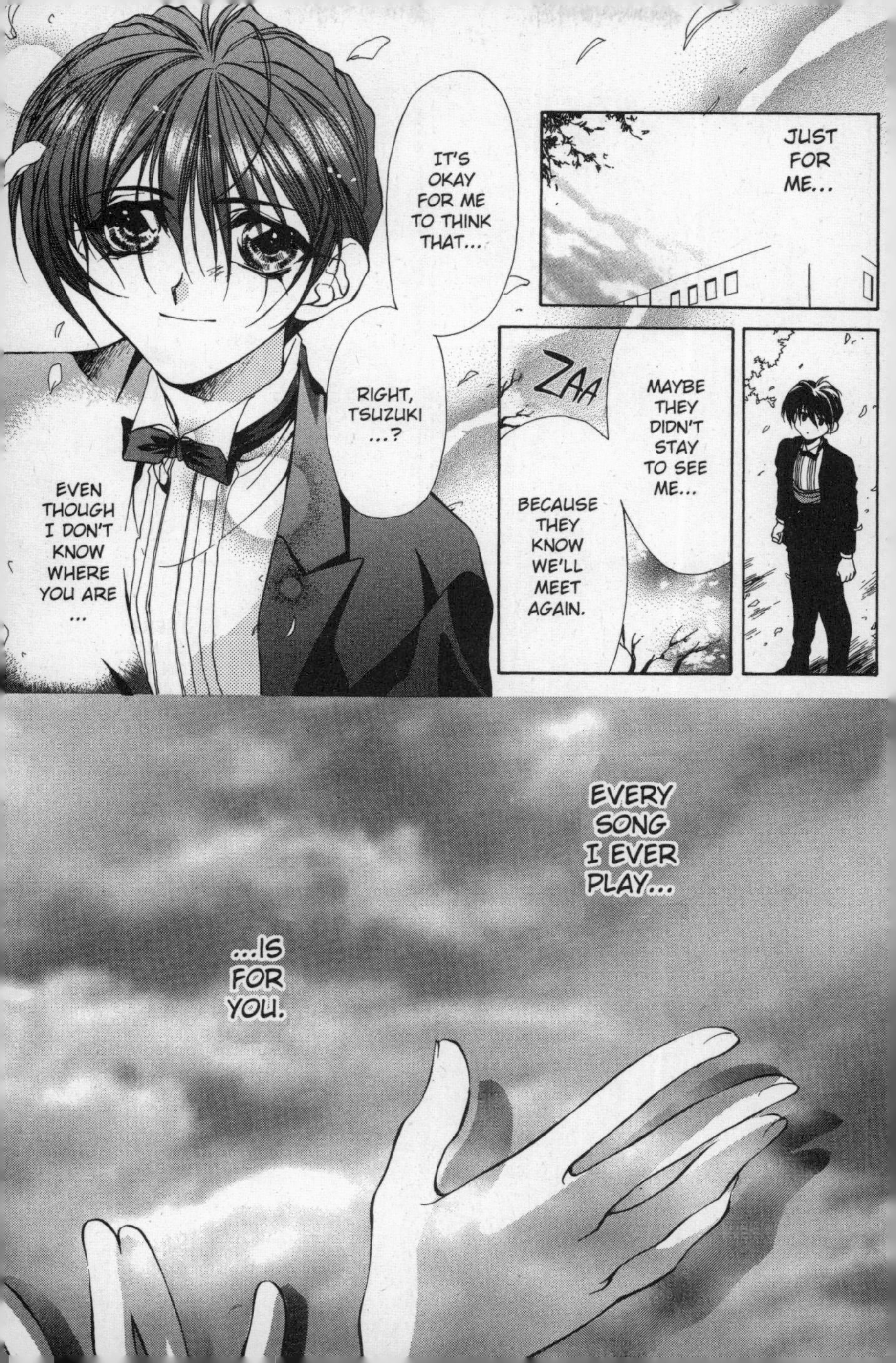
JUST FOR ME...
MAYBE THEY DIDN'T STAY TO SEE ME...
ZAA
BECAUSE THEY KNOW WE'LL MEET AGAIN.
IT'S OKAY FOR ME TO THINK THAT...
RIGHT, TSUZUKI ...?
EVEN THOUGH I DON'T KNOW WHERE YOU ARE ...
EVERY SONG I EVER PLAY...
...IS FOR YOU.

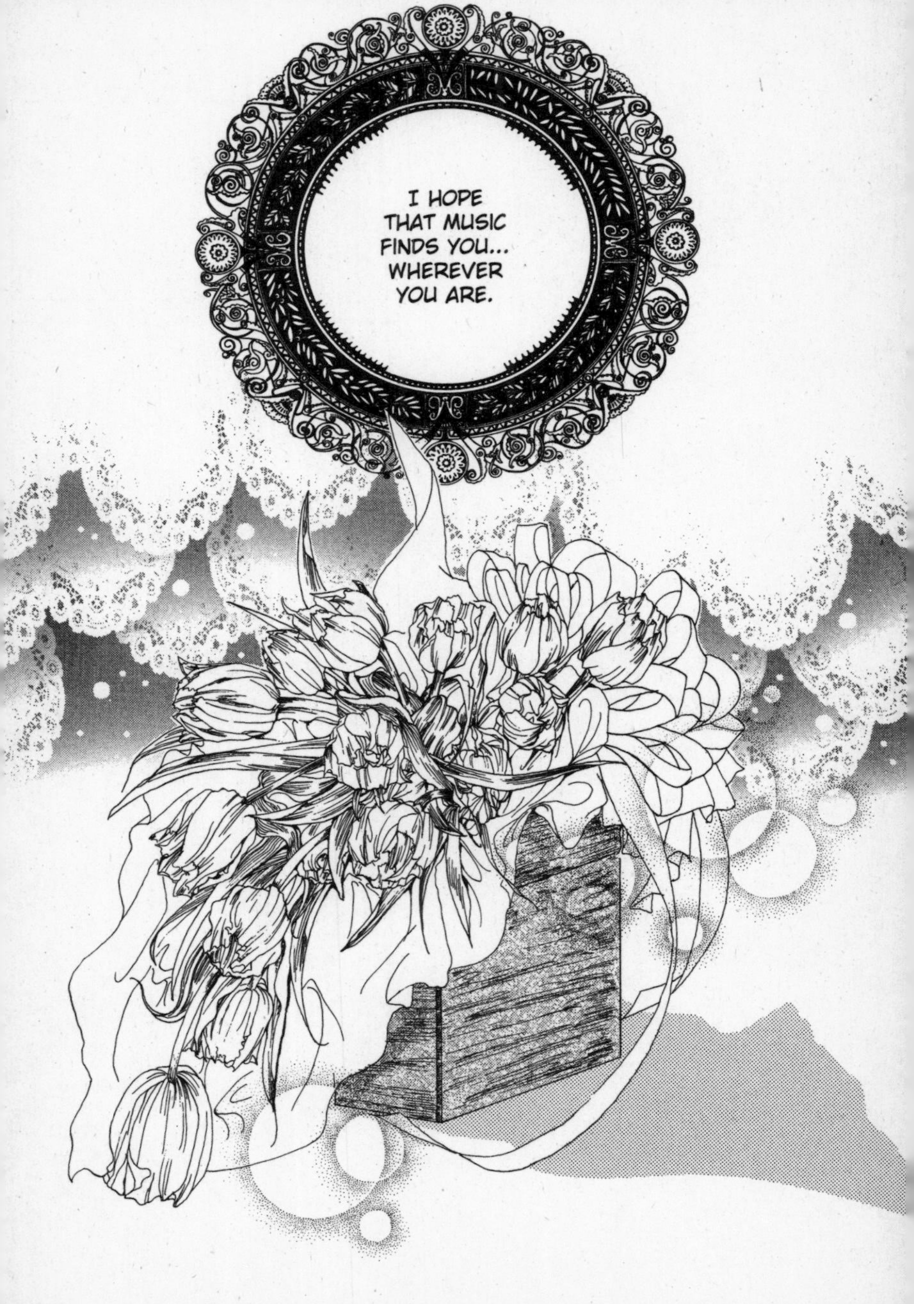
I HOPE THAT MUSIC FINDS YOU... WHEREVER YOU ARE.

END/THE DEVIL'S TRILL

Since food is a big part of Descendants of Darkness (Asato Tsuzuki loves his sweets, after all), we thought readers would be interested in a little bit more information about the foodstuffs mentioned in this particular volume. Space permitting, the book's scriptwriter has agreed to continue contributing a handy glossary of relevant miscellanea for each new book.

- Editor

English Adaptation Notes
by Kelly Sue DeConnick

Curry – Though it originated in India, the combination of spices called "curry" most likely made its way to Japan during the Meiji era (1869-1913), and it's since become a lunch and dinnertime staple. The aromatic spices that Tsuzuki refers to might include cumin, coriander, cinnamon, laurel, octagonal fennel, nutmeg, mace, all spice, cardamom and/or clove. Curries get their distinctive color through a combination of turmeric, saffron and paprika, while peppers, ginger, garlic and mustard provide the heat. Japanese curry rice is generally a thicker dish than Indian curry and it's commonly served with fukujin-zuke or rakkyo pickles. That's right: pickles. Mmm, pickles.

Dried Octopus – A snack food or cooking ingredient that can be eaten warmed or soaked and added to something like a Hairy Marrow and Dried Octopus Soup. Dried octopus is believed by some to strengthen the circulation of the energy called 'Ki.'

Gorgonzola Cheese – An Italian blue cheese named for the village of Gorgonzola, near Milan, where it's been made since the 9th century. The blue veins in the cheese are actually molds that grew in the cool caves where the cheeses were aged way back when. Nowadays, mold spores are mixed right in with the curds to maintain consistency standards.

Hammurabi – The sixth ruler of the 1st dynasty of Babylon. The Code of Hammurabi consists of 280-some legal judgments that, though bizarre and heavy-handed by today's standards, were an advance over previous systems that allowed for charming customs like marriage by capture. Parts of the code are preserved in the Louvre in Paris. You can also find them on the Washington State University website (http://www.wsu.edu/~dee/MESO/CODE.HTM) if you are really, really bored if you have a bizarre fascination with the picayune details of Babylonian life. (Apparently, you could hire an ox driver for six gur of corn per year and the fine for stealing a water wheel was five shekels. Now you know.)

Konbucha – A drink made by infusing dried konbu (a kind of kelp) in hot water. It has a bit of a salty taste and some people consider it a restorative, or a tonic. Variations include konbucha flavored with shiso leaves (shiso is an herb, like basil or mint) and konbucha reconstituted from a powder. It's associated with Okinawa because of its popularity there.

Salted Cuttlefish - Cuttlefish are soft-bodied marine cephalopods (like squid or octopus), with a large head ringed by tentacles and an internal cuttlebone. You can keep them as pets, or failing that, they make a great high-protein snack food.

Shiro Amakusa - A charismatic young samurai who led an uprising of Japanese Roman Catholic peasants in the Shimabara Rebellion of 1637. It didn't end well for Amakusa, but he did score a 15 meter-tall statue that still stands in Aino Amakusa Village in Kumamoto Prefecture. While in the village, you can also tour a Chikuwa fish paste factory and see just how fish paste is made. Be sure to pick up some sea bream paste for your loved ones back home.

Dispatches of Darkness v2
Steps & Violins

© artwork by Julie Da[v]

You're sixteen years old and you just lost your grip and screamed at your mom because, frankly, she's an idiot and while she insists that YOU DON'T LISTEN, in truth, she doesn't listen—she hasn't understood a word that's come out of your mouth for the last four years. She sends you to your room (which is where you were headed anyway), you throw yourself down in a full-body pout and snap your head in between two giant headphones like plugging a cord into a socket and then, through the dual miracles of Noise Reduction and Stereo Sound you are transported. Both calmed and validated, you are taken to a place inside yourself where things make sense, and people understand you and your body moves with a kind of deliberate pulse that you will spend the rest of your life returning to because it is the teat of sanity that keeps you from climbing a tower and showing those fools that none of this really matters.

What is that? What do you call that thing that comes into your head through your ears and wakes up your insides and moves you just as sure as if it were a cruise ship both in to and out of yourself? Why, it's the devil, of course.

What? You think it's not? Okay, you're right: it's not. It's music. But for as long as there's been a bassline, the devil's been getting credit for making you shake your butt. Or grow your hair. Or kill yourself. Or whatever. Judas Priest did not backmask Satanic messages into their albums. I know it's scintillating to think they did, but they didn't. Rob Halford doesn't want you to kill yourself. He wants you to live, and get a job, and make enough money that you can continue to buy his records. Robert Johnson did not sell his soul to the devil at the crossroads to learn to play guitar. And Ozzy Osbourne wasn't sacrificing bats to the dark side—he was snorting his weight in cocaine. And Tartini? Tartini had a dream.

That's the core of it right there: like dreams and conch shells, music doesn't so much put ideas into your head as it does amplify and reflect what's already going on in there. When you're frustrated, and you'd like nothing better than to put your fist through a wall, the best thing in the world to vent that steam is music that sounds and feels like putting your fist through a wall. It doesn't hurt anybody and it saves on blood and spackle. Likewise, if you've been blessed with the temperament of milquetoast and a fourth grade reading capacity, I'd lay five bucks that says there's nothing you'd rather do than spend the afternoon watching a Celine Dion simulcast and sipping on wine from a box. That's not the devil either, honey. That's just a sad fact. You can take that to the bank.

Kelly Sue DeConnick
June 2004

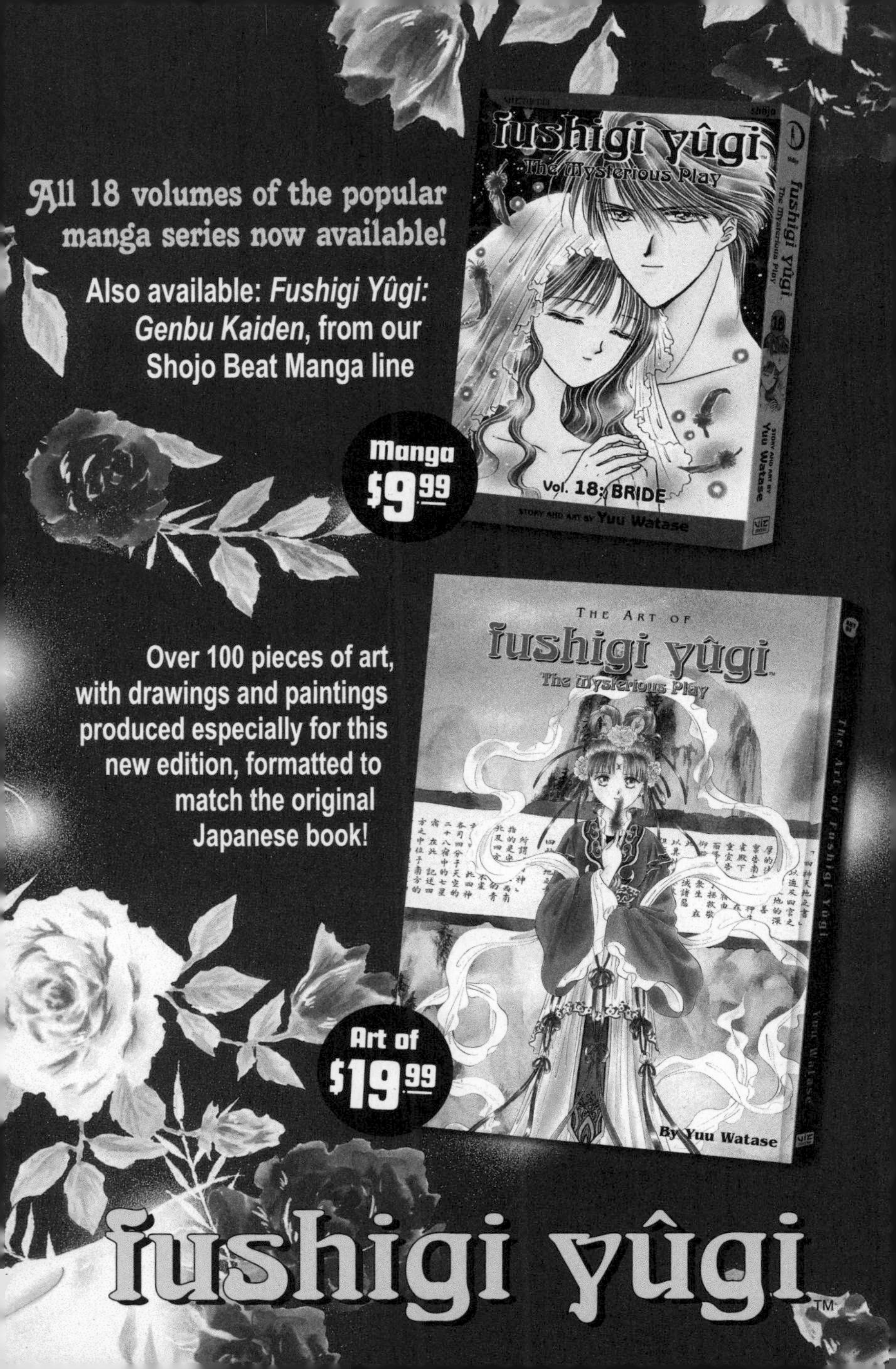
All 18 volumes of the popular manga series now available!
Also available: *Fushigi Yûgi: Genbu Kaiden*, from our Shojo Beat Manga line
Manga $9.99
fushigi yûgi The Mysterious Play
Vol. 18: BRIDE
Story and Art by Yuu Watase
Over 100 pieces of art, with drawings and paintings produced especially for this new edition, formatted to match the original Japanese book!
Art of $19.99
The Art of fushigi yûgi The Mysterious Play
By Yuu Watase
fushigi yûgi™

GET THE COMPLETE
FUSHIGI YÛGI COLLECTION

viz
media

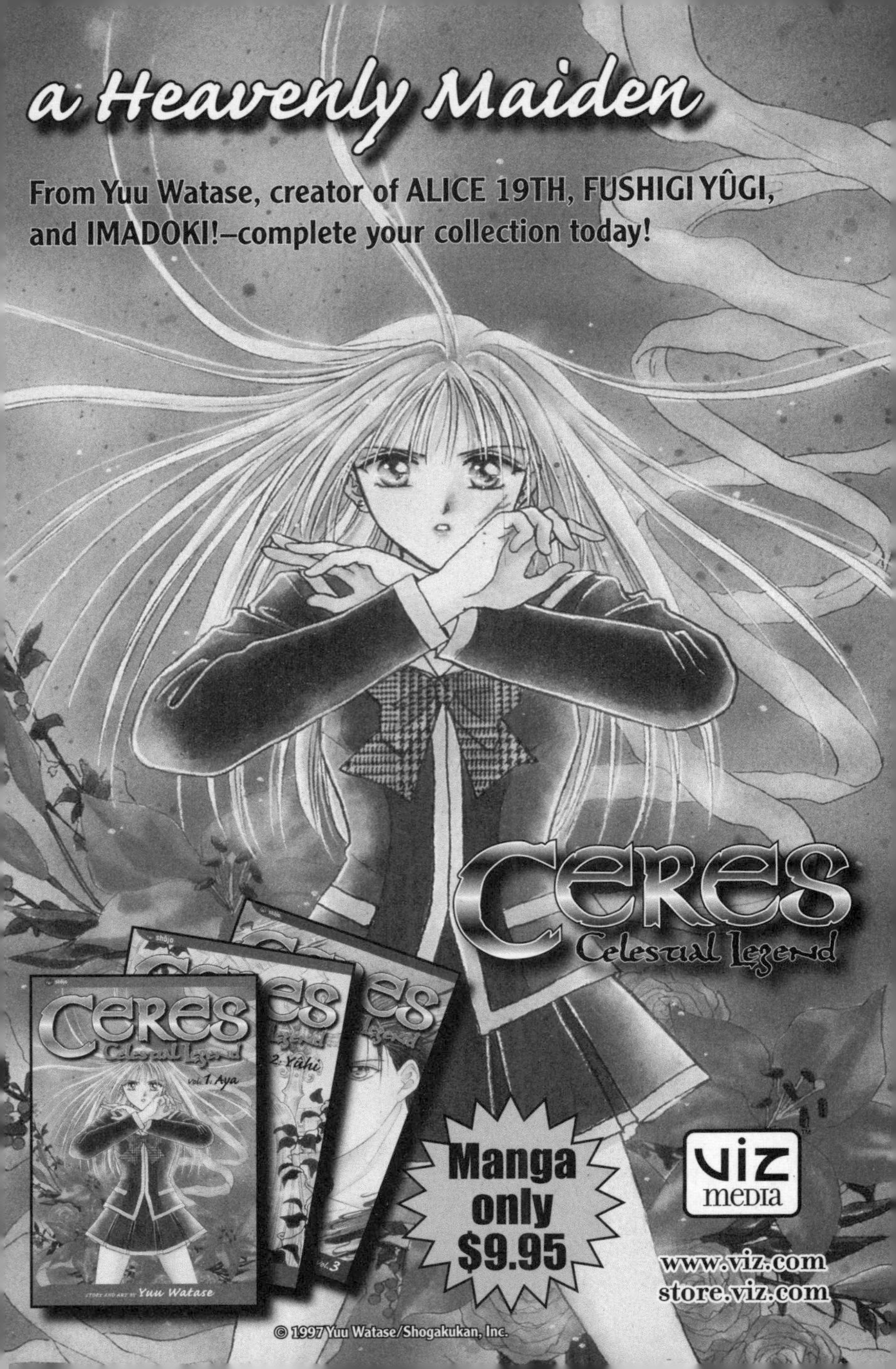

Hell Hath No Fury Like

When an angel named Ceres is reincarnated in 16-year-old Aya Mikage, Aya becomes a liability to her family's survival. Not only does Ceres want revenge against the Mikage family for past wrongs, but her power is also about to manifest itself. Can Aya control Ceres' hold on her, or will her family mark her for death?

Complete anime series on two DVD box sets— 12 episodes per volume

only $49.98 each!

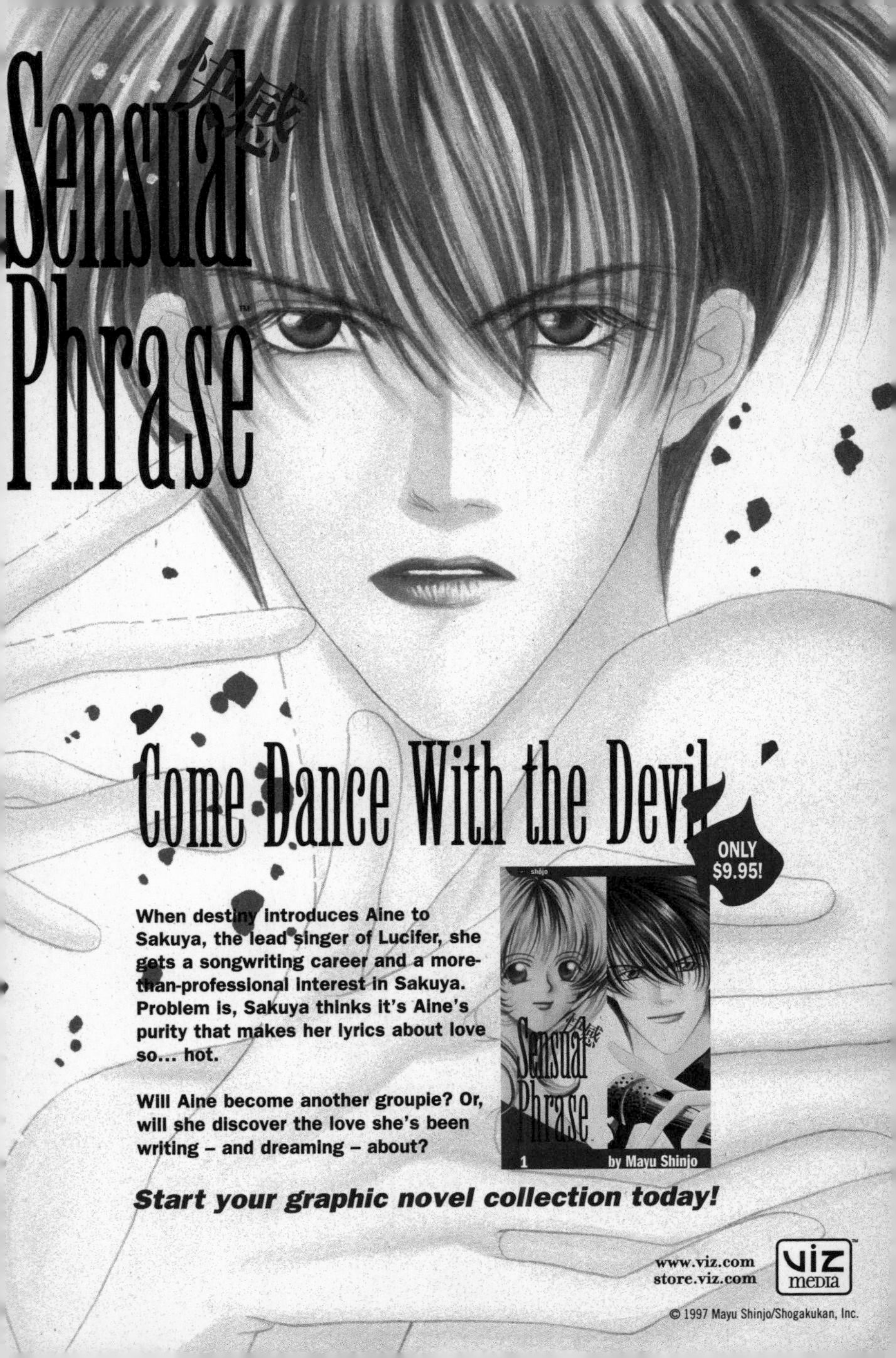
Sensual Phrase™
Come Dance With the Devil
ONLY $9.95!
shōjo
Sensual Phrase
1
by Mayu Shinjo
When destiny introduces Aine to Sakuya, the lead singer of Lucifer, she gets a songwriting career and a more-than-professional interest in Sakuya. Problem is, Sakuya thinks it's Aine's purity that makes her lyrics about love so... hot.
Will Aine become another groupie? Or, will she discover the love she's been writing – and dreaming – about?
Start your graphic novel collection today!
www.viz.com
store.viz.com
VIZ MEDIA
© 1997 Mayu Shinjo/Shogakukan, Inc.

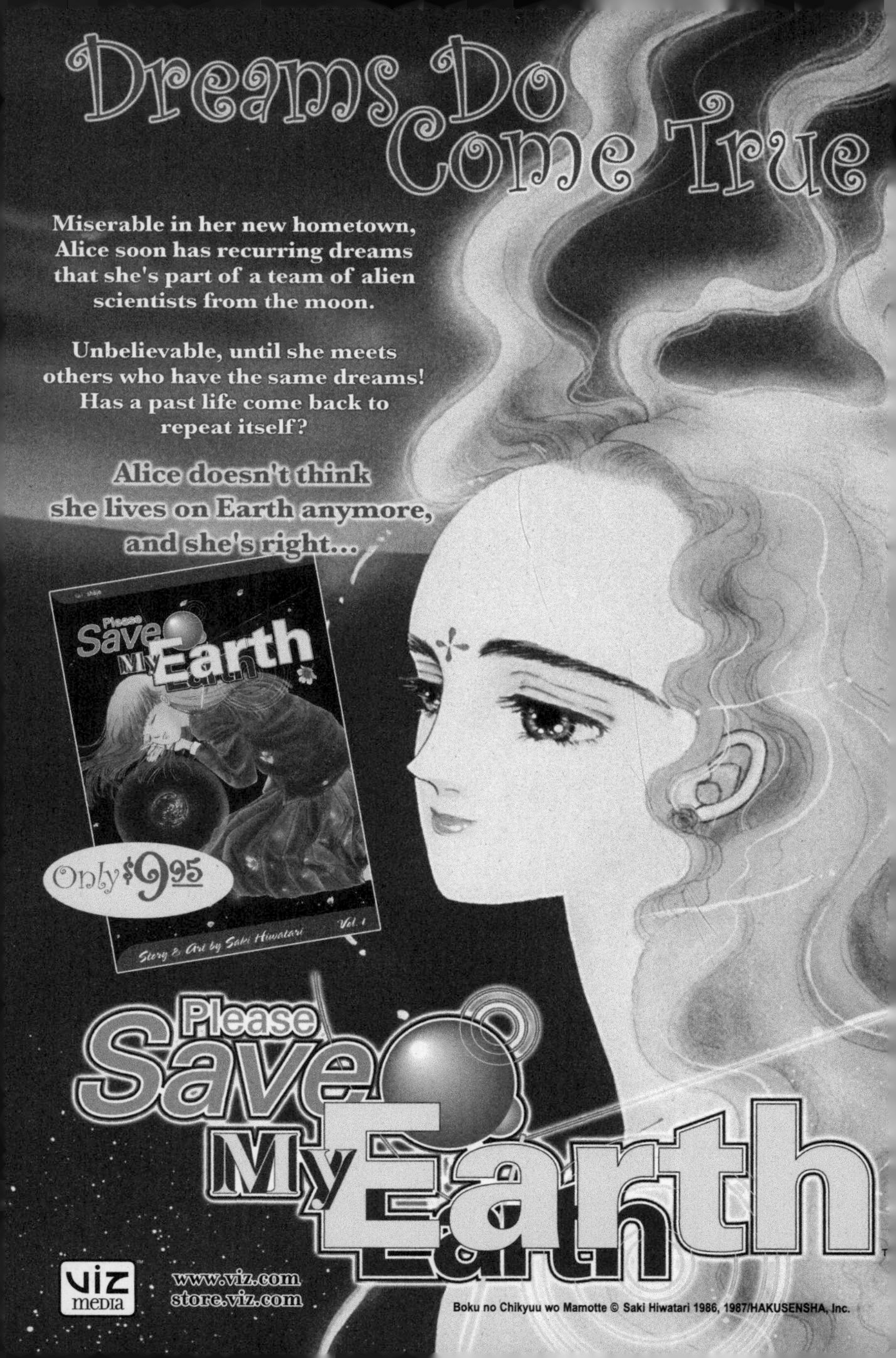
Dreams Do Come True
Miserable in her new hometown, Alice soon has recurring dreams that she's part of a team of alien scientists from the moon.
Unbelievable, until she meets others who have the same dreams! Has a past life come back to repeat itself?
Alice doesn't think she lives on Earth anymore, and she's right...
Please Save My Earth
Vol. 1
Story & Art by Saki Hiwatari
Only $9.95
Please Save My Earth
viz media
www.viz.com
store.viz.com
Boku no Chikyuu wo Mamotte © Saki Hiwatari 1986, 1987/HAKUSENSHA, Inc.

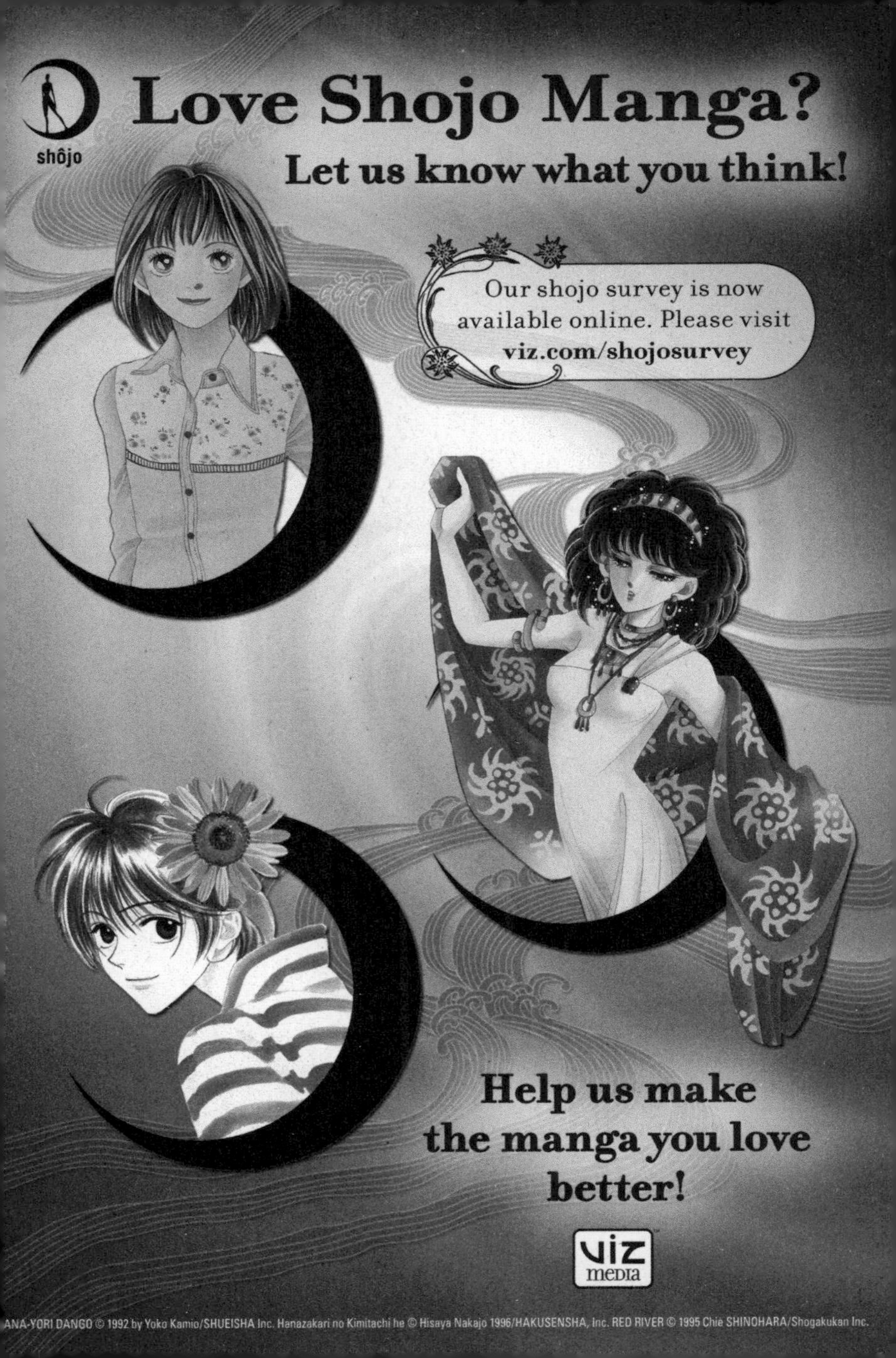
shôjo
Love Shojo Manga?
Let us know what you think!
Our shojo survey is now available online. Please visit viz.com/shojosurvey
Help us make the manga you love better!
viz media
ANA-YORI DANGO © 1992 by Yoko Kamio/SHUEISHA Inc. Hanazakari no Kimitachi he © Hisaya Nakajo 1996/HAKUSENSHA, Inc. RED RIVER © 1995 Chie SHINOHARA/Shogakukan Inc.